1971

University of St. Francis
GEN   370.8 S873 2ed.
Stone
Commitment to teaching

W9-DEI-675

THE CROWELL SERIES IN AMERICAN EDUCATION

JAMES C. STONE, *Advisory Editor for Education*

Foundations
of Education

COMMITMENT TO TEACHING, VOLUME I

COMMITMENT TO TEACHING

James C. Stone and Frederick W. Schneider

Volume I   FOUNDATIONS OF EDUCATION, SECOND EDITION

Volume II   READINGS IN THE FOUNDATIONS OF EDUCATION, SECOND EDITION

Volume III   TEACHING IN THE INNER CITY: A BOOK OF READINGS

James C. Stone

PROFESSOR OF EDUCATION

UNIVERSITY OF CALIFORNIA, BERKELEY

Frederick W. Schneider

PROFESSOR OF EDUCATION

SAN JOSE STATE COLLEGE

THOMAS Y. CROWELL COMPANY   ·   NEW YORK   ·   ESTABLISHED 1834

Foundations
of Education

Second Edition

COMMITMENT TO TEACHING, VOLUME I

LIBRARY
College of St. Francis
JOLIET, ILL.

Copyright © 1971 by
THOMAS Y. CROWELL COMPANY, INC.
ALL RIGHTS RESERVED

Except for use in a review, the reproduction or
utilization of this work in any form or by any
electronic, mechanical, or other means, now known
or hereafter invented, including photocopying and
recording, and in any information storage and
retrieval system is forbidden without the written
permission of the publisher.

L. C. Card 72-146069
ISBN 0-690-20197-4

Designed by Barbara Kohn Isaac

Manufactured in the United States of America

370.8
8873
2ed
1

Foreword

In the usual fashion, we selected a distinguished educator to write the Foreword. We were pleased with his effort, until by chance we saw "A Fable for Our Modern Wise Men" by Martin Buskin in the Long Island, New York, Newsday. We concluded that the fable was written with our book in mind.

And so it came to pass that in all the cities the wise men came together and said one to the other, "Come let us reason together and decide how all the children shall be taught. For surely there is much to be done if they are someday to become all wise men."

And there were some wise men who said, "Let us make sure that all the black children and the white children learn together, for that is surely the most just way to learn." But there were other wise men who said, "Surely you know that the white parents do not want the black and white children to learn together. So let us be reasonable. Let the white and black children learn separately, but let us make sure that they all have teachers who speak the truth and teach them well." But the wise men could not agree on this problem and their talk grew hot and angry. And many days and weeks passed.

And then some wise men said, "Let us talk of other matters. We must make sure that the teachers have all the tools they need to teach." And then some wise men complained that all the tools were made for the teachers of the white children and not for the teachers of the black children. And other wise men said that good teachers should be able to use any tools and that it would drain the treasury to make special tools. And the wise men could not agree on this problem and many weeks passed as they talked.

Outside, in the village streets, the children waited while the wise men argued. And when a child cried, "When shall we learn, and how shall we

v

59222

learn?" one of the wise men called out sharply, "These are great problems that take time to solve. The wise men are talking. And those who know nothing should be quiet." And the children waited.

And then one of the wise men said, "We must make sure that if one of our teachers is no longer good and true he be taken away from the children." And then many wise men grew angry and cried, "How can you know when a teacher is no longer wise? Is a teacher an ox, that you use until you grow tired of his groans and wheezes and turn out to the fields to starve? We have seen no one here wise enough to say when a teacher should be taken away from children." And the wise men argued long and loud on this problem. And many weeks and months passed.

And then a wise man said, "And how shall we know what to teach our children? If a new book is made and the street hawkers shout that it will speed the learning of children, should that book be used by the teachers?" And some wise men said, "If the mothers and fathers think the book is good, then the book is good." And other wise men said that only wise men know when a book is good. And other wise men said that the book must be used on a small group of children first. And they argued. And the children waited outside.

And many months and years passed. And the wise men grew old and hoarse. And some left and others came to take their place. And still they argued. And the questions were always the same. How shall the children be taught? Should there be special tools? Who is to tell when a teacher can no longer teach? Who is to decide what books shall be used? And as time passed, the noise of the wise men's voices grew louder and soon it was as if each one talked only to himself.

And then one day, after many years had passed, there was a new noise, deeper and more angry than the voices of the wise men. One of the old ones looked out of the window of the palace and his face turned gray with fright. The children were no longer there. In their place were adults, young, strong—and furious. They held signs that said nothing, for they did not know how to express themselves. They chanted slogans of hate and destruction, for they had not learned how to reason. And one by one, each frightened wise man turned to the other and said, "While we talked, they have lost their childhood. We have waited too long."

This book is for teachers who will not wait.

SOURCE: Martin Buskin, "A Fable for Our Modern Wise Men," *Newsday*, December 23, 1968. Reprinted by permission of Newsday, Inc.

Preface

Considerable time and effort have gone into the design of this book. If it is unique—and we are convinced it is—it is because of the way in which it was developed. Like its sister volumes in the Commitment to Teaching series (*Readings in the Foundations of Education,* Second Edition, and *Teaching in the Inner City,* both of which follow generally the organization of the present volume), this is a student-centered, student-designed book.

Several hundred beginning students in education at San Jose State College responded in writing to the question: What would you most have liked to know about education when you were considering it as a career choice?

A group of students completing their student teaching and another group completing their year of internship teaching at the University of California, Berkeley, were interviewed with regard to the general question: Looking back over the field of education, what topics would you most have liked to know about, and in what order?

The results of the two surveys agreed both as to the concepts that should be covered and the priority that should be given them. So we have here a book organized and structured from the viewpoint of college and university students of teacher education as learners. In this, *the student-interest approach to education,* the authors believe their book is a first. For this, we are indebted to these students and beginning teachers—too numerous to list—for their invaluable assistance.

The publication of the second edition of a book is a momentous occasion for the author. In the case of the present volume, it is proof that our student-centered approach, which we began in the early 1960's, was the right one. And if it was right then, it is more right today.

We began our work on the second edition with students' reaction and recommendations again in view, with the notion that a little scissoring here and a little pasting there would do the job. On this score we were completely wrong—and the students agreed with us. So what we now offer the reader is a *rewritten* rather than a *revised* edition.

In our rewriting we have been impressed by the durability and consistency of certain social issues and educational problems. The following quotation dramatizes the persistency of the subject matter of education:

In France, the political cauldron seethes and bubbles with uncertainty. England is being sorely tried in a social and economic struggle. The United States is beset with racial, industrial and commercial chaos drifting we know not where. Russia hangs like a storm cloud on the horizon of Europe, dark and silent. It is a solemn moment and no man can feel indifference.

The quotation is from *Harper's Magazine,* October 10, 1847.

We have also, in our rewriting, been deeply impressed by how much has happened since the early 1960's. So much has changed, so much will continue to change, in society, in education, in the schools. Teachers, too, must continue to change—to learn as their students learn, grow as they grow, seek wisdom as they seek wisdom.

To the end of a neat blending of timelessness and timeliness we hope our second edition will make a contribution.

JAMES C. STONE
FREDERICK W. SCHNEIDER

Contents

1. The Milieu   1

The Nature of Culture   2

Education in a Democratic Society   5

Cultural Change   7

Implications for Education   15

Commitment to Teaching   19

Conclusion   22

QUESTIONS FOR DISCUSSION   22

ACTIVITIES AND PROJECTS   23

REFERENCES   24

2. The Goals   28

The Public versus the Educators   28

The Objectives of Education   30

The Teacher's Role   50

Conclusion   50

QUESTIONS FOR DISCUSSION   51

ACTIVITIES AND PROJECTS   52

REFERENCES   52

3. Teaching   55

How Teachers Feel about Teaching   55

Why Do You Want to Teach?   58

Importance of Teachers in Our Society   62

The Job of Teaching   67

The Emphasis on Individualized Instruction   74

The Practical Aspects of Choosing Teaching: A Summary   79

QUESTIONS FOR DISCUSSION   84

ACTIVITIES AND PROJECTS   84

REFERENCES   86

4. Pressures and Problems of Teaching   89

Day-by-Day Teaching: The True Picture   89

The Teacher's Roles   98

Professional and Public Relationships   101

Conclusion   108

QUESTIONS FOR DISCUSSION   108

ACTIVITIES AND PROJECTS   109

REFERENCES   110

5. Pressures and Problems of the School   114

Pressures of Time and Facilities   114

Husbanding Your Resources   128

Conclusion   133

QUESTIONS FOR DISCUSSION   133

ACTIVITIES AND PROJECTS   134

REFERENCES   135

6. The Pupils as Learners   140

Learning and Psychological Propositions   143

Principles of Learning   147

The Problem-Solving Process   149

Methods of Inquiry   152

Discovery and Learning   154

Motivating and the Environment   156

The Ordinalist Concept of Human Development:

   Jean Piaget   157

Evaluation and Testing   161

Conclusion   164

QUESTIONS FOR DISCUSSION   164

ACTIVITIES AND PROJECTS   165

REFERENCES   167

7. The Pupils as Boys and Girls   170

Pupil Differences   171

All Must Be Educated   175

Grouping the Pupils   181

Personality Differences in Children   184

Social-Class Differences of Pupils   185

The Demand for Conformity   186

Hopes and Aspirations versus Realistic Expectations   187

Conclusion   188

QUESTIONS FOR DISCUSSION   189

ACTIVITIES AND PROJECTS   190

REFERENCES   191

8. The Pupils—Class and Caste   196

Social Stratification   197

Color Caste   204

Social-Class Differences in School   209

Educational Discrimination and Compensation   210

Segregation and Integration   215

Conclusion   219

QUESTIONS FOR DISCUSSION   220

ACTIVITIES AND PROJECTS   221

REFERENCES   221

9. The Past   224

Historical Perspective of Education   226

Development of American Education   232

Are the Questions Asked about Education Today New?   250

Are the Questions the Result of Misunderstandings?   251

Are the Questions Unhealthy?   252

Will These and Other Questions Continue?   253

The Adequacy of American Education   254

Conclusion   260

QUESTIONS FOR DISCUSSION   260

ACTIVITIES AND PROJECTS   261

REFERENCES   262

10. The Philosophies   265

Traditional versus Modern   267

The Philosophy of Idealism   268

The Philosophy of Scholasticism   271

The Philosophy of Realism   276

The Philosophy of Experimentalism   279

The Philosophy of Existentialism   285

Conclusion   289

QUESTIONS FOR DISCUSSION   291

ACTIVITIES AND PROJECTS   292

REFERENCES   293

11. The System   297

Organization of the Schools   297

Financing and Control   299

State Certification   303

Employment Practices   311

Getting a Job   311

School-District Selection Procedures   317

Promotion, Transfer, Mobility, Professional Mortality, Tenure,
   Retirement   318

In-Service Growth   322

Conclusion   327

QUESTIONS FOR DISCUSSION   327

ACTIVITIES AND PROJECTS   328

REFERENCES   329

12. The Profession 334

The Making of a Profession   335

Professionalization   336

Individual Responsibility   344

New Careers, Roles, and Staffing Patterns   346

Commitment   353

The Profession Tomorrow   357

QUESTIONS FOR DISCUSSION   361

ACTIVITIES AND PROJECTS   362

REFERENCES   363

INDEX   367

Foundations
of Education

We have modified our environment so radically
that we must now modify ourselves in order to
exist in this new environment.

NORBERT WIENER

1

The Milieu

By accident of birth, every man becomes both a product and a prisoner
of a culture. By the nature of social institutions, schools become the
mouthpiece of a culture. Given these two *pro forma* truths, it should be
obvious why we open this volume with a consideration of the social milieu: the environment in which schools and their clients live, work, have
their being, and acquire their values and their ways of behaving.

Education—the instruction of the young by the older generation, the
passing on and improving of the cultural heritage, the preparation of youth
for adult responsibilities—is carried out in different ways by different societies at different times. Not only do the ways differ, but the nature of the
heritage to be passed on and the type of preparation for adulthood also
differ from one society to another, from epoch to epoch and from nation
to nation.

Now it appears that we may be on the brink of a new cultural epoch.
What it will look like, what its cultural components will be, how its "products" and "prisoners" will think, feel, and behave—all this is still a matter
of some speculation, but in any case we are sure to see accompanying
changes in the formal educational structures of our society. How are education and culture likely to affect each another in an epoch of change? It is
this question that we will consider in this chapter.

American Culture—Indigenous or Borrowed?

Our solid American citizen awakens in a bed built on a pattern which originated in the Near East but which was modified in Northern Europe before it was transmitted to America. He throws back covers made from cotton, domesticated in India, or linen, domesticated in the Near East, or wool from sheep, also domesticated in the Near East, or silk, the use of which was discovered in China. All of these materials have been spun and woven by processes invented in the Near East. He slips into his moccasins, invented by the Indians of the Eastern woodlands, and goes to the bathroom, whose fixtures are a mixture of European and American inventions, both of recent date. He takes off his pajamas, a garment invented in India, and washes with soap invented by the ancient Gauls. He then shaves, a masochistic rite which seems to have been derived from either Sumer or ancient Egypt.

Returning to the bedroom, he removes his clothes from a chair of southern European type and proceeds to dress. He puts on garments whose forms originally derived from the skin clothing of the nomads of the Asiatic steppes, puts on shoes made from skins tanned by a process invented in ancient Egypt and cut to a pattern derived from the classical civilizations of the Mediterranean, and ties around his neck a strip of bright-colored cloth which is a vestigial survival of the shoulder shawls worn by the seventeenth-century Croatians. Before going out for breakfast he glances through the window, made of glass invented in Egypt, and if it is raining puts on overshoes made of rubber discovered by the Central American Indians and takes an umbrella, invented in southern Asia. Upon his head he puts a hat made of felt, a material invented in the Asiatic steppes.

On his way to breakfast he stops to buy a paper, paying for it with

The Nature of Culture

Let us first consider what we mean by *culture* and then the role that education plays within the culture.

As used in the social sciences, the term "culture" refers to man's entire *social heritage,* all the knowledge, beliefs, customs, and skills he acquires as a member of society. A man who grew up apart from human association would lack culture because he had not communicated with other men and would, therefore, not share the knowledge of earlier generations. He would, however, solve problems and learn from experience, as do other animals. By the acquisition of coins, an ancient Lydian invention. At the restaurant a whole new series of borrowed elements confronts him. His plate is made of a form of pottery invented in China. His knife is of steel, an alloy first made in southern India, his fork a medieval Italian invention, and his spoon a derivation of a Roman original.

He begins breakfast with an orange, from the eastern Mediterranean, a cantaloupe from Persia, or perhaps a piece of African watermelon. With this he has coffee, an Abyssinian plant, with cream and sugar. Both the domestication of cows and the idea of milking them originated in the Near East, while sugar was first made in India. After his fruit and first coffee he goes on to waffles, cakes made by a Scandinavian technique from wheat domesticated in Asia Minor. Over these he pours maple syrup, invented by the Indians of the Eastern woodlands. As a side dish he may have the egg of a species of bird domesticated in Indo-China, or thin strips of the flesh of an animal domesticated in eastern Asia which have been salted and smoked by a process developed in northern Europe.

When our friend has finished eating he settles back to smoke, an American Indian habit, consuming a plant domesticated in Brazil in either a pipe, derived from the Indians of Virginia, or a cigarette, derived from Mexico. If he is hardy enough he may even attempt a cigar, transmitted to us from the Antilles by way of Spain. While smoking he reads the news of the day, imprinted in characters invented by the ancient Semites upon a material invented in China by a process invented in Germany. As he absorbs the accounts of foreign troubles he will, if he is a good conservative citizen, thank a Hebrew deity in an Indo-European language that he is 100% American.

Ralph Linton, *The Study of Man* (New York: Appleton, 1936), pp. 326–27. Reprinted by permission of Alfred A. Knopf, Inc.

culture, by tapping the heritage of his past, man becomes distinctively human. Man has, therefore, been called the culture-bearing animal.[1]

Cultures differ because of indigenous factors, such as the physical environment, and because of invention and patterns of borrowing from other cultures. Aside from their artifacts, or the concrete things man has made, cultures are more significantly distinguishable one from another by the abstract concepts—beliefs, customs, and ideals—that they create and that, unlike man, have a certain immortality. Because societies place such im-

[1] Leonard Broom and Philip Selznick, *Sociology,* 3d ed. (New York: Harper, 1963), p. 52.

3

portance on these values and ideals, they establish specific agencies or *social institutions,* such as the family, the church, and the school, to promote and safeguard their perpetual survival. These enduring elements have a particular relevance for education because they provide the framework of a given society's educational system; they shape education, and in turn they are shaped by the educational enterprise. Education's role, then, in preserving the social order has traditionally been viewed as the instrument of cultural transmission and socialization.

Every society is a unique product of its own history and its relation to other societies. Nevertheless, societies, in spite of their bewildering variety, also have common characteristics. They are social systems, and consequently require the performance of certain universal functions if they are to continue to exist. Education is a process concerned with some of these universal functions. This is true about education in all societies. In other words, it is possible to identify the universal functions of education. There are two major ones:

1. All societies maintain themselves by the exploitation of a culture, that is, a set of beliefs and skills that are not carried in the genetic constitution of individuals but must be learned. This social heritage must be transmitted through social organizations. Education has this function of *cultural transmission* in all societies.

2. Individuals must have personalities fashioned in ways that fit into the culture. Education, everywhere, has the function of *the formation of social personalities.* By transmitting the culture through appropriate molding of social personalities, education contributes to the integration of society as a mechanism that enables men to adapt themselves to their environment, to survive, and to reproduce themselves.

A. H. Halsey, "The Sociology of Education," in *Sociology: An Introduction,* ed. Neil J. Smelser (New York: Wiley, 1967), p. 385.

Some questions come immediately to mind. Are these major universal functions of education still relevant to an epoch of change where change becomes itself a life style? Do the schools need now to be totally revolutionized in both structure and function in order to meet the survival demands of our present and future society, or will such evolutionary changes as expanding the present role of the school be sufficient? Consider these questions carefully, for your answers to them are crucial in determining how you will approach the teaching act itself.

We will return to these issues in a later section. First, let us observe how the American educational system has put these universal functions into operation within our particular society.

Education in a Democratic Society

The essential values of a society, as we have said, affect the nature of its educational system. Thus the American commitment to democratic values strongly influences the schools. For example, the concepts, inherent in our Constitution, that every citizen should be able to participate intelligently in the political process and that every citizen should have equal opportunities in the society have encouraged mass public education. These cultural values, then—political franchise and egalitarianism—are implicit in the very formation of our educational institutions. Moreover, within the schools themselves, other values and skills of the culture are transmitted, like the patriotic ideals of national loyalty and the belief in democratic government, the economic ideal of free enterprise, and such social ideals as individualism, self-reliance, and to some extent brotherhood. Accompanying every general ideal or value are related norms to be instilled: thus, "the formation of social personalities."

Now this is the model of how the schools in our democracy are intended to function. Today, however, our society, both in school and out, faces complex problems and deficiencies that we are not adequately handling and that are, in turn, affecting the nature of our democracy. We sense a growing national mood of anxiety arising from apparently endless international conflicts, from continuing social instability and campus disorders, from the threat of economic depression and rising unemployment, and from insufficiencies in health, education, and welfare, to mention but a few. And with all this, the political situation continues to hinder the achievement of long-term solutions.

Although this mood appears to cut across various segments of our society, it is the youth in particular who seem to feel most keenly this demoralization and despair about the future. We were struck recently, for example, by a lengthy newspaper article on the valedictory speeches that were given at the various commencement exercises of San Francisco's high schools.[2] "Struck," because these speakers—serious, troubled, yet the most

[2] "The Class of 1970," *San Francisco Sunday Examiner and Chronicle,* June 7, 1970.

articulate members of their graduating class—were unanimous in reflecting their depression about the present and their pessimism regarding the future. "Struck," too, because we cannot think of an event more symbolic of youth's quest for high idealism and optimism than the traditional high-school graduation ceremonies. In fact, one girl, a straight-A student, even declined to make the traditional, formal speech but, apparently after much persuasion, consented to read instead from Matthew Arnold's "Dover Beach":

> . . . for the world, which seems
> To lie before us like a land of dreams,
> So various, so beautiful, so new,
> Hath really neither joy, nor love, nor light,
> Nor certitude, nor peace, nor help for pain;
> And we are here as on a darkling plain
> Swept with confused alarms of struggle and flight,
> Where ignorant armies clash by night.

What is going on in the schools that is contributing to such cynicism and alienation—outcomes the very opposite of the schools' purposes? Some of the answers can be found in the response of the schools to the values of American culture itself. An increasing number of young people today feel not only that the educational institutions are hypocritical in their support of this culture's stated ideals but also that some of these cherished values themselves need to be questioned, given the problems we face as a nation today. Here, for example, is how one youthful critic sees our schools *actually* functioning:

School is where you let the dying society put its trip on you. Our schools may seem useful: to make children into doctors, sociologists, engineers—to discover things. But they're poisonous as well. They exploit and enslave students; they petrify society; they make democracy unlikely. And it's not *what* you're taught that does the harm but *how* you're taught. Our schools teach you by pushing you around, by stealing your will and your sense of power, by making timid square apathetic slaves out of you—authority addicts.

Schooling doesn't have to be this destructive. If it weren't compulsory, if schools were autonomous and were run by the people in them, then we could learn without being subdued and stupefied in the process. And, perhaps, we could regain control of our own society.[3]

If, as Farber implies, schools dehumanize their students by authoritarian controls, by postponing responsible thinking, by rewarding the status quo,

---

[3] Jerry Farber, "The Student and Society," in *The Student as Nigger* (North Hollywood, Calif.: Contact Books, 1969), p. 14.

and by stubbornly resisting change, then we too must conclude that this educational system is more appropriate to a totalitarian than a democratic society. Of course there are many people who share a different attitude toward youth's criticisms of the present "system":

> Every generation makes mistakes, always has and always will. We have made our share. But my generation has made America the most affluent country on earth; it has tackled, head-on, a racial problem which no nation on earth in the history of mankind had dared to do.
>
> It has publicly declared war on poverty and it has gone to the moon; it has desegregated schools and abolished polio; it has presided over the beginning of what is probably the greatest social and economic revolution in man's history.
>
> It has begun these things, not finished them.
>
> It has declared itself, and committed itself, and taxed itself and damn near run itself into the ground in the cause of social justice and reform.
>
> Its mistakes are fewer than my father's generation—or his father's or his. Its greatest mistake is not Vietnam; it is the abdication of its first responsibility, its pusillanimous capitulation to its youth, and its sick preoccupation with the problems, the mind, the psyche, the raison d'être of the young.
>
> Since when have children ruled this country?
>
> By virtue of what right, by what accomplishment should thousands of teenagers, wet behind the ears and utterly without the benefit of having lived long enough to have either judgment or wisdom, become the sages of our time? [4]

And there are many people who share a different opinion of today's graduates! See, for example, the quotation from George Herman below. The real question, however, is whether the judgment and wisdom of the past will be sufficient for the eventualities of the future—which brings us now to a discussion of cultural change and existing trends now shaping our future.

Cultural Change

To speak of the unprecedented "rapidity" or "acceleration" of change has become almost a cliché. Still, beyond their personal recognition that "things are changing faster than ever," most people have difficulty grasping the concept within the enormous perspective of social and technological evolution. It might be helpful, therefore, to use Postman and Weingartner's clock metaphor to illustrate what the "change revolution" really signifies:

[4] Ross K. Toole, "A Professor Speaks Out," *San Francisco Sunday Examiner and Chronicle,* April 5, 1970.

College Graduation

Something I read in the paper stuck in my mind until I went back and dug it out of the trash basket and thumbed through it and found the item in question. It was a quote from a girl graduating from Cornell and here is part of it: "I had made a commitment to myself that I was never going to be a suburban housewife. I'm not going to allow the world to run my life and I'm never going to allow my ideas to be stifled by what other people are thinking."

I guess I found in that quotation the quintessence of graduation thought: "I'm never going to be like the rest of them—old and tired, partly defeated by life, drinking a little too much at noisy parties, and taking a few too many medicines." And somewhere in the back of my mind I found the faintest hint of that mental fragrance of our youth, like the memory of a fragrance in an antique perfume bottle. It's the echo of Marjorie Morningstar, a rewording of Shakespeare's Puck in *A Midsummer Night's Dream,* a rediscovered fragment from an ancient Greek poem by Meleager.

"I'm not going to allow the world to run my life." It is a cry as ancient as man, and it rings with not so much hope as despair. Even as children we have eyes and we can see that almost no one escapes the pressures of life. I suspect that one reason college students have such dislike and contempt for visiting graduates is because they are a constant reminder that the brief childhood excursion will end in time in the need to earn certain things from society. Among these things are life, to be earned from the doctors and their super-conformist machines, the hospitals. Liberty, to be earned from the majority and their laws and enforcers. And the pursuit of happiness, to be earned in self-approval and the approval of those one respects, and worst of all, loves.

Earning all of this is a hard job, called growing up. It is like what the psalmists called a refiner's fire—it melts and deforms some of us, it refines and purifies others, and it changes everybody no matter how proud his or her boast.

George Herman, in a CBS News radio broadcast, June 9, 1970. Used with permission.

Imagine a clock face with 60 minutes on it. Let the clock stand for the time men have had access to writing systems. Our clock would thus represent something like 3,000 years, and each minute on our clock 50 years. On this scale, there were no significant media changes until about nine minutes ago. At that time, the printing press came into use in Western culture. About three minutes ago, the telegraph, photograph, and locomotive arrived. Two minutes ago: the telephone, rotary press, motion pictures, automobile, airplane, and radio. One minute ago, the talking picture. Television has appeared in the last ten seconds, the computer in the last five, and communications satellites in the last second. The laser beam—perhaps the most potent medium of communication of all—appeared only a fraction of a second ago.

It would be possible to place almost any area of life on our clock face and get roughly the same measurements. . . . It is happening in every field of knowledge susceptible to scientific inquiry.[5]

They go on to say that, while of course there is nothing new about change, what is new is the "degree of change"; in other words, the whole character of change itself has changed.

This is really quite a new problem. For example, up until the last generation it was possible to be born, grow up, and spend a life in the United States without moving more than 50 miles from home, without ever confronting serious questions about one's basic values, beliefs, and patterns of behavior. Indeed, without ever confronting serious challenges to anything one knew. Stability and consequent predictability—within "natural cycles"—was the characteristic mode. But now, in just the last minute, we've reached the stage where change occurs so rapidly that each of us . . . has continuously to work out a set of values, beliefs, and patterns of behavior that are viable, or *seem* viable, to each of us personally. And just when we have identified a workable system, it turns out to be irrelevant because so much has changed while we were doing it.[6]

Thus it may be a foolish enterprise even to attempt projections into the future; but nevertheless, since soothsaying has lately become a fascinating and popular sport, practiced by as many bold theorists as tarot-card readers, we take it that we too may join the game.

The method generally involves attempting to identify significant current behaviors and practices that seem to indicate long-range trends. Although each catalog varies according to its creator's method and point of view—his optimism or pessimism, his radicalism or conservatism—certain directions seem to be fairly constant among intelligent observers. What follows is our attempt to synthesize some of these observations,[7] for a picture of the context out of which are developing the future values of our culture.

[5] Neil Postman and Charles Weingartner, *Teaching as a Subversive Activity* (New York: Delacorte, 1969), p. 10. Copyright © 1969 by Neil Postman and Charles Weingartner. Reprinted by permission of Delacorte Press.

[6] Ibid., p. 11.

[7] We have borrowed the organization here from Charles C. Collins's paper, "Human Values and Changing Work Patterns," for the Junior College Leadership Program, University of California, Berkeley, March 1970.

Certain situations will continue to affect the *physical being* of our planet.

Continuing threat of war, both large scale and small scale. The combined powers of the world today possess together such instruments of nuclear, chemical, and biological warfare as to destroy all the inhabitants as well as a good part of the territory of the planet. We need not explicate the gruesome consequences of this situation.

Continuing population explosion. Even at a 1.7 percent annual increase, there will be 330 million Americans by the turn of the century, and a world population of 7 billion, more than double the present 3.4 billion.[8] Although the situation ought to be eased somewhat by birth-control programs, what this growth implies, regarding not only the prospect of increased famine but also the need for, at the least, greater regimentation (and less individuality) in the social structure, can well be imagined.

Environmental pollution. Consider also how our lives are becoming increasingly infested with junk, smog, garbage, sewage, oil slicks in the ocean, contaminated rivers and lakes, devastated natural-wilderness areas, and visual (or aesthetic) pollution. Although, with ecological consciousness now on the rise, we are beginning to take some steps toward preserving our environment, we can yet foresee continuing resistance from private enterprise and from those who feel that environmental controls will impede the growth of the economy.

Other situations will continue to affect the existing *social order.*

The communications (or media) and technological revolutions. Since the fantastic diffusion and differentiation of automated machinery and its products are apparent to anyone exposed to the media today, we need not spell out the specific trends in this direction. What is perhaps not so obvious is the equally fantastic pervasiveness with which these "revolutions" touch all aspects of our lives—at home, at work, and at leisure. Our society, whose culture will surely continue to be characterized by the connection of machines and computers and by more rapid communications devices, will increasingly require a higher level of education, a higher degree of conformity, and a greater amount of leisure time from its citizenry. Of the conditions we have mentioned and shall mention, this may be the most crucial in determining our future values and life styles—and most crucial, too, because the vastness and intricacy of technology make it so difficult to understand, much less control.

Burgeoning bureaucracies. The implications of the growth of bureaucracy, closely related and indispensable as it is to the expansion of the

[8] Wayne H. Davis, "Overpopulated America," *New Republic,* January 10, 1970, p. 14.

The Principle of Population

I think I may fairly make two postulata.

First, That food is necessary to the existence of man.

Secondly, That the passion between the sexes is necessary and will remain nearly in its present state.

These two laws, ever since we have had any knowledge of mankind, appear to have been fixed laws of our nature, and, as we have not hitherto seen any alteration in them, we have no right to conclude that they will ever cease to be what they now are, without an immediate act of power in that Being who first arranged the system of the universe, and for the advantage of his creatures, still executes, according to fixed laws, all its various operations.

.   .   .   .   .

Assuming then, my postulata as granted, I say, that the power of population is indefinitely greater than the power in the earth to produce subsistence for man.

Population, when unchecked, increases in a geometrical ratio. Subsistence increases only in an arithmetical ratio. A slight acquaintance with numbers will shew the immensity of the first power in comparison of the second.

By that law of our nature which makes food necessary to the life of man, the effects of these two unequal powers must be kept equal.

This implies a strong and constantly operating check on population from the difficulty of subsistence. This difficulty must fall somewhere and must necessarily be severely felt by a large portion of mankind.

.   .   .   .   .

This natural inequality of the two powers of population and of production in the earth and that great law of our nature which must constantly keep their effects equal form the great difficulty that to me appears insurmountable in the way to the perfectibility of society. All other arguments are of slight and subordinate consideration in comparison of this. I see no way by which man can escape from the weight of this law which pervades all animated nature. No fancied equality, no agrarian regulations in their utmost extent, could remove the pressure of it even for a single century. And it appears, therefore, to be decisive against the possible existence of . . . society. . . .

Thomas R. Malthus, *An Essay on the Principle of Population* (1798) technocracy, are not to be underestimated. Moreover, the existence of giant bureaucratic agencies and corporations in our society will become particularly critical because by their very nature—in their structure and function, in their firm commitment to conventional assumptions and standard practices—they are highly resistant to change.

Liberation movements.   Blacks, Third World minorities, women, students, and other oppressed groups who, through discrimination in employment, housing, and education, have been denied self-determination are becoming increasingly militant in their demands. This is partly because of the serious social regressions that we have been experiencing since the later 1960's. The frightening result may be a continuance not only of the use of violent means to achieve the radical social change required for liberation of these groups but also of the contingent polarization of the society's haves and have-nots.

Generation gap.   Parents and teachers of earlier youth probably served more readily as models of moral and ethical behavior than they apparently do today. The acceleration of change has drastically widened the distance between generations, creating in many cases two separate cultures existing on tenterhooks under the same roof (at home and at school). Margaret Mead, speaking of the younger generation, has written: "What they want is, in some way, to begin all over again. They are ready to make way for something new by a kind of social bulldozing." [9] When the older generation sees the way of life to which it is committed being ploughed under, it is no wonder that communication between the young and the old is so tenuous.

Loss of national confidence.   Recent public-opinion polls continue to verify the fact that a large number of people in this country do not believe the statements of their leaders or approve of their actions. Since the whole theory of democracy is based on an essential trust of those who govern by those who are governed, the continuation of the "credibility gap" could imply a mass political-psychological crisis in the society. Closely related to this is the threat to our national concept of self posed mainly by the war in Vietnam. Again the American people are haunted by doubts and perplexities about the righteousness of their government's policies.

Alienation.   Because what is true of the nation is also true of the individuals within the nation, more and more people seem to find themselves aliens in their own culture, estranged from themselves and remote from other individuals. This condition, no doubt, largely explains the increase in

[9] Margaret Mead, "Youth Revolt: The Future Is Now," *Saturday Review,* January 10, 1970.

On Patriotism

And while each of us pursues his selfish interest and comforts himself by blaming others, the nation disintegrates. I use the phrase soberly: the nation disintegrates.

This is a time for the highest order of patriotism. This is a time to ask what it is we stand for as a people. It is a time to re-examine our founding documents and to reflect on what to tell each other are the American virtues. It is a time to search our hearts.

It is very, very easy for leaders to appeal to the prejudice and fear and anger that is in us. It is easy for leaders to speak to the selfishness that is in us, to tell us that nothing in this country need be changed, and to find villains who may be blamed for our troubles.

But there is in us as Americans something better than fear and anger and prejudice, something better than the lazy, comfortable inclination to blame others.

There is in us, if our leaders will ask for it, the courage and stamina to face our problems honestly, to admit that we ourselves are partly to blame for them, and to identify paths of constructive action.

John W. Gardner, former Secretary of Health, Education, and Welfare, from a speech that was to have been given on May 13, 1970, to the Illinois Constitutional Convention at Springfield. (The speech was canceled at the request of the convention officers when the text became available in advance.)

crime and drug abuse, on the harmful side, as well as the growing interest in religious and utopian communities and sensitivity training, on the healthier side.

The situations outlined above are probably not the whole picture, but they do at least seem to be the context out of which the youth of our culture is deriving its values and life styles; they are therefore meaningful portents for the coming years when the younger generation will become the generation in power, the generation that will define our society. While there is nothing sacrosanct about the values of the young, especially in a world of great flux, we might take a brief look at what their emerging values appear to be now.

Their orientation is in the here and now. They are less concerned than past generations with tradition and historical verities and less willing to defer gratification to the future.

They have a strong identification with the physical world, an aesthetic appreciation of its beauty, and a desire to preserve and maintain it, if not repair it.

They do not value materialism.

They do not value nationalism or flag-waving patriotism, although most are seriously concerned about the erosion of democratic ideals in this country.

They tend not to commit themselves to the future and are heedful of keeping their options open.

They espouse the notion "Do your own thing" in place of the competitive Protestant-capitalist work ethic.

Their attitudes toward their fellow beings are romantic and humanistic.

Some of them, out of desperation, have adopted the values of nihilism and anarchy.

They question the values and assumptions of science and technology. There is a growing polarization between them and their elders around this matter.

This last point deserves a little discussion, since, as we have indicated earlier, it is so central to the future form of our culture. On the one hand, there are those such as Harry S. Broudy, editor of *The Educational Forum*, who feel optimistic about the morality of science and the future benefits of life in a technocratic society:

Before leaving the scientific frames of thinking, let it be noted that science is customarily regarded as providing the means, but not the ends, of life. Science, it is contended, can help you win a war but not to decide whether a war is worth fighting. In connection with what has been said about the current crisis in values, about the generation gap, we shall have to turn to science for ends as well as means. Science can determine value possibilities, and in turn, moral obligation. For example, once it becomes possible to do something about the prevention of cancer, there may be an obligation to do it. Once science tells us about the effects of smoking, the means of controlling population, controlling air pollution, and eliminating poverty on a large scale, our moral obligation is likely to expand. For when there were no adequate means for accomplishing these goals, there was no moral obligation to undertake them, however sympathetic and idealistic one might have been. In other words, science has a major role in determining and defining the possible behavioral forms of virtue, of human excellence, as well as in increasing our creature comfort by means of technology.[10]

[10] Harry S. Broudy, "A Philosophy of the Ideal School," in *The Ideal School*, ed. Gloria Kinney (Wilmette, Ill.: Kagg Press, 1969), pp. 10–11.

And, on the other hand, there are those such as Theodore Roszak, author of *The Making of a Counter-Culture,* who believe that the deterministic values of science and technology will be the total undoing of individual freedom in our society:

If there is one especially striking feature of the new radicalism we have been surveying, it is the cleavage that exists between it and radicalism of previous generations where the subjects of science and technology are concerned. To the older collectivist ideologies, which were as given to the value of industrial expansion as the capitalist class enemy, the connection between totalitarian control and science was not apparent. Science was almost invariably seen as an undisputed social good, because it had become so intimately related in the popular mind (though not often in ways clearly understood) to the technological progress that promised security and affluence. It was not foreseen even by gifted social critics that the impersonal, large-scale social processes to which technological progress gives rise—in economics, in politics, in education, in every aspect of life—generate their own characteristic problems. When the general public finds itself enmeshed in a gargantuan industrial apparatus which it admires to the point of idolization and yet cannot comprehend, it must of necessity defer to those who are experts; only they appear to know how the great cornucopia can be kept brimming over with the good things of life.[11]

The arguments for and against the scientific world view are in some sense exemplary of the kind of dialectic we see unfolding constantly between every old and new value now under question. We can still only contemplate the outcome for our culture of this continuing process.

Implications for Education

In a delightful parody on education, *The Saber-Tooth Curriculum,* Harold Benjamin tells the story of a primitive people whose very existence was dependent upon their ability to catch fish with their bare hands, club little woolly horses, and drive away the saber-toothed tiger with fire. Consequently the skills of "fish-grabbing," "woolly-horse-clubbing," and "saber-tooth-tiger-scaring-with-fire" formed the basic curriculum of the school of that primitive society.

In time, a change occurred in the physical environment of these paleolithic people. A great glacier descended from the north, muddying the streams, so that "no matter how good a man's fish-grabbing education had been, he could not grab fish when he could not find fish to grab." The

[11] Theodore Roszak, *The Making of a Counter-Culture* (Garden City, N.Y.: Doubleday, 1969), pp. 205–6.

great glacier also caused the little woolly horses to migrate to a drier climate and killed the saber-toothed tigers. Under these changed conditions, the tribe would have perished had there not been some inventions. Survival now became dependent upon the people's ability to catch fish in the muddy water with newly invented nets, to snare the elusive antelopes that had replaced the horses, and to trap bears in pits. Meanwhile, "back at school," they continued to teach the skills of fish grabbing, horse clubbing, and tiger scaring.

> Traditions are a splendid thing; but we should create traditions, not live by them.
>
> Franz Marc, quoted in Carl Rogers and Barry Stevens, *Person to Person: The Problem of Being Human* (Lafayette, Calif.: Real People Press, 1967), p. 115.

Now there were a few thoughtful tribesmen who criticized the schools. "These new activities of net-making, snare-setting, and pit-digging are indispensable to modern existence," they said. "Why can't they be taught in school? *After all, you will have to admit that times have changed.*"

But the wise old men who controlled the schools pointed out that the school curriculum already was too crowded with teaching the intricate details of the "standard cultural subjects"—fish grabbing, horse clubbing, and tiger scaring. No, they couldn't possibly consider adding such "fads and frills" as net making, antelope snaring, and bear killing, because "the essence of true education is timelessness. It is something that endures through changing conditions like a solid rock standing squarely and firmly in the middle of a raging torrent. You must know that there are some eternal verities, and the saber-tooth curriculum is one of them." [12]

The story of the "saber-tooth curriculum" beautifully illustrates our earlier discussion of the growing forces for and against radical change in our society and in our society's schools. While the events of the next few years will probably set the direction of movement for decades to come, certain educational trends seem predictable, given the evidence at present that many educators, aware of changing social realities, are questioning their goal priorities and given, of course, the survival of our society. Let us comment briefly on four of these trends:

Movement toward an atmosphere of shared learning.   As we have said, education traditionally functions by means of an older person's imparting

[12] Harold Benjamin, *The Saber-Tooth Curriculum* (New York: McGraw-Hill, 1939), p. 44.

his cultural wisdom and skills to a younger person. However, as we have also suggested, this presupposes a constant environment in which the cultural heritage that is passed on is still relevant; and this further implies the *authoritarian* role of the teacher and the *subordinate* role of the pupil. If it is true that today's fundamental social and philosophical questions arise, not from our classical heritage, but from our contemporary experience— from the advances of technology, from the schisms in our social order, from the rapidity of change itself—then no one becomes *the* authority, and everyone, teacher and pupil alike, shares in the quest for knowledge. Thus arises a kind of "community of learners" in which the teacher not only functions to facilitate the students' acquisition of knowledge and attitudes but also is himself involved in the process.

Expansion of the role of education in society. Not only will more and more people become involved in education but the educational period will also be expanded through such programs as early-childhood education; parent, family, and adult education; and vocational retraining. The educational enterprise will thus move away from the autonomy of the schools into industry, community, and home. The concept of a "learning society" will probably also modify the sequence of school-then-work.

Departure from traditional methods of instruction. The traditional classroom-lecture approach will probably be augmented or entirely replaced by individualized learning opportunities leading either to specified behavioral objectives or open-ended growth. The extent to which students shall determine the learning content of their own education is still questionable, but we believe it is desirable that they should do so. Another concept gaining adherents is that of emphasizing the *process* of learning rather than the *product,* the view of education not as a means to an end but as an activity valuable in itself. Consonant with the new curriculum will be new school-staffing patterns, with the instructional roles distributed among teams of curriculum designers, guidance personnel, teachers, assistant teachers, aides, and so on.

New conscious role for education in society. Previously we have spoken of educational systems as *deriving* from cultural values and goals and *responding* to cultural change. Now, however, students and faculty— themselves acting as change agents—are becoming very much involved in accomplishing social goals, thus directly changing the culture itself. Of course, the sponsorship of research in institutions of higher education has always yielded new ideas and technological innovations that, although in a piecemeal way, do add up to change the nature of our culture. Still it has only been recently that schools have tackled the very fabric of society itself, for example in the university "reconstitution" movements throughout the country. We are bound to see particularly the colleges acting more and more as revolutionary forces within the society.

Crap Detecting

In the early 1960s, an interviewer was trying to get Ernest Hemingway to identify the characteristics required for a person to be a "great writer." As the interviewer offered a list of various possibilities, Hemingway disparaged each in sequence. Finally, frustrated, the interviewer asked, "Isn't there any one essential ingredient that you can identify?" Hemingway replied, "Yes, there is. In order to be a great writer a person must have a built-in, shockproof crap detector."

It seems to us that, in his response, Hemingway identified an essential survival strategy and the essential function of the schools in today's world. One way of looking at the history of the human group is that it has been a continuing struggle against the veneration of "crap." Our intellectual history is a chronicle of the anguish and suffering of men who tried to help their contemporaries see that some part of their fondest beliefs were misconceptions, faulty assumptions, superstitions, and even outright lies. The mile posts along the road of our intellectual development signal those points at which some person developed a new perspective, a new meaning, or a new metaphor. We have in mind a new education that would set out to cultivate just such people—experts at "crap detecting."

.   .   .   .   .

Survival in a stable environment depends almost entirely on remembering the strategies for survival that have been developed in the past, and so the conservation and transmission of these becomes the primary mission of education. But, a paradoxical situation develops when change becomes the primary characteristic of the environment. Then the task turns inside out—survival in a rapidly changing environment depends almost entirely upon being able to identify which of the old concepts are relevant to the demands imposed by the new threats to survival, and which are not. Then a new educational task becomes critical: getting the group to unlearn (to "forget") the irrelevant concepts as a prior condition to learning. What we are saying is that "selective forgetting" is necessary to survival.

Neil Postman and Charles Weingartner, *Teaching as a Subversive Activity* (New York: Delacorte, 1969), pp. 2–3, 208. Copyright © 1969 by Neil Postman and Charles Weingartner. Reprinted by permission of Delacorte Press.

Commitment to Teaching

While Americans sit by the fire and spin, debating the various alternatives, what more should the teacher be doing? As early as 1932, George S. Counts raised the question of the professional practitioner's place in the scheme of things, in his book *Dare the School Build a New Social Order?* Nearly forty years later, the question is still appropriate. What direction the future of the American school takes will be determined largely by its teachers. It depends on their wisdom, their insight, their character, their devotion to the task of educating the next generation. And it is the teacher who must guarantee the basic goal of our educational system: to foster individual fulfillment and to nurture the development of free but responsible human beings.

So, as Farber said, it is not so much *what* we are to teach—for the ostensible goal of education in our democracy has been the same since its inception—but *how* we are to help our students become both more free and more responsible through the learning act. We believe that this can be done only by allowing students not only to exercise their own powers but also to take responsibility for their behavior. For if the present and future society we have described requires anything at all for its survival, at the very least it will require thinking, creative, independent, responsible, and humane persons. The teacher must reflect these qualities in his own personality, for if education is to begin to resemble shared learning experiences or a "community of learners," as we suggested before, then the value of teacher behavior as a model comes to be of paramount importance.

Moreover, given the changes likely in our culture and the concomitant changes in the schools, teachers, perhaps more than other members of society, must themselves be committed to and personally involved in the process of change. It is this kind of dynamism that we hope will define the educational future not only for our students but for ourselves as well.

Within this context the teacher will need to develop a certain style that will not only reflect his personal dedication to change but will also allow his pupils the same opportunity to learn and grow freely and responsibly. This style will probably need to resemble somewhat the so-called inquiry method, or at least be based on similar assumptions. By this method students are allowed to pose their own questions and are then assisted in finding their own answers.

The greatest value of inquiry-centered education is the message it holds for the student. It says: "You and your mind are to be valued. There is

Élan, Élite, Ethos

I want to start with one aspect of national purpose, the aspect that I call *élan*. . . . What I mean by *élan* is the feeling of commitment, the feeling of being on fire, a sense of mission, a sense that there are things worth dying for and worth living for.

We've got to recapture what seems to me the *élan* of American history, and that's the authentic idea of a revolutionary America. I think it means we've got to stop being afraid of the term "revolution." I found that the image of America (which many people in other countries have) . . . is the image of a fat, rich, prosperous, complacent country which was the last bulwark of the *status quo,* and they didn't like it.

If we think in terms of this authentic revolutionary tradition and if we keep alive, as I hope we will keep alive, the life of the mind and the spirit so as to give meaning to these dynamic energies of ours, then I think that we can answer the problem of *élan*. And with this energy we have great tasks to perform. I think that I can put them all in a single phrase, and the phrase for me is that of finishing the unfinished business of democracy.

I break down the concept of national purpose into a second portion. To this also I give a foreign name, *élite,* the idea of an educated, creative *élite*. . . . If we are to win what I regard as the crucial race, not the weapons race but the entire *intelligence race,* it can be done only by using our educational plant and resources for development of the best potential of our most promising youngsters.

nothing else but self-education. Man learns principally by encountering his world, getting ideas, playing with them, testing them against reality and revising them. Sometimes others will point out aspects of the world you haven't yet encountered. Sometimes they will suggest new ideas to try out. They will surely try to tell you what is real and what is right. But in the end, you must decide this for yourself, and learn how to make these decisions wisely. To the extent that you relinquish this right and obligation, you become a trained animal." [13]

The teacher in this process will need to develop an open-ended way of thinking, particularly about truth and knowledge. Like the child, he must be willing to test his ideas, and at the end of his search he must be ready

[13] J. R. Suchman, "Some New Roles and Goals in Education," in *The Ideal School,* ed. Gloria Kinney (Wilmette, Ill.: Kagg Press, 1969), pp. 89–90.

The problems of the school system of a generation ago, two generations ago, three or four or five generations ago are no longer the problems of today. We've gone through a great educational revolution, a revolution of trying to give a substratum of necessary cohesion to the society. We are, as Walt Whitman said, not just a nation but a nation of nations. America was built up by streams of immigration from every part of the world. And it was necessary during our history to use our educational system in such a way that youngsters coming from families with different religions, with different ethnic traditions, with different cultural traditions, should have something in common, they should have some cohesion, some cement. The problem today is different. It is that of a creative America.

In every realm of activity, in every discipline in our lives, there is a small group of people who are training themselves, educating themselves, stretching themselves in order to transcend themselves. I see emerging a new creative America which will develop a democratic élite and make use of it for strengthening the culture.

I've spoken of *élan* and of a creative American *élite*. I end by suggesting a third element of the larger concept of national purpose. That is an *ethos*, a sense of values to live by and to die by if necessary.

Max Lerner, "Humanist Goals," in *Education: An Instrument of National Goals*, ed. Paul R. Hanna (New York: McGraw-Hill, 1962). Copyright 1962, McGraw-Hill Book Company. Reprinted by permission.

to recognize that his conclusions are "real and right," but perhaps only for him and only for the time being. In other words, the teacher must be aware of his own experiential limitations but at the same time open to new experiential possibilities.

Thus we are back where we started—with the milieu. Perhaps, as Suchman suggests, this is what education is all about anyway: the opportunity to enter into a dialogue with your milieu—examining it, asking it questions, looking for meanings within its context and within yours, and being aware of its constantly unfolding possibilities and of yours.

So if we have been successful, you now know that change is happening, change is inevitable, change is necessary, change is even changing, and that we are all going to have to adapt ourselves to this condition as the one certainty of life. But won't this make teaching much more interesting, much more fun? Isn't changing just a much better way to live and learn?

Conclusion

We began by examining the nature of culture and how education has traditionally functioned within societies. In the context of our democracy with its particular values and ideals, we then questioned whether these educational functions, based on the passing on of cultural traditions, were relevant for an epoch of change. We also looked at some of the challenges to education and criticisms of how it *actually* functions in our country compared with how education for democracy *ought to* function. We then examined what some of the trends for the future might be, what youth's attitudes are toward these, and what the implications are for education in a changing culture. Finally, we briefly described some requisites for teachers in the "new" education.

Questions for Discussion

1. How did your family, your church, and/or the school you attended influence your personal value system? Did you adopt the value systems of these institutions, did you react against them, or have you independently formulated your own? Describe how your awareness of your values has developed.

2. Devise a strategy for finding out the nature and extent of the influence of the family, the church, and the schools on the pupils you have or will have in your class.

3. Is the idea of cultural change equally acceptable to all groups? Think of examples of groups that resist change. What accounts for their resistance? Considering these obstacles to progress, how can educators help to promote the needed changes in society?

4. Do you believe that there are values or goals that are eternal, never changing? If so, what are they? Show how they have remained constant from culture to culture, from epoch to epoch, and why you believe they will continue to survive.

5. Do you believe that evolutionary changes will be sufficient to meet the challenges of the future, or do you think revolution is inevitable? How do you support your belief? What are the consequences, the advantages and disadvantages, of each kind of change? Given your belief, what strategy ought you to adopt as an educator to insure the desired changes?

6. Can you remember the details (or mood at least) of your high-school commencement? How does it compare with the account of the commencements on pages 5–6?

7. Compare the statements by Farber and Toole, pages 6 and 7. If you can see their positions as opposite poles on a continuum, where do you fit into that continuum? How do you know?

8. Do you experience the "generation gap" in your relations with your parents or the significant adults in your life? If so, what are the polarities involved? Do your parents feel as Toole does? How do they show it? If they are more sympathetic to your search, how do they show that? If you do not feel remote from the older generation, how do you explain that?

9. Think back on the teachers you have had through the years. Were the ones that stand out in your mind as being excellent traditional or discovery oriented? How do you account for your admiration of them? How much of what they taught you do you remember? Is it certain attitudes or skills you remember, or certain subject matter? From your own experience, then, how do you feel about fact-and-memory education as opposed to the inquiry method?

10. Reread the discussion of "crap detecting," page 18. What old concepts or values would you like to unlearn? Which concepts do you feel all of society needs to "forget"?

11. Do you believe, as Suchman does, that "there is nothing else but self-education"? If so, what do you plan to do in order to actualize your belief in the classroom?

Activities and Projects

1. It might be interesting to study the latest in the peer culture of elementary or secondary students. How can you find this out? Consider your sources of information in drawing your conclusions.

2. Using a consistent method, try to determine how each of the following groups regards the teaching of American ideals:
   Boy Scouts of America
   AFL-CIO
   National Association of Manufacturers
   American Legion
   League of Women Voters
   American Civil Liberties Union
   Students for a Democratic Society

John Birch Society
Black Panther Party
Women's Liberation Front

3. Make a special study of education in some other culture or nation, noting especially how its schools are "the mouthpiece of the culture." Is there some way you can ascertain if these schools are actually functioning to promote the culture's ideals and values?

4. Think about the community in which you were raised as a child. List the changes that have taken place since then in the economy, the population, the buildings, the age and social class of the residents, the social and political climate, and so on. Then for each change try to assess to what extent the school played a significant part in it or how the school responded to it.

5. Visit an Americanization class in the adult-education program in your community. What did you observe? What generalizations can you draw from this experience about the promotion of American values?

6. Analyze the front page of the local newspaper over a period of several weeks. What values are being headlined? How are they being headlined? Do the events support the trends mentioned in this chapter? What implications does your study have for the schools?

7. Devise a method for assessing high-school students' attitudes toward the future (how they see society, how they see themselves as adults fitting into society, and so forth). Then carry out your project. What predictions would you make based on this study?

8. How might you as a class demonstrate the polar positions on student rights expressed by Farber and Toole, pages 6 and 7?

9. How might you as a class demonstrate the polar positions on the promise of technology expressed by Broudy and Roszak, pages 14–15?

10. Consider what was said about the inquiry method in this chapter. Devise a strategy for finding out the attitudes of elementary and high-school teachers toward the notion of absolute truth and knowledge and toward inquiry. What generalizations can you draw from this study, and what are the implications for the "new education"?

References

Culture

BENEDICT, RUTH. *Patterns of Culture.* New York: New American Library, 1959.

BROOM, LEONARD, and PHILIP SELZNICK. *Sociology*. 3d ed. New York: Harper, 1963.

LINTON, RALPH. *The Study of Man*. New York: Appleton, 1936.

MEAD, MARGARET. *Coming of Age in Samoa*. New York: New American Library, 1963.

————. *Cultural Patterns and Technical Change*. New York: New American Library, 1959.

SMELSER, NEIL J., ed. *Sociology: An Introduction*. New York: Wiley, 1967.

SPINDLER, GEORGE D. *Education and Culture*. Pt. 2, "Education in American Culture"; Pt. 3, "Education Viewed Cross-Culturally." New York: Holt, Rinehart & Winston, 1963.

Changing Culture

CALDER, NIGEL, ed. *The World in 1984*. 2 vols. Baltimore: Penguin, 1965.

CHASE, STUART. *The Most Probable World*. New York: Harper, 1968.

DRUCKER, PETER. *The Age of Discontinuity*. New York: Harper, 1968.

EHRLICH, PAUL. *Eco-Catastrophe!* San Francisco: City Lights, 1968.

————. *The Population Bomb*. New York: Ballantine, 1968.

ELLUL, JACQUES. *The Technological Society*. New York: Knopf, 1967.

FABUN, DON. *The Dynamics of Change*. Englewood Cliffs, N.J.: Prentice-Hall, 1967.

GALBRAITH, JOHN KENNETH. *The New Industrial State*. Boston: Houghton Mifflin, 1967.

HARRINGTON, MICHAEL. *The Accidental Century*. London: Penguin, 1966.

HEILBRONER, ROBERT L. *The Future as History*. New York: Grove, 1960.

HELMER, OLAF. *Social Technology*. New York: Basic Books, 1966.

HUTCHINS, ROBERT M. *The Learning Society*. New York: Praeger, 1968.

KAHN, HERMAN, and ANTHONY J. WIENER. *The Year 2000: A Framework for Speculation on the Next 33 Years*. New York: Macmillan, 1967.

Changing Values

BAIER, KURT, and NICHOLAS RESCHER. *Values and the Future*. New York: Free Press, 1969.

BELL, DANIEL, ed. *Toward the Year 2000: Work in Progress*. Boston: Beacon, 1969.

BOULDING, KENNETH. *The Meaning of the 20th Century: The Great Transition*. New York: Harper, 1964.

FROMM, ERICH. *The Revolution of Hope: Toward a Humanized Technology*. New York: Bantam, 1968.

GARDNER, JOHN W. *Self-Renewal: The Individual and the Innovative Society*. New York: Harper, 1963.

59222

LIBRARY
College of St. Francis
JOLIET, ILL.

MICHAEL, DONALD N. *The Unprepared Society: Planning for a Precarious Future.* New York: Basic Books, 1968.

ROSZAK, THEODORE. *The Making of a Counter-Culture: Reflections on the Technocratic Society and Its Youthful Opposition.* New York: Doubleday, 1969.

Changing Education

BECKER, ERNEST. *Beyond Alienation: A Philosophy of Education for the Crisis of Democracy.* New York: Braziller, 1967.

BENJAMIN, HAROLD. *The Saber-Tooth Curriculum.* New York: McGraw-Hill, 1939.

COUNTS, GEORGE S. *Dare the Schools Build a New Social Order?* New York: Day, 1932.

CURTI, MERLE. *The Social Ideas of American Educators.* Paterson, N. J.: Littlefield, 1959.

GLASSER, WILLIAM. *Schools without Failure.* New York: Harper, 1969.

GOODMAN, PAUL. *Compulsory Miseducation and the Community of Scholars.* New York: Random House, Vintage Books, 1962.

HOLT, JOHN. *How Children Fail.* New York: Dell, 1964.

KINNEY GLORIA, ed. *The Ideal School.* Wilmette, Ill.: Kagg Press, 1969.

LEONARD, GEORGE B. *Education and Ecstasy.* New York: Delacorte, 1968.

MEAD, MARGARET. "Changing Teachers in a Changing World." In *The Education of Teachers,* ed. G. K. Hodenfield and T. M. Stinnett. Englewood Cliffs, N. J.: Prentice-Hall, 1961.

MORPHET, EDGAR L., and CHARLES O. RYAN, eds. *Designing Education for the Future.* 7 vols. New York: Citation Press, 1967–69.

PARKER, J. CECIL, and LOUIS J. RUBIN. *Process as Content: Curriculum Design and the Application of Knowledge.* Chicago: Rand McNally, 1966.

POSTMAN, NEIL, and CHARLES WEINGARTNER. *Teaching as a Subversive Activity.* New York: Delacorte, 1969.

RAFFERTY, MAX LOUIS. *What They Are Doing to Your Children.* New York: New American Library, 1968.

RUBIN, LOUIS J., ed. *Life Skills in School and Society.* Yearbook of the Association for Supervision and Curriculum Development. Washington, D. C.: Association for Supervision and Curriculum Development of the National Education Association, 1969.

SANFORD, NEVITT, and JOSEPH KATZ. *Search for Relevance.* San Francisco: Jossey-Bass, 1969.

SCOBEY, MARY-MARGARET, and GRACE GRAHAM. *To Nurture Humaneness: Commitment for the 1970's.* Yearbook of the Association for Supervision and Curriculum Development. Washington, D. C.: Association for Supervision and Curriculum Development of the National Education Association, 1970.

TOYNBEE, ARNOLD J. "Education: The Long View." In *American Education Today,* ed. Paul Woodring and John Scanlon. New York: McGraw-Hill, 1963.

NOTE: In addition to the works listed above, and following each of the subsequent chapters in this book, the reader is referred to volumes 2 and 3 in the series of which this is volume 1, *Commitment to Teaching,* edited by James C. Stone and Frederick W. Schneider: volume 2, *Readings in the Foundations of Education,* second edition; volume 3, *Teaching in the Inner City* (New York: Crowell, 1971 and 1970, respectively). The selections in each of these volumes are arranged in parts corresponding generally to the chapters of the present volume.

There are doubts concerning the business [of education] since all people do not agree in those things which they would have a child taught, both with respect to improvement in virtue and a happy life; nor is it clear whether the object of it should be to improve the reason or rectify the morals. From the present mode of education we cannot determine with certainty to which men incline, or what tends to virtue, or what is excellent; for all these things have their separate defenders.

ARISTOTLE

2

The Goals

The Public versus the Educators

Historian Arnold Toynbee has told us that the survival of civilizations is to be seen in the cycle of challenge and response. In 1957 the Russian launching of Sputnik galvanized the American public into an examination of the existing educational system. This examination resulted in a flood of critics who proclaimed that our "el-hi" schools were not doing their jobs in keeping up with the "knowledge explosion" and exhorted educators to concentrate on the "training of the mind" and to cut all the frills from the curricula. Changing the slogan "Johnny can't read" to "Johnny can read" became a major concern, and new curricula in the "basic" subjects (English, mathematics, foreign languages, social studies, and science) were introduced into the schools. Vast sums of federal money were poured into the schools for innovative, remedial, and compensatory programs as an attempt to equalize educational opportunities.

More than a decade later some of the same concerns were being considered in relation to the Right to Read program, but the entire educational system was under scrutiny from a different standpoint. What had seemed to be the scope of the reforms for the 1960's was increasingly being acknowledged as inadequate for future decades. For instance, in remarks delivered to the University of Pennsylvania Graduate School in 1970, James C. Allen, Jr., former United States Commissioner of Education, pointed out:

> To think of the world of the future, even the future as imminent as the year 2000, is to step into fantasy land. The statistics used to substantiate the "knowledge explosion" syndrome are being so outdistanced now as to make them seem almost turtle-like in the speeded-up pace of man's grasp of the universe. Our men on the moon, with their "giant leap for mankind," have shown us that there really are no limits to the what-next's we can expect."

Thus education for a world that staggers the imagination will not be easy and obviously cannot be accomplished by clinging to traditional ways and concepts. A relevant education for a rapidly changing future world would be an education not just for limited specialities but for general adaptability—or, in other words, for turning out from the schools not a finished product, but, rather, a mind and spirit prepared for continued and continuous learning. What is relevant in education is what is significant in education, which should equal the universals in education.

Unanimity on these points does not exist either within or without the educational establishment, however. In a vein similar to Allen's, John Holt comments, "Today the child who has been taught in school to stuff his head with facts, recipes, this-is-how-to-do-it, is obsolete before he leaves the building. Anything he can do, or be taught to do, a machine can do, and *soon will do,* better and cheaper." [1]

Yet on the opposite side of the fence are those like California's former State Superintendent of Public Instruction, Max Rafferty, who insists "that the schools exist to teach organized, disciplined, systematic subject matter to children." He strongly states "that the schools are the only societal agencies specifically charged with the vital performance of this function . . . and . . . that if the schools do not teach subject matter, the children are never going to learn it." [2]

---

[1] John Holt, "Why We Need New Schooling," *Look,* January 13, 1970, p. 52.

[2] Max Rafferty, *Max Rafferty on Education* (New York: Devin-Adair, 1968), p. 6.

If one carefully analyzes the conflicting statements and points of view, he becomes aware of the divergent philosophies of education underlying the differences. In other words, there exists a conflict or a lack of agreement on what schools should accomplish.

Is the purpose of education to prepare for life, for jobs, for citizenship, for college? Has intellectual training and development been neglected in favor of life adjustment, or the "whole" child? Or is a major objective of education to enhance the child's social-facilitating behavior, which includes his ability to get along with others, and the image of himself as a contributing person in a humanistic society? Is intellect more important in a scale of values than good citizenship, getting along with others, loyalty to our democratic traditions, ability to get and keep a job? These are the questions that are still before us today just as they have been over the last hundred years—in fact, ever since the establishment of public schools.

Just as each age creates its women's fashions, so it has its own particular ideas about education. For example, following World War I and the shocking number of young men found physically unqualified for military service came a period when "healthful living" was the first aim of the schools. And following the uproar that resulted from the Russians' launching of the first satellite, the new fashion in education—its central purpose —came to be the "training of the mind." Later, as the country began to face some of its social problems, concern was given to providing means for "the culturally disadvantaged" to join the mainstream of American education. Thus, to the question "What should be the purposes of education?" each generation has offered an answer appropriate to the social conditions and climate of opinion of its epoch. An understanding of this historical development is necessary as we work out our answer in the second half of the twentieth century.

The Objectives of Education

WHAT KNOWLEDGE IS OF MOST WORTH?

We begin this review and analysis of statements of the purpose of education with an essay by Herbert Spencer, a sociologist who has been variously described as "the founder of sociology as a science," "*the* philosopher of the nineteenth century," and "the father of modern social science." Whatever his title, the question he has raised—"What knowledge is of most worth?"—is certainly the basic issue for education. Since Spencer first asked it in 1860, it has continued to provoke, dismay, and stimulate educators.

To Spencer, the basic issue is the "relative values of knowledges." The school's task is to discover what subjects are of most worth and to design a curriculum that gives these subjects top priority. His criterion of true education is utilitarian: "Of what use is it?" The true aim of education is "preparation for complete living." John Dewey and his followers were to say the same thing a half century later, and this philosophy is apparent in several of the later statements included in this chapter.

If there requires further evidence of the rude, undeveloped character of our education, we have it in the fact that the comparative worths of different kinds of knowledge have been yet scarcely even discussed—much less discussed in a methodic way with definite results. Not only is it that no standard of relative values has yet been agreed upon; but the existence of any such standard has not been conceived in any clear manner. And not only is it that the existence of any such standard has not been clearly conceived; but the need for it seems to have been scarcely even felt. Men read books on this topic, and attend lectures on that; decide that their children shall be instructed in these branches of knowledge, and shall not be instructed in those; and all under the guidance of mere custom, or liking, or prejudice; without ever considering the enormous importance of determining in some rational way what things are really most worth learning. . . . Before devoting years to some subject which fashion or fancy suggests, it is surely wise to weigh with great care the worth of the results, as compared with the worth of various alternative results which the same years might bring if otherwise applied.

Spencer discusses the need to establish priorities:

In education, then, this is the question of questions, which it is high time we discussed in some methodic way. The first in importance, though the last to be considered, is the problem—how to decide among the conflicting claims of various subjects on our attention. Before there can be a rational *curriculum,* we must settle which things it most concerns us to know; or, to use a word of Bacon's, now unfortunately obsolete—we must determine the relative value of knowledges.

To this end, a measure of value is the first requisite. And happily, respecting the true measure of value, as expressed in general terms there can be no dispute. Every one in contending for the worth of any particular order of information, does so by showing its bearing upon some part of life. In reply to the question, "Of what use is it?" the mathematician, linguist, naturalist, or philosopher, explains the way in which his learning beneficially influences action—saves from evil or secures good—conduces to happiness. When the teacher of writing has pointed out how great an aid writing is to success in business—that is, to the obtainment of sustenance—that is, to satisfactory living; he is held to have proved his case. And when the collector of dead facts (say a numismatist) fails to make clear any appreciable effects which these facts can produce on human welfare, he is obliged to admit that they are comparatively valueless.

All then, either directly or by implication, appeal to this as the ultimate test.

How to live?—that is the essential question for us. Not how to live in the mere material sense only, but in the widest sense. The general problem which comprehends every special problem is—the right ruling of conduct in all directions under all circumstances. In what way to treat the body; in what way to treat the mind; in what way to manage our affairs; in what way to bring up a family; in what way to behave as a citizen; in what way to utilize all those sources of happiness which nature supplies—how to use all our faculties to the greatest advantage of ourselves and others—how to live completely? And this being the great thing needful for us to learn is, by consequence, the great thing which education has to teach. To prepare us for complete living is the function which education has to discharge; and the only rational mode of judging of any educational course is, to judge in what degree it discharges such function. . . .

When Spencer answers his own question "What knowledge is of most worth?" by citing the subject of science, he means the natural *and* social sciences:

To the question with which we set out—What knowledge is of most worth? —the uniform reply is—Science. This is the verdict on all the counts. For direct self-preservation, or the maintenance of life and health, the all-important knowledge is—Science. For that indirect self-preservation, which we call gaining a livelihood, the knowledge of greatest value is—Science. For the due discharge of parental functions, the proper guidance is to be found only in—Science. For that interpretation of national life, past and present, without which the citizen cannot rightly regulate his conduct, the indispensable key is—Science. Alike for the most perfect production and highest enjoyment of art in all its forms, the needful preparation is still—Science. And for purposes of discipline —intellectual, moral, religious—the most efficient study is, once more— Science. The question which at first seemed so perplexed, has become, in the course of our inquiry, comparatively simple. We have not to estimate the degrees of importance of different orders of human activity, and different studies as severally fitting us for them; since we find that the study of Science, in its most comprehensive meaning, is the best preparation for all these orders of activity. We have not to decide between the claims of knowledge of great though conventional value, and knowledge of less though intrinsic value; seeing that the knowledge which we find to be of most value in all other respects, is intrinsically most valuable; its worth is not dependent upon opinion, but is as fixed as is the relation of man to the surrounding world. Necessary and eternal as are its truths, all Science concerns all mankind for all time. Equally at present, and in the remotest future, must it be of incalculable importance for the regulation of their conduct, that men should understand the science of life, physical, mental, and social; and that they should understand all other science as a key to the science of life. . . .[3]

[3] Herbert Spencer, *Education: Intellectual, Moral and Physical* (New York: Appleton, 1860), pp. 4–5, 6–7, 49–50.

THE SEVEN CARDINAL OBJECTIVES

One of the first and best-known specific definitions of the school's purposes was formulated in 1918 by the Commission on Reorganization of Secondary Education. The commission proposed for the schools a set of Seven Cardinal Objectives:

1. Health
2. Command of fundamental processes
3. Worthy home membership
4. Vocational competence
5. Effective citizenship
6. Worthy use of leisure time
7. Ethical character

To evaluate this statement properly, one must recall its setting. World War I was ending, and Americans were disturbed over the large number of young men rejected for service in the armed forces because of physical unfitness and inability to read and write. If such disabilities and inabilities were to be reduced, the schools obviously had a major job to perform, and the commission sought to give emphasis to this job by the place it gave in a hierarchy of purposes to health and command of the fundamental processes.

THE AIMS OF EDUCATION

About the same time, Alfred North Whitehead, then a University of London professor of mathematics, came to Harvard as professor of philosophy and, in 1922, published *The Aims of Education*. While the statement had a greater initial impact on higher rather than elementary or secondary-school education, it is included here because of its contrast in point of view to the Seven Cardinal Objectives, as well as because of the importance it has attained with today's greater emphasis on the intellectual side of education and on teaching subject matter per se by a deductive rather than by the traditional inductive process.

One main idea runs throughout Whitehead's chapters: students are alive, and the purpose of education is to stimulate and guide their self-development. It follows from this that teachers also should be alive, with living thoughts. The whole book is a protest against dead knowledge, against inert ideas. "There is only one subject-matter for education, and that is Life in all its manifestations."

Culture is activity of thought, and receptiveness to beauty and humane feeling. Scraps of information have nothing to do with it. A merely well-informed man is the most useless bore on God's earth. What we should aim at producing is men who possess both culture and expert knowledge in some special direction. Their expert knowledge will give them the ground to start from, and their culture will lead them as deep as philosophy and as high as art. We have to remember that the valuable intellectual development is self-development, and that it mostly takes place between the ages of sixteen and thirty. As to training, the most important part is given by mothers before the age of twelve. A saying due to Archbishop Temple illustrates my meaning. Surprise was expressed at the success in after-life of a man, who as a boy at Rugby had been somewhat undistinguished. He answered, "It is not what they are at eighteen, it is what they become afterwards that matters."

In training a child to activity of thought, above all things we must beware of what I will call "inert ideas"—that is to say, ideas that are merely received into the mind without being utilised, or tested, or thrown into fresh combinations.

In the history of education, the most striking phenomenon is that schools of learning, which at one epoch are alive with a ferment of genius, in a succeeding generation exhibit merely pedantry and routine. The reason is, that they are overladen with inert ideas. Education with inert ideas is not only useless; it is, above all things, harmful—*Corruptio optimi, pessima*. Except at rare intervals of intellectual ferment, education in the past has been radically infected with inert ideas. That is the reason why uneducated clever women, who have seen much of the world, are in middle life so much the most cultured part of the community. They have been saved from this horrible burden of inert ideas. Every intellectual revolution which has ever stirred humanity into greatness has been a passionate protest against inert ideas. Then, alas, with pathetic ignorance of human psychology, it has proceeded by some educational scheme to bind humanity afresh with inert ideas of its own fashioning.

Let us now ask how in our system of education we are to guard against this mental dryrot. We enunciate two educational commandments, "Do not teach too many subjects," and again, "What you teach, teach thoroughly."

Note that at the turn of the century, Whitehead was discussing the "discovery method" that modern curriculum reformers emphasize:

The result of teaching small parts of a large number of subjects is the passive reception of disconnected ideas, not illumined with any spark of vitality. Let the main ideas which are introduced into a child's education be few and important, and let them be thrown into every combination possible. The child should make them his own, and should understand their application here and now in the circumstances of his actual life. From the very beginning of his education, the child should experience the joy of discovery. The discovery which he has to make, is that general ideas give an understanding of that stream of events which pours through his life, which is his life. By understanding I mean more than a mere logical analysis, though that is included. I mean "understanding" in the sense in which it is used in the French proverb, "To under-

stand all, is to forgive all." Pedants sneer at an education which is useful. But
if education is not useful, what is it? Is it a talent, to be hidden away in a nap-
kin? Of course, education should be useful, whatever your aim in life. It was
useful to Saint Augustine and it was useful to Napoleon. It is useful, because
understanding is useful.

I pass lightly over that understanding which should be given by the literary
side of education. Nor do I wish to be supposed to pronounce on the relative
merits of a classical or a modern curriculum. I would only remark that the understanding which we want is an understanding of an insistent present. The
only use of a knowledge of the past is to equip us for the present. No more
deadly harm can be done to young minds than by depreciation of the present.
The present contains all that there is. It is holy ground; for it is the past, and it
is the future. At the same time it must be observed that an age is no less past if
it existed two hundred years ago than if it existed two thousand years ago. Do
not be deceived by the pedantry of dates. The ages of Shakespeare and of Mo-
lière are no less past than are the ages of Sophocles and of Virgil. The communion of saints is a great and inspiring assemblage, but it has only one possible hall of meeting, and that is, the present; and the mere lapse of time through
which any particular group of saints must travel to reach that meeting-place,
makes very little difference.

Passing now to the scientific and logical side of education, we remember
that here also ideas which are not utilised are positively harmful. By utilising
an idea, I mean relating it to that stream, compounded of sense perceptions,
feelings, hopes, desires, and of mental activities adjusting thought to thought,
which forms our life. I can imagine a set of beings which might fortify their
souls by passively reviewing disconnected ideas. Humanity is not built that way
—except perhaps some editors of newspapers.

In scientific training, the first thing to do with an idea is to prove it. But
allow me for one moment to extend the meaning of "prove"; I mean—to prove
its worth. . . .

Whitehead expresses a pragmatic philosophy of education that seems
to have been ignored in his time by the followers of John Dewey:

    . . . Education is the acquisition of the art of the utilisation of knowledge.
This is an art very difficult to impart. Whenever a text-book is written of real
educational worth, you may be quite certain that some reviewer will say that it
will be difficult to teach from it. Of course it will be difficult to teach from it.
If it were easy, the book ought to be burned; for it cannot be educational. In
education, as elsewhere, the broad primrose path leads to a nasty place. . . .
    . . . There is no royal road to learning through an airy path of brilliant gen-
eralisations. There is a proverb about the difficulty of seeing the wood because of the trees. That difficulty is exactly the point which I am enforcing.
The problem of education is to make the pupil see the wood by means of the
trees.

The solution which I am urging, is to eradicate the fatal disconnection of subjects which kills the vitality of our modern curriculum. There is only one subject-matter for education, and that is Life in all its manifestations. Instead of this single unity, we offer children—Algebra, from which nothing follows; Geometry, from which nothing follows; Science, from which nothing follows; History, from which nothing follows; a Couple of Languages, never mastered; and lastly, most dreary of all, Literature, represented by plays of Shakespeare, with philological notes and short analyses of plot and character to be in substance committed to memory. Can such a list be said to represent Life, as it is known in the midst of the living of it? The best that can be said of it is, that it is a rapid table of contents which a deity might run over in his mind while he was thinking of creating a world, and had not yet determined how to put it together. . . .

Emphasizing the value of trained intelligence (and sounding much like a writer of the 1960's), Whitehead says:

. . . When one considers in its length and in its breadth the importance of this question of the education of a nation's young, the broken lives, the defeated hopes, the national failures, which result from the frivolous inertia with which it is treated, it is difficult to restrain within oneself a savage rage. In the conditions of modern life the rule is absolute, the race which does not value trained intelligence is doomed. Not all your heroism, not all your social charm, not all your wit, not all your victories on land or at sea, can move back the finger of fate. To-day we maintain ourselves. To-morrow science will have moved forward yet one more step, and there will be no appeal from the judgment which will then be pronounced on the uneducated. . . .[4]

The Purposes of Education in American Democracy

Following the Great Depression of the early 1930's, there developed among Americans a renewed concern for the individual—a special concern for the dignity and worth of each man and his rights, not only the traditional freedoms but also rights in the economic sphere. These new concerns called for reevaluation of the purposes of the school; and in response to the times, the Educational Policies Commission of the National Education Association (NEA) developed a statement of aims known as *The Purposes of Education in American Democracy.*

This highly influential statement opens with a quotation from John Dewey:

[4] Alfred N. Whitehead, *The Aims of Education* (New York: Macmillan, 1929), pp. 13–16, 18, 19, 26. Reprinted by permission of The Macmillan Company.

If philosophy is for anything—if it is not a kind of mumbling in the dark, a form of busy work—it must shed some light upon the path. Life without it must be a different sort of thing from life with it. And the difference which it makes must be in us. Philosophy, then, is reflection upon social ideals, and education is the effort to actualize them in human behavior.

The use of the quotation was not incidental: the philosophy of Dewey is reflected in the four major goals for the school, and the goals are stated in behavioral terms—that is, as outcomes that will be apparent in the way students act. The complete list of objectives in the statement follows:

I. The Objectives of Self-Realization

The Inquiring Mind. The educated person has an appetite for learning.
Speech. The educated person can speak the mother tongue clearly.
Reading. The educated person reads the mother tongue efficiently.
Writing. The educated person writes the mother tongue effectively.
Number. The educated person solves his problems of counting and calculating.
Sight and Hearing. The educated person is skilled in listening and observing.
Health Knowledge. The educated person understands the basic facts concerning health and disease.
Health Habits. The educated person protects his own health and that of his dependents.
Public Health. The educated person works to improve the health of the community.
Recreation. The educated person is participant and spectator in many sports and other pastimes.
Intellectual Interests. The educated person has mental resources for the use of leisure.
Esthetic Interests. The educated person appreciates beauty.
Character. The educated person gives responsible direction to his own life.

II. The Objectives of Human Relationship

Respect for Humanity. The educated person puts human relationships first.
Friendships. The educated person enjoys a rich, sincere, and varied social life.
Cooperation. The educated person can work and play with others.
Courtesy. The educated person observes the amenities of social behavior.
Appreciation of the Home. The educated person appreciates the family as a social institution.
Conservation of the Home. The educated person conserves family ideals.

Homemaking. The educated person is skilled in homemaking.
Democracy in the Home. The educated person maintains democratic family relationships.

III. The Objectives of Economic Efficiency

Work. The educated producer knows the satisfaction of good workmanship.
Occupational Information. The educated producer understands the requirements and opportunities for various jobs.
Occupational Choice. The educated producer has selected his occupation.
Occupational Efficiency. The educated producer succeeds in his chosen vocation.
Occupational Adjustment. The educated producer maintains and improves his efficiency.
Occupational Appreciation. The educated producer appreciates the social value of his work.
Personal Economics. The educated consumer plans the economics of his own life.
Consumer Judgment. The educated consumer develops standards for guiding his expenditures.
Efficiency in Buying. The educated consumer is an informed and skillful buyer.
Consumer Protection. The educated consumer takes appropriate measures to safeguard his interests.

IV. The Objectives of Civic Responsibility

Social Justice. The educated citizen is sensitive to the disparities of human circumstance.
Social Activity. The educated citizen acts to correct unsatisfactory conditions.
Social Understanding. The educated citizen seeks to understand social structures and social processes.
Critical Judgment. The educated citizen has defenses against propaganda.
Tolerance. The educated citizen respects honest differences of opinion.
Conservation. The educated citizen has a regard for the nation's resources.
Social Applications of Science. The educated citizen measures scientific advance by its contribution to the general welfare.
World Citizenship. The educated citizen is a cooperating member of the world community.
Law Observance. The educated citizen respects the law.
Economic Literacy. The educated citizen is economically literate.
Political Citizenship. The educated citizen accepts his civic duties.

Devotion to Democracy.   The educated citizen acts upon an unswerving loyalty to democratic ideals.[5]

THE TEN IMPERATIVE NEEDS OF YOUTH

In 1944, the National Association of Secondary School Principals published *Planning for American Youth.* Written during World War II, the book reflects progressive education's "life adjustment" concept [6] as well as wartime conditions. In the Foreword, the authors state: "The war has reminded us of many virtues and ideals that we had forgotten. One of them is the duty we owe to our youth in the provision of their education, not education merely in terms of books, credits, diplomas, and degrees, but education in terms of preparation for living and earning."

Planning for American Youth points out how birth and environment have made boys and girls different and how they must all have equal opportunities to live and learn, but it emphasizes that *all* youth have certain educational needs in common.

"Youth have specific needs they recognize; society makes certain requirements of all youth; together these form a pattern of common educational needs." It is the job of the school to see that these needs are met and satisfied. The Ten Imperative Needs of Youth are:

1. All youth need to develop salable skills.
2. All youth need to develop and maintain good health and physical fitness.
3. All youth need to understand the rights and duties of the citizen of a democratic society.
4. All youth need to understand the significance of the family for the individual and society.
5. All youth need to know how to purchase and use goods and services intelligently.
6. All youth need to understand the influence of science on human life.

[5] Educational Policies Commission, *The Purposes of Education in American Democracy* (Washington, D.C.: Educational Policies Commission of the National Education Association and the American Association of School Administrators, 1938), pp. 50, 72, 90, 108.

[6] "Progressive education" is the name of the movement resulting from the attempts to implement John Dewey's philosophy of education (see chap. 11 below). His concept was to educate the "whole" child—intellect, emotions, etc.—and to do so by capitalizing on the child's own interests. "Life adjustment," as the name implies, means education of the student for life as he is living it now—today—rather than education as preparation for adulthood—tomorrow.

7. All youth need an appreciation of literature, art, music, and nature.
8. All youth need to be able to use their leisure time well and to budget it wisely.
9. All youth need to develop respect for other persons.
10. All youth need to grow in their ability to think rationally.[7]

It is important for the reader to understand that ever since the publication of *The Purposes of Education in American Democracy* and *Planning for American Youth,* the question has been appropriately raised of the extent to which these statements by professional groups of educators—the National Education Association and the National Association of Secondary School Principals—represent the purposes of the schools as seen by the public itself.

THE FIRST WHITE HOUSE CONFERENCE ON EDUCATION

In a monumental attempt to utilize the insights of the American public at large on the problems of public education, President Eisenhower called the first White House Conference on Education. Two-thirds of the three thousand persons called to Washington for this three-day conference were laymen, a group of distinguished Americans who had had experience either as members of local boards of education or college boards of regents. In a significant document entitled *The Committee for the White House Conference on Education, A Report to the President,* the group sought to identify the purposes of education:

WHAT SHOULD OUR SCHOOLS ACCOMPLISH?

1. A general education as good as or better than that offered in the past, with increased emphasis on the physical and social sciences.
2. Programs designed to develop patriotism and good citizenship.
3. Programs designed to foster moral, ethical, and spiritual values.
4. Vocational education tailored to the abilities of each pupil and to the needs of the community and Nation.
5. Courses designed to teach domestic skills.
6. Training in leisure-time activities such as music, dancing, avocational reading, and hobbies.
7. A variety of health services for all children, including both physical and dental inspections, and instruction aimed at bettering health knowledge and habits.

[7] *Planning for American Youth: An Educational Program for Youth of Secondary School Age* (Washington, D.C.: National Association of Secondary School Principals, 1949).

8. Special treatment for children with speech or reading difficulties and other handicaps.
9. Physical education, ranging from systematic exercises, physical therapy, and intramural sports, to interscholastic athletic competition.
10. Instruction to meet the needs of the abler students.
11. Programs designed to acquaint students with countries other than their own in an effort to help them understand the problems America faces in international relations.
12. Programs designed to foster mental health.
13. Programs designed to foster wholesome family life.
14. Organized recreational and social activities.
15. Courses designed to promote safety. These include instruction in driving automobiles, swimming, civil defense, etc.

During the past two generations, this list of school goals has grown with increased speed. This is a phenomenon which has excited both admiration and dismay. After several decades of experimentation, should this broadening of the goals be recognized as legitimate?

This Committee answers *Yes.* Nothing was more evident at the White House Conference on Education than the fact that these goals, representing as they do an enormously wide range of purposes, are the answer to genuine public demand. These goals have, after all, been hammered out at countless school board meetings during the past quarter-century throughout the land. The basic responsibility of the schools is the development of the skills of the mind, but the overall mission has been enlarged. Schools are now asked to help each child to become as good and as capable in every way as native endowment permits. The schools are asked to help children to acquire any skill or characteristic which a majority of the community deems worthwhile. The order given by the American people to the schools is grand in its simplicity: in addition to intellectual achievement, foster morality, happiness, and any useful ability. The talent of each child is to be sought out and developed to the fullest. Each weakness is to be studied and, so far as possible, corrected. This is truly a majestic ideal, and an astonishingly new one. Schools of that kind have never been provided for more than a small fraction of mankind.

Although it is new, this ideal of schools which do everything possible for all children is a natural development in the United States. The moving spirit of this Nation has been from the beginning a sense of fairness. Nowadays equality of opportunity for adults means little without equality of educational opportunity for children. Ignorance is a greater obstacle than ever to success of most kinds. The schools have become a major tool for creating a Nation without rigid class barriers. *It is primarily the schools which allow no man's failure to prevent the success of his son.*

In still another way, this new ideal for the schools is a natural development of this country: it recognizes the paramount importance of the individual in a free society. Our schools are asked to teach skills currently needed by the Nation, but never at the expense of the individual. This policy of encouraging each child to develop his individual talents will be of the greatest use to the Nation, for in the long run, if no talent is wasted in our land, no skill will be lacking.[8]

The purposes of education identified by the White House Conference group are all-encompassing in their coverage. For the first time in the world's history, the schools are to educate all youth to an extent never before conceived. No other nation has ever tried it. If American schools have failed for some, have neglected some of the most able, it should not be surprising. In fact, it would be most remarkable if American schools did well by all. In this connection, the English author Denis Brogan was prompted to remark that the American school "is undertaking to do more than it can (which is very American) and doing much more than it seems to do (which is also very American)." [9]

THE COUNCIL FOR BASIC EDUCATION

One of the groups agreeing thoroughly with Brogan that the schools are "doing too much" while feeling that at the same time they fail to give priority to "the proper goals" is the Council for Basic Education. Its chief spokesman has been James D. Koerner, who says that

almost all children are capable of sustained academic study and that it is the proper business of a public school system to give this study to them through the medium of what Matthew Arnold called "the best that has been thought and said in the world." In this system all students run on the same track but at their own best speeds; and all concentrate their education in a relatively few areas that encompass the most significant of man's knowledge.

Koerner then addresses himself to the question of these "areas that encompass the most significant of man's knowledge" and the criteria by which one identifies them:

In the process of his own intellectual development—as he uncovered great knowledge, mostly through trial and error over eons of time—man finally was able to refine particular techniques for investigating phenomena, techniques that over long periods were found to produce results that were more fruitful than those produced in other ways. Through man's passion for classifying and codifying his knowledge, in order to continue improving it, some few fields

[8] *The Committee for the White House Conference on Education, A Report to the President* (Washington, D.C.: U.S. Government Printing Office, 1956), pp. 8–10.

[9] Denis Brogan, *Unity and Liberty* (New York: Knopf, 1944), p. 135.

have attained pre-eminence because they are generative, because they form the nucleus of other, secondary fields, because they represent pinnacles of human achievement, and because they now constitute bodies of knowledge of proven power and research techniques of proven effectiveness.

These basic fields include the major languages of mankind, the instrument without which all of us would still live like pre-Neolithic sub-men; they also include that other indispensable language, the language of mathematics, without which all of us would likewise still be primitives; they include history, which in its largest sense encompasses all the records of all the ages, without which the race would be as intellectually impotent as a man without a memory; and they include the natural sciences, which by becoming highly qualified and capable of extremely reliable predictions about the major phenomena of nature, have radically transformed the modern world. These fields, I suggest, are clearly the chief ones in which man has recorded his experience on earth and his understanding of life. One might justly argue that other fields are nearly as basic, or that what is basic in one age is not so in another, and that the pattern of educational programs must change accordingly. My only point is that the foregoing fields have been the chief means by which man has become what he now is and that they remain paramount at this particular point in his history. As such they have earned a pre-eminent place in the education of each new generation. In the common schools of our society, the question of priorities is compelling, for there is time only for those subjects which best serve the need of all men, as citizens and human beings.[10]

Clearly, the council would assign to the schools those goals that they alone could achieve. Thus, by implication, it would leave other goals for other social institutions to achieve. And it would also place the academic (or "solid") subjects in a position of paramount importance, thus—again by implication—relegating all other subject fields either to the scrap heap or at least to a position of less importance.

Another well-known critic of the educational status quo during the late 1950's and early 1960's was Arthur Bestor, then professor of history at the University of Illinois. Bestor reacted vigorously to what he called the "soft" effects of the progressive-education movement of the 1920's and 1930's. Like Koerner, Bestor proposed and argued for a return to the "solid" subjects—to the teaching of the intellectual disciplines as the distinctive function of the school. By implication, vocational, social, and other objectives would be eliminated. Through his many publications— *Educational Wastelands, Backwoods Utopias,* and *The Restoration of Learning*—he gained a reputation as the most serious and influential critic

---

[10] James D. Koerner, "Theory and Experience in the Education of Teachers," *Sixteenth Yearbook* (Washington, D.C.: American Association of Colleges for Teacher Education, 1963), pp. 15, 16–17.

of education to appear during the 1950's and 1960's. His point of view is in sharp contrast to the Educational Policies Commission statement and the Ten Imperative Needs of Youth, with their "life adjustment" philosophy of the objectives of education:

"In its education," Admiral Rickover has said, paraphrasing Lord Haldane, "the soul of a people mirrors itself." A mirror, one must remember, is undiscriminating. It reflects the good and the bad, the beautiful and the ugly, with crystalline impartiality. Education is such a mirror. Defects in our educational system are reflections of weakness and shortcomings in our national life. This is a hard truth to accept, but a truth nonetheless. The danger lies in confusing explanation with justification. Because racial discrimination can be explained historically is no reason for viewing it in any other light than as an abomination. So with defects and weaknesses in American education. To explain them is not to condone them.

.   .   .   .   .

The school, the college, and the university were created to perform a specific and recognized function. Their facilities and techniques—classrooms, libraries, laboratories, recitations, lectures, seminars, and examinations—were designed and developed for the particular purpose of intellectual training. To enable the school to carry out any other function, it must be altered and adapted, and its performance in the new role is usually haphazard, fumbling, and defective. Moreover, if intellectual training is pushed aside or neglected by schools and colleges, society is thereby impoverished of intellectual training, because it possesses no other resources, no other agencies, no other techniques for making up the loss. That the primary function of the educational system is to furnish intellectual training is as completely self-evident as any statement that can possibly be made about the function of a social institution, whether one approaches the matter from the point of view of logic or history or sociology.

The distribution of functions that I have described is never more than approximate, of course. Most institutions perform, in an incidental and indirect way, functions that belong primarily to institutions of another sort. Thus business and industry, not only in the "breaking in" of employees but also in advertising, attempt a good deal of social indoctrination, particularly in what are held to be the "economic virtues." The home carries on a good deal of intellectual training. The school, even in its strictly academic work, maintains, and therefore helps to inculcate, the ethical standards of the surrounding culture, whenever issues involving these standards—for example, the matter of honesty in examinations—arise in the classroom. In providing the intellectual foundations for professional work, moreover, the school at times cannot avoid crossing the line that theoretically separates intellectual training from apprenticeship. A blurring of lines, in the degree which these examples represent, is both natural and inescapable, and it raises no question worth discussing.

That American public schools have enormously expanded their functions is so obvious a fact that I do not suppose the point calls for elaboration or demonstration. Those who most vigorously oppose the point of view I take on educational policy do not deny this expansion of scope; indeed they acknowledge it and take pride in it. One of the most influential statements of the function of the public school, *Planning for American Youth,* a program published by the National Association of Secondary School Principals, says: "Youth have specific needs they recognize; society makes certain requirements of all youth; together these form a pattern of common educational needs. . . . It is the Job of the School to Meet the Common and the Specific Individual Needs of Youth."

The "needs" that are particularized (in the ten points that make up the body of the statement) include those forms of training that I have described as job training and social conditioning. The responsibility of the school, in other words, is supposed to extend to all the areas in which society has customarily furnished some form of deliberate training.

. . . . .

Is it really necessary or desirable for the school to expand its responsibility to this extent? In fact, is the school capable of discharging such extended responsibility? Can it perform the tasks involved without fatally neglecting its primary social obligation—that of providing intellectual training?

Bestor discusses "life adjustment," but in terms of a "mature and disciplined intellect":

The adjustment to life that we must strive for through the school is the kind of adjustment that results from applying the varied resources and the developed powers of a mature and disciplined intellect to each successive problem as it arises. Adjustment in this highest sense is an outcome of education. It is not an outcome that can be reached by short cuts, by a miscellany of experiences, by playroom imitations of the mere externals of adult activity. "There is no *royal road* to geometry," said Euclid to his sovereign, Ptolemy I. "There is no royal road to intelligent citizenship" is the message that educators should deliver to the sovereign people of today. Serious, sustained, systematic labor, in libraries, laboratories, and classrooms, is the only way of producing educated men and women in the twentieth century, as in every preceding century.[11]

RESTRUCTURING EDUCATION

While the critics of the 1950's and 1960's were concerned with the reconstruction of education within the same educational system, those of the 1970's are raising the question of whether the educational system might not need total *restructuring* in order to keep pace with the truly revolutionary technological advances that are being made in everyone's lives. In Marshall McLuhan's words, each person lives in an "all-at-once" world, where

[11] Arthur Bestor and J. L. Childs, "Education and the American Scene," in *Education in the Age of Science,* ed. Brand Blanshard (New York: Basic Books, 1959), pp. 55, 56, 60–63, 71. Reprinted by permission.

the senses are being bombarded with the rapid dissemination of information, both factual and emotional, through electronic media systems. To the question "What makes a good education?" we answer, "We must get rid of the notion that education is different and separate from life, something that happens only in the school. Everything that happens to us educates us, for good or bad." To answer the question "What makes a good education?" we must ask, "What makes a good life?"

James E. Allen, Jr., echoes this idea: "The time has arrived for us to think seriously of making major shifts in our education, [instead of] hoping that we can cram into the head of youth all that it needs to know at graduation time. Rather we should make life itself a part of the continuing education process." [12]

With this broader emphasis on what constitutes education, consideration must be given to the total spectrum of human interest, experience, and value. The schools must be concerned with not only the cognitive aspects but also the affective aspects of man. Thus far in the history of education, educators have known far more about the processes of learning that are geared to the cognitive instructional goals than those relating to emotional experience. They have recognized that students need more than the achievement and communication of knowledge and that in dealing with the cognitive functions students need to be disciplined in different ways of knowing and perception; in the inductive, deductive, and intuitive processes; and in the techniques of analysis and generalization. They are less sure what part education should play regarding the affective functions of the student—his motives, passions, and aesthetic and moral sensibilities, his feelings of concern, appreciation, sympathy, or attachment. As more and more automated instruments are introduced into the curricula to teach basic skills needed for literacy and computation, there is a greater need for methods of evaluating these techniques not only for their effectiveness in communicating knowledge but also for their impact on the emotions, the imagination and creative powers, and the artistic and moral sensibilities.

Two of the basic elements sought for the schools of the future are more individuality and more flexibility to allow each person to achieve *personal* effectiveness, whether it be as a worker, as a member of a family, as a citizen taking part in the affairs of his community, or as an individual fulfilling private aspirations and potentialities.

Bruner has speculated on some of the changes that must take place in our modes of educating in a technological society. Basically, he sees that educators will be more likely to search out the underlying ideas to teach

[12] James E. Allen, Jr., "The Educational Third Dimension," address delivered before the Galaxy Conference on Adult and Continuing Education, Washington, D.C., December 9, 1969.

Goals of the "New" Education

If the purpose of education is a quest for answers to questions posed by students, society, and scholars, then the heart of teaching is the ability to deal with questions—i.e. how to stimulate, direct, redirect, and guide them. As a basis for this goal—the quest for answers — ". . . there are certain standards that must be used. These standards may also be stated in the form of questions:

Will your questions increase the learner's *will* as well as his capacity to learn?

Will they help to give him a sense of joy in learning?

Will they help to [give him] confidence in his ability to learn?

In order to get answers, will the learner be required to make inquiries? (Ask further questions, clarify terms, make observations, classify data, etc.?)

Does each question allow for alternative answers (which implies alternative modes of inquiry)?

Will the process of answering the questions tend to stress the uniqueness of the learner?

Would the questions produce different answers if asked at different stages of the learner's development?

Will the answers help the learner to sense and understand the universals in the human condition and so enhance his ability to draw closer to other people?"

Neil Postman and Charles Weingartner, *Teaching as a Subversive Activity* (New York: Delacorte, 1969), p. 66. Copyright © 1969 by Neil Postman and Charles Weingartner. Reprinted by permission of Delacorte Press.

than the technical surface that is so likely to change. He suggests three forms of activity that will be special about the education of the future:

The first is that we shall probably want to train individuals not for the performance of routine activities that can be done with great skill and precision by devices, but rather to train their individual talents for research and development. . . . Here I mean research and development in the sense of problem-finding rather than problem-solving. If we want to look ahead to what is special about a school, we should ask how to train generations of children to *find* problems, to look for them. . . .

A second special requirement for education in the future is that it provide training in the performance of "unpredictable services." By "unpredictable

The Goals of the Davis School System

The Davis joint unified school district board of trustees . . . believes every graduate of the Davis schools should obtain [these goals]:

1. Reflect a variety of interests, using leisure time constructively, and [be able] to meet the challenge of increasing longevity.
2. Exhibit interest in and appreciation of at least some aspects of aesthetics.
3. Show discrimination in receiving and acting upon mass communication.
4. Tailor his thinking to the implications of exploration and use of both the oceans and outer space.
5. Evidence concern for his own and for public's health and safety.
6. Treat with respect persons of varied racial and national origins, and differing creeds and socio-economic levels.
7. Read, speak, listen, and write at levels acceptable to those with whom he needs to communicate.
8. Exercise his rights and responsibilities as a citizen; show respect for the rights of individuals and concern for the welfare of society.
9. Demonstrate mental and emotional balance; be able to live with diversity and uncertainty, to deal with success and with failure.
10. Exhibit respect for his or her own role as a male or female person, and for the sex role of others.

services" I mean acts that are contingent on a response made by somebody or something to your prior act. Again this falls into the category of tasks that we shall do better than automata for many years to come. I include here the role of the teacher, the parent, the assistant, the stimulator, the rehabilitator, the physician in the great sense of that term, the friend, the range of things that increase the richness of individual response to other individuals. I propose this as a critical task, for as the society becomes more interdependent, more geared to technological requirements, it is crucial that it not become alienated internally, flat emotionally and gray. . . .

Third, what human beings can produce and no device can is art—in every form: visual art, the art of cooking, the art of love, the art of walking, the art of address, going beyond adaptive necessity to find expression for human flair.[13]

[13] Jerome S. Bruner, "Culture, Politics, and Pedagogy," *Saturday Review,* May 18, 1968, pp. 19, 20.

11. Demonstrate that he seeks resolution of issues through a problem-solving approach.

12. Support the conservation of natural resources; show concern for the quality and the quantity of the world's physical and human resources.

13. Operate on the basis of some understanding of the scientific principles which underlie our living.

14. Show a sense of history and be able particularly to evaluate this nation's unique role in history.

15. Earn a satisfactory living, and handle his financial affairs with competence.

16. Exhibit attitudes and skills which will make it possible for him to meet the challenges of occupational changes.

17. Indicate that he has a design for living, has a philosophical basis for the making of moral judgments.

18. Conduct himself as one who has a sense of his own worth as a member of the human family.

19. Exhibit physical fitness of a quality commensurate with his needs as an active, productive human being.

20. Demonstrate that through his education his own potentialities as an individual have been enhanced; reflect a love of learning which will form a basis for life-long development of these potentialities.

"School Goals Get Approval," *Davis Enterprise*, May 29, 1970.

We see these three new goals as a challenge to a society that has a capacity to produce technical routine and raises the question whether teachers will be daring enough to go beyond the teaching of technical routine to the cultivation of the uniquely human.

AT THE LOCAL LEVEL

While many of the statements of purpose included in this chapter have been made at national and state levels, local boards of education, local citizen groups, and local teacher groups have also been wrestling with the problem of identifying and establishing a priority for their efforts. The most significant of such statements have been those resulting from a team effort by citizens and teachers working together. A recent example of a local school system's statement of its goals is the one for the Davis, California, schools, which appears on these pages.

The Teacher's Role

This great debate on the aims of education has not ended. As mentioned previously, the ends of education will change and grow as society itself changes and evolves, and with these changes will come conflict among laymen, among educators, and among laymen, students, and educators.

No matter what the current trend, certain constants remain for the teacher: (1) teachers need to formulate their own statement of purposes as a guide to daily instruction of pupils in their classes; (2) teachers' purposes will change in emphasis as the pupils they teach reflect differing socioeconomic levels of the community; and (3) teachers will be asked to do more than there will be the means readily and successfully to achieve.

As a guide to enable teachers to cut their way through the discussions and arrive at decisions concerning their own beliefs about the ends of education, the following quotation from Norman Cousins, editor of the *Saturday Review,* is offered: "Education fails unless the three R's at one end of the schools' spectrum lead ultimately to the four P's at the other—PREPARATION FOR EARNING, PREPARATION FOR LIVING, PREPARATION FOR UNDERSTANDING, PREPARATION FOR PARTICIPATION in the problems involved in the making of a better world." [14]

Conclusion

The schools are supported by the people for the education of their children. Thus they want to say what the basic job of the school is. Teachers, as professional practitioners of their craft, also have well-established ideas on the subject of the purposes of education. And each of these groups, plus the many groups between the laymen and the professionals, now including the students, has expressed its views in relation to the temper of the times. So in this chapter, we have reviewed statements reflecting the range of concerns from Deweyists to basic educationists, from the disciples of the 1900's to the critics and innovators of the 1970's. Each new age will bring new demands on the schools and renewed efforts to define their distinctive and unique role.

The job of the teacher is to recognize the historical and sociological tenets of school purposes and to resolve for himself the question of what his teaching is designed to accomplish. Only in this way will he be able to direct the education of others; only in this way will he be able to choose the means of

[14] *The Clearing House,* November 1956, p. 158.

arriving at his goals; only in this way will he be in a position to determine the extent to which the ends of education have been achieved for his class or any individual in it.

> The goal of education is not to increase the amount of knowledge but to create possibilities for a child to invent and discover, to create men who are capable of doing new things.
>
> Jean Piaget, quoted in *Time*, December 12, 1969, p. 62.

Questions for Discussion

1. Is the true purpose of education to prepare for life, for jobs, for citizenship, for college? Is your answer the same for all students, or might the purpose be different for some?

2. Do you agree with Spencer's criterion that the most useful knowledge is of most worth?

3. For each of the Seven Cardinal Objectives list the school subjects that contribute the most to it. How do you rationalize or explain your classification?

4. Despite Whitehead's protest against "inert ideas," is there still considerable dead knowledge in the school curriculum? Where? Why? So what?

5. What relationship does the 1938 Educational Policies Commission (EPC) statement of purpose bear to the 1970 list of goals of the Davis school district? Do you agree that there is a real philosophical difference between it and the progressive-education influence reflected in the 1938 statement?

6. Assume agreement with the White House Conference statement "It is primarily the schools which allow no man's failure to prevent the success of his son." What implications does this have for education?

7. Some have said that James Koerner's concept of purpose is appropriate for bright, college-bound students, but not for others. Do you agree or disagree? Why?

8. Can Americans enjoy the luxury of both quantity and quality in education?

9. Analyze the Davis statement on pages 48–49 above. Does it reflect the influence of Bestor, of the Ten Imperative Needs of Youth, of both, or of neither? Does it reflect the concerns of Allen and Bruner?

10. Do teachers' purposes change as the pupils they teach reflect differing socioeconomic levels of the community? Should they?

11. Is there a direct relation between the liberal education given by elementary and secondary schools and that available in liberal-arts colleges? Why?

12. In what ways could the affective functions of the student be considered in the schools?

Activities and Projects

1. Write the State Department of Education of your state for a statement of objectives and purposes. How does it compare with the EPC statement reproduced in this chapter?

2. Organize your class into a little White House Conference to discuss the question "What should our schools accomplish?" Conclude with an analysis of similarities and differences in the points of view expressed.

3. Secure a statement of purpose from your local school. How does it compare with the Davis statement?

4. Make up an opinionnaire using statements from the Council for Basic Education. Use it with (a) a group of retired people (senior citizens) and (b) college seniors. Compare the results.

5. Do driver training, civil defense, and ROTC belong in the school curriculum? Justify your answer on philosophical grounds.

6. Within the same school, interview a teacher of each of the following subjects regarding their purposes: (a) foreign language, (b) physical education, (c) remedial reading. In what ways do their purposes agree and disagree?

7. Go to a series of school-board meetings and write a report of the purposes that seem inherent in the system *from what the members say in discussions.*

References

Public versus Profession

BLANSHARD, BLAND, ed. *Education in the Age of Science.* New York: Basic Books, 1959. Pp. 55–75.

THE COMMITTEE FOR THE WHITE HOUSE CONFERENCE ON EDUCATION. *The Committee for the White House Conference on Education, A Report to the President*. Washington, D.C.: U.S. Government Printing Office, 1956 and 1965.

HARRIS, LOUIS. "What People Think about Their High Schools." *Life,* vol. 66, no. 19 (1969).

KOERNER, JAMES. *The Miseducation of Teachers*. Boston: Houghton Mifflin, 1963.

LEONARD, GEORGE B. *Education and Ecstasy*. New York: Delacorte, 1968.

RIESMAN, DAVID. *Constraint and Variety in American Education*. Lincoln: University of Nebraska Press, 1956.

STONE, JAMES C., and R. ROSS HEMPSTEAD. *California Education Today*. New York: Crowell, 1968. Chap. 6.

Classical Points of View

ADLER, MORTIMER, and MILTON MAYER. *The Revolution in Education*. Chicago: University of Chicago Press, 1958.

RUSSELL, BERTRAND. *Education and the Modern World*. London: Allen & Unwin, 1932.

SIMON, LOUIS. *Shaw on Education*. New York: Columbia University Press, 1958.

SMILEY, MARJORIE B., and JOHN S. DIEKHOFF. *Prologue to Teaching*. New York: Oxford University Press, 1959. Pt. 3.

SPENCER, HERBERT. *Education: Intellectual, Moral and Physical*. New York: Appleton, 1860.

TOYNBEE, ARNOLD J. *Education in the Perspective of History*. New York: Harper, 1960.

WHITEHEAD, ALFRED N. *The Aims of Education and Other Essays*. New York: New American Library, 1949.

Goals: The 1920's to the 1980's

AIKIN, WILFORD M. *The Story of the Eight-Year Study*. New York: Harper, 1942.

BRUNER, JEROME S. "Culture, Politics, and Pedagogy." *Saturday Review,* May 18, 1968.

CONANT, JAMES BRYANT. *The American Education*. Washington, D.C.: Educational Policies Commission of the National Education Association, 1961.

FANTINI, MARIO D. "Schools for the Seventies, Institutional Reform." *Today's Education,* April 1970, pp. 43–45.

———, and GERALD WEINSTEIN. *The Disadvantaged: Challenge to Education*. New York: Harper, 1968.

HAVIGHURST, ROBERT J., and LINDLEY J. STILES. "National Policy for Alienated Youth." *Phi Delta Kappan,* April 1961, pp. 283–91.

HABACH, RENÉ. "The Student of Tomorrow, Toward a New Global Horizon." *UNESCO Courier,* January 1970, p. 17.

KEARNEY, NOLAN C. *Elementary School Objectives.* Report Prepared for the Mid-Century Committee on Outcomes in Elementary Education. New York: Russell Sage Foundation, 1953. Pp. 42–113.

MOORMAN, ELLIOTT DUANE. "The Benefit of Anger." *Saturday Review,* June 21, 1969.

NATIONAL EDUCATION ASSOCIATION. *The Central Purpose of American Education.* Washington, D.C.: Educational Policies Commission of the National Education Association, 1961.

YOUNG, WILLIAM C. "Education for the 70's." *The Clearing House,* March 1970, pp. 387–90.

Role of the Teacher

BRUNER, JEROME S. *The Process of Education.* Cambridge, Mass.: Harvard University Press, 1960.

KELLEY, EARL C. *In Defense of Youth.* Englewood Cliffs, N.J.: Prentice-Hall, 1962.

POSTMAN, NEIL, and CHARLES WEINGARTNER. *Teaching as a Subversive Activity.* New York: Delacorte, 1969.

ROSS, LEONARD Q. *The Education of Hyman Kaplan.* New York: Harcourt, 1937.

The art of teaching is the art of assisting discovery.

MARK VAN DOREN

3

Teaching

How Teachers Feel about Teaching

One of the best ways to learn about teaching, or about any profession, is to talk with someone in the field. Accordingly, so that the prospective teachers reading this book might have the benefit of knowledgeable opinions, the authors asked a number of teachers, some with one year of experience and others with a number of years in the classroom, to present unsigned statements of how they feel about teaching and of what it means in their lives. Most of the respondents indicated that the work was hard and seemingly endless, with modest monetary returns, but that it was rewarding in many ways that defy verbal description. It seems that, for the most part, those who remain in the field for several years become attached to their work and plan to devote the remainder of their active professional years to it.

Teaching is dynamic work, with ever-new challenges daily as teachers work with children and youth in the nation's classrooms. Attesting to this idea is the following statement from a primary teacher with more than twenty years of experience:

Teaching has a constantly changing face. As a teacher, I seem to be something different to each pupil in the classroom, and often my role changes from hour to hour as each child's needs change. One great reward of teaching is trying to fulfill the needs of the pupils. Each child is a real challenge; my small part in each child's life represents some of the rewards of teaching. The association with the child in the classroom is a concrete value upon which a teacher can count. Maybe this teacher is learning more than she is teaching.

The satisfaction—the reward—of seeing children progress in their learning because of something the teacher has done or has caused to be done in the classroom is certainly one of the abstract compensations enjoyed by every teacher. One teacher in the early high-school grades, who entered the profession after spending a number of years in business and personnel work, expresses this feeling as follows:

I considered other professions, such as petroleum engineer and commercial aviation, since I have been actively flying since 1951, but I chose teaching because I like working with boys and girls. I felt there would be more satisfaction in teaching than any of these other professions since I would be contributing to the development of young people. . . . It is very satisfying to see a young person grow and develop partially under my guidance. Teaching is very interesting work, because one is constantly meeting new challenges. After having taught for six years, I am happy that I chose this profession and still can not think of any other profession I would rather be in.

Teaching provides individuals with the opportunity of being of service to mankind, and this, to some, is a strong motivation when the time comes for choosing their life's work. A thirty-eight-year-old man with fourteen years of teaching experience in the upper grades feels that teaching is the field in which he can serve his fellow men most effectively. He writes:

Teaching is the most complex profession in the world. To be a teacher, one is presented with the most challenging, frustrating, and yet highly rewarding occupation. To deal with human minds is the greatest responsibility on earth. To help young people succeed and taste the joy of achievement is most gratifying. To experience with them the thrill of victory and the agony of defeat is really living for others. I feel that it is in teaching that I can make my greatest contribution to the good of mankind.

Paradoxically, as is true of society itself, the most constant aspect of teaching is that it is continually changing. Nothing, or very little, is done in exactly the same way twice. A teacher who works with twenty-five or more unique—and alive!—youngsters must expect anything to happen at any moment and be able to make the appropriate adjustment to the situation. One bright young woman, just completing her first year in the middle grades, has this to say:

I like teaching very much, but my opinion of teaching changes from day to day just as the children I teach change from day to day. . . . Teaching isn't all a joy. At 3:30 or 4:00, when others are leaving their jobs, a teacher has papers to correct, children to keep after school to catch up with their lessons or other reasons, meetings to attend, lesson plans to be altered for the next day's work, parents to contact, work to be typed and duplicated and research to be done. These are things that must be done more than several times a week—many of them nightly. This list hasn't even begun to include the extra chores by which a teacher is confronted, such as report cards, cumulative record folders, etc.

It is very disappointing when a teacher encourages children to ask questions and come in for extra help in projects or for class work only to have to turn them away to attend a teachers' meeting, parent conference, etc.

A teacher can be compared to a frustrated mother of 30 (plus) children, trained to see their needs, to know how to meet them, and unable to meet all of them. A teacher will never be able to go home at night and feel that he or she has completed his or her work. There is always more work to be done.

Since teachers work with active ingredients and many times unknowns, reactions are often unexpected. Children don't always seem to appreciate what is being done for them. In fact, some days pass when one isn't quite sure if they have learned anything the day before or not. Unlike some chemical reactions, teachers are not catalysts; they are very much affected by the children they teach. Thankfully, every day is different, and every child is an individual.

Teaching is one of the most creative occupations in the world. Many times rewards don't come when they are needed most, and the work load seems overpowering. But I am a teacher, and I wouldn't trade occupations with anyone else.

Although one particular aspect of teaching may be the predominant motivating force, professional educators choose teaching for a number of reasons—not just one. Such is the situation of a kindergarten teacher who has taught more than twenty years:

I teach because I love children. I feel pride in teaching because it is a profession and is given respect and importance in the community. I enjoy contact with children and their parents. I have much freedom within my job—I can choose when and what I will do today and no one is checking to see if I am earning my salary every minute; I get to drive myself. There are many hours of homework, but I don't mind; I earn more money than I could in an office, without the homework.

From these statements, it is clear that teaching means different things to different teachers. This is to be expected, since each teacher is unique, an individual with a personality peculiar to his own self, just as each child is unique. To some teachers, the work is one exciting challenge after another; to others the experiences in the classroom are nothing short of drudgery. Underlying all the statements, however, are certain threads of consistency: the work is hard and demanding of time and energy; there are new challenges each day; and there are compensations not reflected in the monthly paycheck.

Why Do You Want to Teach?

At this point in your development, you have, at least tentatively, chosen teaching to be your life's work. Why have you chosen this profession? Some of you are members of a teaching family; perhaps your father or mother, or both, are educators, and perhaps their parents, too, and it is natural for you to fall in line. Some of you have decided to become a teacher because back in elementary or high school you idolized one or more of your teachers and then and there vowed to become like them. Some of you have chosen teaching because you feel that the working conditions will be to your liking; some of you sincerely wish to be of service to your fellow human beings; some of you have been forced into teaching by well-meaning parents or other adults who feel that this will always be a good job if you need one or that it will be an excellent stepping-stone to get into something else. Just as teachers now in service have chosen the profession for a number of reasons, so have you.

Perhaps it would be interesting and valuable to know the varied reasons for entering the profession given by others at approximately the same point in their preparation as you. For that reason, the authors have solicited statements from students in the initial stages of their professional training that reveal some of the reasons for their choice. It is interesting to note a rather close relationship between what teachers indicate the profession means to them, as presented in the preceding section, and what educational trainees believe teaching will mean to them.

One student in a beginning professional class said:

I want to teach because I love working with children. . . . I want to see children grow and learn and know that in some way I helped them. The security, the pleasant surroundings, and the convenient hours which can be worked around a family all helped me decide to go into teaching. However, my main reason was that children are the most interesting and complex things in the world and to teach them is one of the most enjoyable jobs in the world.

Another student in an introductory education course expressed this mature point of view:

What profession offers a person the opportunity to shape and guide the thoughts, values, and knowledge of thousands of future citizens . . . the chance to know intimately thousands of fresh young minds . . . a position in which year after year he is looked up to as an "oracle of all wisdom"? Teaching offers the closest thing to a real fountain of youth. A teacher cannot help but share some of the young ideas and outlooks offered by the students. Just as courtesy and good manners are "catching," so is the youthful enthusiasm of children. To be truly effective in the classroom, a teacher must keep up with world affairs, new discoveries, the latest song and dance hits, the current World Series. This aspect of teaching makes it appeal to an active person whose desire to grow "with the times" is as keen as his willingness to learn from youngsters the interests and fears and joys of a new generation.

It has been said that a person in the teaching profession can stay young; he *must* stay young! The student just quoted has this point of view in mind, and, in addition, alludes to the idea that in teaching one may continually quench his thirst for more and new knowledge.

From a student in her first professional course—a young mother who has decided to fulfill the education requirements for teaching—come these reasons:

The desire to teach was firmly established approximately eight years ago when I first became aware of the teaching process, as my oldest child learned to read and write. The opportunity to help open up this new world to children appealed to me then, and has remained a fervent desire. Teaching brings a thrill, as children respond to the newness of any situation. . . . To teach, to serve mankind, is a worthy goal. It does require proper preparation, though, and if one intends to operate within the framework of the public schools, a certain amount of formal education is necessary. After definitely settling in my own mind what my goal was, it was necessary to find out the legal requirements, and fit these requirements into my established life as a wife and mother. This has required a great deal of careful planning and adjusting, both on my part and the part of my family.

As this student points out, it is important for one with home responsibilities to do some careful planning as he contemplates pursuing a teacher-education program. It is no less important for a person who does not have such responsibilities to plan carefully for his future work. He needs to look in a mirror and study himself to ascertain whether he is really suited for working with children; he must consider all aspects of the teaching-learning situation to see whether he has the stamina and patience such a situation requires; he must try to determine just what he wants to give to the job as well as what he expects to get from it.

At this point it should be evident that the decision to become a teacher has about as many origins as there are persons making the decision. In any event, such a decision—and also that of whether to teach at the elementary or secondary level—may have been made long before any future-teacher groups in high school or college provided you with the inspiration to become a member of this profession. Some research indicates that even childhood experiences may determine teaching-career choices; teaching re-creates a common and pervasive childhood environment.

Whatever the origin of your decision, you should remember that when you have elected to go into teaching, or into any other position or profession, you have made one of the most important decisions in your life, and you should make every effort to be sure that your decision is the right one for you.

What Will You Learn about Yourself?

Once your decision is made and you proceed with your teacher-education program and as you finally take your place in front of one of the nation's classrooms, there are many things that you will need to learn.

Who Am I?

Who am I?

I'm the fellow who gave up a dinner date to go to the PTA meeting.

The one who gets the blame if Johnny fails, but not often the credit when he gets an A.

A dispenser of discipline and band aids.

The patriot; the leader; the egg-head, the confidant, the inspiration, the bore, the "tough" guy, the easy mark, the tyrant, the hero —all depending on who's describing me at the moment.

My biggest thrill is the first home run, the first A from the child who had been my poorest pupil . . . the first realization that I'm trying to help, not harass . . . the shy, rare words thanking me for a job well done.

I have one of the hardest, most exciting jobs in the world.

I rarely get credit for the daily miracles I perform—but the "front office" gets bombarded if I pull a boner.

I'm drowning in paper work, blue ink, red pencils, book reports, misspelled words.

Resolutely I face the future, indignant parents, summer study, and the school dance I agreed to chaperone.

I'm a frontline soldier in the war against ignorance—my ammunition, not bullets, but books.

Who am I? I'm a teacher.

The Newsletter, Dade County, Florida, Public Schools.

Among them is a number of things about yourself. Indeed, you will no doubt learn to know yourself better than you have before. You will learn that as a teacher you will face many problems, and you will have to learn how to solve them. You will learn that as a teacher your time is not exactly yours to do with as you please; it must be sacrificed to help students and parents. You will learn how to cooperate with administrators and fellow teachers in trying to evolve the finest educational program for children and youth in your community. You will learn that teaching is a profession with no room for selfish people. You will learn whether you are realistic or foolhardy in the choice of your life's work and that you must be honest in your evaluation of yourself and your goals if the results are to satisfy your needs and interests. You will learn the importance of an honest assessment of your strengths and weaknesses. You will certainly learn whether you are able to get along with many different kinds of people. You will, of course, learn whether you have the ability to motivate youngsters and to arrange an environment in which maximum learning will take place in each individual in your classroom. You will have in true focus your real values and ideals in life. As you progress toward becoming an effective member of the profession, you certainly will learn self-control and unselfishness, and you will develop a better sense of humor than you probably now possess. As you become more and more involved in pursuing later courses in education and then begin teaching in the classroom, you will find yourself in a testing period far more important and more difficult than any final examination you have faced up to this point.

What Will You Learn about Others?

A teacher who makes an attempt to learn the mystery of human behavior can go a long way toward understanding the intricacies of man's relationship to society and to the culture. In becoming acquainted with individual students of varied backgrounds and environments, a teacher can gain a much greater insight into the complex social problems within the communities of the states and nation.

As a teacher, you will find out what people in the school and community expect from you, and if you are dedicated to your work, you will find out how you can respond to their expectations. You will learn that it is necessary to try to understand other people of all ages, to accept them for what they are with all of their idiosyncrasies. As you work with children, colleagues, and lay persons in your community, you are bound to gain increasing insight into other people's attitudes, beliefs, interests, goals, and efforts, and this insight will help you understand why they behave as they do. Through working with others, you may be able to modify and clarify your own ideals and beliefs.

What Will You Learn about Knowledge?

In the ever-changing world and universe in which we live today, you, as a guide of children's growth and learning, have an obligation to your students and to the people in your community to keep abreast of innovations and advancements in all areas of living. A basic foundation of knowledge in such areas as literature, composition, mathematics, science, social sciences, and fine arts is, of course, essential as you begin to teach. You will need to know the *what, how,* and *why* not only of the "three R's" but also of our form of government, of our democracy based on the rights of the individual.

There will no doubt be times when you will be frustrated by how little knowledge you actually possess, even though you hold at least one college degree. These times will provide you with the opportunity to learn to appreciate the amount of knowledge that has accumulated throughout history and to recognize the struggle that pioneers in all fields of knowledge have had and are having in discovering, organizing, and presenting this knowledge for all the world to use. No doubt you will come to have a deep appreciation for the opportunity to probe, no matter how lightly, into a vast reservoir of information.

You will learn that knowledge, if it is to have full value, must be realized and comprehended by each individual learner; only in this way will the knowledge be a working part of him. It will be your responsibility to help the pupil prepare himself for acquiring knowledge, to teach him to think for himself, to help him increase his capacity to understand, and to aid him in recognizing truth for himself.

In the classroom you and your pupils will discover knowledge principally through the various disciplines to be studied. It is most important that you and your class learn to approach the disciplines directly in such a manner that the students may be active, not passive, learners—in effect, producers of knowledge, not mere passive consumers of it.

Importance of Teachers in Our Society

The importance of teachers and teaching in the schools of our country is undeniably great. One has only to read a popular magazine or a daily newspaper to sense the general public's interest in and demand for quality programs in schools. Indeed, the future of our democratic way of life is dependent upon the kinds of learning experiences our future leaders and citizens have as they progress through the elementary and secondary-school classrooms in the United States. Authorities in all fields of knowledge are collaborating in an effort to provide the ultimate in programs for the education of students of all ages in America and abroad, and teachers are in a pivotal position for organizing and implementing these programs for classroom use.

It is of great concern, then, that only the best possible people be assigned to the classrooms of the nation to guide the growth and learning of children and youth. Teachers are assuming no small responsibility when they set out to help pupils learn the subject matter of the various disciplines as well as acquire the numerous skills and attitudes that accompany this knowledge, because these are essential for productive, happy, and creative lives in a democratic culture where dynamic changes occur almost daily.

A recent survey taken by the research firm of Louis Harris for *Life* indicated that 60 percent of those Americans polled thought the last place to cut federal spending should be in aid to education. According to the data from the Harris polls in *Life* (August 15, 1969), education ranks above the following items that the public would not cut from the federal budget: pollution control, poverty programs, aid to cities, and highway financing. The survey, which included a cross section of Americans, young and old, rich and poor, urban and rural, gives a fair indication of the esteem in which persons in this nation hold schools and the education of the country's youth and children.

NUMBER AND TYPES OF TEACHERS

In most communities in the United States, the schools constitute the largest business, and the corps of teachers and other school personnel is the largest working force in the area. According to United States Office of Education statistics for the 1967–68 school year, for example, there were 1,942,785 teachers in public elementary and secondary schools; of this number, 1,079,253 were in elementary-school classrooms and 863,532 in secondary schools.[1] Approximately 220,000 teachers man classrooms in private elementary and secondary schools; there are about 135,000 administrators, supervisors, consultants, research experts, and other specialists in elementary and secondary education; about 375,000 professional personnel are employed in higher-education institutions; and more than 25,000 serve on the staffs of professional organizations. These figures total well over 2,500,000 persons allied in one way or another with the profession of

[1] See *The 1970 World Almanac and Book of Facts* (New York: Newspaper Enterprise Association, 1969), p. 349; and *1970 Information Please Almanac Atlas and Yearbook* (New York: Dan Golenpaul Associates, 1969), pp. 656, 657, 660.

teaching. The NEA Research Division's 1969–70 report listed a total of 1,997,870 classroom teachers, an increase of 47.4 percent since 1959–60.

As indicated above, the field of education offers persons who enter it many kinds of opportunities to serve in interesting, dynamic positions. Possibly the most interesting and challenging of all jobs is that of the class-room teacher, and in this category the schools employ individuals at the preschool (nursery and kindergarten), elementary, secondary, and college or university levels. Within these levels are found teachers of separate or combined grades; teachers of special subjects such as art, music, English, foreign languages, social studies; teachers of physically and mentally hand-icapped children and youth; and critic teachers in laboratory or experi-mental schools.

Types of Teachers

There are five types of teachers . . . in the public schools. Each is easily recognized.

1. The Rebel—is against the entire system, but has no suggested plan of change.

2. The Retreatist—wants out of teaching, is constantly seeking other employment, and leaves, usually, with his or her leave bank empty.

3. The Ritualist—has retired on the job, and continues to repeat the same lessons year in and year out. This teacher can quote page, paragraph, and sentence of the text.

4. The Conformist—goes along with what is current without making an effort to contribute. In many cases this person and the ritualist are related.

5. The Innovator—sees the need for change and seeks to bring it about without antagonism. This effort ranges from his/her class-room to the district.

Romeo Eldridge Phillips, "Whose Children Shall We Teach?" *Educational Leadership*, February 1970, p. 472. Reprinted by permission.

Aiding the important work that teachers perform in the classroom are other personnel in positions where classroom-teaching experience often is a prerequisite. Many teachers aspire to such positions as superintendent of schools, principal or vice-principal of a school, general or special supervi-sor, librarian, speech correctionist, school psychologist, guidance counselor, nurse, curriculum consultant, athletic coach, research director, registrar, business manager, head of department, dean of boys or dean of girls, or director of audiovisual materials. Most large school systems employ all these types of personnel in addition to many others, whereas smaller systems do not offer so many different kinds of positions. In general, the smaller the district, the fewer the personnel available in certain of the special services.

There are also employment opportunities for educators in certain of the national, regional, and local professional organizations such as the National Education Association, in state departments of education, in civic or private or religious organizations, in federal agencies, and in foreign service.

THE INFLUENCING OF BEHAVIOR BY TEACHERS

Teachers are in constant contact with impressionable children and youth in the classrooms of this country; the effectiveness of any school depends upon the knowledge, skills, convictions, character, and ability in human relations of the teachers on the staff.

Good teachers exude a contagious enthusiasm, faith, and confidence in life and learning that are needed by young people as they strive to solve their problems and reach their goals. Often only in the school classroom do children and youth find the intelligent, sympathetic guidance needed to chart a course through the bafflement and bewilderment of world and national politics, changes in ways of living and in social institutions, and emotional disturbances in homes and communities.

The job of the teacher—in fact, the job of all persons employed in a school system—is to facilitate and motivate learning by the learners. In a real sense, learning is change of behavior, because as a result of learning, a person's behavior is changed. Thus, the job of teachers and other school personnel is to influence desirable changes in pupil behavior. To do this job effectively, teachers not only must be knowledgeable in subject areas and adept in how to teach them, but also must be aware of backgrounds —the physical condition of the pupils, the skills and knowledge they possess, and their socioeconomic status. Only after these things are known about his pupils can the teacher really proceed, with the cooperation of the children, to the business of initiating and directing experiences that result in optimum learning.

Good teachers use methods that are effective in helping all students grow toward understanding their social environment and ways to improve it, and that provide opportunities for student participation in the democratic planning and carrying out of learning activities. Children should learn to use the scientific method of problem solving, so that when they leave school they will be able to meet all problems head-on and follow through to satisfactory solutions. It is important, too, for teachers to encourage creativity in pupils' approaches to problems and learning situations.

TEACHERS OF TOMORROW

The foreseeable future promises to be a period of changing values and extended horizons in all areas of living and learning, a critical era in history, bringing with it a burning need for individuals who can make intelligent decisions. As we have noted previously, the years immediately ahead will demand that teachers be able not only to "hand down the culture" but, more importantly, to provide each child with an opportunity to develop his abilities to the fullest, so that he can help the nation and himself solve problems that do not even exist in today's complex world society.

As the world's population continues to explode, throwing people into extremely close proximity, teachers of tomorrow must be increasingly concerned with human values, motives, and aspirations, which must have scientific, historical, traditional, and artistic roots in order to condition and help shape human behavior into socially acceptable channels. More than this, though, teachers of the future must be able to inspire their pupils to be creative in their approach to problems they will be facing at that time. Students must be taught *how* to learn; this is much more important than having the ability to parrot facts and figures that ten or fifteen years or less hence will be outmoded or obsolete.

Since the will of the student to learn is in some measure prompted by emulation of his most effective teachers, it is imperative that tomorrow's teachers be well grounded in a liberal education, which really means preparation for enlightened citizenship and character development. The behavior and character of the nation's future teachers, tempered by their knowledge of the humanities and social and physical sciences, will have a deep and abiding influence upon the quality of our future citizens.

Professional authorities currently propose that tomorrow's teachers help solve education's problems by individualizing instruction, giving individual attention to each pupil instead of continuing the current broad, massive approaches to teaching. They further suggest that teachers should constantly search for methodology effective for all children, not just the narrow, middle-class-oriented approaches so commonly used at present. Classroom teachers in the future will necessarily avoid literal equality of educational opportunity if that term is construed to mean treating all children exactly alike.

Tomorrow's teachers will need to increase their efforts to teach the humanistic values necessary for society. The democratic ideal demands that members of the society have a sincere interest in their fellow men and in social and political affairs; people in a democracy must understand the interdependence of all men.

Armed with a background of substantial academic preparation and sound professional education in psychological, curricular, and applied aspects of teacher preparation and carefully screened for their work, the nation's future teachers will be the most competent corps of professional persons the schools have ever known. The advances in knowledge and the demands of the profession and the public will insist upon such competency. The survival of mankind may depend upon such competency!

The Job of Teaching

The aim of teaching is assisting children and youth in their effort to develop an open mind and an adaptability in the matter of ends—in short, the cultivation of competence in young people to fashion their own lives well. To this end, pupils must be afforded the opportunity to exercise significant autonomy in choice, discrimination, and judgment in the classrooms so that possible passivity and, often, boredom may give way to vibrant, meaningful, thought-provoking activities. Children should be involved in observing and inquiring with tools they already possess, so that they may be helped to create and assimilate sharper tools and more adequate knowledge.

The teacher who brings the most to his classroom is the one who has an understanding of the political, social, physical, and intellectual world; who helps children develop skills, knowledges, understanding, good work and study habits, aesthetic appreciation, and their own innate and creative abilities; who is sensitive to individual differences within the class group as a whole; who understands child growth and development and learning principles, especially as they apply to the age group he is teaching; who frees the child to recognize, express, actualize, and experience his own uniqueness. And in addition to these relationships with children, the effective teacher also has normal relationships with other adults in political, social, intellectual, and spiritual areas of life.

Public- and private-school teachers generally strive to accomplish these many objectives at one of three levels: (1) the elementary school, (2) the junior high school, and (3) the secondary school, including the senior high school and the first two years of college. To set forth the many actual duties and responsibilities of teachers at any one of these levels would be a task of impossible magnitude; a cursory overview of the three levels should be sufficient at this point.

TEACHERS AT WORK: THE ELEMENTARY SCHOOL

When a teacher's education prepares him for elementary-school teaching, he will probably be assigned to one of the grades between kindergarten and grade six, or grade eight if this is the terminal grade in the district's elementary-school organization. The usual range of chronological ages of pupils in the elementary school is five years to eleven years in the K–6 school, or five to thirteen in the K–8 school. The learning activities of boys and girls in the elementary school stress physical, social, and emotional growth and also emphasize the development of social relations, ethical behavior, and character, as well as the more traditional areas of social studies, science, language arts, mathematics, and fine arts. As children progress through the elementary grades, their teachers attempt to help bring about desirable changes in behavior commensurate with their particular age and grade level. It should be emphasized at this point that a teacher will find quite a wide range of ability and achievement among children in his classroom, regardless of what grade or subjects he may be teaching; in fact, it should be added, if the teacher does an effective job of teaching, the range should widen perceptibly.

Children begin their formal education in the first four years of the elementary school, usually referred to as the primary grades, consisting of kindergarten and grades one, two, and three. Grades four, five, and six, usually considered the intermediate grades, continue the learning begun in the primary grades and proceed to learning activities of ascending difficulty. Typically, especially in the primary grades, the classrooms are self-contained; that is, one teacher teaches the same children each day in all subject areas. For the past several years, however, a number of elementary schools in America have been experimenting with different types of organizational structure. The three types most in evidence currently are known as (1) the ungraded, nongraded, multigraded, or continuous-progress plan; (2) the dual-progress, platoon, or core plan; and (3) team teaching.

Under the ungraded plan, children generally are grouped according to achievement levels instead of in grades, and each child advances step by step through the various levels at his own particular rate. Teachers do not teach at grade levels; they teach usually in the primary or the intermediate department. They advance each child to the next achievement level as rapidly as he is qualified for it, even if school has just gotten underway in the fall or is ready to be dismissed for the summer vacation; there are no promotion crises in the ungraded school. A typical elementary school under this plan may comprise as many as seventeen to twenty different levels of achievement, based primarily upon the child's reading abilities, though other aspects of his development are considered also. The ungraded plan of organization thus (1) provides for the continuous growth and learning of each child through flexible groupings; (2) eliminates, or minimizes, grade-level lines; and (3) provides a plan of promotions that considers a child's development in all aspects of his being, not just the intellectual aspect.

A program of instruction containing some aspects of both the graded and ungraded plans and both the self-contained and departmentalized plans is the dual-progress plan. Here the grades are retained in language arts, social studies, and physical education, while grade lines are ignored in other subjects such as arithmetic, science, music, arts and crafts, recreation, and health. Proponents of this plan hold that every person in our culture should have a definitely set knowledge of the basic tools of everyday living—language arts and the social studies; they hold, also, that no such universal obligation exists in subjects like arithmetic, music, art, and science, in which children progress only as their abilities permit. A home-room teacher is responsible for registration, counseling, and teaching reading and social studies for a half day; children are then assigned for the other half day to special teachers for all their other subjects.

The team-teaching plan operates in this general manner. Instead of each teacher having charge of a class of twenty-five, thirty, or thirty-five pupils, two or more teachers who are subject-matter specialists pool their pupils for part of each week in a large classroom, and one of the team presents a series of lessons in his special field. Meanwhile, other teachers on the team prepare lessons and curriculum materials for the next sequence. At times, small groups of twelve to twenty pupils meet for discussion; at other times, pupils do individual study in libraries or laboratories. Some teams include teacher assistants and clerks who take care of the more or less routine duties for the team. The team-teaching plan makes use of large classes, perhaps of seventy-five to a hundred pupils, small groups, and individual study. Television teaching is usually accomplished via the team plan, and many teacher teams employ such innovations as teaching machines and programmed lessons.

The newer plans of organization are not restricted to elementary schools in this country; in fact, a number of secondary and junior high schools in various sections of the nation are experimenting with all these innovations.

TEACHERS AT WORK: THE JUNIOR HIGH SCHOOL

The transition school in a large number of communities in the United States is known as the junior high school; here youngsters between the ages of twelve and fourteen or fifteen attend grades seven, eight, and nine. During these years young adolescents are making rapid changes in their growth patterns, so that teachers must provide dynamic learning experiences to fit a wide variety of interests and needs and varying psychological-readiness levels. Broad fields of humanities, social studies, the arts, and the sciences are provided for youngsters in the junior high school, and students have opportunities for experiences in many fields that they may study in more detail in the secondary or senior high school.

The typical organizational plan in the junior high school is departmental; however, the core program, similar to the dual-progress plan described above, has met with its greatest success at the junior-high-school level. Teachers who are subject-matter specialists but at the same time are well grounded in methodology, curriculum, and early-adolescent psychology, are usually found in the junior-high-school classrooms of the country.

Educational and social guidance plays an important role in the junior high school; teachers must help students assume a healthy, natural acceptance of adolescent growth patterns, so that learning will be fostered with a minimum of emotional stress and embarrassment. Junior-high-school teachers strive to help boys and girls grow naturally through the early adolescent years rather than risk permanent emotional damage by forcing students through premature adult patterns.

In the democratic junior-high-school classroom, a prime responsibility of the teacher is to see that his pupils learn how to work effectively together, to recognize and to respect their responsibilities toward one another, and to control their own desires while working for the benefit of the entire group. In short, the important responsibility of the junior-high-school teacher is to provide learning experiences through which students may not only acquire knowledge but also make some long strides toward becoming ready for effective citizenship in our democratic culture.

Most teachers in junior high schools have been enrolled in teacher-education programs for secondary-school teachers while preparing for their profession. In many instances they are not adequately educated for teaching young adolescents; often they are not prepared to cope with the interests and intellectual, social, emotional, physical, and spiritual needs of youngsters who are in between the child stage and the adolescent stage. A possible answer, besides the provision of a special educational program for junior-high-school teachers, might be found in a rapidly rising new organization structure, the middle school—where teachers are, by and large, prepared for upper-elementary-grade teaching.

Teachers at Work: The Middle School

A fast-growing upper-elementary organizational plan, touted as serving the educational needs of the in-between-age students, is the middle school.

Final structure for the middle-school program has not as yet materialized, but it consists generally of accommodations for students between the ages of nine and fourteen, with the greatest number being those between ages ten and thirteen. Typically, the program involves grades four or five through six, though other age-grade patterns are in existence.

Flexibility characterizes the program and organization of the middle school. In most of the schools, grades five and six retain the self-contained arrangement typical of the elementary school, while grades seven and eight are essentially departmentalized, thus assuming a feature of the secondary school. Several reasons for the middle school have been advanced by its proponents. First, it was felt that such a school would afford its children a haven from unwholesome pressures of too-early senior-high-school activities or junior-high-school interscholastic events. Related to the concept of upper-grade pressures is the emergence of increasing demands from secondary-school professional organizations to restore the traditional four-year high school; also, junior-high-school critics believe that early-secondary-education problems have found better solutions in the middle school.

In the middle school, increasing emphasis is placed upon student self-scheduling, self-understanding, and self-learning and also on modifications of encounter groups that encourage topics and issues identified by preadolescents themselves. Such activities require adequate space and time as well as an adequate psychological approach on the part of teachers.

Characteristic of the middle school is the adoption of today's educational innovations. Teachers, then, must adapt and adopt from the myriad of new approaches to learning those techniques most applicable to their classes; they must decide whether or not to have their classrooms become stages for experimentation in the extreme and for numerous innovations in various aspects of the curriculum.

TEACHERS AT WORK: THE SENIOR HIGH SCHOOL

Students aged fifteen through seventeen or eighteen, in grades ten, eleven, and twelve, are taught usually by teachers who have had college subject-matter majors, with strength in professional-education foundation and methods courses. In these upper grades the teachers help the students continue to perfect the knowledges, skills, and attitudes that will eventually enable them to succeed as effective members of our democratic society. Besides gaining increased power in written and oral communication and expression, increased understanding of science principles and social-sciences areas, and increased maturity in physical- and mental-health habits and social responsibility, senior-high-school students begin to prepare themselves in vocational areas for which they seem best suited. Teachers at this level help students plan their educational programs and their life careers to mesh with their capabilities.

The secondary-school teacher's work usually involves teaching several subjects, but often, especially in middle-sized to large school districts, the subjects lie within one broad field. For example, a teacher of English may have classes in American literature, English literature, composition, grammar, or linguistics; a teacher of business subjects may teach typewriting, shorthand, secretarial practice, accounting, or office procedures. If a young person preparing for a teaching position tends to prefer subjects in one broad field rather than subjects in several different fields, and working with adolescent youth rather than with youngsters of elementary-school age, he should seriously consider the senior-high-school field.

The typical senior high school is organized according to the departmentalization plan; that is, teachers are members of the social-sciences department, the physical-sciences department, the music department, the business department, the industrial-arts department, etc. Most teachers at this level are subject-matter specialists in one field or another. This does not, however, make any less important their learning to know their students as individuals so that they may help them satisfy their needs and interests. A knowledge of how to care for individual differences is especially important with teen-age youngsters, because in these upper grades of the public schools the widest range in achievement levels is apparent.

TYPES OF METHODOLOGY

In considering teaching methodologies used at all grade levels in the schools, prospective teachers may encounter such terms as *discovery, inquiry, strategy teaching,* and *expository techniques.* The first three terms may be considered, for purposes of this discussion, as almost synonymous and have come to be known generally as *discovery teaching.* This kind of teaching stands somewhat in opposition to the fourth kind named above, expository teaching. For the sake of convenience a brief discussion of the two techniques—expository and discovery—will be presented, though most good teachers do not use one approach exclusively; they employ what, in their judgment, will be the most effective techniques in a particular subject area with a particular group of pupils, or with individual learners.

In general, the exposition method assumes that the teacher presents ideas and information in such a manner that students can organize a body of knowledge and retain it for a long period of time. While it is admitted that the teacher is the one who provides for the selection, organization, presentation, and translation of subject matter in an appropriately developmental manner, nevertheless proponents of the method maintain that expository learning cannot be considered as passive learning. Students necessarily relate new material to their cognitive structures through establishing relationships of likeness and dissimilarity to knowledge acquired previously, and through translating new knowledge into their own personal context of experience and vocabulary. The job of the teacher is to provide assistance to students as they strive to achieve higher-order ideas, if they do not have the necessary preliminary concepts and principles. Some proponents of the exposition method claim that 95 percent of pupils can master all learning tasks, given the proper amount of time.

Expository teaching often makes use of a motivational technique some of the plan's advocates call *advance organizers*—a procedure in which certain explanatory principles are introduced prior to formal instruction, thus facilitating and expediting such instruction. Since expository teaching is efficient and less time-consuming than discovery teaching, it is utilized in many schools—especially in secondary classrooms and in departmentalized elementary schools where teachers' time with students is limited or where classes are quite large. Among proponents of the method of exposition are D. P. Ausubel and J. B. Carroll.

Opposed to expository teaching is the method of discovery, in which students achieve the instructional objective with little or no guidance from the teacher. The discovery technique is described more fully in chapter 6, which is devoted to the theme of learning. Some authorities differentiate the discovery techniques into guided and unguided approaches. In the latter technique, the teacher may give neither principle nor problem solution. Guided discovery lies between expository teaching and unguided-discovery teaching: it attempts to use an eclectic approach to classroom methodology.

STUDENT-TEACHER PLANNING

Considerable emphasis is placed in modern elementary and secondary schools on student-teacher planning, on the psychological basis that motivation, adaptability, and learning speed may be increased when all involved in the learning situation participate in its planning. In all areas of living, children and adults are constantly planning to make intelligent decisions. In the classroom, more subject-matter competence is required of the teacher when student-teacher planning is used than when it is not. Students and the teacher, in the planning procedure, attempt to answer such questions as the following:

1. What do we already know about this topic?
2. What do we need to know, or would be well to know, about the topic?

3. Why do we need to know these things about the topic?
4. How do we go about learning what we need to know?
5. Where do we find out what we need to know?
6. When do we do the things we need to do to find out about the topic?
7. Who will do what parts of the job of finding out what we need to know?

While all the questions included here are important, probably the most significant one is the "Why." It is especially important that children understand the reason for pursuing the material and that they set, within bounds, their own goals, because if optimum learning is to take place, children need to see that success in some new undertaking is possible, though not necessarily certain. Teachers who provide too much direction often create attitudes of apathetic conformity, defiance, or defeat in their pupils. An appropriate amount of permissiveness must be provided by teachers, so that increased curiosity, self-confidence, enterprise, and creativity may be generated among the students. Teachers must also provide an appropriate amount of encouragement to students; "Success breeds success" is especially applicable to achievement in school.

The Emphasis on Individualized Instruction

Individualized instruction, including programmed learning and computer-assisted instruction (CAI), has, in recent years, been receiving endorsement from increasingly larger numbers of teachers and school administrators.

Attempts at grouping children for instruction, including various kinds of homogeneous arrangements and the nongraded, dual-progress, and team-teaching plans described in preceding paragraphs, are all efforts to individualize instruction for pupils. Programmed lessons, of course, involve the pursuit of knowledge on a completely individualized basis on the part of each pupil.

A "new" system of learning, hailed in some quarters as the first successful operation of individualized instruction on a systematic, step-by-step basis throughout a K–6 elementary-school program, with plans underway for expansion into junior and senior high schools, is a program called Individually Prescribed Instruction, more familiarly termed IPI.

The IPI system, which was first put into operation in September, 1964, at Oakleaf Elementary School in Oakleaf, Pennsylvania, a blue-collar suburb of Pittsburgh, was operating in 1968 in eighty-eight schools in twenty-six states involving some thirty thousand students. In 1968 the Learning Research and Development Center sponsored by the United States Office of Education at the University of Pittsburgh (which created IPI) had a thousand schools on the waiting list for implementation of IPI, but directors indicated that the program would not be ready for massive implementation until 1970 or 1971. According to Harold Howe II, then United States Commissioner of Education, in an address before the 1968 annual meeting of the American Association of School Administrators, individualized instruction should be promoted in every school in the United States. He indicated that results of IPI were most impressive; many students perform two to four grade levels above the norm for their age, and the atmosphere of self-directed learning appears to boost attendance and virtually eliminate discipline problems.

The subjects taught in the IPI program are mathematics, reading, primary science, and spelling—all completely individualized to the point that each youngster in a mathematics class of thirty-five pupils could be doing something different at a given time. These subjects were chosen because they are basic tools of intellectual development that must be used in any future job or future learning. Since there are no grades or basal-series books in the four subject areas, it is conceivable that a third-grade pupil might be working at sixth-grade arithmetic, or a fifth-grade youngster might be reading at a second-grade level.

A typical second- and third-grade reading class might have sixty to sixty-five pupils; they use a large learning-center room equipped with record players with attached earphones along the walls, and, possibly, two adjoining smaller classrooms. Serving as coordinators and tutors for this large group are at least two teachers and perhaps a librarian and perhaps a teacher's aide. Most pupils work independently; some listen to records and complete workbooks, or repeat sounds as directed by the voice on the record, while others work with printed programmed materials. Some get new materials for their "next step" from numbered files in the room. One teacher might be working with a small group of three or four pupils in one of the adjoining rooms, while another might be tutoring a single student on some aspect of a current lesson. A teacher's aide might be correcting a test to be returned to a pupil immediately so he will know his mistakes before he forgets what he was doing wrong. Following such tests, a pupil, if he has demonstrated that he has learned by scoring 85 percent or better on the test, moves on to a new "prescription" assigned by the teacher. Each prescription involves several potential alternatives: for example, it could direct the pupil into a variety of learning activities such as assignment to a teacher for tutor instruction; assignment with a few pupils to a teacher for small-group instruction; assignment to work pages; listening to a tape or disc; or viewing a filmstrip or film.[2]

Instituting an IPI program increases the per-pupil cost of education between $37 and $115, depending upon the quality of the program before the introduction of IPI. While evidence of IPI's effect upon pupil achievement is fragmentary, limited testing and in-depth pupil observation indicate remarkable success. Extensive comparative research studies will not be made until 1973 or 1975, when IPI programs will have been perfected to the point of readiness for testing. One study, however, conducted in Urbana, Illinois, compared the achievement in arithmetic and reading of two similar groups of pupils, aged five through seven. In the academic year 1966–67, two groups of two hundred pupils each were studied, one given the IPI mathematics and reading programs and the other given the regular ungraded program without IPI. The California Achievement Test was administered to both groups at the end of the year. At the lower-primary level, IPI pupils in the 110–119 I.Q. range received a grade-placement score of 2.97 in reading comprehension and 2.42 in arithmetic fundamentals. Similar non-IPI pupils received a grade-placement score of 1.18 in reading comprehension and 1.97 in arithmetic fundamentals. At the 140+ I.Q. level, IPI pupils scored 2.94, compared to 2.44 for non-IPI pupils in reading comprehension. In the middle-primary level, IPI pupils in the 120–129 I.Q. bracket received a grade-placement score of 5.12 in reading comprehension compared to 4.12 for non-IPI pupils.[3]

Project PLAN (Program for Learning According to Needs) is an attempt to mobilize tools, technology, and methodology of modern education behind teachers as they systematically and comprehensively attempt to organize teaching according to each individual student's needs. Basic to the program is the fact that each student is provided instruction only when there is measured discrepancy between his current knowledge, skills, or performance level and the level called for by one of the instructional objectives. These objectives, derived for possible selection by a panel of subject-matter experts in the various subject areas, are compared by teacher consultants with existing instructional materials relevant to the achievement of these goals, and then instructional units are designed and created to achieve as many of these objectives as possible. Actual selection of units is made by student, teacher, school district, and parents; the teacher, in conference with each pupil about his year's program, indicates which objectives are required and which are recommended for him to at-

[2] *Individually Prescribed Instruction,* an *Education U.S.A.* Special Report (Washington, D.C.: National School Public Relations Association of the National Education Association, 1968).

[3] Ibid., p. 23.

tain. Based on his own frame of reference, the student then selects the order of the objectives he will follow, when sequence is optional, and then selects instructional units to pursue. Thus, the selection of objectives for each student is based on the following: current interests, aspirations, and capabilities of the student; comparisons of current student performance with the expectations and standards of society; and reasonable expectations based on comparison of student capabilities with occupational requirements.

Proponents of Project PLAN indicate that it includes several procedures for the individualization of instruction as well as of educational objectives. Effective use of the computer is envisioned in the program: the student is provided information on the basis of which he can increase the comprehensiveness and accuracy of his self-knowledge; he is provided the option of choosing among relevant instructional procedures the one or ones judged by him to be most suitable for himself; his present performance and that required by an objective are continually being compared by the system. The student does not receive instruction in what he already knows; he is provided information by which he can assess his own progress so that he may better organize his own time and activities.[4]

Project PLAN was instigated in September, 1967, by the American Institute for Research in the Behavioral Sciences, Palo Alto, California, the Westinghouse Learning Corporation, and twelve cooperating school systems in the United States. The computer makes individualized instruction available to a large number of students because it stores, processes, and retrieves information very rapidly. It stores large amounts of detailed information about each student, teacher, course, and learning unit; it scores tests and gives back results very quickly; it takes much of the burden of clerical tasks off the teachers and counselors.

In a fifteen-week study, financed by the United States Office of Education, made at Pennsylvania State University's Center for Cooperative Research with Schools, more than a hundred sixth-grade pupils who were taught spelling with computer-assisted instruction (CAI) were found to score significantly higher on achievement tests than students who received conventional instruction. Even more significant gains were made by the normally poor spellers who require, but do not always get, extra teacher attention. This project indicated that it may be possible to use CAI to pinpoint the way a child best learns spelling.

Projections for the future use of the computer in education are rather glowing, while cherished beliefs about teaching and improved learning are

[4] R. F. Mager, "On Project PLAN," duplicated (Palo Alto: American Institute for Research in the Behavioral Sciences, 1967).

being disproved. Among examples of past beliefs being struck down: smaller classes do not improve learning, according to one hundred studies; there is no existing evidence that reading is best taught by phonics or the whole-word method; people learn no better from films than from an average instructor. Educational authorities predict the widespread use of CAI in elementary and high schools by 1980, after technical problems and high costs are alleviated. They believe that the computer—as an aide to the teacher—will teach a large share of fundamental subjects such as arithmetic, spelling, and reading; will individualize instruction and make it more efficient; and will teach remedial and special-interest work while relieving teachers of routine chores. With CAI, it is hoped that instruction can truly be tailored to fit the special requirements and capabilities of each learner so that he may reach optimal achievement in any area he pursues.

OTHER NEW APPROACHES

There are other approaches to teaching too numerous to include in this chapter. It is encouraging to note that a number of school districts in the nation are experimenting with their own unique innovative plans and techniques. Space permits mention of only two additional types of approach to instruction that currently seem to be gaining considerable popularity over a wide area of the country.

In line with the need mentioned earlier for schools to teach the humanistic values necessary for tomorrow's society, a plan titled Self-Enhancing Education (SEE) has made inroads in schools in some sections of the country. SEE is concerned with communication techniques and processes believed to be of universal application in the interaction of adults with adults, children with children, and adults with children. Major learning problems treated by the program include: becoming aware of the communication techniques and processes traditionally used in human interaction; considering the limitations of the traditional patterns; and learning how to achieve activation of additional communication techniques and processes believed to be helpful in overcoming traditional limitations. It is through such a program as SEE is endeavoring to provide that elementary and secondary schools may teach civilized human relations, including a respect for the attitudes, sensitivity, pride, and personal worth of one's fellow man.

A technique still in the beginning stage but heralding an important new movement in education is the use of educational or simulation games. Even though research thus far indicates that children do not learn more through games, the value of simulation appears to be in its use as a springboard for discussions following its use. Briefly, in the games, pupils assume the role of decision makers in a simulated environment and compete for certain objectives according to specified procedures or rules. An illustration of this procedure is presented in the Foreign Policy Association's booklet *Simulation Games for the Social Studies Classroom,* in an example titled "Dangerous Parallel." Here pupils learn about foreign policy by acting as ministers of six fictional countries facing a situation much like that leading to this nation's involvement in the Korean War.

Advising that games should not be used in isolation but should reinforce other methods and materials, proponents hold that such simulations increase feelings of political efficacy and perceptions of social and political complexity, that facts and principles are more effectively taught through the games than through more traditional techniques, and that knowledge learned through simulation seems to be retained longer than that gained through more traditional means. Opponents of the games approach believe the technique teaches a simplistic view of reality, with the result that the pupil thinks he knows all about a particular subject when in reality he has had only a minor orientation to it. They also believe that the games dehumanize pupils by allowing for the manipulation of others and the furtherance of self-interest, and they are concerned that pupils may learn unfortunate values from a method where success may be measured by obtaining worldly goods or votes through shrewd and sometimes deceptive means.

> If you treat people as they are, they will remain as they are. If you treat people as they ought to be and should be, they will become what they ought to be and should be.
>
> GOETHE

The Practical Aspects of Choosing Teaching: A Summary

The previous sections of this chapter have dealt with a number of aspects of teaching and the teaching profession. At this point the authors present what might be termed some "practical" aspects of the job of teaching, some reactions to certain questions that naturally will come to the minds of young people contemplating entering into the profession of teaching.

WILL I BE IN A FIELD WHERE I'M NEEDED?

Since before World War II there has been a shortage of qualified teachers for the public schools in the United States, but the opening of school in the fall of 1969–70 gave indication for the first time in more than twenty years that the general teacher shortage had come to an end. An announcement to this effect came from the National Education Association, the largest professional teaching organization, but the association hastened to add that shortages of qualified teachers continued in some subjects or teacher assignments and in some localities, especially in rural areas, and that many additional teachers would continue to be needed throughout the nation to provide top-notch education for all pupils. It is a fact of life, however, that surpluses of elementary and secondary teachers may result if students continue to elect these fields in the same proportion as in the past. This, of course, represents a sharp change in prospects in the field of teaching, long a shortage occupation.

As a matter of fact, it has always been true that a first-year teacher may not be able to find a position in the exact location he desires, or at the exact grade level or in the subject-matter field for which he feels he is best suited. Many school systems traditionally find little difficulty in filling their staff vacancies; others experience considerable difficulty and must occasionally resort to employing teachers with emergency licenses who are not completely qualified. Also certain academic areas, such as social studies and physical education, seem to have had adequate supplies, while certain other areas, such as languages, English, and elementary grades, have been in short supply.

A prospective teacher should consult the annual publication of the NEA Research Division, entitled *Teacher Supply and Demand in Public Schools,* for an up-to-date analysis of supply and demand in the profession. The picture is constantly changing, and the current situation may change within the very next few years. Such factors as birth rates, economic conditions, trends in the profession, and the status of certain instructional fields cause supply and demand to vary. Some of the personnel in the education department of your college have information regarding the supply and demand of teachers nationally and in the specific locality in which you prefer to teach; it would be well for you to confer with them regarding the current status and the trends that appear to be emerging.

WILL I HAVE ENJOYABLE WORK?

Most teachers enjoy their work. Like any type of work, teaching has its share of headaches, disappointments, and problems, but these are outweighed by the challenges it presents and by the satisfactions it affords.

There are unfortunately a few persons in the profession who for one reason or another do not enjoy teaching. Perhaps they do not enjoy working with children and youth; perhaps they do not understand why young people do the things they do; perhaps they do not like the dynamic atmosphere of the public-school classroom. Whatever their reason, they should not remain in the profession; there are few things worse than being discontented with one's life's work. For this reason prospective teachers should take advantage of every opportunity to work in children's or youth groups and should take introductory courses in education early in their college careers as "self-screening" measures.

WILL I MAKE A REASONABLE SALARY?

Teachers' salaries generally have been improving in recent years, and there are indications that they will continue to improve in the future. Historically the wages of teachers have been pitifully low, but the organized efforts of educators and others, especially since World War II, have caused the general public to become increasingly concerned over the low remuneration of teachers, with the result of improved salaries and other economic benefits.

The national range in teachers' salaries is great. With a little under $8,000 being the estimated current national average for classroom teachers, salaries range from about $4,500 to more than $16,000. In general, teachers' starting salaries compare favorably with those of other professions and occupations, but it is only fair to say that over a period of years they do not as a rule keep pace with the incomes of persons in such professions as medicine and law.

Larger school systems pay higher salaries than smaller ones; the NEA Research Division reported that the average large-system salary for teachers in 1968–69 was $6,069, as compared to $5,674 in 1967–68. In these systems in 1968–69, the range for beginning teachers with baccalaureate degrees was $5,040–$7,500. According to the United States Office of Education, the average for all teachers in all districts in the nation in 1967 was $7,630. Cities in northern and western states, as a rule, have higher teacher-salary schedules than cities in the southern states. There is a trend within the various states toward a minimum salary for beginning teachers, and also toward the establishment of single salary schedules within districts so that teachers with the same background of experience and education receive the same salary. It is advisable for teacher applicants to consider, in addition to the annual salary, the cost of living: a salary of $6,000 in one community may mean almost as much purchasing power as a salary of $7,000 in another.

WILL I HAVE A REASONABLE AMOUNT OF LEISURE TIME?

In teaching, as in most other lines of work, practitioners need time for activities that will give them release from their regular occupational duties and responsibilities. While there are many occasions that keep teachers at school after hours, and while many hours are spent in planning and preparing after the dismissal bell rings, teachers do—and should—have their evenings and weekends relatively free of professionally associated duties. For two or three months in the summer, also, teachers have the opportunity to participate in activities other than those directly associated with school, though many improve themselves professionally by attending summer sessions on college campuses, by reading, by travel, or by participating in children's and youths' camps and other activities. It is important for teachers to plan their lives so that they have a proper balance of work and rest and relaxation or participation in activities that are different from their usual routine.

ARE THERE REAL OPPORTUNITIES FOR SERVICE?

As indicated in a previous section of this chapter, opportunities for service to children and adults abound in the field of teaching. There are also opportunities to serve organizations of various kinds in the profession, the community, the state, and the nation. Teachers make up the membership of committees and official staffs of national, state, regional, and local professional organizations. They serve as Sunday-school teachers or other church-affiliated officials; workers with Boy or Girl Scouts; members of service clubs and other organizations in the community; and organizers of social, recreational, and religious activities. Some enter into political affairs, and a few run for public office. Opportunities for teachers to serve are legion; oftentimes they face the problem of limiting themselves to the most worthwhile activities so that they do not spread themselves too thinly and thereby accomplish little, if anything, of importance.

AM I PROPERLY EQUIPPED TO DO THE JOB?

To the sincere prospective teacher, the idea of being responsible for guiding the learning activities of twenty-five or more youngsters in the classroom is a challenge of considerable magnitude, and it is natural for him to question whether he is prepared to undertake such a responsibility. Dedicated teachers have always pondered this question from the first day they teach until the day they retire.

Good teaching requires physical and mental stamina, so the successful teacher will maintain satisfactory personal health. Good teaching demands a broad background in the liberal and practical arts, so the effective teacher will include in his prebaccalaureate and postbaccalaureate college program a series of courses and other experiences that will make him a well-educated individual. Good teaching calls for an adequate background in the profession and knowledge of how to guide learning activities for young people, so in his college curriculum the professional teacher will have an adequate balance of education courses that will include psychological, historical, social, and philosophical foundations of education, a study of the curriculum, and methodology.

The effective teacher keeps in mind that the pupils must learn things today that will be beneficial to them in tomorrow's world. Thus he must keep abreast of happenings and trends in all areas and places of living. Most important of all, he must gain and maintain the ability to teach children how to learn so that the experiences they have in today's classrooms will transfer to the world outside the classroom when they become adults. Today's children will need to know how to survive in tomorrow's completely different world.

Effective teachers will keep up with happenings and trends in all areas of living, especially in fields closely allied to their profession. New knowledge is continually being disseminated in the fields of psychology, growth and development, learning, methodology, and audiovisual materials. It is imperative that teachers keep abreast of this knowledge through such activities as reading in professional books and journals and attending professional meetings as well as evening classes and summer sessions at colleges and universities.

CAN I HAVE PRIDE IN THE PROFESSION?

Teachers in America's public schools have had no small part in making this the great nation it is today. Their pupils have graduated from their classes to become world leaders in science, medicine, government, politics, art, music, and communications. Their pupils have contributed to making this country the one with the highest standard of living in all the world. Public-school teachers have done, and are doing, a highly commendable job in the classrooms of the nation.

The profession itself has risen in public esteem in recent years. The myriad written and spoken words attest to the fact that public respect for the profession has risen to peak proportions. This has resulted in increased moral and financial support of teachers and their work. Respect for educators by persons in business, industry, and the home has never been higher than at the present time.

Prospective teachers have every right to be proud of the accomplishments of their predecessors and of those currently employed in carrying on work of greatest importance. It is of utmost urgency, for our culture and for the profession, that tomorrow's teachers continue to hold high the standards of a profession that has made great strides since the early days of our country's history.

Questions for Discussion

1. Why have you chosen teaching as the profession you wish to follow? Before you can adequately answer this question, you must do two things: write down on paper your philosophy of life and, also, write down your philosophy of education.
2. To what position in the schools do you ultimately aspire? Why?
3. Specifically, how can a teacher teach his pupils *how* to learn?
4. Explain why the range of achievement in academic areas should widen within a grade or subject area if the teacher is performing effectively.
5. Of the three types of experimentation in organizational structure at the elementary-school level described in this chapter (ungraded, dual-progress, and team-teaching), which do you believe holds the most promise? Explain your answer. Do you feel that any of these plans might be adaptable to the junior-high- or senior-high-school levels? Which ones and why?
6. Do you believe that the new middle-school type of organizational structure might be preferable to the junior-high-school arrangement? Explain your answer.
7. Which of the two individually prescribed instruction programs described in this chapter appeals most to you? Why?
8. In what ways does the work of the elementary teacher differ from that of the secondary teacher? From the junior-high teacher?
9. What are some of the ways teachers can keep up with the immense amount of new knowledge that is forthcoming almost daily?
10. How many teachers are employed in your community? How does this compare with the number of doctors, dentists, and filling-station operators?

Activities and Projects

1. In some of the authors' foundation courses, certain students have found it interesting and informative to return to the public school that they attended or from which they were graduated and interview some of their former teachers about the profession. If such a project interests you, be certain you are equipped with a set of questions for which

you wish answers; remember, teachers are busy people, and for them time is a precious commodity. If your former school is not convenient, try this project at one that is. Either way, be certain to arrange an appointment in advance of your visit. An oral report of your interview will be of interest to others in your college class.

2. Refer to some self-rating scale for determining fitness for teaching, such as the one in Robert W. Richey, *Planning for Teaching,* or E. E. Samuelson, et al., *You'd Like Teaching,* to see how you rate as a prospect for the profession.

3. If you aspire to an administrative position, such as a principalship, interview a person in that position regarding its advantages and disadvantages and report your findings to the class.

4. Make a list of qualities you think teachers should possess. Talk to your friends about the qualities they think teachers should possess. Which ones predominate? Are there any evidences of differences in those proposed by women and those by men? How does your list compare with an authority's list?

5. Check over your transcript of college work thus far. Is 75 to 90 percent of it in the liberal arts? How do you feel your major subject area will help you in teaching classes at the elementary or secondary level? What professional courses you have taken so far do you feel will most benefit you on the job? Least?

6. Check with the teacher-placement office in your college and determine which teaching areas seem to be currently most in demand. In which does the supply seem to be adequate? How does your particular teaching interest stand in the supply-and-demand figures?

7. Secure the salary schedule from the district in which you are interested in securing a position. How does the beginning salary compare with the national average? Approximately how does the starting wage compare with the first-year income for doctors, lawyers, and ministers in your area?

8. Look through several college bulletins in your library and compare their teacher-education programs. How does your program compare with those described? What are the respective percentages of work in the liberal arts and in professional education in each instance?

9. Choose the field of your greatest interest from these: science, medicine, government, politics, art, music, communications. By consulting encyclopedias and other references, choose the world's leaders in the area of your choice. Which are products of America's public schools?

References

Planning for Teaching

ADAMS, SAM, and JOHN L. GARRETT, JR. *To Be a Teacher: An Introduction to Education.* Englewood Cliffs, N. J.: Prentice-Hall, 1969.

ANDERSON, ROBERT H. *Teaching in a World of Change.* New York: Harcourt, 1966.

BURRUP, PERCY E. *The Teacher and the Public School System.* 2d ed. New York: Harper, 1967. Chaps. 7, 16.

CALVERT, ROBERT, JR., and JOHN E. STEELE. *Planning Your Career.* New York: McGraw-Hill, 1963.

CHARLES, M. R. *A Preface to Education.* New York: Macmillan, 1965. Chap. 9.

COLLIER, CALHOUN, W. ROBERT HOUSTON, ROBERT R. SCHMATZ, and WILLIAM J. WALSH. *Teaching in the Modern Elementary School.* New York: Macmillan, 1967. Chap. 16.

FRASIER, JAMES E. *An Introduction to the Study of Education.* New York: Harper, 1965. Chap. 12.

HASKEW, LAURENCE D., and JONATHON C. MCLENDON. *This Is Teaching.* 3d ed. Glenview, Ill.: Scott, Foresman, 1968. Chap. 1.

HICKS, WILLIAM VERNON, and FRANK H. BLACKINGTON III. *Introduction to Education.* Columbus, Ohio: C. E. Merrill, 1965, Chaps. 1–3, 5.

JOHNSON, MAURITZ, JR. *American Secondary Schools.* New York: Harcourt, 1965. Chap. 8.

LEE, J. MURRAY. *Foundations of Elementary Education.* Boston: Allyn & Bacon, 1969. Chap. 1.

POIRIER, GÉRARD A. *Students as Partners in Team Learning.* Berkeley: Center of Team Learning, 1970.

RICHEY, ROBERT W. *Planning for Teaching.* 4th ed. New York: McGraw-Hill, 1968. Chaps. 2, 18.

The Work of the Teacher

BROWN, B. FRANK. *The Appropriate Placement School: A Sophisticated Nongraded Curriculum.* West Nyack, N.Y.: Parker, 1965.

COLLIER, CALHOUN, W. ROBERT HOUSTON, ROBERT R. SCHMATZ, and WILLIAM J. WALSH. *Teaching in the Modern Elementary School.* New York: Macmillan, 1967. Pt. 2.

FOREIGN POLICY ASSOCIATION. *Simulation Games for the Social Studies Classroom.* New Dimensions, vol. 1. New York: Foreign Policy Association, 1968.

FRASIER, JAMES E. *An Introduction to the Study of Education.* New York: Harper, 1965. Chaps. 7–9.

FRAZIER, ALEXANDER, ed. *A Curriculum for Children.* Washington, D.C.: Association for Supervision and Curriculum Development of the National Education Association, 1969.

FROST, JOE L., and G. THOMAS ROWLAND. *Curricula for the Seventies.* Boston: Houghton Mifflin, 1969. Chaps. 5, 8–12.

GRAMBS, JEAN DRESDEN. *Schools, Scholars, and Society.* Englewood Cliffs, N.J.: Prentice-Hall, 1965. Pp. 127–55.

HARRISON, RAYMOND. *Supervisory Leadership in Education.* New York: American Book, 1968. Chap. 4.

HAVIGHURST, ROBERT J., and BERNICE L. NEUGARTEN. *Society and Education.* Boston: Allyn & Bacon, 1967. Pp. 431–81.

HILLSON, MAURIE, ed. *Elementary Education.* New York: Free Press, 1967.

JOHNSON, JAMES A., HAROLD W. COLLINS, VICTOR L. DUPUIS, and JOHN H. JOHANSEN. *Introduction to the Foundations of American Education.* Boston: Allyn & Bacon, 1969. Sec. 5.

KNELLER, GEORGE F. *Foundations of Education.* New York: Wiley, 1963. Chap. 16.

LEE, J. MURRAY. *Foundations of Elementary Education.* Boston: Allyn & Bacon, 1969. Chaps. 5, 6.

NATIONAL EDUCATION ASSOCIATION. *Life Skills in School and Society.* Washington, D.C.: Association for Supervision and Curriculum Development of the National Education Association, 1969. Chaps. 4–9.

RATHS, JAMES, JOHN R. PANCELLA, and JAMES S. VAN NESS. *Studying Teaching.* Englewood Cliffs, N.J.: Prentice-Hall, 1967. Chaps. 1–9.

RICHEY, ROBERT W. *Planning for Teaching.* 4th ed. New York. McGraw-Hill, 1968. Chaps. 5, 6.

SHUMSKY, ABRAHAM. *In Search of Teaching Style.* New York: Appleton, 1968.

SKINNER, B. F. "Why Teachers Fail." *Saturday Review,* October 16, 1965. Pp. 80–81, 98–102.

SOLTIS, JONAS. *An Introduction to the Analysis of Educational Concepts.* Reading, Mass.: Addison-Wesley, 1968. Chaps. 3, 4.

WALLEN, NORMAN E., and ROBERT M. W. TRAVERS. "Analysis and Investigation of Teaching Methods." In *Handbook of Research on Teaching,* ed. N. L. Gage. Chicago: Rand McNally, 1963. Pp. 448–501.

WEBSTER, STATEN W. *Discipline in the Classroom.* San Francisco: Chandler, 1968. Chaps. 5, 6.

Economics of Teaching

BURRUP, PERCY E. *The Teacher and the Public School System.* 2d ed. New York: Harper, 1967. Chap. 13.

COLLIER, CALHOUN, W. ROBERT HOUSTON, ROBERT R. SCHMATZ, and WILLIAM J. WALSH. *Teaching in the Modern Elementary School.* New York: Macmillan, 1967. Chap. 1.

DORROS, SIDNEY. *Teaching as a Profession.* Columbus, Ohio: C. E. Merrill, 1968. Chap. 9.

FOY, RENA. *The World of Education.* New York: Macmillan, 1968. Chap. 14.

HASKEW, LAURENCE D., and JONATHON C. MCLENDON. *This Is Teaching.* 3d ed. Glenview, Ill.: Scott, Foresman, 1968. Chap. 9.

MARTIN, DONALD L. "Teachers Unions and Educational Change: Some Economic Implications." In *Inventing Education for the Future,* ed. Werner Z. Hirsch. San Francisco: Chandler, 1967.

NATIONAL EDUCATION ASSOCIATION. *Economic Status of Teachers.* Washington, D.C.: Research Division of the National Education Association, published annually.

―――. *Teacher Supply and Demand in Public Schools.* Research Report. Washington, D.C.: Research Division of the National Education Association, published annually.

RICHEY, ROBERT W. *Planning for Teaching.* 4th ed. New York: McGraw-Hill, 1968.

WAYSON, W. W. "The Political Revolution in Education, 1965." *Phi Delta Kappan,* March 1966, pp. 33–39.

WOELLNER, ROBERT C., and M. AURILLA WOOD. *Requirements for Certification of Teachers, Counselors, Librarians, Administrators for Elementary Schools, Secondary Schools, Junior Colleges.* Chicago: University of Chicago Press, revised annually.

All the high hopes which I entertain for a more
glorious future for the human race are built upon
the elevation of the teacher's profession and the
enlargement of the teacher's usefulness.

HORACE MANN

4

Pressures and Problems
of Teaching

Day-by-Day Teaching: The True Picture

THE TYPICAL WORK DAY

Mrs. M., third-grade teacher at Willow School, arrives at the school building at 8:00 A.M., goes immediately to the teachers' lounge where she picks up
the principal's "Bulletin for the Day," hurriedly reads it, and then takes
out of her folder five Ditto masters she has prepared at home last night.
She runs off on the duplicator forty copies of each master for distribution to her children; they will use the sheets for seat work later in the day.
Mrs. M. then goes to her room to get supplies ready for the children and
to ready the room for the opening of the class sessions.

When the 8:30 bell rings, Mrs. M. greets the children who have lined
up at the classroom door, according to their usual procedure. She allows
them to enter the room, and for five minutes the boys and girls sit quietly,
resting their heads on their desks. Until 9:00, the classroom time is spent
by the entire class repeating the Pledge of Allegiance, conducting a health
inspection, and collecting cafeteria money. Between 9:00 and 9:45, the
teacher and children plan together for the day's work in social studies, and

the teacher distributes and explains the duplicated sheets in language usage, spelling, and writing. On days when time allows, part of this time is used in conversational Spanish or English activities.

At 9:45, Mrs. M. takes the children to the playground, where she supervises their playing a game she has introduced earlier in the year, and at 10:00 the children return to the classroom for reading instruction. During the ensuing hour, Mrs. M. first works with reading group III while group I works on the language work-study sheets and group II works on work-study sheets for social studies; she then works with reading group II while group I works on social-studies work-study sheets and group III works on language work-study activities; and finally, she works with reading group I while group II works on language work-study sheets and group III completes the social-studies sheets. On alternate days, the children work on science instead of social studies.

The twenty-minute period beginning at 11:00, which Mrs. M. has designated as the directed-writing and spelling period for the entire group, usually proves to be insufficient, because the class is in the process of making the transition from manuscript to cursive writing. Between 11:20 and 11:30, the teacher always, and wisely, allows time for an evaluation of the morning's work; a list of "Things We Learned This Morning," drawn out from members of the class, is written on the chalkboard for all to see.

During the lunch hour, Mrs. M. has half of the period for rest and relaxation, but she spends the other half hour in supervising in the cafeteria, a duty that falls her way for three weeks each semester. On three other weeks during the semester, Mrs. M. has "yard duty" on the playground for half of her lunch-hour time.

At 12:25 the bell sounds and the children once more line up at the classroom door; Mrs. M. admits them to the room and they rest once more for a five-minute period. At 12:35, Mrs. M. begins the arithmetic lesson, which she teaches by entire-group and small-group activities. During the forty-five-minute period between 1:05 and 1:50, Mrs. M. again calls each of the three reading groups to the reading circle for fifteen-minute sessions each, but this time the emphasis is upon recreational reading, instead of developmental reading as it was in the morning. While the teacher is discussing with each group their recreational-reading activities, the other groups are doing additional recreational reading at their seats. Between 1:50 and 2:20, Mrs. M. leads the class in an art lesson with tempera paints; on other days at this period she provides experiences for the class in music, literature, dramatization, story telling, or choral speaking. During the final ten minutes before dismissal at 2:30, all completed papers are turned in by the children, and another evaluation period ensues, in which the children provide statements under a chalkboard heading of "Things We Learned Today."

During the day, two mothers come to visit the classroom—one in the morning and the other in the afternoon. Of course, some time must be spent with each mother discussing her child's achievement. Twice during the day children from nearby rooms come to the room to borrow certain pieces of equipment, each time interrupting Mrs. M. in whatever she happens to be doing, and once the principal pops into the room to ask Mrs. M. if she will serve on the refreshments committee for the next meeting of the Parent-Teacher Association. On this afternoon, as on each Wednesday afternoon, Mrs. M. joins her colleagues in a regular faculty meeting that runs from 3:00 to 4:15. Faculty meetings at Willow School are not the drudgery they are in some schools, however, as time is spent in worthwhile in-service education activities involving participation by all teachers on the building staff.

By the time Mrs. M. returns to her room and picks up papers to be graded at home that evening, it is a little after 4:15, and she has completed an eight-hour-and-fifteen-minute day. It seems that despite her best organization it is never possible to complete the day at the building in less time than that, what with parent conferences, organizational meetings, and other kinds of activities. Furthermore, Mrs. M. often returns to the school building in the evening to attend programs by pupils in the school, PTA meetings, and gatherings of other organizations and groups in the school community.

Mr. S. is a business-education teacher in Pioneer Senior High School. He leaves his home at 7:35 each morning to reach his one-mile-distant school by 7:50; when he arrives at the building he reads the principal's bulletin to teachers and makes last-minute preparations for the first class session, which begins at 8:05. During the first class session, on office practice, Mr. S. has students work on clerical-office-practice sets; and when they complete the various jobs, they turn them in to the teacher to be checked.

Mr. S.'s preparation period comes between 9:00 and 9:45. After listening to the daily bulletin read from the principal's office, he studies shorthand for a class period later in the day; checks some student papers handed in during the previous period; goes to see the Dean of Girls about curriculum offerings in the business-education department next year, including class size, total enrollments, and number of sections; and talks with his student teacher, who reports to the school each day.

Between 9:50 and 10:45, Mr. S. supervises the student teacher as the latter teaches a clerical-office-practice class, helps students who need individual attention in the course, and then confers with the student teacher's college supervisor, who has come to observe the student's work in the classroom. Mr. S.'s lunch hour this year is between 10:50 and 11:35; on this day during lunch he confers with another business-education teacher regarding subject offerings for the next year, about certain techniques of teaching shorthand, and about the possibility of building a class in secretarial practice.

From 11:40 to 12:20 Mr. S. teaches the class in Typing III and IV, in which students learn how to do tabulation reports of an accounting and executive nature, and from 12:25 to 1:15 he teaches the second section of the same class. The beginning shorthand class meets between 1:20 and 2:15; for the first five minutes of the period students practice brief forms with their flash cards; then Mr. S. dictates homework and new matter to the class. Juniors in the class remain a few minutes after class is dismissed for a checkup with Mr. S. to find out whether they have been recommended for next year's secretarial-practice class.

The period between 2:20 and 3:15 is free on all days except Wednesdays, when Mr. S. sponsors the American Field Service Club in the high school. At this day's meeting, a foreign student in a neighboring high school speaks to the club about her homeland of Barbados.

After the 3:15 dismissal bell, Mr. S. grades the shorthand papers, counsels a student about transferring to an earlier morning class in shorthand, talks with four students about the next speaker for the American Field Service Club's meeting, writes two letters asking for free teaching materials, closes the windows in the classroom, and checks it for orderliness. On the way to the parking lot, Mr. S. talks with another business-education teacher regarding textbook orders, curriculum reports, and the school's proposed semester examinations. By this time, the clock reads 4:00, and Mr. S. has completed a day of better than seven and one-half hours at school, and in the evening at home he spends another two hours grading papers and planning for the next day's classes.

The two examples given above are true stories in the lives of two teachers, one at the elementary-school level and one at the secondary level. They are mythical typical days, because teachers, pupils, and schools vary so greatly from day to day that in teaching it is impossible to call anything typical. But the preceding accounts of two actual teachers' days should give the reader some conception of what teachers do during the day. At least it can be seen that for a certainty the teacher's day is not what is commonly thought, a 9:00 to 2:30 job in which the teacher spends his time "hearing lessons" and disciplining children, and which ends for the day when the children go home. It can be seen that the usual day in teaching is about eight hours long, plus whatever time is spent on school work after regular school hours.

THE TYPICAL WORK WEEK

The length of the typical work week for teachers is about fifty hours. Here again, no actual week is typical, but a survey of the time devoted to various teacher activities resulted in the following:

ELEMENTARY SCHOOL (Average work week, 47 hours, 50 minutes)

Duty	Total Hours	Percent of Work-Week Time
Class instruction	28 hours, 15 minutes	59
Out-of-class instructional duties	11 hours, 52 minutes	25
Preparing materials	3 hours, 30 minutes	
Correcting papers	3 hours, 26 minutes	
Preparing for lessons	2 hours, 48 minutes	
Helping individual pupils	1 hour, 9 minutes	
Contacting parents	59 minutes	
Miscellaneous	7 hours, 43 minutes	16
Performing monitorial duties	2 hours, 33 minutes	
Preparing grade cards and reports	2 hours, 18 minutes	
Attending official meetings	57 minutes	
Other	1 hour, 55 minutes	

SECONDARY SCHOOL (Average work week, 47 hours, 58 minutes)

Duty	Total Hours	Percent of Work-Week Time
Class instruction	23 hours, 4 minutes	48
Out-of-class instructional duties	12 hours, 59 minutes	27
Preparing materials	1 hour, 49 minutes	
Correcting papers	4 hours, 45 minutes	
Preparing for lessons	3 hours, 41 minutes	
Helping individual pupils	1 hour, 37 minutes	
Contacting parents	1 hour, 7 minutes	

SECONDARY SCHOOL (*continued*)

Duty	Total Hours	Percent of Work-Week Time
Miscellaneous	11 hours, 55 minutes	25
Sponsoring clubs and student activities	2 hours, 14 minutes	
Conducting study halls	2 hours, 7 minutes	
Preparing grade cards and records	1 hour, 49 minutes	
Performing monitorial duties	1 hour, 10 minutes	
Coaching athletics, etc.	59 minutes	
Attending official meetings	57 minutes	
Other	2 hours, 39 minutes	

It is evident from the authors' survey that actual teaching in the classroom is roughly only one-half of the teacher's job as measured in hours expended. It is also clear that teachers, like most others in professional work, spend much more than the traditional forty-hour week in meeting the demands of their jobs. Unfortunately, many lay persons are unimpressed with the many hours spent in preparation for classes, in completing reports, in supervising student activities, and in many other assignments too numerous and varied to categorize in the teacher's work load. They have the erroneous impression that because children spend about six hours a day in school, that amount of time constitutes the teacher's work load for a day, with Saturdays and summers off in addition!

THE TYPICAL SUMMER

Teaching is the one profession that affords its members a long summer-vacation period. Because most school systems in the United States dismiss pupils for the summer vacation in mid- or late June, teachers are relatively free from their classrooms until early or mid-September. Although the trend is toward extending the school year, it will probably be some time before teachers can no longer look forward to a two- to three-month summer vacation that they can pretty well use as they see fit. Like the school day, there is no typical pattern of teacher activities during this free period.

More school districts each year are offering their teachers opportunities to supplement their annual income by jobs in the district's summer sessions for the enrichment of many pupils' programs and for special makeup or remedial classes. Many teachers, too, gain salary increments through completing district in-service education classes and courses on college campuses; the large college enrollments during summer sessions are made up predominantly of teachers who are taking advantage of this time to improve their professional status and to grow. An increasing number of teachers are combining travel and further education in colleges and universities in different parts of this country and abroad. Many teachers supplement their income by working in jobs outside the teaching profession during the summer months; others take part in such creative activities as writing, painting, composing, and playing or singing in musical organizations.

The mythical typical days in the lives of two teachers with which this chapter began clearly point up the fact that persons in the profession have a multitude of responsibilities, both inside and outside the classroom. Their duties are many and varied: most of them are challenging and interesting; some of them are routine and dull.

TYPICAL DAILY PLANNING

An analysis of the two teachers' days at the opening of this chapter reveals something of the amount of behind-the-scenes effort expended by teachers so that their pupils may participate in many kinds of learning experiences. Most teachers spend literally hours of time in study and in planning and organizing teaching-learning procedures.

Teachers must plan for certain instructional units to be taught their pupils; often this presents a need for either writing a resource unit or choosing one that will be adaptable to the present group of children in the class. From the units, the teachers plan individual lessons with the needs and interests of the class members in mind. Teachers must determine which types of instructional materials and audiovisual aids will most effectively carry out the activities of the individual lessons, and must see that they are on hand when needed.

In good schools today, teachers employ many types of instruction methods at both elementary- and secondary-school levels, and do not depend on one single approach to accomplish their objectives. Much use is made of teacher-pupil planning and problem-solving and inquiry techniques, and from them spring such procedures as dramatizations, film presentations, demonstrations, presentations by resource persons, field trips, laboratory experiences, and individual and group evaluations. If the teachers give more than lip service to the idea that learning is an *individual* matter, then relevant pupil-centered and cooperative group projects to which all children can contribute will be the bases of methodology. Since there is no one

My First School

The question was settled; the die was cast. The matter which had been under consideration by myself and friends for some length of time was finally decided. *I was to teach.*

With a vigorous and confident hand, I grasped the reins of government in the little domain of my classroom. All went well for a time. But then, to my dismay, my pupils began to exhibit signs of restlessness and insubordination. I tightened the reins of discipline, assumed more sternness of demeanor, but in vain. The hitches and jerks in the machinery would come.

Weeks and months passed, and, in spite of all my effort, the school would often be noisy; the children, unruly. I was utterly heartsick and discouraged until, gradually, permanent thought and experience took the place of anxiety and discouragement. I discovered I had been reaching after the unattainable, that I had been wasting my strength in vain endeavor to keep quiet, and to drill into perfection that which God never meant should be quiet.

A healthy growth can best be secured by that very restlessness which is the bane of the teacher's experience. Indeed I may say, the teacher's proper task is not to destroy restlessness, but to seek to turn it into the right channel, and thus promote the development of both

best way to teach, teachers must be encouraged to experiment in the classroom and to use their ingenuity in instructional approaches.

Classroom management is an important aspect of a teacher's daily work. This many-faceted area includes a number of things discussed previously —planning for units and lessons, arranging for instructional materials, and deciding upon appropriate methodology. Attendance checking, assignment making, and paper collecting are also obvious parts of this important teacher responsibility. Another aspect of classroom management, one that looms large on the horizon of many teachers, particularly first-year teachers, is that of discipline. Some teachers seemingly have more than their share of behavior problems; others apparently have very few or none at all. The difference, generally, is that those who have few or no behavior problems have learned to avoid them subtly by creating classroom environments where industry and interest abound, or they have learned to sense impending misbehavior and have taken steps to prevent its happening. Despite the most subtle planning to avoid behavior incidents, they still occasionally arise. When they do, teachers, realizing that all behavior has a cause, should attempt to find the cause of the problem and insofar as possible take steps to alleviate or eliminate the cause. The causes that make children behave in socially unacceptable ways are legion, but teachers who physical and mental faculties. He or she who learns to do this has found the "philosopher's stone" in teaching.

My short experience has brought to my mind the fact that a very great evil in country schools is keeping the children in school too long, and especially too long at a time. But I enforce the policy of keeping them busy, let it be whatever you choose—printing, drawing, writing on a slate, or whatever is assigned.

And then when they have done the best they can and all that has been asked of them for the time, I let them go out to play to work off the superabundant vitality that is in them. Fresh air and exercise is what they need to keep their bodies sound and their minds bright and active for work in the school room.

This, my humble experience in my first effort to "teach the young ideas how to shoot," I give for what it is worth. If it will be any help or any encouragement to my fellow teachers, who like myself have just begun to tread the thorny pathway of the profession and whose hearts groan, as did mine, for light, sympathy, and help in their calling, my object will be attained.

Written sometime between 1880 and 1883 by Amanda Crabtree, as quoted in *NEA Journal*, March 1963, p. 61. Reprinted by permission.

do not attempt to find specific causes for misbehavior and to remedy them are not worthy of their titles. Unless causes of misbehavior are found and acted on, children can hardly be expected to grow into socially acceptable ways of behavior.

During the course of each learning experience, teachers and pupils must evaluate their progress toward whatever are the agreed-upon objectives of the class. Procedures and techniques must constantly be appraised so that the teacher and the class will know whether they can be continued or whether others should be employed. Tests of various kinds, written reports, anecdotal records, checklists, and questionnaires are among the tools used in evaluation, and it is the responsibility of the teacher to administer and interpret the results of these evaluative media.

Reporting to parents is an extremely important part of the teacher's work. This demands of a teacher the ability to measure pupils' achievements and accomplishments accurately and to report to parents objectively regarding children's growth in skills, knowledges, understandings, attitudes, and behavior. Such reporting can hardly be done effectively through many of the traditional systems of grading. Individual teacher-parent conferences provide possibly the most mutually beneficial method of reporting, since parent and teacher may learn from each other what procedures may be taken by each for the ultimate benefit of the child. The traditional letter marks or percentage scores are frequently confusing and misleading, and the written paragraphs, while superior to the marks, have their grave limitations also. It is unfortunate that now, in the third quarter of the twentieth century, the trend in reporting seems to be back in the direction of the five-level letter marks: A, B, C, D, and F.

Other aspects of a teacher's daily work are also obvious from an analysis of the activities described at the beginning of this chapter. Many times each day, teachers who have proper rapport with pupils are called upon to counsel children and youth as they attempt to solve problems involving educational, social, or vocational plans. Also, in most schools in the country, teachers have the opportunity to direct at least one activity that is termed, variously, cocurricular or extracurricular; these activities are concerned with many areas, such as music, speech, journalism, athletics, hobbies, or social life. The daily work of the teacher also includes professional study and cooperative professional contacts and projects with other teachers on the school's staff.

The Teacher's Roles

The teacher "wears many hats." Some fit very well; others do not. But the teacher must wear them all, for associating and working with pupils and parents and other lay persons and professional colleagues forces him to fill many different roles, a number of which have been indicated previously. In the light of the massive changes taking place in today's society, coupled with the projection of greater and more rapid changes in the future, the teacher's role is constantly changing in the direction of increasing educational leadership. Technological advances do not pause to solve the problems they create; mass-communication techniques have shrunk the world beyond the wildest expectations of people a quarter century ago. With these changes have come problems of hate, poverty, unrest, and environmental deterioration, and whether or not these—and other problems, many of which are currently unforeseen—are met and solved, to the benefit of our world, depends not a little upon how teachers in our schools prepare children and youth to live and work effectively after they leave the classrooms of the nation.

Besides being a director of learning, a motivator, a confidant, a disciplinarian, an agent for change, and a resource person, the teacher at different times also finds himself in the roles of clerk, baby-sitter, executive, recreational leader, and joiner.

THE CLERK

There is a great deal of paper work involved in the teacher's job; in fact, the record keeping required of teachers seems to increase almost annually. Much of the work is of a clerical nature, but a great amount of it, such as making entries in cumulative records, is highly professional and is necessary for an effective teaching-learning situation. Daily attendance records are usually kept by teachers; these are important since the state money allotments are based on average-daily-attendance records. Pupils' cumulative records must be kept up-to-date in areas where teachers are involved. Lunch records, excuses for pupil absences or tardiness, teacher registers, pupil permits to take field trips—all of these, as well as others, bid for their time in the daily life of the teacher.

What Is a Teacher?

The teacher is a prophet. He lays the foundations of tomorrow. *The teacher is an artist.* He works with the precious clay of unfolding personality. *The teacher is a friend.* His heart responds to the faith and devotion of his students. *The teacher is a citizen.* He is selected and licensed for the improvement of society. *The teacher is an interpreter.* Out of his maturer and wider life he seeks to guide the young. *The teacher is a builder.* He works with the higher and finer values of civilization. *The teacher is a culture-bearer.* He leads the way toward worthier tastes, saner attitudes, more gracious manners, higher intelligence. *The teacher is a planner.* He sees the young lives before him as a part of a great system which shall grow stronger in the light of truth. *The teacher is a pioneer.* He is always attempting the impossible and winning out. *The teacher is a reformer.* He seeks to remove the handicaps that weaken and destroy life. *The teacher is a believer.* He has abiding faith in the improvability of the race.

Joy Elmer Morgan, *NEA Journal,* March 1958, back cover. Reprinted by permission.

THE BABY-SITTER

Some parents apparently feel that one of the responsibilities of the teacher is to "sit" with their children. One of the authors vividly recalls an incident wherein a mother brought her child back to school after he had had a "not-too-sick" experience with chicken pox, and the relief the parent expressed now that the child would be back on the school's hands and out from under her feet. What teacher has not had a parent suggest, "Anything the school can do for the child will be appreciated, as I can't do a thing with him"? On the other hand, the teacher has a legal role *loco parentis,* "in place of the parent," in which the laws and traditions of this country have given him parental status for supervision of pupils on playgrounds and on trips of various kinds.

THE EXECUTIVE

As employees of a local school district, teachers are expected to abide by and to enforce the state laws and the rules and regulations of the local board of education as they apply to the school and the classroom. At the same time, however, it is important for teachers to remember that, even though they are employees of a local district and as such are agents of the state, they are legally liable for any injuries caused by negligent acts, just as are any other persons in this nation. The teacher, too, is the real executive officer in the classroom: even though the activities are cooperatively planned and executed, the teacher, in the final analysis, is the person responsible for what goes on in the classroom.

THE RECREATION LEADER

Because of a teacher's background of training and his ability to work with youngsters and adults, he is often called upon to take an active leadership role in recreational activities in the community. Whether he is sought out in this capacity, he most certainly will be, at times, the recreational leader of the boys and girls in his classroom, especially in the elementary school. With the desired goals of social and physical well-being, recreational activities in the classroom or school consist of games, sports, and certain recreational clubs that are usually promoted through contests or tournaments. A relatively new and increasingly important recreational activity in the schools—one in which increasing numbers of teachers are being involved—is camping and outdoor education. Many colleges are increasing their programs in which pupils work, play, live, and learn together under the direction of public-school and student teachers.

THE JOINER

Teachers, of course, are key persons in the important community area of education, but they are also participants in other community activities such as the church, civic organizations, and other clubs and political groups. They also join the professional organizations at national, state, and local levels.

Most school districts expect teachers to become associated with churches in the community, and studies have shown that, whereas less than half of the general population of the nation are members of religious organizations, over 90 percent of the country's teachers participate in church activities. Teachers are sought for membership in local service clubs in most communities, and they are often asked to give leadership to such agencies as the Community Chest, the Red Cross, and Boy Scout and Girl Scout troops. Members of teaching staffs generally take their political responsibilities seriously, and many of them run for and are elected to political offices. Most teachers belong to two or three professional organizations, such as the NEA, state teachers' associations, and national, state, and local groups affiliated with the NEA. Some school districts apply considerable pressure to get teachers to join professional groups.

Professional and Public Relationships

PARENTS AND COMMUNITY GROUPS

Schools, like other institutions, cannot long continue to operate at a high level of efficiency if they do not have the good will and support of the patrons they serve. While the schools do not "sell" in the same sense that commercial institutions do, they nonetheless must develop a grass-roots understanding and appreciation of their programs through interaction with parents and other lay persons. Since almost everyone in America has attended public schools at one time or another, and since millions of people have children now attending their classes, the schools are close to the people and are likely to remain so for a long time to come. The schools must maintain an effective program of keeping the people informed of their needs, purposes, and achievements and at the same time develop a sensitivity to the needs and desires of the community.

It is inevitable that teachers, whether they are new to the system or are veterans of some tenure, will have many contacts with parents and various groups of lay persons in the community. Parents have a special concern for the school and, in most cases, feel an interest akin to the teachers' in the education of their children. In a sense, teachers pick up the educational task from the children's first teachers, their parents, and carry on from that point in collaboration, it is hoped, with them. The further teachers can go in developing good relationships with the parents, the greater will be the possibility of an effective team approach to the education of the children.

Whether or not the school is considered a "good" one depends to a large extent on the stories children bring home to their mothers and fathers. If the learning experiences at school have been satisfying, meaningful, relevant, interesting, and pleasant for children, the principal struggle for satisfactory parent-teacher relationships will be won, and the way will be open to effective team effort in the education of children and youth.

With proper rapport between teachers and parents will usually come the necessary effective cooperation to achieve the optimum in the children's learning; parents will often contact the teachers and will contribute, as well as receive, much information of mutual benefit in the education of the children. Parents and teachers should share alike the goal of the fullest development of the children, and both have much to contribute toward this end.

Teachers invariably feel a sense of frustration when the need comes to communicate with parents at "reporting" time, especially if the reporting system involves letter grades or percentage marks. The reporting time could and should be a time when some of the most effective interaction takes place between teachers and parents for the benefit of the children. But it can be so only if parents and teachers are able to sit down together in mutual trust and confidence and exchange information about the children that will materially affect their growth and development. Thus the reporting time becomes a two-way exchange, in which those concerned with an evaluation of the children's achievement may discuss ways of improvement—rather than a one-way affair, in which teachers tell parents in ways often not understood, or else misunderstood, about the progress of the children.

Parents may be brought into closer cooperation with the school in ways other than individual conferences. Often they serve on committees with teachers and administrators, such as curriculum, report-card, and social committees. Many interested teachers and parents affiliate with the local chapter of the National Congress of Parents and Teachers, an organization founded in 1897, consisting of more than twelve million members, and dedicated to the education and welfare of children and youth. Meetings of local PTA's can be used constructively for informing parents and teachers of school affairs and activities and their purposes. It cannot be denied that parent-teacher organizations of this type have made some outstanding contributions over the years to public-school education.

An organization existing in many communities, called the community coordinating council or simply the community council, is made up of lay leaders from most of the civic and social organizations in the area. Such a council is often active in studying the educational programs of schools in the community, and it is not unusual for such a group to make recommendations to the local board of education or to the local school district's corps of administrative officials. Teachers are usually represented in one way or another on community councils; at any rate, it is well for teachers to know of such groups and their purposes and activities.

It is not unusual for the school district's board of education to appoint committees for special purposes. It is popular at this time, for example, for boards to appoint committees to study the programs of the schools in the local district and to make recommendations for changes or improvements. Members of such committees sometimes visit teachers' classrooms to evaluate the activities they find there. Sometimes these committees are composed of teachers as well as lay persons, but at other times teachers are not included.

Space does not permit a complete listing of the numerous clubs and societies in the community with which the schools must work from time to time. Certain of these are "youth-serving" groups, such as church-sponsored organizations, Boy Scouts and Girl Scouts, Hi-Y, Rainbow Girls, DeMolay, and 4-H, in all of which teachers are often solicited to serve. Adult groups active in most communities having, in one way or another, education as one of their purposes include Kiwanis, Rotary, and Lions in the service-club area; Masons and Knights of Columbus among the religious-social-philanthropic groups; American Legion, Veterans of Foreign Wars, and Daughters of the American Revolution in the patriotic-club category; and the League of Women Voters and the Fortnightly Club in the study and social groups. All these organizations have varying degrees of influence and have upon occasion been quite effective in exercising this influence on the school curriculum and curriculum materials, personnel, finance, and methodology.

Labor organizations in the various American cities have historically been strong supporters of public education and have been very effective at times in organizing public opinion about certain educational issues. Commercial and industrial groups, such as the powerful United States Chamber of Commerce and the National Association of Manufacturers, have, particularly in recent years, joined the group of public education's best friends. A review of the legislative records of both major political parties —Republican and Democrat—reveals that, in general, they have favored strong educational systems in the fifty states.

The importance of involving parents in the education of their children was underscored in a recent report of the Department of Health, Education, and Welfare. That department's Task Force on Parent Participation recommended that (1) parents should be on advisory boards that establish policy on health, education, and welfare programs affecting their children; (2) public-welfare agencies, schools, and hospitals should provide jobs for parents and youth, emphasizing new careers for the disadvantaged and on-the-job training; and (3) "human services" should be available in the neighborhood and should cover the needs of the entire family.

BOARDS OF EDUCATION

A district is a division to which the state legislature delegates most of the actual administration of the schools within its boundaries; its size may vary from less than a square mile to several thousand square miles embracing an entire township or an entire county. And the legally constituted community group charged with complete responsibility and authority for the operation of the schools in a single district is the board of education. Composed usually of five to seven members elected in most states by popular vote in the community, the board usually serves without pay and spends much time exercising duties in connection with the schools. Legally, the board can exercise direct supervision of the school program, and in some communities, particularly in small ones, individual members actually take this right seriously. However, when the board of education is not in session, its members have no more authority in school matters than have other citizens, unless the board has delegated them such authority.

In actual practice, the board does not as a rule become involved in the actual running of the school, but rather serves as a policy-making, legislative, and evaluative organization, delegating the executive powers to the school's superintendent and his staff; the superintendent is the board's chief executive officer. The board generally approves or rejects the superintendent's nominations for teaching positions in the district, though it is not uncommon practice in small districts for the teacher applicants to be interviewed by members of the board individually or as a group.

The board approves or disapproves the superintendent's budget and other matters that come to its attention from school employees through the district's chief school officer. State legislatures and state departments of education, which are charged by law with education within the state, generally delegate most of this responsibility to the local board of education.

ADMINISTRATORS; SUPERVISORS; OTHER TEACHERS

When a teacher accepts a position in a school district, he will come in contact with other persons employed in the district in many different capacities. Here he will find fellow teachers, administrators, supervisors, custodians, nurses, cafeteria employees, and, in some instances, doctors, dentists, psychologists, and others.

From the day the teacher is interviewed throughout his entire tenure, he is constantly associating on the job with school administrators. In small districts, he may come in daily contact with the superintendent of schools;

Teacher Evaluation

TEACHER: *Socrates*

A. PERSONAL QUALIFICATIONS

Rating
(high to low)

	1	2	3	4	5	Comments
1. Personal appearance	☐	☐	☐	☐	☑	Dresses in an old sheet draped about his body.
2. Self-confidence	☐	☐	☐	☐	☑	Not sure of himself—always asking questions.
3. Use of English	☐	☐	☐	☑	☐	Speaks with a heavy Greek accent.
4. Adaptability	☐	☐	☐	☐	☑	Prone to suicide by poison when under duress.

B. CLASS MANAGEMENT

	1	2	3	4	5	Comments
1. Organization	☐	☐	☐	☐	☑	Does not keep a seating chart.
2. Room appearance	☐	☐	☐	☑	☐	Does not have eye-catching bulletin boards.
3. Utilization of supplies	☑	☐	☐	☐	☐	Does not use supplies.

C. TEACHER-PUPIL RELATIONSHIPS

	1	2	3	4	5	Comments
1. Tact and consideration	☐	☐	☐	☐	☑	Places student in embarrassing situation by asking questions.
2. Attitude of class	☐	☑	☐	☐	☐	Class is friendly.

D. TECHNIQUES OF TEACHING

	1	2	3	4	5	Comments
1. Daily preparation	☐	☐	☐	☐	☑	Does not keep daily lesson plans.
2. Attention to course of study	☐	☐	☑	☐	☐	Quite flexible—allows students to wander to different topics.
3. Knowledge of subject matter	☐	☐	☐	☐	☑	Does not know material—has to question pupils to gain knowledge.

E. PROFESSIONAL ATTITUDE

	1	2	3	4	5	Comments
1. Professional ethics	☐	☐	☐	☐	☑	Does not belong to professional association or PTA.
2. In-service training	☐	☐	☐	☐	☑	Complete failure here—has not even bothered to attend college.
3. Parent relationships	☐	☐	☐	☐	☑	Needs to improve in this area—parents are trying to get rid of him.

RECOMMENDATION: *Does not have a place in Education. Should not be rehired.*

John Gauss, *Phi Delta Kappan,* January 1962, back cover. Reprinted by permission.

in large districts, he may see the superintendent only once or twice a year, if that often, and then only in large district-wide staff meetings. The teacher may see the assistant superintendent in charge of instruction a bit oftener, but here again, very little individual contact with him will be possible.

The administrator with whom the teacher has the most direct contact is the building principal. The national trend is toward the principalship as a supervisory as well as administrative position; in fact, national and state principals' organizations have subscribed to the idea that at least fifty percent of the principal's time should be spent in supervision, teacher evaluation, and general improvement of instruction. If all principals would adhere to this recommendation, it is clear that a great deal of their work would be devoted to helping teachers.

It is natural for a beginning teacher to want to know what will be his relationship with the principal, what each can expect from the other. As a starting point, it is reasonable to expect that, since administrators are former teachers, they are acquainted with most of the problems of instructors; as principals, they are now charged with the coordination of all teachers' efforts in and contributions to the instructional program. Given the administrator's teaching background, the beginning teacher can reasonably expect him to be an educational leader, one whose professional leadership the teacher can follow. The teacher can also expect the administrator to be competent in his position, to be fair in his dealings with all teachers, and to display an understanding attitude toward the instructors' problems, since he himself has experienced similar problems. By his actions, the administrator should also allow the teacher to share in much of the administrative problem solving and action concerning school affairs.

In return, the administrator can expect the teacher to be competent in teaching the subjects and guiding the learning activities of children at whatever grade level the teacher is assigned. He should expect the teacher to assume a professional attitude and an ethical countenance in his dealings with others, and to participate in projects of various types that will immediately or eventually benefit the school system.

Qualified public-school teachers are generally well versed in academic and professional areas, but they often need to be relieved of their timidities and freed from traditional controls that inhibit the teaching-learning activities in the classroom. This is the responsibility of the instructional supervisor, and he works at these objectives cooperatively with classroom teachers and administrators. At the same time, many teachers are not fully qualified because of a lack in academic and professional backgrounds; here, too, are areas in which supervisors can help facilitate growth. Modern supervision emphasizes the key factors in the learning process: the teacher and the student; and it attempts to facilitate the teaching-learning process. Basically concerned with the improvement of this process, supervision sets about to develop a structure in which individuals help each other and feel themselves more adequate and worthy of achieving the goals of education.

Supervisors in most local school districts are usually attached to the central staff, rather than to a single building. In a typical local district, general supervisors deal with general questions of methods, curriculum, and materials, while special supervisors—currently increasing in numbers— are concerned with special subject-matter or grade-level areas. While supervisors work primarily with teachers at improving classroom instruction, they are also responsible for providing classroom personnel with freedom to experiment, to evolve new ideas, to work out their own problems, and to feel that they are important to the successful operation of the entire school program. Effective supervision will give attention to the reduction of teacher loads and the improvement of the teachers' status in the school and community.

Teachers work with other teachers. Often, too, since teachers have similar backgrounds and experiences, the relationships are extended into their social activities. Teachers share ideas individually and in group meetings; they travel together to professional meetings; they participate together in teacher institutes and workshops; and they pool their ideas in college summer-session classes or other professional activities held during times when school is in recess. In some schools, arrangements are made for teachers to visit each other's classrooms or schools in distant parts of the city or in other communities; such activities have proved interesting and helpful in improving the teachers' own instruction.

Demonstration teaching is often a part of a building's in-service education program: teachers or supervisors demonstrate some particular technique or techniques—often with pupils present—for the benefit of their colleagues.

Professional Organizations

There is a large number of professional organizations to which a teacher might belong. Teachers should study the various organizations available to them and decide for themselves the ones with which they want to become affiliated.

Of course, a teacher cannot afford the dues or the time to belong to very many of the professional organizations, so he must weigh them in relation to his own needs, interests, and financial ability. To gain the most from membership in professional groups, just as in other organizations, a teacher must participate actively; this can be a drain on a teacher's time, energy, and finances.

Conclusion

A teacher faces many problems and pressures when he enters into the largest profession in the nation. In the first place, he faces long work days, which often extend late into the night, and weeks that extend well beyond the forty hours usually accepted as a typical work week. Then, too, the teacher assumes a number of different roles as he works with children, parents, and others in the community in directing educational activities and in closely related projects. He has certain obligations and responsibilities toward lay persons and the professional colleagues with whom he associates each day.

Questions for Discussion

1. How can we reconcile the fact that teachers work nearly a fifty-hour week, while the normal work week in other occupations is forty hours —with prospects of thirty-two hours?

2. The one aspect of teaching about which prospective teachers are most apprehensive is discipline, or, more accurately, misbehavior. How do you account for the fact that some teachers just never have any behavior problems, while others have many?

3. Which of the several media for reporting pupil progress do you prefer? Explain why you feel that your preference does the best job of letting parents know how their children are progressing.

4. Can you think of ways that might alleviate some of the burden of responsibilities now assumed by teachers in roles having little direct relation to the teaching-learning situation?

5. What are the education-oriented organizations in your community? With which of these should teachers have some acquaintance? Which seem to be most sincerely devoted to the well-being of children and to their education? Which organizations do you think would be good for elementary-school teachers to join? Why? Which ones would probably be more interested in secondary-age children? Why do you think so?

6. How can a beginning teacher determine what his relationship with his professional colleagues should be? If a beginning teacher wishes to act in a professional manner, how should he consider and deal with the news he hears in a typical teachers' lounge?

7. Compare the work of the elementary teacher and the secondary teacher described at the beginning of this chapter. In what ways should their teacher-preparation programs be different? How should they be similar? Which deals more with subjects and which more with children? Should this be true? Why?

8. How do modern teachers' methods compare with those indicated in the selection "My First School," on pages 96–97, written in the early 1880's? How do they differ and how are they similar? What should be a teacher's goal in this respect?

9. In what ways do you think parents and teachers can work together as a team in the education of children?

10. Do you think it is fair and ethical for communities to insist that their teachers join and attend local churches, spend their wages in local places of business, wear business clothing while in the classroom, and refrain from patronizing certain businesses or amusement places that the general public may patronize? Why or why not?

Activities and Projects

1. Divide a sheet of paper into two columns by drawing a line vertically through the center of the paper. Label the lefthand column "The teacher is . . . ," and then in the column, list each predicate nominative included in the selection "What Is a Teacher?" In the righthand column, entitled "As such, he . . . ," insert as many instances as you can of how teachers personify each of the nominatives. Example:

The Teacher Is . . .	*As Such, He . . .*
1. A prophet	1. Helps pupils become prepared to meet future questions by teaching them how to solve problems scientifically.
	2. Projects into the future, basing projections on experiences of the past and present.
	3. Helps pupils see the possible results of courses of action they take daily.
	4. . . .
2. An artist	1. . . .

2. Visit a meeting of a civic, social, or religious organization that stresses education as one of its major objectives. Make a list of the educational projects of the group and indicate what, specifically, is being taught.

What techniques are being used by those doing the teaching? Can you detect similarities and differences in the methodology used by trained professionals and those doing the teaching in the organization?

3. Interview two or three teachers at the level of your interest (elementary or secondary) on their typical summertime activities. Note similarities and differences.

4. Visit, or write to, two or three schools in different districts and obtain copies of their report cards; contrast these in such areas as the subjects reported on, the type of marks given, the means of parental contributions, the terminology used in explaining the marks, and so on.

5. In collaboration with other members of your class, dramatize a spontaneous teachers'-room meeting of several members of a school's staff. With a different "teacher" assuming each of the various roles of the teacher—the clerk, the baby-sitter, the executive, the recreation leader, and the joiner—discuss recent activities in each of these areas, including the demands made upon each one's time and energies. See if your group can arrive at any courses of action that might relieve the pressures in each area.

6. Attend a meeting of a school's PTA or Parents' Club. Note the activities of the group that you feel contribute to the children's education, and those that do not. What suggestions would you make regarding those that are not learning oriented? In what specific ways do the activities purportedly contributing to the children's education actually do so?

7. Attend a meeting of a local board of education. Make notes of the types of topics considered by the board. Is any time spent in considering topics extraneous to the operation of the school system?

8. Talk to a school principal, after making an appointment with him, regarding what he believes should be the appropriate relationships between the teachers on his staff and himself with respect to (a) the schools and (b) activities of a social nature.

References

Teachers' Relationships with Others

DAPPER, GLORIA. *Public Relations for Teachers*. New York: Macmillan, 1964.

————, and BARBARA CARTER. *A Guide for School Board Members*. Chicago: Follett, 1966.

DeLaney, Jack J. *The School Librarian.* Hamden, Conn.: Shoe String Press, 1964.

DeYoung, Chris A., and Richard Wynn. *American Education.* 6th ed. New York: McGraw-Hill, 1968. Chap. 13.

Elsbree, Willard S., Harold J. McNally, and Richard Wynn. *Elementary School Administration and Supervision.* 3d ed. New York: American Book, 1967. Chaps. 1, 2, 30.

Haskew, Laurence D., and Jonathon C. McLendon. *This Is Teaching.* 3d ed. Glenview, Ill.: Scott, Foresman, 1968. Chaps. 4, 7, 8.

Janowitz, Gayle. *Helping Hands: Volunteer Work in Education.* Chicago: University of Chicago Press, 1966.

Johnson, James A., Harold W. Collins, Victor L. Dupuis, and John H. Johansen. *Introduction to the Foundations of American Education.* Boston: Allyn & Bacon, 1969. Secs. 1, 2.

McCleary, Lloyd E., and Stephen P. Hencley. *Secondary School Administration.* New York: Dodd, Mead, 1965. Chaps. 1–3, 5, 16, 17.

Misner, Paul J., Frederick W. Schneider, and Lowell G. Keith. *Elementary School Administration.* Columbus, Ohio: C. E. Merrill, 1963. Chaps. 14–16.

National Education Association. *Changing Supervision for Changing Times.* Washington, D.C.: Association for Supervision and Curriculum Development of the National Education Association, 1969. Pp. 13–29, 43–63.

———. *The Right Principal for the Right School.* Washington, D.C.: Committee on Selection of School Principals, American Association of School Administrators of the National Education Association, 1967.

———. *Supervision: Emerging Profession.* Washington, D.C.: Association for Supervision and Curriculum Development of the National Education Association, 1969. Pts. 1, 2, 4, 5.

———. *The Supervisor: New Demands, New Dimensions.* Washington, D.C.: Association for Supervision and Curriculum Development of the National Education Association, 1969. Theme B.

Patterson, Cecil H. *The Counselor in the School.* New York: McGraw-Hill, 1967. Pts. 1, 4.

Redfern, George, and Lewis E. Harris. *Improving Principal-Faculty Relationships.* Englewood Cliffs, N.J.: Prentice-Hall, 1966.

Richey, Robert W. *Planning for Teaching.* 4th ed. New York: McGraw-Hill, 1968. Chap. 5.

Schooling, H. W. "Teacher-Administrator Relationships." *NEA Journal,* February 1965, pp. 32–34.

Stinnett, T. M., and Albert J. Huggett. *Professional Problems of Teachers.* 2d ed. New York: Macmillan, 1963. Chaps. 2, 4.

Professional Organizations

BATCHELDER, RICHARD D. "Unionism vs. Professionalism in Teaching." *NEA Journal,* April 1966, pp. 18–20.

BURDIN, JOEL L. "Professional Education Associations and the Federal Government." *Phi Delta Kappan,* February 1968, pp. 315–18.

BURRUP, PERCY. *The Teacher and the Public School System.* 2d ed. New York: Harper, 1967. Chap. 14.

DEWING, ROLLAND. "Teacher Organizations and Desegregation." *Phi Delta Kappan,* January 1968, pp. 257–60.

HASKEW, LAURENCE D., and JONATHON C. McLENDON. *This Is Teaching.* 3d ed. Glenview, Ill.: Scott, Foresman, 1968. Pp. 262–67.

LeBLANC, RICHARD C. "UNESCO and Education." *NEA Journal,* April 1966, pp. 42–43.

NATIONAL EDUCATION ASSOCIATION. *NEA Handbook for Local, State and National Associations.* Washington, D.C.: National Education Association, published annually.

————. "Professional Negotiation: Fact Not Fancy." In *The Shape of Education for 1968–69.* Washington, D.C.: National School Public Relations Association of the National Education Association, 1968.

RICHEY, ROBERT W. *Planning for Teaching.* 4th ed. New York: McGraw-Hill, 1968. Chap. 7.

SHILS, EDWARD B., and C. TAYLOR WHITTIER. *Teachers, Administrators, and Collective Bargaining.* New York: Crowell, 1968.

"What Leaders Think about NEA Refusal to Consider Merger with AFT." *Phi Delta Kappan,* January 1969, pp. 304–5.

ZELUCK, STEPHEN. "The UFT Strike: Will It Destroy the AFT?" *Phi Delta Kappan,* January 1969, pp. 250–54.

Reporting to Parents

BAILARD, VIRGINIA, and RUTH STRANG. *Parent-Teacher Conferences.* New York: McGraw-Hill, 1964.

DAVIS, FREDERICK B. *Educational Measurements and Their Interpretation.* Belmont, Calif.: Wadsworth, 1964. Chap. 13.

HANNA, LAVONE A., GLADYS L. POTTER, and NEVA HAGAMAN. *Unit Teaching in the Elementary School.* Rev. ed. New York: Holt, Rinehart & Winston, 1963. Chap. 15.

HARRISON, RAYMOND H. *Supervisory Leadership in Education.* New York: American Book, 1968. Chap. 15.

HASKEW, LAURENCE D., and JONATHON C. McLENDON. *This Is Teaching.* 3d ed. Glenview, Ill.: Scott, Foresman, 1968. Pp. 95–97, 102, 224–232.

HICKS, WILLIAM VERNON, and FRANK H. BLACKINGTON III. *Introduction to Education.* Columbus, Ohio: C. E. Merrill, 1965. Chap. 13.

LINDVALL, C. M. *Measuring Pupil Achievement and Aptitude.* New York: Harcourt, 1967. Pp. 178–82.

NATIONAL EDUCATION ASSOCIATION. *Evaluation as Feedback and Guide.* Yearbook of the Association for Supervision and Curriculum Development. Washington, D.C.: Association for Supervision and Curriculum Development of the National Education Association, 1967. See especially chaps. 4 and 6 and pp. 108–17.

PHILLIPS, RAY C. *Evaluation in Education.* Columbus, Ohio: C. E. Merrill, 1968.

RICHEY, ROBERT W. *Planning for Teaching.* 4th ed. New York: McGraw-Hill, 1968. Pp. 155–56.

THOMAS, R. MURRAY. *Judging Student Progress.* 2d ed. New York: McKay, 1960. Chaps. 13–15.

The school is an old, dark, brick, two-story con-
traption, a Norman fortress, built as if learning
and virtue need a stronghold, one defended by
old-fashioned weapons, a place of turrets and par-
apets, with narrow slits in the bricks through
which scholars with crossbows can peep out at an
atomic world.

JOHN HERSEY

5

Pressures and Problems
of the School

The preceding chapter pointed up certain pressures and problems encountered by the teacher as he attempts to meet the responsibilities connected with his multifaceted position. It is only fair to advise the prospective teacher that there are yet additional pressures and problems he must
face: as long as there are schools and instructors, there will be pressures of
time and facilities, and there will also be problems of husbanding resources so that the pressures can be satisfactorily met and relieved.

Pressures of Time and Facilities

In their attempt to arrange learning activities so that their pupils can learn
the very most that is possible, teachers invariably find that there simply are
not enough hours in the day or that the facilities available to them are insufficient. Successful teaching requires a great amount of organizational
ability, so that more can be accomplished in a short amount of time, and it

also requires considerable ability to improvise in situations where needed physical facilities are not available.

TYRANNY OF THE CURRICULUM

Generally speaking, when a new teacher joins the staff of a school district, he will find a pretty well established curriculum, and he will be expected to carry on his teaching within the framework of that program. Perhaps a part of the curriculum has been legislated by lawmakers in the state capital; perhaps a part of it has been established by professionals who made up the teaching staff of the school in years past; perhaps a part of it has been previously imposed by boards of education, which, for one reason or another, deemed it necessary that certain things be included in the school's program.

State legislatures with a concern for education and general welfare within their boundaries have enacted laws proposing curriculum additions or changes that have a real effect not only upon what teachers teach in their classrooms but also, in some instances, upon how it is to be taught. Generally these laws have been reasonable, especially when one considers that lawmakers, most of whom are not teachers, do not have an opportunity for a comprehensive and continuing study of the school curriculum.

Prior to 1968 the laws of the state of California were probably the most detailed of any of the states' in matters of curriculum in the public schools: they provided for the entire course of study at the elementary level, and for a part of the secondary-school curriculum. These laws indicated not only the specific courses to be offered in the elementary schools of the state, and several that would be offered in the secondary schools, but also the amount of time per week to be spent in instruction in the disciplines.

When the governor of California signed into law what has come to be known as the George Miller Junior Education Act of 1968, in May of that year, the state school system took a giant step forward in matters of public-school curricula. The state then found itself in line with most other states in the nation that had previously passed similar forward-looking legislation. The new school law, termed "the most significant educational legislation to be enacted in California in the last fifty years," represented a breakthrough from traditional strictures imposed upon school curricula by legislative mandate to a new legislative policy giving increased powers and responsibilities to governing boards and local school officials for the development and conduct of quality programs of instruction.

To exemplify the significant changes in statutory requirements relating to the California public-school curriculum, the only current time requirement in the entire state structure is in the area of physical education: mandatory daily physical-education instruction for a minimum of time was replaced by a required lump sum of no less than two hundred minutes of physical-education instruction for elementary grades in any ten school days, and by a minimum of four hundred minutes of such instruction in any ten school days at the secondary-school level.

The new California Education Code does require that instruction be given elementary-school pupils in the following areas of study: English, mathematics, social sciences, science, fine arts, health, and physical education—but, except for the last, without specification of time. For example, a unit of rudimentary science (one week, one month, or one semester) would satisfy the legal requirements for grade one. An important aspect of the new law is that the local governing board may offer or require subjects to be taught other than those listed in the code.

Before the enactment of the law, all secondary-school students were required to take, between grades seven and twelve, five years of English, five years of history, two years of a foreign language, driver education, and public speaking. Now the law requires simply that the adopted course of study for grades seven through twelve shall offer (make available) courses in English, social sciences, foreign language, physical education, science, mathematics, fine arts, applied arts, and driver education. The code sets the requirements for a diploma from grade twelve, namely: completion of the course of study, including English, American history, American government, mathematics, and science—at least one course in each area—and the minimum amount of instruction in physical education, as well as meeting standards of proficiency required by the governing board. Under the law of 1968, the adopted course of study for both elementary and secondary schools throughout California shall provide for instruction at appropriate grade levels and subject areas in safety, conservation, fire prevention, and health. Integration of these subject areas as a part of other subjects is allowed.

At the elementary-school level, the legislative requirement regarding English includes the subject areas of reading, writing, spelling, speaking, listening, and composition. The social-sciences requirement includes the areas of geography, civics, and history, and the fine-arts requirement includes the areas of music and art. The 1968 law also eliminated the elementary-school foreign-language requirement that had previously been in the course of study beginning in grade six and continuing through grades seven or eight, as the case may be.

Some of the advantages claimed for the current legislative provisions for California public schools are: (1) pupils may more easily be placed in appropriate instructional programs; (2) more flexibility in scheduling of courses is provided for; (3) comprehensive programs to fit pupil and community needs may now be set up; and (4) the opportunity is provided for more involvement of lay persons in the development of curricula in the state schools.

Thus the citizens of California have the opportunity to work cooperatively—professional people with lay persons, in groups and individually—at improving the curriculum of the schools in their communities by conducting research and by recommending additions and changes to the local governing boards of education. This has been the situation in most other states for a considerable time.

But the "do-it-yourself" curriculum building of the past has pretty well served its usefulness. Trends now indicate that in the future the curriculum may be developed on a national basis by teams of recognized scholars, as evidenced by the work and published materials of such organizations as the School Mathematics Study Group and the National Science Foundation, to name only two of many.

Whereas in the past, only the local community was much concerned with the education and welfare of its people, now the nation is concerned. Schools in urban areas, especially, can no longer rely on the limited fiscal and personal assistance their own areas can provide, so they must look to the federal government. Hope for the future lies principally in increased federal monetary assistance to be used at local discretion. A start has been made, Congress having appropriated billions of dollars for education in the past several years. An annual United States Office of Education budget item of $3.5 billion is not unusual today, with the bulk of the money intended for educational systems in the great urban centers or in rural communities, where there is also great poverty.

Most of the federal assistance to school districts, especially in the inner cities, was included in legislation passed by Congress in the mid-1960's. The National Defense Education Acts (NDEA) of 1961 and 1964 show the deep concern of the federal government for education. Millions of dollars were made available by those acts to provide materials and equipment to the schools for experimental programs in the curricular areas of mathematics, science, foreign language, English, reading, history, geography, and civics; in higher education, financial assistance for institutions provides for added preparation of teachers in these subjects and for teachers of disadvantaged youth, school librarians, and educational-media specialists. The provisions of the 1964 NDEA extended through 1967; and, as with the earlier NDEA, the controls over funds were not only very few in number but also very general in scope.

Legislation for another federal program to aid children, especially those in poverty areas, was passed by Congress in 1965: the Elementary and Secondary Education Act (Public Law 89-10). Under the initial act, one billion dollars financed some 22,000 local educational projects in 17,481 local school districts, helping about 8,300,000 children. Some 200,000 new full- and part-time teaching positions were created, and 180,000 sub-professionals, teacher aides, and other personnel were employed full- or part-time. The comprehensive titles under the Elementary and Secondary Education Act provide the potential for implementing programs that may provide quality educational opportunities for all youngsters.

Other congressional legislative actions recently passed at the federal level include the Economic Opportunity Act of 1964, which is, in effect, a youth-training act providing for, among other things, huge sums to fight poverty through work-training and work-study programs. The Higher Education Act of 1965 provided for a National Teacher Corps intended to supply inner-city schools with the services of exceptionally effective teachers, thus enlarging a reservoir of excellent teachers.

The real criterion of whether curriculum *improvement* takes place when there is curriculum *change* is whether the pupils learn; thus, the curriculum is not effective, regardless of its origin, except in the teaching-learning situation. Here lie the real opportunity and responsibility of the teacher in the area of curriculum improvement in the public schools.

TYRANNY OF THE DAILY SCHEDULE

Since the curriculum of today's public schools provides for so many teaching-learning activities, and since it becomes more crowded each year with new areas that seem to deserve a place in an already-crowded program, it is imperative that teachers and children evolve some kind of daily schedule. Effective planning of daily programs is not easy, though it is of utmost importance. Time must be provided for the teacher to work with the class as a whole, with small groups, and with individuals; daily schedules must make provisions for each child in the class. Flexibility with balance and variety are the ingredients of an effective daily schedule that provides for satisfying and adequate learning experiences.

One teacher attended an entire summer session of a state university for the expressed purpose of writing daily plans for her elementary-school class for the next school year, but after the first two weeks of school the following fall, she found that she had to relegate the entire summer's work to the wastebasket. Her plans were not flexible to the point that they provided for *this* particular group of children *this* particular semester. Moreover, they did not allow for learning possibilities that presented themselves unexpectedly. Daily schedules, if they are to provide opportunities for optimum learning, must be flexible enough to allow for such activities as field trips, attendance at concerts or plays, use of television or special radio programs, and special school programs of various types as they arise. They must also be of such a nature that if the activity demands a longer period of time than anticipated, an extension can be made with no serious damage to the program generally.

Balance in the daily program is one of the most important and challenging aspects of the teacher's schedule. Just as the question "What knowledge is of most worth?" constantly plagues the curriculum maker, the question "How much time shall be given to each learning activity?" continually rears its challenge to the classroom-program arranger. Both, obviously, are problems of balance. In figure 1 is presented a configuration on which balance in the program is indicated at the various levels from the primary grades through senior high school. Adequate attention must be given in the schedule to all areas of learning—but the big question is, and has always been, "What is 'adequate'?" It may be that this question can never really be answered for all situations—just as the one posed by the curriculum maker has never really been answered—except with the words "It depends." Inherent in the problem of scheduling the daily school program are such limiting factors as the length of the school day, which varies from about three hours in the kindergarten to six–eight hours in the high school; the legally prescribed features of the program, mentioned in the preceding section; the number of grades in the classroom; and the varying needs and interests of the learners.

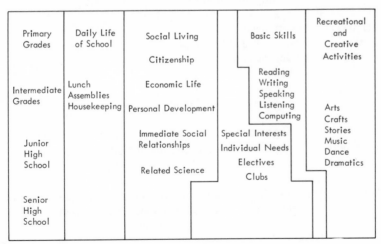

FIGURE 1. Balance in the Total Life of the School.

SOURCE: Lavone A. Hanna, Gladys L. Potter, and Neva Hagaman, *Unit Teaching in the Elementary School,* rev. ed. (New York: Holt, Rinehart & Winston, 1963), p. 105. Adapted from Henry Harap, *Social Living in the Curriculum* (Nashville: George Peabody College for Teachers, 1952), p. 65. Used by permission.

In many schools, teachers will find a program already scheduled and worked out by administrators or teachers. Pupils and teachers in such situations know what happens in which order. This is especially true in high schools and many elementary schools whose "periods" are regulated by a master clock and bell system. Experience has shown that primary children, especially, become accustomed to a routine and that a deviation from the set procedure can be frustrating to them. It is questionable, of course, whether teachers' programs should become so routine that children come to depend on certain things happening in a certain order or at certain hours. Besides, there are bound to be interruptions to upset rigid routines. There is, in fact, a trend away from closely designed daily schedules, especially in elementary schools; certain classes or activities often require more or less time at certain places in their development than at others, and learning experiences should not be chopped off before they are completed.

Hanna suggests the following daily program for elementary teachers who use the unit approach in the social and related sciences: [1]

Time	Subject	Approximate Minutes per Day
9:00–10:00	Unit work	60
10:00–10:10	Recess	10
10:10–11:10	Reading (two groups)	50
11:10–11:30	Physical Education	20
11:30–12:00	Arithmetic	30
12:00– 1:00	Noon [Lunch]	
1:00– 1:40	Language arts	40
1:40– 2:00	Music	20
2:00– 2:10	Recess	10
2:10– 2:30	Appreciations (art, literature, music)	20

The same author suggests the following program for another day when almost all activities might be related to the social studies unit: [2]

9:00– 9:20   Planning
9:20–10:20   Reading—three groups, twenty minutes each (children not in reading group working on letters to be mailed at the "post office")
10:20–10:35 Recess
10:35–10:50 Seeing film on distributing the mail

[1] Lavone A. Hanna, Gladys L. Potter, and Neva Hagaman, *Unit Teaching in the Elementary School*, rev. ed. (New York: Holt, Rinehart & Winston, 1963), p. 106.
[2] Ibid., pp. 106–7.

10:50–11:10   Discussing what they had learned from the motion picture and
              planning the construction period
11:10–11:40   Working in committees in building the "post office"
11:40–12:00   Cleaning up and evaluating
12:00– 1:00   Lunch
 1:00– 1:40   Reading and correcting letters and making spelling list of words
              used in the letters
 1:40– 2:00   Music
 2:00– 2:15   Recess
 2:15– 2:35   Making up an original rhythm expressing "sorting the mail"
 2:35– 3:10   Buying stamps and making change, and computing time it would
              take letters to reach their destination

For school districts employing a split day in which smaller groups are in
reading classes during the first and last hours of the school day, Hanna
suggests the following schedule for grades one and two: [3]

 9:00–10:00   Reading (half of class)
10:00–10:10   Recess
10:10   Arrival of other half of class
10:10–10:40   Language arts: spelling and oral and written expression
10:40–11:00   Music
11:00–11:10   Recess
11:10–11:30   Physical education
11:30–12:00   Arithmetic, science, health, safety
12:00– 1:00   Lunch
 1:00– 2:00   Social studies
 2:00   Dismissal of children who came at 9:00
 2:00– 2:10   Recess
 2:10– 3:10   Reading (half of class—children who came at 10:00)

At the secondary level, flexibility and balance in planning lessons are
still important considerations. In recent years some secondary schools have
experimented with highly flexible scheduling, often involving *modules,* or
units, of time as short as fifteen or twenty minutes. Particular requirements
of the subject content determine the frequency with which the class meets,
the duration of the class, and the size of the class group. Some classes or
activities may take from one to three modules one day and a different
number the next day. Some classes may meet fewer than five times a week;
some students may find themselves in some classes of 7 to 15 pupils and in
groups of 50 to 175 or more in other activities. Large-group, small-group,
and individualized instruction is practiced in high schools using the modu-
lar approach to scheduling.

[3] Ibid., p. 107. This and the two preceding programs are reprinted by permission.

	MODULE	MONDAY	TUESDAY	WEDNESDAY	THURSDAY	FRIDAY
8:30	1	Mathematics	Music	Mathematics	Mathematics	Mathematics
	2		English	English		
	3	English			English	Music
	4	Social studies	Independent study	Physical education	Independent study	Physical education
	5					
	6			Science		Science
	7		Lunch	Lunch		Lunch
	8	Lunch	Science	Health	Lunch	Independent study
	9	Science		Independent study	Science	
	10	Typing	Independent study	Independent study		
	11					
	12					
	13	Independent study	Social studies			Typing
	14		Mathematics		Music	
3:30	15			Social studies		English

FIGURE 2. A Flexible Secondary-School Schedule.

SOURCE: Robert W. Richey, *An Introduction to Education,* 4th ed. (New York: McGraw-Hill, 1968), p. 197. Used with permission of McGraw-Hill Book Company.

Figure 2 depicts a flexible secondary-school schedule in which the cycle is normally a week in length, as opposed to the traditional schedule in which the cycle is the day. In the flexible program, the schedule does not repeat itself for an entire week, whereas in the traditional schedule, the classes and activities for one day are the same as every other day.

In some secondary-school buildings, teachers must realize that the rigid time limits of the daily period are aspects with which they must reckon.

Since there are individual differences among teachers just as among children, the detail of the plan for each day's activities depends upon the individual teacher; generally, a considerable degree of detail provides some assurance for many instructors, especially those in their first year of teaching.

McKean emphasizes that the quickest way for the first-year teacher to start building an instructional time sense is to make daily estimates of the amount of time needed for various parts of the lesson. He suggests that a secondary teacher's time estimate for a one-hour period might be as follows: [4]

[4] Robert C. McKean, *Principles and Methods in Secondary Education* (Columbus, Ohio: C. E. Merrill, 1962), p. 140.

8:30–8:35   Take roll.
8:35–8:40   Read announcements; collect parent questionnaires due today.
8:40–8:55   Pass out assignment sheets for in-class theme. Discuss the assignment. Answer questions. Review the use of *to, two* and *too*, which they are to pay special attention to in this written work.
8:55–9:25   Students work on themes at their seats. Teacher moves about the room to supervise the writing. (Check to see that Rex is using quotation marks correctly.)
9:25–9:30   Collect the papers. (Ask Sandra to stop by the room after school to talk about the class newspaper.) Remind the class that the unit examination will be given Friday.

ADEQUACY OF FACILITIES

Many are the teachers who have learned good practices and procedures in professional-education courses in college, only to go out to teach in school situations where it is impossible to put the practices and procedures into effect because of inadequate facilities. If the principal responsibility of teachers is motivating children and arranging the environment so that they may learn, which is the authors' thesis as explained in chapter 6, then adequate physical facilities should be available to help instructors.

The school building. The building itself is a facility important to the teaching-learning situation. Despite the trend, begun before World War II, to build school plants that are more functional, comfortable, healthful, and long lasting, there remain thousands of buildings throughout the nation that do not meet these criteria and thus are not adapted to modern educational programs. Many pupils are housed in unsafe, unsanitary, poorly constructed school buildings, the remnants of a period when the philosophy was to build the school and then fit the program into it. Not all of the antiquated, drab, dismal, and dark school buildings are located in isolated rural areas of this country. One has only to observe the older buildings in many towns, cities, and large metropolitan areas to see conditions deplorable for teaching and learning. It will take a great deal of planning and many dollars before such situations will be improved.

Modern school buildings present a marked contrast in appearance to those constructed before 1925. But even more important than improved appearance are the better structural and functional features of the newer plants. For example, increased use of windows and glass brick in appropriate portions of the buildings has allowed for more natural light, and increased attention to artificial lighting has also resulted in improvements. School-building planners have provided for better orientation to the site where the plant is located and have promoted one-story structures for greater safety and, in many instances, for outside entrances to each room. Roomier corridors, recessed water fountains and lockers, carpeted floors, acoustically treated ceilings and walls, automatic temperature controls and air conditioning, hygienic furniture, pastel colors throughout—all these features, and many more, combine to make today's modern school plant a proper environment for children's learning.[5]

The classroom.   The most important work in the school building takes place, of course, in the individual classrooms. For the sake of health, working efficiency, and comfort, school classrooms should provide optimum conditions for pupils who spend from 5 to 6 hours within their confines each day. The use of proper lighting, adequate heating and ventilation, combined with newer shades of color in the painted walls, chalkboards, and other items of furniture and equipment, will help protect teachers' and pupils' physical and mental health. Attention should be given to the shape and size of the chairs and tables in the classroom, also. The trend in today's public schools is away from "fixed" seating.

In newer school buildings, the dull, cold, repetitive, institutional quality that characterizes many buildings erected a few years ago has been replaced with facilities consistent with and relevant to the new forces found in progressive schools today. Flexibility seems to be the key, provided by space-dividing devices that enable the teacher to organize instruction in any manner he desires. There is more open floor area with a range of spatial environments to suit different purposes. Rooms with high ceilings and few or no partition walls provide space for large groups or for vigorous action; versatile, medium-sized areas somewhat like the traditional classrooms are available to small groups; and individualized instruction or private tutoring is carried on in small, intimate, low-ceilinged alcoves or carrels. In some secondary-school plans, the plant is divided into five-hundred-student "houses," each composed of a vertical cross section of the student body from first through last year and representing a full range of ability, achievement, and aspiration. Each house develops its own personality and atmosphere, and the emphasis is upon social and psychological development, rather than academic. In most newer schools, the library learning center and the central administrative offices occupy central and separate facilities. In some plans for house-type secondary schools, each house occupies a different floor of a high-rise building. The university counterpart of the house-type school is the "cluster college" concept being initiated on several campuses in the country.

Classroom size is an important aspect of schoolhouse planning. Most

[5] For an interesting report on facilities for individualized instruction, see Ronald Gross and Judith Murphy, *Educational Change and Architectural Consequences* (New York: Educational Facilities Laboratory, 1968).

authorities today recommend that classrooms for both elementary and secondary schools contain a minimum of thirty square feet of floor space per pupil; a room containing at least nine hundred square feet would thus be the minimum suggested for a class of 30 pupils. The authorities' suggestion for primary and activity rooms, in which there is a great amount of pupil movement, is that they contain from one thousand to twelve hundred square feet. There should, of course, be considerable flexibility in room sizes. With today's emphasis upon such organizational structures as team teaching, for example, the classrooms should be of a size to accommodate large groups—up to 75 or 100 in elementary school, and up to 250 in secondary school—and small groups, and should have some facilities to accommodate pupils working on individual research projects.

Ideally, an elementary-school self-contained classroom of approximately twelve hundred square feet will have space for necessary work areas; exhibit, display, and storage areas; boys' and girls' lavatories; a stage for dramatization; and movable shelving and storage cabinets for books and other materials. Laboratory and water facilities will also be provided within the room. Darkening shades and projection screens will be provided for the use of audiovisual materials and, if possible, radios and television receivers will be part of the room's equipment.

Regardless of the type of room in which a teacher finds himself, he can do much to make it educationally livable. Attractively arranged bulletin boards and special areas of the room can be planned by the teacher and children. Furniture and other equipment can be well placed about the room to improve its appearance and functional aspects. Light-colored panels made from materials such as oak tagboard can lighten up drab or dark places within the room. And the teacher can watch himself to see that he does not stand between the pupils and the windows so that pupils have to look into the light as they watch and listen to him.

Effective learning today calls for pupils' doing, as well as reading and listening. This presupposes a flexible situation in which classroom furniture and other equipment can be moved about. Instead of the old types of combined seat-desks (usually screwed to the floor!), tables and chairs, or tablet armchairs, are used in today's modern classrooms so that effective individual and group work and construction projects can be carried out. Bookcases and some storage cabinets on casters provide for moving books and other materials to various parts of the room with maximum efficiency and speed and, at the same time, may serve as dividers for partitioning off special areas. Tack board on the backs of cabinets provides additional bulletin or pinning-board space.

Books and materials.   For more than a hundred years, a dominant factor in instruction in the United States schools has been the textbook. Educational conditions in the early period of American history may explain, in part, the traditional importance attached to textbooks: in most schools teachers were poorly trained, reference material was for the most part non-existent, and formal or memoriter conceptions of education prevailed. Even though several national committees, including the Committee of Ten in 1892, condemned the use of a single textbook in each subject, to this day the textbook largely dominates classroom instruction in American schools.

In many schools, particularly in elementary grades, resourceful teachers now are employing the multiple-textbook approach and are divorcing themselves from the traditional practice of using one textbook for each course. These teachers are accepting the balanced development of intellectual skills and independence of thought in the pupil as the fundamental objective of education and are seeing the fallacy of class adherence to a single textbook, with the assignment-recitation cycle in daily repetition. They hold that in facing the challenge of attempting to meet the needs of pupils, teachers must have at their disposal textbooks at the level of the slower-learning or the retarded readers, the average, and the bright, and, in addition, that they must have many and varied instructional materials of other types.

Broader, more flexible teaching plans are possible with the multiple-textbook approach. Teachers employ groups of pupils equipped with textbooks and other materials appropriate to topics of a common nature and to the range of the pupils' abilities in classroom activities pursued in the development of subject units. Textbooks used in this approach are most often employed in small sets for individual or small-committee reference and are not followed page by page from cover to cover; rather, teachers and pupils select the portions from them that best serve their needs. Mastery of the tools of learning is the goal; and in this endeavor, much use is made of many textbooks, collateral readings, audiovisual aids, excursions, construction activities, and the like, which are intended to be compatible with plans of teachers and pupils—plans that are not restricted to the activities suggested in any of the teaching materials. By this approach, pupils are taught to reserve judgment, seek evidence, and exchange ideas before forming opinions. Value goals sought for children and youth include desirable attitudes, appreciations, abilities, habits, and skills; and attention is given to such attributes as cooperation, leadership, integrity, responsibility, and critical thinking.

In a study made at a midwestern elementary school by one of the authors, it was found through objective tests that pupils using multiple textbooks in the classroom had no significant advantage over pupils using a single textbook as far as acquisition of social-studies subject matter is concerned and that the multiple-textbook group had no significant advantage over the single-textbook group in improvement in such characteristics as co-operation, friendliness, integrity, responsibility leadership, and critical thinking. However, it was found that in the concomitant area of related sciences, the multiple-textbook group had a slight advantage over the single-textbook group; also, probably of more importance, it was found that children of superior mental ability who used the multiple-textbook technique surpassed the children in the control group with superior mental abilities by a 10 percent level of significance. In addition, in areas of work-study skills and understandings, as measured subjectively by the teachers in the experiment, the multiple-textbook approach appeared to hold more merit and potential.

All of this points up the importance of many books and other teaching materials in the truly effective teaching-learning situation. If teachers accept the broader purposes of education—if they want boys and girls to learn to think critically and to understand what they learn—a multiplicity of references and textbooks and various other materials is a necessity. The books and equipment such as maps, charts, globes, various types of projectors, and tape recorders should be stored in or near the classroom, readily accessible to teachers at the time they are needed.

The fact is, however, that many school systems do not have a large supply of books and other materials. Good teachers can teach, and are teaching, acceptably every day under adverse classroom conditions and with inadequate supplies of books and other materials; however, it is reasonable to assume that they would do a better job if they were provided with the tools and facilities they need.

The traveling teacher. Another problem faced by certain teachers when they join a district's staff is that of finding a place to "hang their hats," a place they can call home. Many school districts employ special teachers who travel from building to building to assist in the instructional program in the manner to which they are best suited. Included in this group of teachers are those whose training and experience have been in specialized areas such as exceptional children, including the mentally retarded, physically handicapped, emotionally disturbed, culturally disadvantaged, and academically talented; art, music; physical education; science; foreign language; television teaching; speech correction; occupational therapy; and remedial reading. It is not unusual for teachers with specialities to spend perhaps one or two periods in a building and then move to other buildings for about the same period of time. Very often these traveling teachers seldom teach, but rather spend their time assisting classroom teachers with problems in their special areas. If the prospective teacher plans to specialize in areas such as those named above, it is quite possible that he will find himself employed in a district with no particular home base.

Generally, traveling teachers work directly out of the central offices of the district, which in a sense are their headquarters. Their work, however, is done out in the various schools, so they spend very little time in their offices. They sometimes find it necessary to haul much of their equipment and materials in their automobiles; they can ill afford to dash to the central offices between each school visit to leave materials and pick up additional equipment. Some districts try to provide materials used by special teachers at each building on a more or less permanent basis, but this obviously runs into considerable expense. Various kinds of rooms are provided for the traveling teachers; these may range from a nicely furnished, regular-sized classroom to a clothes-closet type of room, if regular classrooms are deemed impossible to spare. In some schools, the philosophy of the principal with respect to the special areas taught by traveling teachers determines the facilities provided.

Still another type of traveling teacher may be found in areas, especially in fast-growing sections of the United States, where classrooms must be scheduled rather tightly because of space shortages. Thus it is entirely possible for teachers to find themselves without a home base right in their own building and to have to move about to different rooms for their classes so that the available classrooms can be used to the optimum. The extent of such situations in California was indicated in a study made at the University of California. In the 1959–60 class of sixty graduate intern teachers, thirty-seven remained in one location for the entire day, but eleven had two locations, seven had three, three had four, and two teachers worked in five different locations during the day.

Husbanding Your Resources

The Fatigue Problem

It goes without saying that individuals who are able to withstand the rigors of teaching should be in good physical and mental condition. Many states, in fact, require that applicants pass a physical examination before they are issued teaching licenses. And an annual physical examination should be on each teacher's calendar.

Few jobs exceed teaching when it comes to hard work. The strain and stress of guiding the learning activities of twenty-five or more pupils, each unique and each with differing needs and problems, places exceptional pressures on the physical and emotional reserves of teachers. Then there is the length of the work week, up to fifty hours in many instances. Furthermore, many teachers' schedules are overloaded, the pupil-teacher ratio is extremely high in many instances, and innumerable buildings and classrooms are inadequate from the standpoint of structural and physical facilities. All of these factors cause fatigue in the instructors. Financial and job insecurity is often a cause of further mental stress, though the trend toward adoption of tenure regulations and single salary schedules in more and more districts is helping to alleviate these conditions. Further strain in the life of a teacher is caused by the various roles he must play, as described in the preceding chapter.

Despite the stresses and activities of teachers, the profession is not considered particularly hazardous physically. In fact, teachers in most districts are provided special rates for insurance policies.

A teacher should develop, if he does not already possess, an ability to meet an emotionally charged situation in a calm manner, an appropriate sense of humor, a balanced emotional countenance, a respect for and acceptance of himself for what he is, and a sincere interest in and compassion for other people. Superior teachers tend to manifest superior emotional adjustment. The teacher should pursue activities and interests outside the realm of teaching and in company with adults other than teachers; this will provide a healthy avenue for release of pent-up physical and emotional stresses.

THE ENTHUSIASM PROBLEM

There are times when teachers have difficulty in keeping their morale on a high plane, in keeping their enthusiasm operating at high gear. This is true of all jobs, but teaching is particularly susceptible to an elusive characteristic that periodically causes morale to hit new lows and at such times exerts an especially debilitating effect. Some capable persons even leave the profession because of it.

One aspect of teaching that often produces a demoralizing effect on dedicated persons is the intangibility of the educational product. In contrast to the work of persons in other professions or vocations, the results of education cannot be guaranteed. The success of the teacher's work depends largely upon the cooperation and effort of his students. Part of the compensation of teaching is seeing progress in pupils' achievement, but since progress is often not forthcoming for some time—months or even years— and since credit for this progress may never find its way to the right person, teachers often become distressed and feel that their efforts are producing no results.

Teacher Fatigue

Whether he becomes conscious of the problem at the end of two months, two years, or twenty years of teaching, however, there is much the teacher himself can do to avoid battle fatigue. (That's all it is, really.)

He needs a hobby, for one thing. Listening to phonograph records or (if the teacher is a lady) hooking rugs won't do; the mind is still free to brood about school problems. The activity must be absorbing, must call for physical and mental activity, not passivity. Bowling, gourmet cooking with a congenial group, reading, carpentry, painting, and choral singing are all good.

Keep in training. Get enough sleep; eat a balanced diet; get the proper exercise. The demands of teaching are rigorous even for a person in good health. A sick man will crumple out of shape in no time at all.

Try to arrange matters so you don't have to take courses at night while school is going on, ever. This is especially true during your first year. This is entirely too big a dose of new educational experiences to absorb at one time. You won't learn much, either from your professor or from your new students.

You will probably need to pick up courses in summer school (doesn't everybody?). Try to schedule the ones you need so you won't go all summer and return to school in the fall as exhausted as when you left at the beginning of summer. Make the time that you spend on the college campus with real honest-to-goodness adults count. You'll pick up as many new ideas from the other students in your classes as you will from the professor. Have coffee with them; study with them. The best ploy of all is to find a principal in the class who's fifty miles or more from home. (Not a local product; he'll be afraid you might quote him.) Buy him a couple of beers and get him to talk shop. You'll *really* learn about education.

Take a course in something unrelated to your field but that you've always wanted to know more about—music appreciation, ceramics, Egyptology, investments, Elizabethan poets, swimming, archaeology, etc.

Sometimes, too, teachers find that conditions in the schools stymie, or limit, them in the very things that caused them to choose the teaching profession in the first place; they find themselves so busy with other things that they have little time left to guide the learning activities of their pupils. In some schools, the amount of bookkeeping work required of teachers de-

Get away from home. Load up the family and take a float trip down a river, camp out in the mountains, rent an inexpensive cabin on the lake, visit your brother in Florida, teach summer school in another city (*not* your own district!).

Allow yourself a week to get ready for school in the fall when you go back. Go through your files; throw away things you know you won't use again. Develop teaching ideas and new lesson plans; revise your old tests; work out that new bulletin board display. Write companies for catalogs or examination copies of books; write to that expert in your field or a former professor for a point of information you aren't sure about. Set up your calendar for the year. Approximately when will you need to order this? When will you check out that? When will you invite the guest speakers?

Do you like your room arrangement the way it is? Is your desk farther from the door than you'd like it to be? Do the students get afternoon sun in their eyes? Are you tired of the pictures? Change things around.

Most important, try to see it all as a whole. "What am I doing and why?" Teaching isn't like running a grocery store or filling teeth or selling insurance. Maybe it's more like farming than anything else. Every year there's a new crop. "Success" means the crop grew and flourished and "failure" means it didn't. The growing season is grueling, backbreaking work. Teachers and farmers don't rest much over week-ends, as others do, but once a year, during the off-season.

There are good years and bad years. There are years when the seed is right, the soil perfect, the rains on time, and the farmer can do no wrong. Other years everything he does is wrong. Both farmers and teachers learn to accept these cycles, even to exploit them.

One perseveres. Last year's mistakes inspire this year's experiments, which in turn yield next year's wisdom. So, one grows with the growing, finds renewal in the renewed. Perhaps that's why teachers and farmers live longer than other people do. It's a good life, after all.

Jenny Gray, *The Teacher's Survival Guide* (Palo Alto: Lear Siegler, Inc./Fearon Publishers, 1967), pp. 118–120. Reprinted by permission.

mands too much time and energy that could otherwise be spent in a teaching-learning situation. Occasionally, teachers find themselves on faculties headed by authoritarian administrators who block all efforts toward creative teaching. In some communities in recent years, teachers have found themselves responsible for too many pupils or too many classes and have discovered that they attempt to spread themselves too thin, with the result that very little of importance is really accomplished. Very often, too, teachers find themselves being rated by principals or supervisors, not upon their ability in the classroom learning situation, but upon their ability to patrol the halls, playgrounds, or lunchrooms, their promptness in getting in reports, their willingness to take an active part in extramural activities or in community responsibilities. Too often teachers find themselves on a staff with other instructors not so professional and ethical as they should be, and their gripe sessions tend to have a wearing effect upon one who is dedicated to his profession.

Despite these adversities, however, the professional teacher must carry on. Again, he must assume a calm, collected countenance as he pursues his work, making whatever progress he can in the face of adverse conditions and occasionally making inroads into situations that are difficult but possible to alter. Activities such as listening to good music, pursuing creative hobbies, seeing good art and drama, reading good books, raising a garden, actively participating in cultural pursuits, often serve as effective morale boosters for teachers afflicted with the problem of keeping enthusiasm at a high level.

THE LACK-OF-STUDENT-RESPONSE PROBLEM

The final problem to be considered here is one experienced by every teacher in the classroom: the lack-of-student-response situation. Whether the fault lies with the pupils or with the teacher, this phenomenon occurs on occasion in even the best teaching-learning situation. Here, as with all school problems, there is no one simple answer. The teacher must keep constant vigil for signs of the cause of lack of response so that a remedy may be sought in the procedures of the classroom. If the problem is a serious one, the solution may come only after considerable evaluative investigation. It may be a situation that calls for a problem-solving approach.

If the lack of response is caused by low pupil intelligence, the teacher will be obliged to plan curriculums, materials, and methods to provide for these children of low mental ability as well as for average and fast learners. Similar planning on the teacher's part will be necessary if he finds the problem to be caused by retarded maturing in children; effective teachers plan for a variety of approaches if they find the children in their classroom at different levels of maturity.

Some lack-of-response problems may be caused by an absence of motivation for learning in the pupils. Since pupil motives are important determiners of what is learned and how it is learned, good teachers will constantly seek motivational activities that will ensure continual learning.

In some instances of lack of pupil response, the trouble may be that the pupil cannot apply something he has learned in one situation to another situation. Pupils learn things in the classroom so that they may be able to use or apply them in other situations, but the teacher must realize that the student needs to learn to transfer knowledge, that he does not automatically know how to do this. Thus the teacher who would provide for the greatest amount of positive learning transfer will see that his pupils have many opportunities to use their skills and knowledge in a variety of situations and to seek relationships among many in-school and out-of-school activities.

Conclusion

A universal problem of teachers is lack of sufficient time and often absence of adequate facilities. Many problems arise from a too tightly prescribed curriculum and a too crowded daily schedule. There remain too many antiquated and unsatisfactory buildings and classrooms, too few books and other learning materials, to do a completely adequate job of guiding optimum learning activities. Successful teaching calls for the maximum husbanding of physical, emotional, and mental resources and ingenuity.

Questions for Discussion

1. How can a teacher, other than by means of a compartmentalized day or period, meet the provisions of the law in states where the legislatures have prescribed all or most of the curriculum?

2. In what ways do modern school plants facilitate the work of the classroom teacher?

3. Explain why children in the control group in the experimental study referred to on pages 126–27 appeared to gain as much subject matter as did those in a group using the multiple-textbook approach to the social studies.

4. If you found that you were a traveling teacher in your building, what suggestions would you have for facilitating your situation?

5. Compare the pressures and problems of elementary and secondary teachers. Do you feel that some pressures would be unique to either elementary or secondary teachers? What are they? Which pressures

would probably be common to all teachers, regardless of the level on which they teach?

6. How might a teacher's association with adults outside the profession help relieve some of his pressures? What are some of the habits or behavioral tendencies teachers acquire in the school situation that will need to be guarded against when they associate with persons who are not teachers?

7. What do you think are the teacher's responsibilities with respect to improvement of the curriculum?

8. What are some of the traditional teacher urges that would have to be suppressed if a teacher works in a school where the emphasis is upon the democratic approach in all aspects?

9. What kinds of aid do you think teachers need to help them overcome problems of fatigue, lack of enthusiasm, and lack of student response?

10. Do you feel, as is sometimes claimed, that the curriculum in America's elementary and secondary schools has been watered down to adjust to children's needs and interests or to get into the program all that is supposed to be included? Explain.

Activities and Projects

1. Think back on the school you know best. Write down some proposals you would suggest for curriculum improvement in that school if you were a member of its teaching staff.

2. Make appointments to interview two teachers at the level of your choice (elementary or secondary). Ask them to tell you the difference between a textbook and a course of study, and note these differences. Ask to see their courses of study. Write down the major points included in these documents and note briefly the types of things included under each major point.

3. Prepare a one-day schedule for a class of third-grade youngsters in a typical third-grade situation, or a one-week program of five English classes in a secondary school. Note why you arranged the program in the manner you did.

4. Search the literature to find suggested ideal building layouts or plans for either an elementary or a secondary school. Write an essay or draw a plan embodying the best features of all, and explain why you think these features are ideal. Do the same thing for an ideal classroom—one you feel meets the needs of children of the twentieth century.

5. Make a resource unit in any subject area at the grade level of your choice.
6. Search in your college library, or write to the state departments of education, to find the legal curriculum requirements of three or four states, and compare them with the California requirements included in this chapter.
7. Plan an experiment in which you would attempt to find out whether a group of students using multiple textbooks and all available audiovisual aids would gain more from a unit than a group using only a single textbook. How would you conduct the experiment? How would you allow for differences in student ability and teacher bias? How would you follow up such a study?

References

Teachers' Work Load

BERNARD, HAROLD W. *Mental Hygiene for Classroom Teachers.* 2d ed. New York: McGraw-Hill, 1961. Chap. 20.

BURKE, ARVID J. "Do Teachers Have 'Short' Hours?" In *Teaching in America,* ed. Anthony C. Riccio and Frederick R. Cyphert. Columbus, Ohio: C. E. Merrill, 1962. Pp. 125–26.

BURRUP, PERCY E. *The Teacher and the Public School System.* 2d ed. New York: Harper, 1967. Chaps. 7, 8.

"Class Size in Secondary Schools." *NEA Research Bulletin,* February 1965, pp. 19–23.

"Conditions of Work for Quality Teaching." *NEA Journal,* March 1965, pp. 33–40.

DORROS, SIDNEY. *Teaching as a Profession.* Columbus, Ohio: C. E. Merrill, 1968. Chap. 10.

GRAY, JENNY. *The Teacher's Survival Guide.* Palo Alto: Fearon Publishers, 1967. Chap. 6.

HANNA, LAVONE A., GLADYS L. POTTER, and NEVA HAGAMAN. *Unit Teaching in the Elementary School.* Rev. ed. New York: Holt, Rinehart & Winston, 1963.

HASKEW, LAURENCE D., and JONATHON C. MCLENDON. *This Is Teaching.* 3d ed. Glenview, Ill.: Scott, Foresman, 1968. Chap. 1.

JOHNSON, JAMES A., HAROLD W. COLLINS, VICTOR L. DUPUIS, and JOHN H. JOHANSEN. *Introduction to the Foundations of American Education.* Boston: Allyn & Bacon, 1969. Sec. 1, pt. 2.

McKEAN, ROBERT C. *Principles and Methods of Secondary Education.* Columbus, Ohio: C. E. Merrill, 1962.

MOFFITT, FREDERICK A. "The Teacher's Day." *NEA Journal,* October 1962, p. 59.

PROVUS, MALCOLM M. "NEA Time to Teach Project." *NEA Journal,* April 1965, pp. 8–10.

RICHEY, ROBERT W. *Planning for Teaching.* 4th ed. New York: McGraw-Hill, 1968. Chap. 5.

SNOW, ROBERT H. "Anxieties and Discontents in Teaching." *Phi Delta Kappan,* April 1963, pp. 318–21.

Curriculum and Facilities

BERMAN, LOUISE M. *New Priorities in the Curriculum.* Columbus, Ohio: C. E. Merrill, 1968. Chap. 11.

BROWN, B. FRANK. *The Appropriate Placement School.* Englewood Cliffs, N.J.: Prentice-Hall, 1965.

BRUNER, JEROME S. *Toward a Theory of Instruction.* Cambridge, Mass.: Harvard University Press, 1966.

DEYOUNG, CHRIS A., and RICHARD WYNN. *American Education.* 6th ed. New York: McGraw-Hill, 1968. Chap. 15.

DOUGLASS, HARL R., ed. *The High School Curriculum.* 3d ed. New York: Ronald, 1964.

FROST, JOE L., and G. THOMAS ROWLAND. *Curricula for the Seventies.* Boston: Houghton Mifflin, 1969.

GOODLAD, JOHN I. "Changing Curriculum of America's Schools." *Saturday Review,* November 16, 1963, pp. 63–67, 87–88.

KEITH, LOWELL G., PAUL BLAKE, and SIDNEY TIEDT. *Contemporary Curriculum in the Elementary School.* New York: Harper, 1968. Chaps. 3, 6.

LAUX, DEAN M. "A New Role for Teachers?" *Phi Delta Kappan,* February 1965, pp. 265–68.

MICHAELIS, JOHN, and RUTH GROSSMAN. *New Designs in the Elementary School Curriculum.* New York: McGraw-Hill, 1968.

NATIONAL EDUCATION ASSOCIATION. *Curriculum Handbook for School Administrators.* Washington, D.C.: American Association of School Administrators of the National Education Association, 1967.

———. *Imperatives in Education.* Washington, D.C.: American Association of School Administrators of the National Education Association, 1966.

———. *Life Skills in School and Society.* Yearbook of the Association for Supervision and Curriculum Development. Washington, D.C.: Association for Supervision and Curriculum Development of the National Education Association, 1969.

―――. *New Curriculum Developments.* Washington, D.C.: Association for Supervision and Curriculum Development of the National Education Association, 1965.

PARKER, J. CECIL, T. BENTLEY EDWARDS, and WILLIAM H. STEGEMAN. *Curriculum in America.* New York: Crowell, 1962. Chap. 5.

"Pressures and Concerns." *Educational Leadership,* May 1963.

RICHEY, ROBERT W. *Planning for Teaching.* 4th ed. New York: McGraw-Hill, 1968. Chap. 5.

SILBERMAN, CHARLES E. *Crisis in the Classroom.* New York: Random House, 1971.

STONE, JAMES C., and R. ROSS HEMPSTEAD. *California Education Today.* New York: Crowell, 1968. Chaps. 8, 9.

TABA, HILDA. *Curriculum Development Theory and Practice.* New York: Harcourt, 1962. Chap. 1.

What Should Be Taught

BRUNER, JEROME S. *The Process of Education.* Cambridge, Mass.: Harvard University Press, 1961.

―――. *Toward a Theory of Instruction.* Cambridge, Mass.: Harvard University Press, 1966.

DEYOUNG, CHRIS A., and RICHARD WYNN. *American Education.* 6th ed. New York: McGraw-Hill, 1968. Chap. 14.

FRAZER, DOROTHY McCLURE. *Deciding What to Teach.* Washington, D.C.: National Education Association, 1963.

―――, and THOMAS G. PULLEN, JR. "What to Teach?" *NEA Journal,* October 1962, pp. 34–36.

GORMAN, ALFRED H. *Teachers and Learners: The Interactive Process of Education.* Boston: Allyn & Bacon, 1969.

GWYNN, J. MINOR, and JOHN B. CHASE. *Curriculum Principles and Social Trends.* New York: Macmillan, 1969.

HASKEW, LAURENCE D., and JONATHON C. McLENDON. *This Is Teaching.* 3d ed. Glenview, Ill.: Scott, Foresman, 1968. Pp. 86–88.

KOBLITZ, MINNIE W. *The Negro in Schoolroom Literature.* New York: Center for Urban Education, 1967.

NATIONAL EDUCATION ASSOCIATION. *Life Skills in School and Society.* Yearbook of the Association for Supervision and Curriculum Development. Washington, D.C.: Association for Supervision and Curriculum Development of the National Education Association, 1969. Chaps. 4–9.

————. *New Curriculum Developments.* Washington, D.C.: Association for Supervision and Curriculum Development of the National Education Association, 1965.

ROGERS, CARL R. *Freedom to Learn.* Columbus, Ohio: C. E. Merrill, 1969.

SOLTIS, JONAS F. *An Introduction to the Analysis of Educational Concepts.* Reading, Mass.: Addison-Wesley, 1968. Chap. 2.

SOWARDS, G. WESLEY, and MARY-MARGARET SCOBEY. *The Changing Curriculum and the Elementary Teacher.* Rev. ed. San Francisco: Wadsworth, 1969.

TIEDT, SIDNEY, ed. *Teaching the Disadvantaged Child.* New York: Oxford University Press, 1968.

Resources for Teachers

ALEXANDER, WILLIAM R. *Are You a Good Teacher?* New York: Holt, Rinehart & Winston, 1959.

BERNARD, HAROLD W. *Mental Hygiene for Classroom Teachers.* 2d ed. New York: McGraw-Hill, 1961. Chap. 5.

"Discipline." *NEA Journal,* September 1963, pp. 9–20.

GNAGNEY, WILLIAM J. *Controlling Classroom Misbehavior.* What Research Says Series, no. 32. Washington, D.C.: Department of Classroom Teachers of the National Education Association, 1965.

GRAY, JENNY. *The Teacher's Survival Guide.* Palo Alto: Lear Siegler, Inc./Fearon Publishers, 1967. Chaps. 2–5.

HASKEW, LAURENCE D., and JONATHON C. McLENDON. *This Is Teaching.* 3d ed. Glenview, Ill.: Scott, Foresman, 1968. Chap. 7.

HUGHES, MARIE. "What Is Teaching? One Viewpoint." *Educational Leadership,* January 1962, pp. 251–59.

MISNER, PAUL J., FREDERICK W. SCHNEIDER, and LOWELL G. KEITH. *Elementary School Administration.* Columbus, Ohio: C. E. Merrill, 1963. Chap. 16.

RAGAN, WILLIAM B. *Teaching America's Children.* New York: Holt, Rinehart & Winston, 1961. Chap. 2.

RANDOLPH, NORMA, WILLIAM HOWE, and ELIZABETH ACHTERMAN. "Self Enhancing Education: A Training Manual." A Program to Advance Creativity in Education (PACE) Project, under Title III, Elementary and Secondary Education Act. Rev. ed. Mimeographed. Washington, D.C.: U.S. Department of Health, Education, and Welfare, Office of Education, 1968.

RATHS, JAMES, JOHN R. PANCELLA, and JAMES S. VAN NESS. *Studying Teaching.* Englewood Cliffs, N.J.: Prentice-Hall, 1967.

RICHEY, ROBERT W. *Planning for Teaching*. 4th ed. New York: McGraw-Hill, 1968. Pt. 2.

SHUMSKY, ABRAHAM. *In Search of Teaching Style*. New York: Appleton, 1968.

WEBSTER, STATEN W. *Discipline in the Classroom*. San Francisco: Chandler, 1968. Pts. 1, 2.

Education should try to lessen the obstacles, diminish the friction, invigorate the energy, and
should train minds to react, not at haphazard, but
by choice, on the lines of force that attract their
world. What one knows is, in youth, of little moment; *they know enough who know how to learn.*

HENRY ADAMS

6

The Pupils as Learners

Mark is sixteen years of age and is in the eleventh grade. He is a handsome young man, but his physical size has somewhat outgrown his coordination. Mark has an excellent home environment. As with all teen-agers,
the important people in his life are the youngsters with whom he associates. All of them are interested in athletics, dancing, parties, and, yes,
subjects in school; Mark is interested in everything, including the great social and religious issues of the day. While on the surface he indicates that
parents and teachers couldn't interest him less, he secretly is glad they are
around, especially when he has profound problems to talk over with them.
Of slightly higher than average mentality, Mark is quite good in his academic work and keeps it up to date, despite his interest in school affairs
and community activities for young people. He lives in a fairly large city
on the West Coast and attends a senior high school with about sixteen
hundred other students. He has never been a behavior problem; all in all,
he is an extremely well rounded young man.

Johnny is eight years old and in the third grade. He is a handsome
child, with ruddy cheeks, wavy golden hair, and more than his share of energy. His home environment is excellent: he has a pony to ride about on
his parents' acreage at the edge of the midwestern community in which he

lives; his well-to-do parents are interested in his accomplishments in and out of school and are very cooperative with teachers and other school authorities; his home contains the finest in children's books and other facilities to aid in his learning. Yet Johnny is the most consistent "customer" in the principal's office. But there is one thing sure about him: everything he does is open and aboveboard. If he feels like doing something, he does it —and, of course, if it is not accepted behavior, he usually gets caught at it. He has normal ability for his age and apparently achieves up to his ability. Johnny has two older brothers.

Betty is an attractive second-grader, but is also eight years old. Although she has an intelligence quotient (I.Q.) in the normal range as measured by standardized tests, she is a slow achiever. She is shy and withdrawn to the point that she very seldom speaks to anyone, even her peers, unless she is spoken to. Her parents both work, often until late at night, and she has never known any genuine affection from them. She is often left alone at night with her only brother, who is just one year her elder. There is a great amount of bickering between her parents when they are at home with her. Betty lives in a small house in a rural community of about ten thousand in the Midwest, and the house contains only the necessities for substandard living.

Bob is a ten-year-old fifth-grade youngster who, despite his high I.Q., has not achieved as well as expected in school for a variety of reasons. Because of a bad home environment, he has developed an emotional block to learning. He is reading at a second-grade level. In addition, his general physical health is below normal, and socially he is a misfit, an isolate. He has no status at home and at times has been neglected in the classroom— but he tries to gain status with his peers through sheer physical prowess: he is forever starting fights and throwing stones at other children on the playground. He visits the principal's office a great deal because of misbehavior. Bob attends an elementary school with about 650 pupils in a middle-sized community in the eastern states. He is currently being studied by the school psychologist.

Wendy is a seventeen-year-old sophomore in high school. Her parents are in the lower socioeconomic group in an eastern community of about twenty thousand population. Her father is chronically ill, and her mother does not work. She became associated with the "wrong crowd" when she was in junior high school and is currently under the supervision of juvenile authorities. Although Wendy has normal intelligence, she does not achieve to her capacity in her courses; in fact, she is quite lackadaisical about them. If her parents did not make her attend school, she would not be there, because her interests are more worldly than those explored in the classroom. Wendy's teachers have often expressed disgust with her attitude

—but have also been concerned for what will become of her in the future. In the past year, she has been in two automobile accidents while riding with questionable friends; one of the accidents was quite serious, resulting in the hospitalization for a long period of time of a three-year-old child. There are two other girls and one boy in the family.

Jerry is a popular senior in secondary school and a high achiever in his classes. He is a star athlete in three sports, having won a monogram for three years in each. Jerry is taking advanced-placement work in mathematics and science and plans to become an experimental physicist after he completes the course of study in his high school of twelve hundred students in the Midwest. Jerry goes steady with one of the popular pep-squad girls, but he has no marital plans at present and intends not to have any until he is through college and has completed his military service. His is a fine home environment, and his parents have been most cooperative with school authorities ever since he began kindergarten. He is an Explorer Scout and has been active in Sunday School and church activities. In school he sticks to business and has never caused behavior problems for his teachers. He is an only child.

Mary, a twelve-year-old in the fifth grade, is mentally retarded (I.Q. about 65) and, of course, makes little or no progress in academic subjects. Most of her schoolwork entails such activities as learning how to keep herself clean and neat and home-arts activities. Her parents, too, are below average in intelligence and have been a constant thorn in the side of teachers and administrators ever since Mary started at achool. Mary has five brothers, one of whom is also mentally retarded. She lives with her family in a hovel in an unattractive slum area of a city of twenty-five thousand in a southern state. The family receives financial assistance from the county, and charitable organizations provide some food and clothing. Mary's school attendance is quite irregular; she is often ill, especially during inclement weather. Her sex urges are beginning to develop quite strongly, and she constantly chases the boys in her school.

These seven youngsters are actual persons, though the names are fictitious. They differ from one another, and they bring these differences to school. Even within a single building in a single school system, each pupil is different from all the others, with different problems and different interests and different native abilities. Most of the children in a single building come from different home backgrounds; all of them have different needs. But to teachers and other school authorities, all these unique individuals are the same in that they must be encouraged to learn and grow and develop as much as possible during the time they are in school.

If all pupils were alike, their growth patterns identical, their backgrounds and previous education similar and equal, teaching would be a relatively simple occupation. But a glance at the seven preceding descriptions, with the realization that these are but a few of the hundreds of thousands of children over the nation, should convince teachers and prospective teachers that this is certainly not the case. The thing that makes teaching hard work—yet forever exciting and challenging—is the fact that our educational "products" are all different, and when we do a good job of teaching, we help each pupil in our charge grow and learn according to his own individual pattern. Educational products, our boys and girls, are not supposed to look alike when they complete their programs in school; only products that come off an assembly line en masse are intended to take on such aspects of similarity. When a pupil completes a grade or course in school, he is different from what he was when he entered the grade or course; and he should be, if the teacher has done an acceptable job in guiding the learning activities of the pupils in his classroom.

The problem, then, facing conscientious teachers is that of providing experiences that will enhance the growth and development and learning of each individual in the classroom to the extent that he may make maximum progress in accord with his ability. If teachers have a real speciality, it is, or should be, in the area of knowing how children learn and of providing for optimum learning by each pupil in the classroom. Accordingly, then, teachers and prospective teachers should continuously pursue a study of their speciality. They may accomplish this, at least partially, by keeping abreast of developments relating to the learning process and of their relationships to classroom methodology.

Learning and Psychological Propositions

Modern psychologists are by no means in agreement on a single theory of how learning takes place. This is small consolation to classroom teachers in America's schools, who look to psychologists for scientific evidence that will help them in their work of arranging an environment in which boys and girls may learn. Experimental psychologists, such as Watson and Thorndike, have proposed the stimulus-response relationship as a unit of behavior from which learning processes may be inferred; each question a teacher asks is a situation acting on the learner, and his answer is a response to the situation. Thorndike's principles of rewards and punishments —simply that rewards strengthen and punishments weaken stimulus-response associations—have been many times refuted, but recent evidence tends to point up their basic accuracy. Cognitive theorists, such as Tolman and Lewin, on the other hand, do not accept the stimulus-response associations as applicable to human behavior. Instead, they emphasize organization and reorganization of experience occurring in the central nervous systems of the individual; the change that occurs within the learner is the formation of a new realization or expectation. The specific stimulus-response association is, to these theorists, too small a segment to be considered a unit of behavior; their unit is a much larger whole. Jerome Bruner, in his *Process of Education*,[1] examines the work done fifty years ago by the Swiss psychologist Piaget: the child moves as a matter of course from intuitive to intelligent thought, and the teacher's task is to represent in terms of the child's viewpoint that which is being taught.

Despite disagreements among schools of psychology and claims that psychology, as a research discipline, deals with its own problems rather than with those of education, some psychologists have tried to bring forth some meaning for educators from a wealth of empirical data resulting from experimentation, and they do agree on certain propositions important to the field of teaching.

"LAWS" OF LEARNING

The most commonly accepted fundamental psychological proposition appropriate to education is to the effect that rewarded, or reinforced, tendencies are those that will probably recur. Children, or animals for that matter, will react to a situation in much the same manner as to a previous situation if that reaction proved satisfactory or successful.

Part of the teacher's responsibility is to promote fruitful learning experiences involving reinforcement wherever possible. Among the techniques teachers use to this end are self-correction devices such as answer books or handwriting standards and mechanical devices such as certain types of teaching machines, tape recorders by which students can hear themselves as they play back their recitations, and self-correcting tests of various kinds.

Some of the claims made for many of the modern teaching machines imply that reinforcement is strengthened by their use because the reward is immediate. This seems to be psychologically sound, as experimentation has indicated that reinforcement immediately following the behavior sequence is more satisfactory than that which is delayed for a time. For instance, the simple comment "Right" immediately following the behavior sequence is more effective than a larger reward following much later. Generally, reinforcements should be applied as soon as possible; pupils should know as quickly as possible whether what they are doing is correct.

[1] Jerome S. Bruner, *The Process of Education* (Cambridge, Mass.: Harvard University Press, 1961).

Reinforcement

In an auto-instructional program, reinforcements of various kinds are available to the student. When the student makes a response that he "knows" is right, just the fact that he can go on and complete the response is reinforcing; that is to say, the reinforcement is simply the realization that he knows, or the fact that he is able to proceed to make a response. Contrast this reinforcing event with the case of the student who comes to a test question to which he does not know the answer or who reads a passage in a book that he does not understand; not only is there no response available, but emotional reactions (e.g., frustration) can develop, involving the occurrence of behavior that actively interferes with subsequent learning. Even if the student tries to make responses to material that is not completely clear to him, wrong responses don't fit, and no self-reinforcement is available in the form of "I'm right" or "I understand." The situation is completely different when a program not only makes the correct responses available, but, in addition, indicates to the student that each response is indeed correct, thus providing additional reinforcement. The student then proceeds on to new material and this continuous progress is a kind of moving on to new, novel stimulation, an activity which has also been shown experimentally to be reinforcing.

The programmed learning situation includes more than one kind of reinforcement, and includes at least two kinds of student behavior that are being consistently reinforced: each correct response is reinforced, thereby producing the desired relationships between the content of the frames and the responses made to the content; and, in addition, the behavior called paying attention, or attending to stimuli, or reading carefully, is reinforced each time a correct response is made, with the result that the student tends to continue to pay attention and work carefully on each frame. He learns the content of the program, but he is also reinforced for using the program, which results in continued interest and motivation for using the program and responding actively to it.

William A. Deterline, *An Introduction to Programmed Instruction* (Englewood Cliffs, N.J.: Prentice-Hall, 1962), pp. 28–29. Copyright © 1962. Reprinted by permission.

In contrast to reward, which should be used generously, particularly in early stages of learning, punishment should be avoided. In certain children, punished responses may encourage tendencies adverse to increased learning. Also, punishment generally serves to disturb teacher and pupil relationships, rather than to increase the likelihood of correct responses.

Intrinsic rewards are generally considered better than extrinsic ones, and thus teachers should aim at them for their pupils, despite the fact that currently there is an emphasis by some psychologists on the extrinsic approach. When a child has a feeling of success, his chances of attaining real learning are greater than when he receives a star or a candy bar for some achievement or other. Whereas the effects of the extrinsic reward usually depend on the giver of such rewards, the learner always has only himself to contend with when the reward system is intrinsic. It is admitted, however, that in some instances, and with some children, extrinsic rewards may be most effective in certain stages of dealing with youngsters, but the ultimate aim should be to utilize the intrinsic-rewards system.

The law of readiness, also an important psychological proposition, is a concept upon which most authorities agree. Readiness relates to physiological maturity, but, just as important, it relates also to psychological maturity involving the learner's sense of the importance of, and his past preparation for, the new material to be learned. Many claims of superiority are made for foreign schools that begin instruction much earlier in a child's life than do public schools of the United States. In evaluating these claims, one should remember that this early teaching is based on an approach to readiness somewhat different from ours and that it is believed no great harm is done a learner if he spends two years, beginning at age six, learning something that would take him only six months to learn at age ten. In other words, some modern psychologists indicate that just because a youngster *can* learn the structure of a particular subject at any particular age, as indicated by Bruner and others, that is not necessarily an indication that he *should* learn that structure.

INSIGHT, REFLECTIVE THINKING, AND PURPOSE

Insight is important in learning. Indeed, it is the most important part of all learning for cognitive psychologists, who contend that the problem is really solved when a pupil has the proper insight. According to Watson, "the experience of learning by sudden insight into a previously confused or puzzling situation arises when (a) there has been a sufficient background and preparation, (b) attention is given to the relationships operative in the whole situation, (c) the perceptual structure 'frees' the key elements to be shifted into new patterns, (d) the task is meaningful and within the range of ability of the subject." [2] When a student of language arts who is as-

[2] Goodwin Watson, "What Do We Know about Learning?" *NEA Journal,* March 1963, p. 22.

signed a composition to write is taught that an outline is an invaluable aid in organizing the composition, he has gained insight that might otherwise have escaped his attention.

Reflective thinking is also important in children's learning. This process is applicable to either reading or listening. Learning is facilitated when children are asked to read an assignment and then tell, orally or in writing, what they have read. There is some research to support the idea that children learn considerably more when they reflect upon what they have read than when they simply reread material they have already read. If, shortly after learning material, children are asked to recall what they have learned, they will likely forget less than they would if they were not asked to recall it until somewhat later. The rate of forgetting is most rapid when knowledge is first learned.

Principles of Learning

All things considered, perhaps it is not fair to expect a full explanation of learning to come from one discipline, since the complexity of the phenomenon is quite generally accepted. Perhaps a teacher should search for an understanding of the learning process from several disciplines, starting with psychology but also including other behavioral sciences such as sociology and anthropology. The phrase "should search" is used advisedly, because the simple truth is that at the present time there does not exist a clear-cut, concise, generally-agreed-upon definition of learning universally applicable to all situations and all individuals. Perhaps as experimentation and research in all the behavioral sciences proceed, a satisfactory theory of learning will one day evolve. Until that day, however, the best a teacher can do is to operate by the rather comprehensive "lore" of teaching, at the same time keeping watch on the results of experimentation reported in the literature and conducted in the classrooms across the nation.

While there is much disagreement as to how learning *takes place,* there seems to be quite general agreement as to what learning *does.* A widely accepted axiom is that learning, evoked by stimuli from within an individual or by external stimuli acting against him, causes changes in that individual's behavior. The problem arises when we propose to ascertain the nature of the stimuli and when we attempt an explanation of how these stimuli actually affect learning. Whatever it is that happens, the results are obvious every day in classrooms across the nation as teachers observe changes in the behavior of their students, not to mention the considerable learning that goes unnoticed because it does not result in observable change of behavior.

Regardless of which psychological theory of learning a teacher accepts, if indeed he accepts any at all, there are certain aspects of learning that will help him to understand how he may best direct his efforts to facilitate optimum learning.

LEARNING IS AN INDIVIDUAL MATTER

In the first place, learning is an individual and personal matter with each learner. What a challenge it is to each teacher to know that the 30 or 40 or 250 or whatever number of pupils in his class are unique individuals, each with a pattern of growth and development—intellectual, physical, social, emotional, spiritual—all his own! Never before has the teacher had a pupil with the same growth pattern as any pupil currently in his classroom; none of those he will have in his classroom in the future will have the same learning image as any in his room today! Furthermore, what each pupil learns is dependent entirely upon him: he will learn only what he feels is important for him to learn or what he is interested in learning. The claims of some critics of progressive education notwithstanding, an individual cannot open up the head of another and pour in knowledge.

ARRANGING THE ENVIRONMENT AND MOTIVATING PUPILS

A person may, however, facilitate the learning process, and this is where the teacher comes in. One responsibility of the classroom teacher is to arrange the environment and motivate pupils so that they may learn. What a challenge it is, in the light of the idea expressed above, that *each* child's environment must be arranged for him and that *each* child must be motivated to learn whatever has been determined for him to learn!

LEARNING TO LEARN

The real job of the teacher is to facilitate learning, not to be a hard taskmaster; the job of the learner is learning to learn, not to memorize facts and figures that tomorrow will probably become obsolete or outmoded. If children, through opportunities provided by their teachers, can learn to learn, they will continue to learn to cope with new situations and problems throughout their lives. With new knowledge evolving at such a rapid rate now in the last quarter of the twentieth century, the world of the future will be much different from today's, and it is in that future world that today's children will need to learn to live. No one alive at the present moment can foretell what knowledge people will need, but then as now, people will need to know how to solve their problems. It is here that the teacher's real speciality becomes evident: the teacher is, or should be, an expert in instructing others how to learn, an expert in helping pupils learn how to solve their problems.

The Problem-Solving Process

Success at solving their problems and making discoveries for themselves is a thrilling, satisfying, habit-forming experience for children and youth, from the kindergarten through the most advanced levels of college graduate work. Though the problem-solving process results in a great deal of learning in the traditional sense of knowledge being transmitted, even more important is the fact that in the process real use is made of this knowledge. This context also involves attitudes, understandings, feelings, and physical activity.

THE STEPS

It is convenient to present a list of the steps used in the classroom in the problem-solving process. Depending upon the authority, the number of steps varies from three or four to eight or nine, and the order of these varies also. They vary greatly in wording but very little in content.

1. *Recognizing that a problem exists.* In the usual classroom situation, problems often are not easily seen. Normally there must be a change in an otherwise easy, ongoing situation before a problem is recognized. Opportunities for upsetting or provocative situations in which problems are recognized often present themselves during demonstration lessons in the room, on field trips, and in the use of motion pictures.

2. *Clarifying or defining the problem.* This is often one of the most difficult steps in the problem-solving process, because once a problem is recognized by the pupils in a group, each one attempts to clarify or define it from his own frame of reference. Since each member of the group has had different past experiences and since each pupil's social environment is different from that of the other members of the class, each tends to view the problem on the basis of his own perception. At this point in the process, pupils usually set up a tentative goal, and their problem then becomes one of how to achieve this goal; also, there is likely to be a considerable amount of hypothesizing, or the formulation of several possible problem solutions, at this point. This should be encouraged by the teacher.

3. *Collecting data.* Information from many possible sources is collected at this point, if the information seems to have some relationship to the

problem or will help in its solution. The subject matter to be pursued depends upon the particular area in which the problem falls and the goals or purposes the class has in view. Books are, of course, an excellent source from which data may be obtained, as are newspapers, journals published by learned organizations and the government, magazines, lectures, films, and community resources that may be visited by the class or brought into the classroom.

4. *Formulating, modifying, or testing hypotheses.* This step in the problem-solving process involves educated guesses, ideas, or insights and usually includes the organization and analysis of the data collected. Hypotheses may explain the data, or they may point up the necessity for further study or fact finding. At this point, the most logical solutions to the problem are tested; the data that have been collected and the plans that have been made are put to trial. Action is carried on until a plausible solution to the problem is found.

5. *Evaluating results.* When the final solution to the problem is found, the results of the problem-solving process need to be evaluated to determine whether the original purposes were met and whether any unexpected information was uncovered. Not only should the results of the process be evaluated but the process itself should be appraised to see whether it could be improved on.

6. *Generalizing.* Progressing through the various steps in the problem-solving process would be an uneconomical use of time and energy if the learning results were to end with the solution of one problem. The purpose of most learning is to gain knowledge that may be used in other situations. Following the arrival at a solution, then, the teacher should lead the class in applying the results to other circumstances, so that pupils may understand that the findings do not apply only to the one particular problem under consideration. The test of children's learning about any subject or topic is what they are able to do with the knowledge they have gained. Not until a pupil is able to apply what he has learned is he deemed to have learned at all.

POLYA'S PROBLEM-SOLVING FORMULA

Polya presents a simple, logical approach to problem solving, in four steps, which can be expanded to deal with any problem at any grade level. His approach follows:

FIRST	UNDERSTANDING THE PROBLEM
You have to *understand* the problem.	*What is the unknown? What are the data? What is the condition?* Is it possible to satisfy the condition? Is the condition sufficient to determine the

unknown? Or is it insufficient? Or redundant? Or contradictory?

Draw a figure. Introduce suitable notation.

Separate the various parts of the condition. Can you write them down?

SECOND

Find the connection between the data and the unknown. You may be obliged to consider auxiliary problems if an immediate connection cannot be found. You should obtain eventually a *plan* of the solution.

DEVISING A PLAN

Have you seen it before? Or have you seen the same problem in a slightly different form?

Do you know a related problem? Do you know a theorem that could be useful?

Look at the unknown! And try to think of a familiar problem having the same or a similar unknown.

Here is a problem related to yours and solved before. Could you use it? Could you use its results? Could you use its method? Should you introduce some auxiliary element in order to make its use possible?

Could you restate the problem? Could you restate it still differently? Go back to definitions.

If you cannot solve the proposed problem, try to solve first some related problem.

Could you imagine a more accessible related problem? A more general problem? A more special problem? An analogous problem? Could you solve a part of the problem? Keep only a part of the condition, drop the other part; how far is the unknown then determined, how can it vary? Could you derive something useful from the data? Could you think of other data appropriate to determine the unknown? Could you change the unknown or the data, or both if necessary, so that the new unknown and the new data are nearer to each other?

Did you use all the data? Did you use the whole condition? Have you taken into account all essential notions involved in the problem?

THIRD

Carry out your plan.

CARRYING OUT THE PLAN

Carrying out your plan of the solution, check each step. Can you see clearly that the step is correct? Can you prove that it is correct?

FOURTH

Examine the solution obtained.

LOOKING BACK

Can you *check the result?* Can you check the argument?

LOOKING BACK (*continued*)

Can you derive the result differently? Can you see it at a glance?

Can you use the result, or the method, for some other problem? [3]

The concept of education as problem solving is, of course, in sharp contrast to the traditional concept that the educative process is strictly intellectual and is concerned only with ideas forced on the pupil by a textbook author, a teacher, or some other authority. In the traditional sense, the primary object is to gain knowledge; the application of this knowledge is not considered important until after the subject matter is gained. Unfortunately, the traditional approach necessitates the retraining of the learner in the application of knowledge sometime after he presumably gains the knowledge. In the problem-solving conception, application of the knowledge is made at the time it is learned; thus it is more meaningful and the chances of its retention are much greater than in the rote approach.

If pupils are guided by teachers in problem-solving experiences, they will gain knowledge and be able to apply it; they also will be given opportunities for forming scientific attitudes and correct work-study skills, as well as for appropriate activities in critical and reflective thinking. As pupils participate increasingly in problem solving, they will gain skill in the process and will become adept at meeting head-on the myriad problems they encounter in life and working through to successful conclusions.

Methods of Inquiry

Techniques of problem solving, inquiry, and discovery are, as indicated in chapter 3, quite closely related and, in fact, are methods whose titles often are used interchangeably. Also indicated in that chapter is the fact that some authorities are inclined to differentiate discovery techniques into guided and unguided approaches. The method of inquiry proposed by J. R. Suchman is an example of the latter approach.

Suchman found in his investigations in the public schools that a teacher asks from eight to ten times as many questions as the children, a strange state of affairs when one considers the excited curiosity and interest typical of the young child and the fact that children come to the school to learn. Suchman suggests that pupils have been trained out of inquiry and wait passively to receive knowledge presented to them by the teacher.

[3] G. Polya, *How to Solve It* (New York: Doubleday, 1957). Reprinted by permission of the publisher.

As a stimulus to his presentations, Suchman makes considerable use of films in which children are given an experience that is, from their standpoint, unexplainable. For instance, in a film depicting the classical demonstration involving the use of a heated brass ball and a brass ring, an interesting dialogue resulted:

Pupil: Were the ball and ring at room temperature to begin with?
Teacher: Yes.
Pupil: And the ball would go through the ring at first?
Teacher: Yes.
Pupil: After the ball was held over the fire it did *not* go through the ring. Right?
Teacher: Yes.
Pupil: If the ring had been heated instead of the ball, would the results have been the same?
Teacher: No.
Pupil: If both had been heated, would the ball have gone through then?
Teacher: That all depends.
Pupil: If they had both been heated to the same temperature, would the ball have gone through?
Teacher: Yes.
Pupil: Would the ball be the same size after it was heated as it was before?
Teacher: No.
Pupil: Could the same experiment have been done if the ball and ring were made out of some other metal?
Teacher: Yes.

The children are taught to use a three-stage plan in developing logical, systematic approaches. First, they are asked to identify, verify, and measure the parameters of a given problem. In this process, they identify objects, observe the properties of these objects, note the conditions or states of the objects, and discover changes in the conditions. Second, they determine the relevance of particular conditions in producing the events of a scientific episode, for all conditions are not relevant. Third, they formulate and test theoretical constructs that show relationships among the variables of the observed physical event. This action calls for flexibility and imagination in asking questions.

Training sessions of an hour or less are held at intervals of several days. A silent motion picture of a physics demonstration is shown. This picture raises questions about cause and effect, and the children begin immediately to ask probing questions which are to be answered "yes" or "no." "Yes" and "no" questions test hypotheses; therefore the teacher who answers them is helping them to establish the tenability or untenability of their hypotheses. During the first stage, the children ask questions of verification. During stages two and three, they ask questions of an experimental nature, stating a set of conditions and postulating a result. Here, the teacher's answer tells whether the postulated result will or will not occur. If the teacher cannot give an unequivocal answer, he says, "That all depends," or "Tell me more," indicating that the child's "experiment" has not been sufficiently controlled. When children try to tap the teacher's understanding, the teacher's response may be, "What could you do to find out for yourself?"

After the period of inquiry through questioning, a critical review of the process is conducted by teacher, pupils, and any observers who may be present. From this review, the children are expected to learn improved strategies of inquiry. The children apparently have little interest in improving their inquiry skills *per se,* but they are willing to improve them in the context of understanding cause-and-effect relationships. The children used in the experiments have often been at sixth grade level.[4]

Discovery and Learning

A great deal is being made in today's classrooms of the principles that are involved in the discovery method as a technique of learning. These principles, so evident at this time in the areas of science and mathematics, are based on the fact that things to be learned have an internal connectedness and that, in order to be really learned, they must be fitted together in a meaningful manner. Actual discovery is, of course, a rare phenomenon; in the classroom it usually involves gaining new insights as a result of the pupil's going beyond his current knowledge by rearranging the facts involved. It seems evident that if children are to be given opportunities for discovery, they must be trained in the problem-solving process, which was discussed earlier in this chapter.

The discovery concept is one in which children may become "active" learners as opposed to "passive" ones. According to this idea, children may participate in making knowledge, rather than simply consume knowl-

---

[4] The foregoing account of Suchman's method of inquiry was drawn, and is reprinted by permission, from the following sources: A. Harry Passow, ed., *Nurturing Individual Potential,* Papers and Reports from the ASCD Seventh Curriculum Research Institute (Washington, D.C.: Association for Supervision and Curriculum Development of the National Education Association, 1964), p. 46; *Individualizing Instruction,* Yearbook of the Association for Supervision and Curriculum Development (Washington, D.C.: Association for Supervision and Curriculum Development of the National Education Association, 1964), pp. 166–67; and J. R. Suchman, "Inquiry Training in the Elementary School," *The Science Teacher* 27 (1960): 42–47. See also J. R. Suchman, "The Child and the Inquiry Process," in *Intellectual Development: Another Look,* Papers and Reports from the ASCD Eighth Curriculum Research Institute (Washington, D.C.: Association for Supervision and Curriculum Development of the National Education Association, 1964), pp. 59–77.

edge already made. Bruner relates an incident that illustrates this process:

Children in the fifth grade of a suburban school were about to study the geography of the Central states as part of a social studies unit. Previous units on the Southeastern states, taught by rote, had proved a bore. Could geography be taught as a rational discipline? Determined to find out, the teachers devised a unit in which students would have to figure out not only where things are located, but why they are there. This involves a sense of the structure of geography.

The children were given a map of the Central states in which only rivers, large bodies of water, agricultural products, and natural resources were shown. They were not allowed to consult their books. Their task was to find Chicago, "the largest city in the North Central states."

The argument got under way immediately. One child came up with the idea that Chicago must be on the junction of the three large lakes. No matter that at this point he did not know the names of the lakes—Huron, Superior, and Michigan—his theory was well-reasoned. A big city produced a lot of products, and the easiest and most logical way to ship these products is by water.

But a second child rose immediately to the opposition. A big city needed lots of food, and he placed Chicago where there are corn and hogs—right in the middle of Iowa.

A third child saw the issue more broadly—recognizing virtues in both previous arguments. He pointed out that large quantities of food can be grown in river valleys. Whether he had learned this from a previous social studies unit or from raising carrot seeds, we shall never know. If you had a river, he reasoned, you had not only food but transportation. He pointed to a spot on the map not far from St. Louis. "There is where Chicago *ought* to be." Would that graduate students would always do so well!

Not all the answers were so closely reasoned, though even the wild ones had about them a sense of the necessity involved in a city's location.

One argued, for example, that all American cities have skyscrapers, which require steel, so he placed Chicago in the middle of the Mesabi Range. At least he was thinking on his own, with a sense of the constraints imposed on the location of cities.

After forty-five minutes, the children were told they could pull down the "real" wall map (the one with names) and see where Chicago really is. After the map was down, each of the contending parties pointed out how close they had come to being right. Chicago had not been located. But the location of cities was no longer a matter of unthinking chance for this group of children.[5]

What did the children learn? Bruner's answer is: A way of thinking

[5] Jerome S. Bruner, "Structures in Learning," *NEA Journal*, March 1963, p. 26. Reprinted by permission.

about geography, a way of dealing with its raw data. They learned that there is some relationship between the requirements of living and man's habitat. If that is all they got out of their geography lesson, that is plenty. Did they remember which is Lake Huron? Lake Superior? Lake Michigan? Do you?

Foshay relates how the discovery or knowledge-making technique might be used in an American-history class. He suggests that when the class has proceeded to the immediate post–Civil War period, the teacher might pursue the "ideal of intellectual excellence that is represented by an attempt to study the disciplines directly" by carrying the children to a confrontation of the historian's problem and raising with them various questions: "What kinds of events after Lincoln would be most worth knowing?" "How can we discover what these events were?" (We can read, ask, search, tell one another.) "What do historians say these events were?" (Not one historian, but several; for not all historians choose to deal with the same events, and the sooner we understand this, the more liberated we are from a naïve view of our past and of the historian's place in understanding it.) "What are the principal ways the period has been interpreted by the historians?" "Do you, as a student, think of other ways?" "What information do you think the historians might include that they appear to have omitted?" "Why do you suppose they omitted this information? Because they couldn't find it? Because it didn't fit with their interpretation?" [6]

What a radical departure is this method from the old subject-centered method of teaching history! Through techniques such as those indicated in the two examples cited, teachers may confront the disciplines directly and bring pupils into knowledge-making activities instead of strictly knowledge-consuming lessons.

Motivating and the Environment

Reference was made earlier in this chapter to the importance in learning of motivation and environmental arrangement, both of which are significant aspects of the teaching act. Actually, the two are not mutually exclusive. One of the first accomplishments the teacher must strive for in motivating pupils is the creation of a learning environment, an environment in which youngsters will be stimulated toward interesting, appropriate, and attainable goals. This is no mean accomplishment, to say the least. It means that the teacher must learn the needs, interests, and capacities of

[6] Arthur W. Foshay, "A Modest Proposal for the Improvement of Education," in *What Are the Sources of the Curriculum? A Symposium* (Washington, D.C.: Association for Supervision and Curriculum Development of the National Education Association, 1962), pp. 7–8.

each pupil in his class. He must establish close rapport with each individual in his group and at the same time supervise the peer interaction within the class. It means that the teacher must generate and communicate a vast amount of interest, enthusiasm, and creativity.

Four psychological aspects of motivation might be mentioned at this point. First is intention to learn: it seems obvious that the least teachers can do in motivating children is to let pupils know what they are expected to learn; deliberate intention to learn is an effective aid to learning. Second, ego involvement aids learning: every pupil needs to experience some degree of success and social approval. Third, frequent testing is sometimes used as a motivational technique: although this is a somewhat questionable technique, especially at the elementary level, many teachers believe that it motivates pupils to study harder and acquire more knowledge. Fourth, knowledge of results, or of one's performance rating: this may build up favorable attitudes toward improvement.

Within each individual are certain basic needs and drives that, when properly channeled, motivate him toward acceptable goals. Included among these are the need for physical security and freedom from fear; for self-sufficiency and independence, personal improvement and competition with self and others; for group status; for personal satisfaction from accomplishment; for pride and self-esteem; and for emotional release. As a key person in the teaching-learning situation, the teacher must understand the needs of children and help them to satisfy these needs.

The learning environment, of course, centers in the classroom. Obviously, it should be attractive and orderly, with proper lighting, ventilation, seating, and appurtenances needed in, or conducive to, the teaching-learning act. In evidence should be attractive bulletin boards; points of interest such as science tables and reading corners; listening centers where pupils can use phonographs, radios, and television equipment; individual study areas; and ample quantities of books, supplies, and other materials. These physical attributes of the classroom are, however, important only to the extent that they facilitate amiable interpersonal relationships and keep lines of communication open to members of the group, that they help the group develop a sense of responsibility, and that they stimulate achievement motivation.

The Ordinalist Concept of Human Development: Jean Piaget

The *normative* concept of human development—that associated with the name of Arnold Gesell and proposing that there are specific age-related achievements (a child at age A should be able to perform task B)—is currently giving way among educators to the *ordinalist* ideas. The ordinalist holds that there is an inherent, invariant sequence of behaviors preliminary to any developmental objective, and that it is the teacher's task to determine where on the developmental continuum the child is presently functioning and to proceed from there to the predetermined goal. That a child is below or above a certain "norm" is not implied in the ordinalist's concept. If teachers subscribe to the idea that human growth and development are not tied to time—yet are invariant and sequential—they may understand that a child's malfunction may be the result of his deprived environment and set about to provide him with experiences which would establish, or reestablish, the central processes appropriate to the tasks that children should perform. This is an especially important concept to teachers of disadvantaged youngsters.

Jean Piaget, a Swiss natural scientist turned educational psychologist, has given impetus to the new emphasis on ordinal concepts of growth and development; his impact on education in the United States has been increasingly potent in the past few years. His work in Europe on human development and the origins of behavior was with James Mark Baldwin, an American psychologist; Jerome Bruner of Harvard University has also made contributions to the newer concepts. Since 1929 Piaget has been associated with the Institut J. J. Rousseau, a teacher-training institution, and in 1932 he was made codirector, a position he continues to hold at this writing (November, 1969). Piaget's most influential book is *La psychologie de l'intelligence,* published in Paris in 1947 and reprinted in 1966; in 1950, Malcolm Piercy and Daniel E. Berlyne published an English translation of the book under the title *Psychology of Intelligence.* In his writings, Piaget has recorded observations of the intelligent behavior of his own young offspring. The reason for the span of time between Piaget's early work and its impact in this country is said to be the zeitgeist of schools of psychology here and in Europe.

The two areas of principal concern in Piaget's psychological theory are "the structure and operations of intelligent behavior" and "the sequential stages of development"—the two separated only for academic convenience.[7] The continual or sequential nature of human growth as present throughout the developmental phenomena, from conception until death, is an underlying assumption of the theory. A human being's progress along his unique continuum is identifiable by his manifested behaviors, which serve as specific points in the developmental cycle.

Piaget's operational theory of the development of intelligent behavior

[7] See T. Rowland and C. McGuire, "The Development of Intelligent Behavior, I: Jean Piaget," *Psychology in the Schools* 5 (1968): 47–52.

holds that such development is the result of an organism's interactions with its environment and also its operation on its environment. To understand that evolution of intellectual operations is complex, mobile, reversible, and unlimited except by the individual operator and the social genetic processes of the operations is to understand the basic problem of the development of intelligent behavior.

Although teachers have long subscribed to the theory of working with and accepting the "whole child" as he is, nevertheless they have not always put this into practice. Piaget's idea would force the teacher to become, in addition to a good practitioner of methodology, a keen observer of children and to plan activities that would move them toward advanced stages of development. Each classroom learning activity has as its objective a global intelligent behavior on the part of pupils—but each behavior is structured and organized of lower-level behaviors, each with its own purpose, integrity, and consistency. In order to achieve that global behavior, students must master those lower-level behaviors that contribute to the ultimate objective.

According to Piaget, the reason for cognitive organization is the learner's need to be in a state of "dynamic equilibrium," a state in which a learning organism is most comfortable while operating at peak efficiency. In the classroom, the group of pupils operates best when pupil behaviors are not disruptive, when there is mutual cooperation, and when pupils are responsive.

A basic function of a behaving organism—seemingly related to survival —is adaptation, says Piaget. This is defined as a balance between assimilation and accommodation, the processes that compose learning, resulting in adjustment to the environment. Piaget says that assimilation is "the action of the organism on surrounding objects, in so far as this action depends on previous behavior involving the same or similar objects." The function is assimilatory so long as a continuous or unified relationship exists between the organism and the object; there is no need for the organism to initiate accommodatory behavior. The converse of assimilation is accommodation, in which the environmental stimuli promote changes in the organism's assimilatory network. If pupils in a class are more rather than less familiar with material being presented by the teacher, little adaptation will be necessary. But where new material is introduced, new learning must prevail; a mature organism will accommodate only proportionately to the increase in complexity of the environment. A simple example of assimilation may be seen in the instance of a child who, when he learns to open a door, has to manipulate the knob or handle, determine whether the door should be pulled or pushed, and decide what the door weighs. When he learns these things in a right way, thus assimilating the experience of door opening, he establishes a pattern of behavior Piaget calls a *schema* —something that can be repeated and generalized. This original schema, though, will have to be modified when the child encounters different kinds of doors with different kinds of handles or knobs, with different inward or outward manners of opening, or with different weights. Whenever new experiences are met with, modifications will be needed: the result is accommodation. The processes of assimilation and accommodation begin at conception and continue throughout life.

Piaget discusses recurrent patterns in development—similar cognitive structures occurring at different times across the ontogenetic span—and refers to them as vertical and horizontal *decalages*. Vertical decalages involve different cognitive functions that may be used by a person on identical subject matter at different levels of achieving. An example might be the case of a child in the classroom who has a successful sensory-motor experience but who, at the same point in his development, cannot represent that same experience symbolically.

Horizontal decalages probably have more significance for the classroom practitioner, as they are more closely related to the transfer of training for which every teacher strives. Piaget defines the horizontal decalage as "the application of familiar schemata to new situations"; in short, children— even those still in the crib—use, and should be encouraged to use, what they already know when facing new situations. It is this concept that is the basis of the new methodological approaches, discovery learning or the inquiry approach, discussed earlier in this chapter.

Four stages of development as categorized by Piaget and his disciplines are: (1) the sensory-motor stage, (2) the preoperational stage, (3) the stage of concrete operations, and (4) the stage of formal or hypothetico-deductive operations. Each stage sees the elaboration of new mental abilities that set the limits and determine the character of what can be learned during that period.

The sensory-motor stage (generally from conception to age two) involves the evolution of abilities needed to construct and reconstruct objects. The preoperational stage (ages two to seven, roughly) is that of elaboration of the symbolic function and those abilities needed in the gradual acquisition of language skills, symbolic play, and graphic representation and drawing. In the stage of concrete operations (about ages seven to eleven), the child acquires internalized actions permitting him to "do in his head" what he previously would have to accomplish through real actions. At this stage the youngster is enabled to think about things and deal with relations among classes of things. During the fourth stage, that of formal or hypothetico-deductive operations (ages twelve to fifteen, usually), adolescents begin to think about their thoughts, construct ideals, and consider the future realistically. They reason about contrary-to-fact propositions; they can understand metaphor.

Following the final stage, no new mental systems emerge, but mental growth is presumably translated into a gradual increase in wisdom.

Evaluation and Testing

The emphasis in this chapter has been on learning and the learners. The newer approaches to explaining how pupils learn—including a consideration of their motivation, values, and unique perceptions—make clear the fact that evaluation is involved in all learning. It seems pertinent, then, that some consideration be given at this juncture to the problem of testing, measurement, or, better, evaluation, since it is so closely allied with the teaching-learning act. The feedback that good teachers get from effective evaluation controls their next steps in providing learning experiences for their classroom charges. As a matter of fact, evaluation is a special variety of feedback organized by effective elementary, secondary, or higher schools.

Most evaluation in a school is half-intuitive and informal, but the part of the evaluative process that "shows" the most is a system of testing or examining. Real evaluation, or course, means more than just testing or measuring: it is a process with qualitative and introspective features in which pupils have an opportunity to reflect on their own experiences for whatever meaning they may discover. It involves relative features of pupils' experiences; it considers all elements of their milieu. It includes self-appraisal and recapitulation of experiences and utilizes, besides tests, such techniques as parent-teacher conferences, counseling, guidance, and case studies. It involves, in addition to judgments of proficiency in subject matter and skills, appraisals in such areas as healthy attitudes, changes in behavior, growth in emotional maturity, understanding of and concern for other persons, and social skills. All of these areas, and others, are included in a good school evaluation program.

While the testing aspect of a school's evaluation program may not be the most important one, still it is true that most teachers feel they must measure what they teach. And they do this principally through standardized and teacher-made instruments. In fact, probably never in history has there been a teacher who has not felt that he must test his charges in the material he has taught. Tests are necessary so that teachers and pupils may get their bearings and determine the direction in which they are moving. The big question remaining, however, is what to test. Adequate evaluation is no longer simply a matter of examining the students' mastery of subject matter, since broader school objectives have affected changes in the school's curriculum and, subsequently, the methods of appraising outcomes. Hence, we have seen in the past three-quarters of a century the development of not only sophisticated instruments for the measurement of achievement but also many tests for the measurement of human aptitude, interest, and personality traits. With the emphasis on scientific means of measurement has come increased attention to problems of establishing the validity and reliability of the measuring instruments as well as of defining objectives and discerning criteria. Teachers, then, should have an understanding of the various techniques of measurement available to them, and they should know which to choose for particular purposes and how to interpret results.

Achievement tests.   In the areas of assessing pupil achievement, in addition to the use of such informal means as watching performances in class, listening to recitations, and grading homework, teachers also utilize the more formal teacher-made or published standardized tests. While the teacher-made instruments are most widely used as procedures for assessing achievement, teachers themselves would be the first to admit that they usually leave a great deal to be desired. Good published tests are valuable for some assessment purposes.

Aptitude tests.   Pupil aptitude is important to teachers as they plan for learning activities in their classrooms. Here, again, much information regarding aptitude is obtained by teachers as they observe the work of pupils in class and as they check on past performances in certain subjects. But there are good aptitude tests available to teachers that may be more valid sources of information than are informal means.

A popular aptitude instrument is the general intelligence test, which is usually given at several selected stages in the pupils' progress through the school. Scores from such tests can be helpful to teachers and other school personnel provided they are very carefully used and interpreted. It is probably best for teachers to consider an intelligence-test score as just another indicator of a pupil's aptitude for learning.

In addition to the general intelligence test, teachers also have available certain instruments designed to measure aptitude for specific subjects or vocations. A special type of aptitude test is the reading-readiness test, commonly used in early elementary grades and designed to assess a pupil's aptitude for beginning formal instruction. Other tests of this ilk are available also in areas such as arithmetic and writing. Subject- or vocational-aptitude test scores may be considered as being of some assistance in deciding whether to pursue certain courses or vocations.

An interesting situation regarding aptitude tests presents itself to those practitioners who accept the "new" definition of aptitude as the amount of time required by a learner to master a learning task, as proposed by such modern psychologists as John Carroll and B. S. Bloom. Note that no reference to "ability" is made in this definition.

Interest tests. Since good teachers attach a great deal of importance to capitalizing on pupils' interests in planning for learning activities, it is important that they have some means at their disposal to ascertain the real interests. Informally, the teacher may use free art, free composition, or other techniques to determine these interests. In addition, there are published tests that may be of some help in making such determinations, though they should not be considered as the sole, final, absolute measure of pupils' interests. Interpretation of interest-test results usually requires the assistance of guidance and counseling personnel or of one with special training in test interpretation.

Personality tests. Personality tests, published under a number of different titles and purporting to measure areas such as values, attitudes, personality, preferences, and temperament, are available. These, however, should definitely be administered and interpreted by trained clinical psychologists, who may then confer with teachers regarding personality problems.

Most schools of education or departments of psychology in colleges and universities offer courses in tests and measurements. It would be well for all teacher candidates and those already in service to take at least one such course so that they will have a better understanding of how to construct and administer their own tests and how to interpret the results of the vast number of published tests at their disposal.

Teachers in training should be advised that a national assessment-of-education program, initially intended to provide information on the current status of knowledge, is under way in the United States. The national program seeks to obtain objective information on how much Americans learn, both in school and from the many other sources of education open to them. The examinations will be given in schools and will cover the subjects taught. The fifty states will be covered through four regions—Northeast, Southeast, Central, and West—and no comparisons of scores will be made on a unit smaller than the region.

Conclusion

There are a number of theories on how learning takes place, none of which a teacher needs to adopt in its entirety. It is important, however, for a teacher to study the psychological propositions that receive general agreement and, after research and experimentation on his own part as well, arrive at some sound conclusions regarding methodology in the classroom. Problem-solving and discovery methods, when approached from the standpoint of teaching learners how to learn, offer some promising procedures that may help students face the important problems of the time when they will be living as adults in a precarious world.

At the same time, teachers should consider a number of possible limitations if they are thinking of building a lesson entirely on children's questions. The inquiry or unguided-discovery approach is effective only if the process results in better-informed or more capable students. It is difficult for youngsters to ask questions about something with which they have little or no acquaintance or experience. They also need time to grow in the process of framing good questions. Too, the teacher needs to recognize the constant "hand waver" and know whether or not his contributions or questions represent the majority of the class members. The teacher may also wish subtly to "direct" the trend of the questions by inserting some of his own among those of the class members; occasionally he may propose, "Have you ever considered . . . ?" Discovery in their own experimentation often causes some of the best questions to evolve from children and youth themselves.

Children's interests can be overemphasized and underdeveloped; there is little or no time for nonsense in the school program, and interests oftentimes are really only passing whimsies that need direction by the teacher.

Questions for Discussion

1. Do you agree with the idea that if a teacher has done an effective job, the range of differences in achievement among the pupils in his classroom will be wider at the end of the year than it was at the beginning? What is the rationale behind this idea?

2. In what ways do modern teaching machines implement the well-known laws of learning?

3. Why is it necessary for the teacher to have more knowledge of subject matter when teacher-pupil planning is employed than when it is not? When would be the appropriate times for a teacher to use teacher-pupil planning?

4. What is the relationship between the problem-solving approach and the reflective-thinking approach to learning? How would you justify the claim of some authorities in education that the only way people learn is by the scientific problem-solving method?

5. It is generally accepted that, broadly, learning means change in behavior. In what ways does learning new words in reading, new axioms in mathematics, or new concepts in physics change one's behavior?

6. What is the teacher's real responsibility with respect to children's learning?

7. Support or refute the idea that nothing is so constant as change.

8. What is meant by the statement that until a satisfactory theory of learning evolves, teachers will have to depend upon the "lore" of teaching?

9. Explain what you conceive as the relationship between aspects of Piaget's psychology and the concept of readiness expressed by Jerome Bruner in his *Process of Education:* "We begin with the hypothesis that any subject can be taught effectively in some intellectually honest form to any child at any stage of development." (This opening statement of Bruner's book became the most quoted single sentence in the educational literature of the decade of the 1960's.)

10. What advice could you give to parents who want to "help" their children with schoolwork in the evenings and during the summer recess?

Activities and Projects

1. Visit a fifth-grade elementary-school classroom after first making arrangements with the principal and a teacher to do so. Notice the difference in physical appearance of the children, making notes of these differences. No names need be involved. If convenient and permissible, have the teacher tell you about the differences in mental abilities and achievement of the children in the class, again omitting all references to personalities. Note the wide range and discuss it in your class, trying to arrive at some ideas as to how individual differences found in the elementary classroom in only one area—that of the social studies, for example—might be provided for.

2. Arrange with the professor of your class to allow you to pursue the teacher-student planning procedure with your classmates, with you serving as the teacher. Plan with them as though you were in a high-school history class, and use as a unit topic "The Post–Civil War Era." Using the steps listed in chapter 3 under the topic "Student-Teacher Planning" (pages 73–74), go through the actual planning procedure.

3. Assume you are the science teacher in a junior high school, and you are studying the subject of air. The problem has arisen of why the length of the trombone's slide determines the varying tones of the instrument. With you serving as teacher and your classmates as students, proceed through the steps of the problem-solving process as outlined in this chapter.

4. Practice the reflective-thinking process by asking your classmates to read silently with you any paragraph in this chapter. Then ask each one to comment on any concept or concepts he obtained from the paragraph, or any sentence in the paragraph. Encourage everyone to contribute, in his own words, what he learned from his reading; encourage, too, those students who did not learn the same concepts to express their ideas. Motivate the discussion to continue until some definite concepts are agreed upon by the class.

5. Attend a class session in an elementary or secondary school in which television or teaching machines are being used in the teaching-learning situation. Note the role of the teacher, and try to determine what new skills are needed on his part. How does this situation differ in class organization from a typical one?

6. Compare some textbooks used in today's schools with some used in the nineteenth century (these are usually available in the education library of your college). What are some of the outstanding differences? How do you account for these differences? What inferences can you make with respect to differences in authors' conceptions of pupil motivation and arrangement of environment?

7. In psychological journals or in abstracts of doctoral dissertations in your college library, look up several studies that attempt to determine the amount of subject matter retained by elementary or high-school pupils after they have completed certain courses. How do you account for the "forgetting" rate?

8. Arrange to visit for a half-day in an elementary or secondary-school classroom. Can you pretty well tell what the teacher's philosophy of education is? Upon what do you base your answer?

References

Learning and Programmed Learning

"Are Schools Changing Too Much Too Fast?" *Changing Times,* September 1966, pp. 6–10.

BRICKMAN, WILLIAM W., and STANLEY LEHRER, eds. *Automation, Education, and Human Values.* New York: School and Society Books, 1966.

BROWN, B. FRANK. "The Non-Graded High School." *Phi Delta Kappan,* February 1963, pp. 206–9.

BRUNER, JEROME S. *The Process of Education.* Cambridge, Mass.: Harvard University Press, 1961. Chap. 6.

BUSHNELL, D. D., and DWIGHT W. ALLEN, eds. *The Computer in American Education.* New York: Wiley, 1967.

CAMPBELL, COLIN. "A Comment on Whether Teaching Implies Learning." *Harvard Educational Review* 35 (Winter 1965): 82–83.

COLE, LUELLA, and IRMA NELSON HALL. *Psychology of Adolescence.* 6th ed. New York: Holt, Rinehart & Winston, 1964.

DEYOUNG, CHRIS, and RICHARD WYNN. *American Education.* New York: McGraw-Hill, 1968. Pt. 5.

FRAZIER, ALEXANDER, ed. *A Curriculum for Children.* Washington, D.C.: Association for Supervision and Curriculum Development of the National Education Association, 1969.

FROST, JOE L., and G. THOMAS ROWLAND. *Curricula for the Seventies.* Boston: Houghton Mifflin, 1969. Chap. 3.

FURTH, HANS G. *Piaget for Teachers.* Englewood Cliffs, N.J.: Prentice-Hall, 1970.

GLACER, ROBERT, ed. *Teaching Machines and Programmed Learning.* Washington, D.C.: National Education Association, 1965.

HANNA, LAVONE A., GLADYS L. POTTER, and NEVA HAGAMAN. *Unit Teaching in the Elementary School.* New York: Holt, Rinehart & Winston, 1963. Chap. 2.

HASKEW, LAURENCE D., and JONATHON C. MCLENDON. *This Is Teaching.* 3d ed. Glenview, Ill.: Scott, Foresman, 1968. Chaps. 2, 3.

HILL, WINFRED F. *Learning: A Survey of Psychological Interpretation.* San Francisco: Chandler, 1963.

KOMISAR, R., and J. MACMILLAN, eds. *Psychological Concepts in Education.* Chicago: Rand McNally, 1968.

MEIERHENRY, W. C. "Implications of Learning Theory for Instructional Technology." *Phi Delta Kappan,* May 1965, pp. 435–38.

MISNER, PAUL J., FREDERICK W. SCHNEIDER, and LOWELL G. KEITH. *Elementary School Administration*. Columbus, Ohio: C. E. Merrill, 1963. Chap. 5.

NATIONAL EDUCATION ASSOCIATION. *Perceiving, Behaving, Becoming: A New Focus for Education*. Washington, D.C.: Association for Supervision and Curriculum Development of the National Education Association, 1962.

PIAGET, J. *The Origins of Intelligence in Children*. New York: International University Press, 1952.

————. *Psychology of Intelligence*. Translated by Malcolm Piercy and Daniel E. Berlyne. London: Routledge & Kegan Paul, 1950; Totowa, N.J.: Littlefield, ILP Paperback no. 222, 1966.

RICHEY, ROBERT W. *Planning for Teaching*. 4th ed. New York: McGraw-Hill, 1968. Pp. 183–89, 199–200.

ROBINSON, LLOYD E. *Human Growth and Development*. Columbus, Ohio: C. E. Merrill, 1968. Chap. 10.

ROUCEK, JOSEPH S., ed. *Programmed Teaching*. New York: Philosophical Library, 1965.

SHUMSKY, ABRAHAM. *In Search of Teaching Style*. New York: Appleton, 1968. Chap. 6; pp. 149–50.

STOLUROW, LAWRENCE. *Teaching by Machine*. Washington, D.C.: U.S. Department of Health, Education, and Welfare, 1961.

THOMAS, C. A., I. K. DAVIES, D. OPENSHAW, and J. B. BIRD. *Programmed Learnings in Perspective*. Chicago: Aldine, 1965.

Problem Solving, Inquiry, and Discovery

BLACKIE, JOHN. "How Children Learn." *NEA Journal,* February 1968, pp. 40–42.

BRUNER, JEROME S. "The Act of Discovery." *Harvard Educational Review* 31 (Winter 1961): 21–32.

————. "Structures in Learning." *NEA Journal,* March 1963, p. 26.

DAWSON, KENNETH E., and MORRIS NORFLEET. "The Computer and the Student." *NEA Journal,* February 1968, pp. 47–48.

ENNIS, ROBERT H. *Logic in Learning*. Englewood Cliffs, N.J.: Prentice-Hall, 1969.

FENTON, EDWIN. *Teaching the New Social Studies: An Inductive Approach*. New York: Holt, Rinehart & Winston, 1966.

GOLDMARK, BERNICE. *Social Studies: A Method of Inquiry*. Belmont, Calif.: Wadsworth, 1968. Chap. 7; pp. 19–20, 43.

GUILFORD, J. P. "Creative Thinking and Problem Solving." *California Teachers Association Journal* 60 (January 1964): 9–10.

HANNA, LAVONE A., GLADYS L. POTTER, and NEVA HAGAMAN. *Unit Teaching in the Elementary School.* New York: Holt, Rinehart & Winston, 1963. Chap. 8.

HASKEW, LAURENCE D., and JONATHON C. MCLENDON. *This Is Teaching.* 3d ed. Glenview, Ill.: Scott, Foresman, 1968. Pp. 321–23.

MASSIALAS, BYRON G., and C. BENJAMIN COX. *Inquiry in Social Studies.* New York: McGraw-Hill, 1966.

RICHEY, ROBERT W. *Planning for Teaching.* 4th ed. New York: McGraw-Hill, 1968. Pp. 188–89, 528–89.

SHUMSKY, ABRAHAM. *In Search of Teaching Style.* New York: Appleton, 1968. Pp. 53–60, 229–31.

STROM, ROBERT D. *Psychology for the Classroom.* Englewood Cliffs, N.J.: Prentice-Hall, 1969.

SUCHMAN, J. R. "The Child and the Inquiry Process." In *Intellectual Development: Another Look,* ed. A. Harry Passow and Robert R. Leeper. Washington, D.C.: Association for Supervision and Curriculum Development of the National Education Association, 1964. Pp. 59–74.

Intelligent teaching requires an understanding of individual children, their potentialities, their interests and aspirations, their problems and difficulties, and their sources of strength.

RALPH W. TYLER

7

The Pupils as Boys and Girls

A review of the descriptions of the seven children found at the beginning of chapter 6 reveals that each is unique, each is different from each of the others. Even when children, like Mary and Bob, are at the same grade level—a situation in which we should expect to find some uniformity—we discover vast differences between them. There have never been two children alike, and there never will be. When this fact is considered along with the fact that there are hundreds of thousands of children attending public and private schools in this country, with hundreds of thousands more to come, it is easy to see that teachers and administrators indeed have their problems in planning educational programs that will be applicable to each child. Variations exist among and between children in physique, chronological age, sex, achievement, intelligence and ability, nationality, interests, personality, and socioeconomic backgrounds, to name only a few.

Entire volumes have been written on individual differences among children. In this chapter, only a few of the more important considerations will be pointed out.

Pupil Differences

PHYSICAL DIFFERENCES

One of the most obvious differences among children is that of physique: height, weight, and proportion. If one were to line up along a wall all the children of any one grade level, he could not help but be amazed at the wide variations that exist, for children of both sexes and of all age groups.

Boys and girls remain about the same height until age eleven, when girls are usually taller than boys; however, by age fifteen, this trend reverses, boys showing averages higher than girls. Heights overlap from age to age: the tallest six-year-old youngsters are equal in height to the shortest eleven-year-olds, and the tallest eleven-year-old children are taller than the shortest eighteen-year-old youths. We find marked irregularities in rate of growth; that is, most youngsters apparently experience growth spurts and plateaus in development toward adulthood. The most rapid growth occurs during a child's preschool years: at age three a child has attained half his adult height. As he grows older, his growth rate decreases except for the adolescent growth spurt at ages thirteen to fifteen.

Wide ranges in weight for children at all ages are also in evidence. Occasionally, a six-year-old first-grader is heavier than a sixteen-year-old eleventh-grader. Children have usually attained half their adult weight at age twelve or thirteen. Whereas children reach their adult weight in the late teens or early twenties, it is obvious that weight may continue to increase until late adulthood.

A wide range of body build also exists among children at any age. Amount of fat and sturdiness of bones and muscles varies among boys and girls alike. The change in proportion as children grow older is almost endless. So long as weight stays within reasonable limits for a child's particular build, there is no cause for undue concern or anxiety.

CHRONOLOGICAL AGE DIFFERENCES

In a typical school district, a wide range in chronological ages naturally exists. Typically, kindergarteners begin to attend school at age five, though some districts operate nursery schools where the lowest age may be three or four. In the same district may be found high-school seniors at ages seventeen to nineteen, or students finishing junior college at ages eighteen and higher. Often there is considerable variation in chronological age at any given grade level, though the chronological age seems to be the most consistent criterion for grade placement in the public schools.

Sex Differences

While there are no significant differences, generally, in mental ability between boys and girls in school, there are some noticeable differences between them in other areas. For school-age children, the period of most rapid growth—between ages fourteen and fifteen for boys and between ages twelve and thirteen for girls—closely coincides with the beginning of sexual maturity. But the age range at the onset of sexual maturity also varies widely among individuals; there will probably be some girls in each grade between four and eleven who have reached sexual maturity, and some who have not. An equally wide range probably exists for boys.

If a boy and a girl have the same intelligence, the girl will usually do the better work. Girls like literature and lean toward love and "cute" stories, whereas boys generally prefer mathematics and mechanical studies and are more interested in adventure and danger stories.

Schools have generally not been aware of sex differences in establishing their educational programs; however, as teachers, supervisors, and administrators pursue their educational planning, they should consider some differences that are important. Waetjen has pointed to research indicating the following differences between boys and girls: boys burn up more oxygen than girls; they show higher I.Q. variations; up to age eight they do not use visual clues as well as girls; they can transfer their learnings better than girls; they perceive their environment more thoroughly, while girls are often misled by extraneous clues; nearly twice as many of them receive unsatisfactory marks, the sex of the teacher making no difference in the grades given; they are more analytical and do better work in mathematics and science; they are less dependent upon verbal methods of learning than girls, who do better work in the language arts.[1]

In the development of standards and motives for intellectual mastery, children at the tender age of six strive to maximize their similarities to whatever standards their schoolmates set for their sex; boys and girls favor those behaviors that they themselves define as feminine or masculine. They decide which behaviors are male or female by implicitly computing the ratio of males to females associated with a particular event: a lopsided ratio in one direction assigns the event to the sex role of the majority party. Interest in sports is masculine; reading and sewing—and school!—

---

[1] Walter B. Waetjen, address to the national meeting of the Association for Supervision and Curriculum Development, St. Louis, March 1963.

are feminine. School is included in the feminine category, probably because 90 percent of the teachers in elementary schools are women.

Several inferences can be made from these facts. One would bolster the arguments of the proponents of segregation of the sexes, particularly in the school's primary grades. In a sexually segregated classroom, each child might learn to maximize in the school experience the sex role appropriate to himself. A male teacher would have a strong impact on a boy. In a study of two midwestern high schools, sociologists discovered that boys who play in time-consuming sports such as football make better grades than nonathletes.

ACHIEVEMENT DIFFERENCES

There are striking individual differences among schoolchildren in measures of academic achievement. Children are found in grade four, for example, who on achievement tests may rate grade three in reading, grade five in arithmetic, and grade two in spelling. Or the differences may be much greater, in both individuals and groups. A child in grade four may rate grade seven in vocabulary, grade five in fundamental knowledge, grade six in fundamental operations, and grade four in problem solving. When a well-known reading-achievement test was administered recently to a group of freshmen entering an eastern university, it was found that the range of achievement spread from grade four to college graduate, with the median being grade ten. Some college students are unable to read as well as pupils leaving junior high school.

In actual situations, it has been found that the spread in the range of achievement increases as children progress through school. In classrooms the range should widen if the teacher is doing an acceptable job of guiding the learning of children. Interesting, too, is the fact that if the teacher expects the child to exhibit intellectual growth, the child will generally exhibit such growth!

INTELLIGENCE AND ABILITY DIFFERENCES

Mental-age differences among children in a single grade may total five or six years. Typically, mental ages ranging from twelve to sixteen will usually be found in a ninth-grade group, and from seven to eleven in a fourth-grade class. Students with I.Q.'s ranging from 80 to 130 may be found in a typical high-school freshman class; in primary grades in elementary schools, I.Q.'s may be as low as the 50's and 60's. Since the I.Q. is not a constant factor, but tends to become more stable as children grow older, it behooves teachers not to accept any quotient—particularly one obtained in the lower grades—as a measure of brightness throughout a child's elementary-school years. Since extrinsic or accidental factors may play a part in obtaining measures of intelligence, too much precision should not be attributed to the I.Q.; it is only one approximate index to a pupil's level of intelligence.

The results of I.Q. tests have become less absolute as additional limitations to the basic concept have become uncovered. They do not, for example, identify the bright youngsters who are very highly creative, and it is, of course, these youngsters who make direct contributions to cultural progress. In addition, I.Q. scores vary significantly for the same child: different tests can give different results. Also, I.Q.'s can be raised substantially with suitable treatment techniques.

Conventional I.Q. tests have changed considerably since Alfred Binet, a famed French psychologist, devised the first intelligence test in 1905. The early tests depended heavily upon recognition of words and grasping relationships between words, and most tests still do; but some have expanded to include nonverbal skills. Early test results were supposed to have revealed something "fixed," since I.Q. scores tend to remain stable during a person's lifetime. But recently psychologists and educators have been viewing I.Q. as the joint product of an individual's genetic makeup and his personal experiences.

Nationality Differences

Among boys and girls of different racial origins, the differences in learning capacity and character development are not significant; but they are significant with respect to such environmental aspects as interests, attitudes, and language abilities.

Several years ago, the public school systems of both New York and Washington, D.C., dropped the use of group I.Q. tests because of complaints that the tests were biased in favor of white middle-class youngsters. The controversy over I.Q. tests was renewed during the late 1960's with an article in the *Harvard Educational Review* by Arthur R. Jensen, an educational psychologist at the University of California, Berkeley, which argued that, judged by the results of I.Q. tests, black pupils may be intellectually inferior to white youngsters in some respects. Unlike most educators, Mr. Jensen avers that genetic factors are strongly implicated in the average Negro-white intelligence difference. Opponents of the genetic point of view contend that the results of I.Q. tests indicate skills children acquire in the society, which lower-class children, regardless of their national origin, do not get. Recently in Los Angeles, Mexican-American youngsters' I.Q.'s were raised when they were retested in the Spanish language. Recent studies have indicated that low I.Q. scores among ghetto children are to some extent traceable to vitamin deficiencies during the prenatal period. There is some evidence, also, that minority-group children are somewhat inhibited when being tested by a white person. It seems clear that an I.Q. score does not reveal what a youngster is capable of if his cultural setting could be enriched.

> Having gone through some turbulent stages,
> I have a conviction that's flat:
> A youngster's most difficult stage is
> Wherever he's presently at!
>
> ANONYMOUS

INTEREST DIFFERENCES

It has been said that all there is to teaching is meeting the needs and interests of children, or rather, helping them meet their needs and interests. Perhaps teaching is more than that, but the statement nevertheless points up the significant role of interests in the teaching-learning situation. They are of paramount importance in planning for teaching.

Teachers are constantly changing their approaches because children's interests are so variable; and as children mature, their interests widen and change. What may appear a real interest today will tomorrow turn out to be only a passing whimsy. Alert teachers are, however, able to detect a thread of consistency in children's interests as they observe their work over a period of time. School personnel have at their disposal interest inventories, which are helpful in determining pupils' real interests.

All Must Be Educated

The descriptions of the pupils at the beginning of the previous chapter and the discussion of individual differences above serve to point up the tremendous responsibilities of teachers and other school personnel as they set about to help each child progress through school. As indicated earlier, these children are in the schools *now,* and dedicated professional workers all over the nation strive every day to help them meet their needs and prepare to become responsible citizens in our democratic society. In keeping with the spirit of the Educational Policies Commission's theme, we must seek to see that all the children of all the people become educated.

TEACHING THE AVERAGE PUPIL

The superintendent and staff of a large Illinois elementary-school district, after hearing so many parents relate that theirs were "superior" children, decided to find out how many "average" pupils were in the district. The entire student body of the district, numbering over ten thousand, were tested against carefully drawn-up criteria to measure their "averageness." When the data were all in and tabulated, a total of only *one* pupil met the criteria for being of average ability. This true incident illustrates the fact that there really are no "average" pupils in a school, despite the fact that teachers have been accused of teaching "to the average" of their classes.

What is probably meant by the assertion that teachers teach to pupils of average ability is that teachers tend to teach a general diffusion of knowledge so that the largest possible number of pupils—the approximately 68 percent of children who fall within the statistical limitations of one standard deviation on either side of the mean—may benefit from the instruction. Granted such a trend is not ideal, because it results in neglect of pupils beyond the limitations suggested here; but it is natural for it to exist, and teachers need to be on constant guard against relating instruction principally toward this group. What is needed in American schools is quality education for all children, regardless of where they fall along the ability continuum.

In the light of the wide ranges of ability and achievement indicated previously, it is impossible to standardize instruction for students of average ability, because they simply do not exist. The idea of uniform mass instruction of homogeneous groups of children using single textbooks in the various subject areas fails to recognize the existence of individual differences in each classroom.

Grade levels do not actually indicate definite steps in academic achievement; course-work requirements at any grade level cannot be prescribed for all children. To retain children at a grade level for more than one year simply on the basis of their nonacademic achievement alone is a direct violation of the laws of learning and of child growth and development. The idea that if teachers do a good job of taking care of individual differences, all children in the class will be brought up to a certain predetermined standard, is ridiculous; in fact, as stated earlier, good teaching results in widening the range of achievement within a group and in increasing the heterogeneity of groups. The problem of meeting "average" pupil needs is the same as that of meeting superior pupil needs: how can we best meet the needs of all children and youth in classes of widely varying capabilities?

Knowing how children can best meet their needs requires that teachers know what these needs are. Certainly a teacher can more readily discover the needs of children if the number in the class is kept within reason. The optimum pupil-teacher ratio recommended by the Association for Supervision and Curriculum Development at a recent national convention (20 to 1 for both elementary and secondary schools) would facilitate teachers' efforts to gain knowledge about their pupils and help them meet their needs. A testing program that would indicate status and growth of pupils in the academic areas necessary for living in our culture would also help teachers in these efforts. Such a testing program would enable the teacher to know better the books pupils are able to read and the kinds of problems they are able to solve. The practice of elementary teachers' remaining with the same group of youngsters for as many as three years provides further opportunity for them to become acquainted with the needs of pupils.

TEACHING THE SLOW LEARNER AND THE HANDICAPPED

There are many children attending America's public schools who deviate from the normal in ability, intelligence, physique, or socioeconomic background to such an extent that special-education programs must be provided for them if we are to educate all the children of all the people to the optimum of their capacities. While all children have the same basic needs, it is more difficult for maladjusted and handicapped children to meet their needs than for the more normal boys and girls to do so. All children, regardless of the condition of their minds and bodies, should be considered as individuals who can make contributions to democratic group living; all must learn to live in the culture in which they find themselves. Thus in their curricula many schools in the nation include programs for mentally retarded, physically handicapped, emotionally disturbed, and disadvantaged children who live in their districts.

Causes of retardation are legion. Children who do not make progress in school subjects may be mentally retarded, physically incapacitated, emotionally or socially disturbed, or disadvantaged because of a low socioeconomic environment. Teachers may find children whose intelligence measures well below the 90–100 I.Q. range considered by most authorities to be "normal." Rarely, however, will a teacher find a pupil in public-school classrooms whose I.Q. is below 50. There are also children in the public schools who have orthopedic, heart, hearing, sight, speech, and certain other types of physical defects. Occasionally teachers encounter children in their classes who are psychotic, nervous, retiring, or socially negative or who have problems of truancy, incorrigibility, or delinquency. Chiefly in the core sections of the nation's largest cities, teachers may find pupils under their tutelage who live with the barest of necessities in a totally inadequate home and neighborhood environment.

Tantamount to an educational program for the maladjusted and handicapped is a proper philosophy, or attitude, regarding these children on the part of teachers, administrators, parents, and children; sympathetic understanding of the special problems of maladjusted and handicapped children must be developed. These boys and girls must be afforded opportunities to develop good work habits, dependability, adequate body and eating habits, and attributes of good citizenship, as well as opportunities to develop their intellectual capacities. If possible, maladjusted and handicapped children need to be integrated into activity classes in art, physical education, and music, at least for certain periods of time, so that they may learn to get along with others—a skill they will use all their lives.

In many communities in the nation, slow-learning and handicapped children have opportunities to attend special-education programs in which the school tries to adjust its offerings so that their abilities can be developed to the maximum. Such programs attempt to provide handicapped boys and girls with a broad basic education and with opportunities to develop certain skills, habits, and attitudes so that they can adjust to society to the best of their abilities.

Some school districts provide special-education programs in segregated classes or special schools where children may be free from academic competition and may pursue individual problems at their own rate. In such an environment, too, children may be free from the stigma that sometimes exists in a regular school or classroom situation. Opponents of the segregation plan, on the other hand, maintain that children often revolt against the isolation and distinction of special classes, that teachers sometimes feel less responsibility for handicapped children and thus stress academic subject matter rather than social development, and that such a plan tends to accentuate problems of behavior in an environment where exemplary behavior is the predominant need.

Special requirements for teachers in special-education classes have been set by more than half the states: some require an advanced graduate degree, and most require some teaching experience. Needless to say, effective teachers in such classes need a large amount of enthusiasm, a maximum degree of patience and understanding, and an exceptional ability to motivate children. They should approach special-education classes from the aspect more of practicability than academic emphasis.

Teaching the Superior Student

Although professional educators and lay individuals have long recognized a need to educate mentally superior children in ways different from those used for "normal" children, only in the past twenty years has much been actually accomplished in this respect. Because mentally superior children have been able to make progress pretty much on their own, teachers have been inclined to neglect them to the point that they have often been satisfied with a level of achievement considerably below their capabilities.

While many schools accept for classes for the mentally superior any child who is gifted in some particular ability, most educational institutions accept favorable teacher observations and an I.Q. score of 110 or above as the most objective criteria for a pupil's participation. Whatever the method of selection, an important part of a school's program is its screening procedure. Studies have revealed that mentally superior children are generally superior in most other aspects also; they are well adjusted socially and are above average in physical health. Often they show unusual insight and possess remarkable ability to apply their learning to other situations.

While the literature and observations do not indicate the existence of any typical program for the education of mentally superior children— undoubtedly because of widely varying philosophies among teachers, administrators, and lay persons—there are generally three types of plans provided by schools for these children and youth: enrichment, acceleration, and special classes. None of these is considered the final answer, however.

In programs of enrichment, the regular classroom program is embellished to a point where the mentally superior children in the class are challenged at their level of achievement. Children of higher mental acuity often provide much of their own enrichment, but this should not be left to chance; teachers need to plan for stimulating and nurturing the cognitive abilities of these boys and girls. The school should provide opportunities for the mentally superior to utilize individual research skills or otherwise to expand and develop more deeply their special interests.

A much-publicized and highly successful program of enrichment is provided for the superior students in the Major Work–Honors program in the Cleveland, Ohio, public-school system. Originated in 1921, the program has grown to include Enrichment, Major Work, and Special Major Work classes at the elementary-school level; Major Work and Honors classes at the junior-high-school level; and Honors and Advanced Placement classes at the senior-high-school level. All of these classes are designed to challenge eligible students through a multidimensional teaching approach involving special curricula, enrichment, and acceleration of course content. As of early 1969, the program was effective in nine elementary-school Major Work centers, twenty-five elementary-school Enrichment centers, five junior-high-school Major Work–Honors centers, and five senior-high-school Honors centers. The curriculum for the Major Work–Honors and Advanced Placement classes differs from that for the regular school classes. Emphasis is placed on developing high levels of thinking, such as analysis, synthesis, application, and evaluation. The enrichment of this program is left to the discretion of the specially trained teachers in charge of the classes, with due consideration of the desires, needs, and interests of the pupils. Foreign languages, presently including French, German, and Russian, are offered to students in the Major Work and Enrichment classes.

Possibly the oldest, mechanically the simplest, and currently the most discouraged method of handling mentally superior youngsters is acceleration. Under this plan, children are usually provided for in one of three ways: they are advanced to higher grade levels than their chronological ages would normally allow, assigned more advanced subject matter for study, or allowed to enter school earlier than children of "normal" mental ability. In good schools, the social, emotional, and physical development of children is always considered before acceleration actually takes place. The acceleration plan calls for no differentiation of the school's curriculum. An exception, however, is the advanced-placement plan, whereby a superior secondary-school student can gain college credit and advanced placement by taking courses at the college level or passing a college-level course examination. This plan, of course, necessitates major changes in instructional procedures and curriculum content in the high school, as the program provides for special attention to superior students and encourages them to study independently, thus giving them an advanced start on their college work.

Special class groupings, or segregation, is the third technique commonly used by school districts in taking care of mentally superior students. If the district is sufficiently large, this controversial plan may include entire schools, or it may involve only certain classes meeting for an hour or so a week in enrichment-type assignments. Many school districts employ specially trained teachers to plan for these special classes. In New York City, four specialized schools are maintained for gifted high-school youngsters: Brooklyn Technical High School, the High School of Music and Art, the Bronx High School of Science, and Stuyvesant High School, each having its own philosophy, organizational structure, curriculum, and equipment centering around a specific purpose and each having a program designed to meet the superior student's special needs, interests, and abilities. Students are admitted on the basis of highly competitive examinations and interest in the area in which the school specializes.

RELATIONSHIP BETWEEN INTELLIGENCE AND CREATIVITY

With the technological advances of recent years has come a new interest in the identification and development of creativity. Recent studies have indicated that while highly creative persons are generally above average in intelligence, the relationship between intelligence and creativity is not clear-cut. Among some persons in creative groups, the correlation between intelligence and creativity has proved to be essentially zero.

Grouping the Pupils

Grouping in elementary and secondary schools in the United States has always been a matter of considerable concern, which today's demand for improved instruction and greater individualization has made even more pronounced. The problem of grouping has for many years been one of the most persistent of those challenging the ingenuity of the teacher and his professional cohorts.

Children in public-school classrooms are generally grouped according to chronological age, ability, maturity, or special characteristics. When children are grouped by chronological age, they are simply placed in a room with other pupils of their own age; this is currently the typical method of grouping. When grouped by ability, boys and girls are placed in a room with others of their approximate ability; when grouped by maturity, they are placed with children of the same estimated maturational level. Special-characteristic grouping refers to separate groupings of children with special interests or needs, as described previously in this chapter.

A number of elementary and secondary schools separate students according to ability into graded sections or groups within grades, these groups often being designated as H, X, Y, or Z. The H (honors) group contains pupils who are extremely bright or who have the ability to achieve in a superior manner; the X, Y, and Z groups consist of pupils whose achievement indicates that they are fast, average, or slow, respectively. Usually the curriculum of the school is modified to meet the needs of the pupils in each of the groups. Pupils in H groups pursue courses that not only meet the minimum requirements but also offer opportunities to do extremely advanced academic work; those in X groups take courses that meet minimum requirements and also include a great amount of work of an enriching nature; pupils in Y groups take courses that meet minimum requirements and provide for a moderate amount of enrichment; and those in Z sections take courses that provide the minimum essentials. Students may be transferred from one group to another at the beginning of a semester or at the initiation of a new unit of instruction if their progress is sufficient to merit such a transfer.

Further refinement in grouping children for instruction is accomplished in each classroom within the school. Teachers in graded schools organize many kinds of groups, such as ability groups, interest groups, and self-selection groups evolving, generally, from teacher-pupil planning of a unit about to be launched by the class. Primary-level teachers usually group children according to their abilities in reading or arithmetic or in both; three or four groups in a primary room usually mean three or four levels of ability evident in the class. In intermediate and upper grades, some ability grouping is still accomplished, although at these levels, teachers often find that other types of grouping result in more effective learning.

Ability grouping should be arranged subject by subject, so that groups may be as different as they need to be. When considering a group for one field or subject, the teacher should use as much objective data as possible: he should consider the pupils' previous achievement in the field as well as what aptitude and intelligence tests and the teacher's own judgment show are their potentialities. Flexibility in ability grouping will provide children with opportunities for moving from one group to another so that they may at times be leaders and at other times followers and at all times contributors. There may be considerable advantage to some children if they are assigned to longer-lasting groups; such children may need to have the feeling of security that comes from belonging to a more permanent group, or they may need to become involved in the processes of group dynamics applied to a single grouping.

Interest grouping has considerable merit in certain classroom undertakings. Children who are strongly motivated, who want to do a job well just because they want to, often amaze their teachers and their peers with what they accomplish. Teachers need to encourage this type of activity by appealing to pupils' real interests; these are often difficult to ascertain, but they can generally be spotted by watching children as they pursue their informal art and literature activities.

Unit teaching lends itself especially well to self-selection groupings, in which children in the pupil-teacher planning session virtually assign themselves to carry out certain aspects of the unit. The social studies and sciences are particularly fine springboards for units in which all subject areas may be correlated. The work is often accomplished by committees of pupils—some of whom are interested in bookish pursuits, some of whom have particular interest in national heroes or inventors, some of whom

The Creative Person

If . . . one were to attempt to give the briefest summary picture of a creative person, one might say that he appears to be distinguished, most generally, by two fundamental traits, one intellective, the other motivational or attitudinal: (a) an unusual capacity to record and retain and have readily available the experiences of his life history, and (b) the relative absence of repression and suppression as mechanisms for the control of impulse and imagery.

The first of these variables is what commonly goes under the name of intelligence, and the general finding of those who have studied highly creative persons is that, in the main, they are well above average on this dimension and often, indeed, are highly intelligent.

. . . . . .

As in the case of any intelligent person, the items of information which creative persons possess may readily enter into combinations, and the number of possible combinations is increased for such persons because of both a greater range of information and greater fluency of combination.

. . . . .

Yet intelligence alone, as we all too often observe, does not guarantee creativity. Intelligence as measured by an intelligence test must be distinguished from the effectiveness with which a person uses whatever intelligence he has. The effective use of intelligence depends in large measure upon the mechanisms of defense which an individual employs, and more specifically upon his eschewing the mechanisms of repression and suppression.

. . . The creative person, who characteristically does not suppress or repress, but rather expresses, has more available to him, his own unconscious, and thus has fuller access to his own experience.

. . . . .

Thus creative persons not only tend to think well of themselves, but also, more often than their less creative peers, they have the courage to recognize and to make public the less favorable aspects of their being. It would appear that their very good opinion of themselves makes them feel free to describe themselves frankly, critically, and in unusual ways.

Donald W. MacKinnon, "The Courage to Be: Realizing Creative Potential," in *Life Skills in School and Society,* Yearbook of the Association for Supervision and Curriculum Development (Washington, D.C.: Association for Supervision and Curriculum Development of the National Education Association, 1969), pp. 100–3. Reprinted by permission.

have special interest in art or music or mechanics, some of whom are good leaders, and some of whom are good followers. All may experience success by making contributions to the unit's culmination in pursuing the work of the group in which they have chosen membership. Often self-selection comes about because the pupils themselves recognize they have certain interests or needs.

Flexibility should be the key in whatever type of grouping is employed. While most grouping plans are undoubtedly used with the children's best interests in mind, too many of them overlook the uniqueness of each pupil. Flexible grouping is necessary if children are to be moved freely within the classroom so as to be placed among those who are working on projects that best fit their individual needs, interests, and level of maturity. Teachers who use flexible grouping procedures, who see wide ranges of differences among children at any grade level as normal and acceptable, and who know that learning is a different matter with each unique individual in the classroom and fit their instruction to him—such teachers are well on the way to success in the important work of guiding the learning activities of children.

Some of the newer types of school organization discussed in chapter 3 present interesting possibilities in the area of grouping. In the ungraded school, when a child is ready for the next level of achievement he is moved into a suitable group, regardless of the time of year. Both the dual-progress plan and team-teaching situations also provide opportunities for pupils to be members of large groups and small groups, and they present occasions for individual study or research.

Personality Differences in Children

It is a relatively easy matter to ascertain that there are vast personality differences in children and youth. When faced by identical problems or by the same type of frustrations, one child will react in one way while another will react in an entirely different way. Pupils who tend to be introverts, for example, attempt to adjust to their situations by rearranging their own ideas or by thinking the situations through, whereas those who have extrovert tendencies attempt to adjust by rearranging their environment.

Differences in personality seem to result from differences in the perceptual fields of individuals: that is, the way a person behaves will be a direct outgrowth of the way things seem to him at the moment of his behaving. If teachers are to help children improve their personalities, then, it would seem that they must first understand the nature of their pupils' perceptual fields and, second, provide for the kinds of experiences that will foster in the pupils the attainment of what Combs calls the four characteristics of the perceptual fields: a positive view of self, identification with others, acceptance of and openness to experience, and an abundance of information and understanding, which can be called on when needed and put into effective use.[2] Since effective learning experiences, among which are the mastery of symbol systems, problem solving, reasoning, and acquiring and organizing information, contribute to the fulfillment of these four characteristics, teachers must constantly be alert to and attempt to foster the close relationship that exists between learning and personality development.

While studies indicate that individual personalities do not vary a great deal, that they are fairly constant over the years, there are certain psychological authorities who maintain that the primary function of the schools is helping children and youth to develop healthy personalities. With society becoming increasingly affluent in the future, and most people realizing freedom from want, schools should concern themselves with the development of integrated personalities within their students. Thus the individual students, by relating successfully to one another, by analyzing past experiences and making inferences about future behavior, and by having a sufficient understanding of one another's being, might develop and maintain their own sense of identity so as to respond to life's situations according to their own interests, beliefs, and values.

As with other classroom activities, the responsibility for seeing that boys and girls participate in classroom functions without excessive external compulsion and that each has some degree of success falls to the teacher.

Social-Class Differences of Pupils

A glance into the classrooms of the public schools of America provides one with a cross-sectional view of the nation's children, boys and girls who vary as widely in their social backgrounds as in the aspects discussed previously in this chapter. Children from different social groups bring to school varying attitudes and learning patterns; at their graduation from school they will take away learning that they will use in widely varying ways.

Differences in social class are reflected in children's play interests and reading interests; children from higher groups play more varied games,

[2] Arthur W. Combs, "A Perceptual View of the Adequate Personality," in *Perceiving, Behaving, Becoming*, Yearbook of the Association for Supervision and Curriculum Development (Washington, D.C.: Association for Supervision and Curriculum Development of the National Education Association, 1962), chap. 5.

many of them adult-type intellectual games, and their reading materials include better books and periodicals. Upper-class children generally have richer vocabularies and wider ranges of experiences to verbalize. Middle-class children generally hold a high regard for success in language-arts experiences and have been taught that education holds the key to economic and social advancement. Children from lower socioeconomic backgrounds generally have lower standards of academic achievement and conduct than do their peers from higher social strata.

Other aspects of social-class differences will be considered in chapter 8.

The Demand for Conformity

The traditional educational system has motivated boys and girls to conform and to resist change, has centered on rote memorization of facts and figures that have been discovered or agreed upon, has emphasized the "right answer" type of problem-solving activity. Such a system has had small concern for developing pupil creativity; indeed, it has discouraged initiative and originality in students. There are teachers, even in traditional-school situations, who are well-meaning, who plan to give pupils opportunities for reflective thinking and original expression. But thinking and creativity are weak competitors against time and "the system," which insists that certain skills must be learned and certain basic information must be acquired *first*. In the traditional system, ready answers to any questions will be found in "the course."

Traditional-school personnel, most often well-meaning, have censored books, restricted discussion of critical and controversial topics, limited sharing of ideas, and imposed methodology that fosters strict discipline and rote learning. Some sophisticates have advocated that schools should concern themselves only with the universal and lasting truths, and that all else is trivia. Often teachers have been made to feel that they must teach children to ape the opinions of their elders.

Forces often operating against the school have sometimes driven teachers and administrators into neutral corners. Academicians, not classroom teachers, have often selected and organized knowledge for initiating pupils into the various fields of learning; teachers have had to come to depend on textbooks written by scholars in the various fields. Pupils have been forced to accept the written and spoken words of authorities and have been given little or no opportunity to reflect upon or question those words. Too many classrooms have been intimidated by the tyranny of the "one right answer." Sometimes the compulsion to keep the school running smoothly has forced teachers to a regimen in the areas of organization and methodology.

In too many instances, thinking, if it has been stimulated at all, has been of the convergent type.

It is not intended here to imply that everything done in traditional situations is bad; but it seems only too unfortunate that the utilization of newer ideas and techniques is so infrequently in evidence. If our democratic way of life is to be perpetuated, it will be because the citizens of America know how to think critically and reflectively. They must learn how to do this during their years in the classrooms of the nation. We need hold little fear for the future of our democracy if children learn in school to question the things they hear and read about, check the authority of the speaker or the author, arrive at answers only after consulting a number of different sources, and refuse to pass judgment until all the data have been collected and analyzed.

Hopes and Aspirations versus Realistic Expectations

The reader of this book who is looking forward to taking his place shortly as a teacher in a classroom is probably viewing the future with extremely optimistic anticipation. It has been the authors' observation, as they have taught college young people in their introductory or foundations courses in education, that at this point in their professional preparation students are a bit starry-eyed over the picture of themselves guiding the learning activities of public-school youngsters in the near future. It would be farthest from the writers' intention to dampen such eager aspirations; indeed, if they did not think teaching was among the finest of professions, they would not have remained associated with it for these many years. They agree that "a teacher affects eternity; he can never tell where his influence stops."

As teachers-to-be read this book and others, they will undoubtedly get the feeling that they understand and are ready to tackle what is involved in caring for individual differences in children, in motivating children, in helping children meet their needs, in involving children in pupil-teacher planning and in problem-solving processes, and in helping children develop healthy personalities and countenances adequate to confront the exigencies of modern society. If a student beginning the professional-education sequence of course work does not feel this way, he should probably reevaluate his objectives.

At the same time, it is important for prospective teachers to understand that it is much easier to read about the responsibilities and activities of teachers than actually to meet and carry them out. After all, when a teacher faces a group of twenty-five to thirty-five or more unique individuals each day in the actual classroom situation, the problem of motivating and arranging an environment for each child becomes a gargantuan task. Sometimes it seems an almost impossible assignment; sometimes it proves impossible even to get to know certain children during an entire year, much less to get them on their way toward meeting their needs. Sometimes it is "like pulling teeth" to motivate children to become involved in pupil-teacher planning and in problem-solving processes; sometimes a teacher feels that he is making progress backwards when today a child's responses indicate that he has unlearned everything that yesterday he had been "taught" so well. Often it is necessary for teachers to spend so much time and energy on the "5 percent"—the children with misbehavior problems —that they feel the day has been wasted as far as doing any real teaching is concerned. Most of the time teachers end the school day with spent energy, and often with spent temperaments. And many times it is necessary for teachers to return to the school for pupil or parent activities in the evening.

But this IS teaching! It would be unfair to prospective teachers if they were left with the opinion that teaching is a bowl of cherries, that the job is soft and free from frustrations, that it is always carried out in a pleasant and tension-free environment between the hours of 9 A.M. and 2:30 P.M., with all noon hours and vacations free from any concern for the classroom and its population. Good teachers fairly live their work, day and night and during free times. They are always concerned when Stevie isn't grasping reading as he should, or that Mary has missed so many sessions of geometry class; they lie awake nights wondering what is happening in Bobby's home tonight that will make him withdrawn and sleepy in the classroom tomorrow; they awaken early in the morning wondering how they can make American history live for thirty-five boys and girls in class today.

With persistence and consistent endeavor, however, teachers can expect to do an acceptable—in many cases, outstanding—job of guiding the learning of boys and girls in their classrooms. If the teacher maintains an alert and open mind, he will learn things from each class session that will prove helpful to him in all future classes. Soon he will find himself inspired when he sees children make progress, when he sees them learn because of something he has done or has caused to happen. In a short period of time, he will begin to see each class as the best he has ever had. He will then be well on his way toward becoming a successful practitioner.

Conclusion

In our changing society with its changing needs, it is becoming more evident by the day that nothing short of quality education is adequate for the very survival of our free way of life. With greater emphasis on quality than on quantity in education, attention in our schools is focused on individual differences, on challenging each child to achieve his fullest potential, on developing the creative abilities of youngsters, and on meeting the needs of our dynamic society. We are now concerned about teaching the child how to think, rather than what to think; how to solve problems he will meet, rather than ready-made problems provided by a textbook author or a teacher; how to become a self-actualizing, self-directing human being, who takes increasingly greater responsibility for his own education.

Relentless and continuous experimentation has been and is being carried on with respect to how to organize the school and its methodology for the best learning results for the nation's youngsters. When we employ improper grouping and grading practices, we ignore the very laws of child growth and development. It is impossible to maintain a standardized educational product by any name known to man; the teacher must teach children with widely varying abilities, with an emphasis upon methodology and processes that develop creativity, competent thinking, and feelings of personal adequacy in America's boys and girls.

Questions for Discussion

1. What generalizations or conclusions can you draw regarding individual differences among and between children?

2. Why is homogeneous grouping of children generally impractical, in fact, impossible? Admittedly, grouping techniques in reading and mathematics, for example, are attempts toward achieving a higher degree of homogeneity; what happens, however, when children are taught in other subject areas where no attempt at ability grouping is made?

3. Which plan of providing for mentally superior children do you favor —enrichment, acceleration, or special classes? Justify your answer.

4. Can you think of any specific activities that might be used by a teacher in a classroom to develop children's potentialities?

5. What steps can a teacher take to avoid indoctrinating children with his social-status standing—usually upper-middle-class?

6. Do you agree that if our free democratic culture is to survive and prosper, it is necessary for teachers to teach children to think critically and reflectively? Why? How can a teacher achieve these objectives?

7. How can a teacher be flexible in his grouping procedures within the classroom? How would grouping techniques used by a teacher at the high-school level differ from those used by a teacher in a typical elementary-school situation?

8. How and why do teaching-learning situations in America's classrooms vary with the social makeup of the school communities?

9. Why do so many pupils lose interest in school and drop out after they pass the legal age limit? Where are schools failing in their responsibilities to pupils? What are some other agencies or forces besides the school that may be contributing to this situation?

Activities and Projects

1. Visit an elementary-school fourth grade or a seventh grade in a junior high school and notice the differences in height, weight, and proportion between the children. Take notes, contrasting five children whose differences appear greatest, and report on these differences to your college class.

2. If permitted by school authorities, visit three high-school teachers and, avoiding names of students, obtain the range of achievement in the three different subject areas taught by these teachers. Recommended subject areas might be English, history, and typewriting. Note the differences—the range—in each class, and report your findings to your class at college. Discuss with your classmates some possible approaches toward meeting the needs of students in each of the three classes— particularly those at the high and low ends of the achievement continuum.

3. Visit either an elementary or a high school in your area, after making an appointment with the principal. Talk with the principal or a special-education teacher about how that school provides for mentally talented and mentally and physically handicapped children. Combine your findings with those of other members of your college class who have pursued this same project, duplicate what seem to be the most promising techniques, and distribute them to the entire class.

4. Arrange for a debate between class members adept in the art of argumentation on the topic "Resolved, that creativity can be taught in a junior-high-school classroom."

5. Prepare a unit lesson plan for any grade level in the area of the social sciences with which you plan to correlate the other subject areas in the curriculum. Which of the subjects do you find most difficult to correlate? Why do you suppose this is so?

6. Visit a school in which team teaching is carried on. Note the activities being undertaken, and write a paper comparing this method with typical procedures. In the "Conclusions" section of your paper, state the

advantages and disadvantages that you see in teaching by the team approach.

7. Attend some school activity with a child or youth of your acquaintance, and watch his reactions to occurrences. Note how he relates to what he sees and, after the event, note the things he talks about most. Do you feel he might have reacted differently had he attended the activity with another youngster instead of an adult? Why?

8. If possible, visit in the home of a culturally disadvantaged child. Note how his home environment differs from the one in which you grew up, in such aspects as type of house and furniture, availability of reading materials, presence of such media as radio and television, attitudes of parents toward cultural pursuits and the school, and general physical and mental health of family members. Report on what you find to your college class.

References

Individual Differences

ANDERSON, RICHARD C., et al., eds. *Current Research on Instruction*. Columbus, Ohio: C. E. Merrill, 1969.

DE CECCO, JOHN P. *The Psychology of Learning and Instruction: Educational Psychology*. Englewood Cliffs, N.J.: Prentice-Hall, 1968.

FROST, JOE L., and G. THOMAS ROWLAND. *Curricula for the Seventies*. Boston: Houghton Mifflin, 1969. Chap. 2.

FURTH, HANS G. *Piaget and Knowledge: Theoretical Foundations*. Englewood Cliffs, N.J.: Prentice-Hall, 1968.

GINSBERG, HERBERT, and SYLVIA OPPER. *An Introduction to Piaget's Theory of Intellectual Development*. Englewood Cliffs, N.J.: Prentice-Hall, 1969.

GRAMBS, JEAN D., and L. MORRIS McCLURE. *Foundations of Teaching*. New York: Holt, Rinehart & Winston, 1964. Chap. 5.

HARRISON, RAYMOND H. *Supervisory Leadership in Education*. New York: American Book, 1968. Chap. 14.

JERSILD, ARTHUR T. *Child Psychology*. 6th ed. Englewood Cliffs, N.J.: Prentice-Hall, 1968.

JONES, J. CHARLES. *Learning*. New York: Harcourt, 1967.

LEE, J. MURRAY, and DORRIS M. LEE. *The Child and His Curriculum*. New York: Appleton, 1960.

MALLERY, DAVID. *High School Students Speak Out*. New York: Harper, 1962.

MEANS, RICHARD K. *Methodology in Education.* Columbus, Ohio: C. E. Merrill, 1968.

MINUCHIN, PATRICIA P. "Sex Differences in Children: Research Findings in an Educational Context." *National Elementary Principal,* November 1966, pp. 45–48.

NATIONAL EDUCATION ASSOCIATION. *Humanizing the Secondary School.* Washington, D.C.: Association for Supervision and Curriculum Development of the National Education Association, 1969.

————. *Youth Education: Problems, Perspectives, Promises.* Yearbook of the Association for Supervision and Curriculum Development. Washington, D.C.: Association for Supervision and Curriculum Development of the National Education Association, 1968.

PIKUNAS, JUSTIN. *Human Development: A Science of Growth.* New York: McGraw-Hill, 1969.

RICHEY, ROBERT W. *Planning for Teaching.* 4th ed. New York: McGraw-Hill, 1968. Pp. 176–85, 467–68.

ROBISON, LLOYD E. *Human Growth and Development.* Columbus, Ohio: C. E. Merrill, 1968.

SHUMSKY, ABRAHAM. *In Search of Teaching Style.* New York: Appleton, 1968. Chaps. 6–8.

STOFF, SHELDON, and HERBERT SCHWARTZBERG, eds. *The Human Encounter: Readings in Education.* New York: Harper, 1969. Chap. 8.

STROM, ROBERT D. *Psychology for the Classroom.* Englewood Cliffs, N.J.: Prentice-Hall, 1969.

WILSON, JOHN A. R., MILDRED C. ROBECK, and WILLIAM B. MICHAEL. *Psychological Foundations of Learning and Teaching.* New York: McGraw-Hill, 1969.

WYATT, NITA M. "Sex Differences in Reading Achievement." *Elementary English* 43 (October, 1966): 596–600.

Special Education and Disaffected Children and Youth

AUSUBEL, DAVID P. "The Effects of Cultural Deprivation on Learning Patterns." In *Understanding the Educational Problems of the Disadvantaged Learner,* ed. Staten W. Webster. San Francisco: Chandler, 1966. Pp. 251–57.

BARTON, TERRY. "Reaching the Culturally Deprived." *Saturday Review,* February 19, 1966, pp. 77–78, 104–5.

DEHAAN, R. F., and R. J. HAVIGHURST. *Educating Gifted Children.* Rev. ed. Chicago: University of Chicago Press, 1962.

DEYOUNG, CHRIS A., and RICHARD WYNN. *American Education.* 6th ed. New York: McGraw-Hill, 1968. Pp. 267–84.

"Disaffected Children and Youth." *Educational Leadership,* February 1963.

FLIEGLER, LOUIS A. *Curriculum Planning for the Gifted.* Englewood Cliffs, N.J.: Prentice-Hall, 1961.

GETZELS, JACOB W., and PHILIP W. JACKSON. *Creativity and Intelligence.* New York: Wiley, 1962.

HASKEW, LAURENCE D., and JONATHON C. MCLENDON. *This Is Teaching.* 3d ed. Glenview, Ill.: Scott, Foresman, 1968. Pp. 2, 46–47, 196–99, 220–22, 301–2.

INGRAM, CHRISTINE P. *Education of the Slow-Learning Child.* 3d ed. New York: Ronald, 1960.

JOHNSON, JAMES A., HAROLD W. COLLINS, VICTOR L. DUPUIS, and JOHN H. JOHANSEN. *Introduction to the Foundations of American Education.* Boston: Allyn & Bacon, 1969. Pt. 1.

NATIONAL EDUCATION ASSOCIATION. *Life Skills in School and Society.* Yearbook of the Association for Supervision and Curriculum Development. Washington, D.C.: Association for Supervision and Curriculum Development of the National Education Association, 1969.

———. *Perceiving, Behaving, Becoming.* Yearbook of the Association for Supervision and Curriculum Development. Washington, D.C.: Association for Supervision and Curriculum Development of the National Education Association, 1962.

RICHEY, ROBERT W. *Planning for Teaching.* 4th ed. New York: McGraw-Hill, 1968. Pp. 211, 366, 573.

RIESSMAN, FRANK. *The Culturally Deprived Child.* New York: Harper, 1962.

SHUMSKY, ABRAHAM. *In Search of Teaching Style.* New York: Appleton, 1968. Chaps. 8, 9.

THURSTON, JOHN R. "Too Close to Normalcy." *The Clearing House,* January 1964, pp. 296–98.

TORRANCE, E. PAUL. *Gifted Children in the Classroom.* New York: Macmillan, 1965. Pp. 19–37, 38–49.

Creativity

ANDERSON, HAROLD H., ed. *Creativity and Its Cultivation.* New York: Harper, 1959.

California Teachers Association Journal, January 1964, entire issue.

DERELL, G. R. "Creativity in Education." *The Clearing House,* October 1963, pp. 67–91.

DREWS, ELIZABETH MONROE. "Profile of Creativity." *NEA Journal,* January 1963, pp. 26–28.

FABUN, DON. *You and Creativity.* Beverly Hills: Glencoe Press, 1968.

FRAZIER, ALEXANDER, ed. *A Curriculum for Children.* Washington, D.C.:

Association for Supervision and Curriculum Development of the National Education Association, 1969.

FROST, JOE L., and G. THOMAS ROWLAND. *Curricula for the Seventies.* Boston: Houghton Mifflin, 1969. Chap. 6.

GETZELS, JACOB, and PHILIP W. JACKSON. *Creativity and Intelligence.* New York: Wiley, 1962.

HAEFELE, JOHN W. *Creativity and Innovation.* New York: Reinhold, 1962.

HANNA, LAVONE A., GLADYS L. POTTER, and NEVA HAGAMAN. *Unit Teaching in the Elementary School.* New York: Holt, Rinehart & Winston, 1963. Chap. 13.

MACKINNON, DONALD W. "The Courage to Be: Realizing Creative Potential." In *Life Skills in School and Society.* Yearbook of the Association for Supervision and Curriculum Development. Washington, D.C.: Association for Supervision and Curriculum Development of the National Education Association, 1969.

RICHEY, ROBERT W. *Planning for Teaching.* 4th ed. New York: McGraw-Hill, 1968. Pp. 183–84.

SHUMSKY, ABRAHAM. *In Search of Teaching Style.* New York: Appleton, 1968. Chap. 3.

STOFF, SHELDON, and HERBERT SCHWARTZBERG, eds. *The Human Encounter: Readings in Education.* New York: Harper, 1969. Chap. 2.

TORRANCE, E. PAUL. *Education and the Creative Potential.* Minneapolis: University of Minnesota Press, 1963.

Grouping for Instruction

FROST, JOE L., and G. THOMAS ROWLAND. *Curricula for the Seventies.* Boston: Houghton Mifflin, 1969. Chap. 7.

GRAMBS, JEAN D., and L. MORRIS McCLURE. *Foundations of Teaching.* New York: Holt, Rinehart & Winston, 1964. Pp. 111–13.

GWYNN, J. MINOR, and JOHN B. CHASE, JR. *Curriculum Principles and Social Trends.* 4th ed. New York: Macmillan, 1969. Pp. 275–76.

HANNA, LAVONE A., GLADYS L. POTTER, and NEVA HAGAMAN. *Unit Teaching in the Elementary School.* New York: Holt, Rinehart & Winston, 1963. Pt. 2.

HARRISON, RAYMOND H. *Supervisory Leadership in Education.* New York: American Book, 1968. Pp. 68–72.

HASKEW, LAURENCE D., and JONATHON C. McLENDON. *This Is Teaching.* 3d ed. Glenview, Ill.: Scott, Foresman, 1968. Pp. 63–65, 219–20.

HILLSON, MAURIE. *Change and Innovation in Elementary School Organization.* New York: Holt, Rinehart & Winston, 1965. Pts. 5, 6.

KNELLER, GEORGE F., ed. *Foundations of Education.* New York: Wiley, 1963. Pp. 497–99.

RICHEY, ROBERT W. *Planning for Teaching.* 4th ed. New York: McGraw-Hill, 1968. Pp. 357–59.

THORNDIKE, ROBERT L. *The Concepts of Over- and Underachievement.* New York: Teachers College Press, Columbia University, 1963.

"Working in Groups: How? For What?" *Educational Leadership,* December 1963.

I have felt lonely, forgotten or even left out, set
apart from the rest of the world. I never wanted
out. If anything I wanted in.

ARTHUR JACKSON, *aged fifteen*

8

The Pupils—
Class and Caste

Confronting the notion of class and caste within the context of democratic ideals is always a somewhat paradoxical problem. After all, the very
purpose of our American Revolution, in declaring that "all men are created equal," was to do away with the concept of qualitative differences inherent among men. Inevitably, however, the rank ordering of social assets
tends to take place in varying degrees in all societies and in most of the
subsystems within them, including of course the schools. Because of the
original foundations of American society and the progress of the Industrial
Revolution, however, we have desired in this country to replace the traditional stratification system of Western man based on ancestral or *ascribed*
status with the principle of *achieved* status based on an individual's ability
and ambition.

But here is the paradox: While the New World has offered many people
a chance to acquire property and status, it has not, in fact, given everyone that opportunity. Yet simultaneously the impression remains that
ability is all that counts, and if one does not "make it"—all things among
all people being equal—it is assumed to be because of his own failure
rather than the result of inequities in the social system.

It is the operation of these assumptions within schools that produces a profound dilemma for education in and for democracy. On the one hand, in order to perform their socially strategic role of stratifying people and choosing elites, American schools presume to unite the children of all classes with one another under the umbrella of equal educational opportunity; yet on the other hand, there exist among social classes obvious inequalities of access to the educational benefits and the consequent rewards of the society. Virtually all studies have shown, for example, that students' success in school is directly related to their social-class background and their "natural abilities" derived from the culture and motivation of their families.

To what extent the socioeconomic and ethnic divisions within society and education affect one another will be the focus of discussion for this chapter.

Social Stratification

Social stratification is a matter of classifying and evaluating the members of society into categories above or below one another on a scale of superiority and inferiority. It is not, however, a problem only for sociological study; for once a stratification scheme has become well established and recognized, the members themselves of the various strata tend to identify with that class and to develop feelings of solidarity vis-à-vis other strata. They may even develop distinctive organizations or associations restricted to that class level. Because of this, it is important to take a look at the character of the social classes in America.

Social scientists have employed various methods in analyzing social stratification. Perhaps the most influential series of studies has been undertaken by W. Lloyd Warner and his associates,[1] who use what is known as the "reputational approach," by which people are asked to classify one another's community status. These rankings have been found, however, to be closely associated with more objective sets of criteria that include measures of occupation, income, and education. Warner's first classic study was of Yankee City, a New England town with a population of seventeen thousand; later he produced similar studies of southern and midwestern towns known variously as Old City, Elmtown, Prairie City, and Jonesville. The investigators generally identified six social classes in terms of their common and distinguishing characteristics, as follows:

[1] See particularly W. Lloyd Warner and Paul Lunt, *The Social Life of a Modern Community* (New Haven: Yale University Press, 1941); and W. Lloyd Warner, Marchia Meeker, and Kenneth Eells, *Social Class in America* (New York: Harper, 1960).

Upper–Upper	1.4%	The "old" families
Lower–Upper	1.6%	Like Upper–Uppers only newly acquired, "the _nouveau riche_"
Upper–Middle	10%	The professional man, substantial businessman
Lower–Middle	28%	White collar workers
Upper–Lower	33%	Blue collar workers
Lower–Lower	25%	Slum dwellers, the unemployables

FIGURE 3. Social Classes in Yankee City.

SOURCE: Based on data from W. Lloyd Warner and Paul Lunt, _The Social Life of a Modern Community_ (New Haven: Yale University Press, 1941).

1. *The upper-upper class.* This elite group is characterized by aristocracy of birth, inherited wealth, gentility, and good breeding. They usually constitute only about 1 percent of the people in middle-sized communities.

2. *The lower-upper class* (about 2 percent of the population). Although their life styles are similar to those of the upper-upper class, they have acquired their status in their own generation, and while they may derive much of their income from investments and profits, they are usually actively employed as successful entrepreneurs, professionals, or captains of industry. They must have kept their money for several generations before they are accepted as having the distinguished ancestry and traditions of upper-upper-class behavior.

3. *The upper-middle class* (about 10 percent of the population). This class is composed of moderately successful corporation executives, substantial businessmen, doctors, lawyers, and other professionals. These hard-working members of the community represent the leaders in civic affairs—the backbone of the society, but not "society" themselves. They tend to man community projects and serve in political bodies and are the group from which most school-board members and some teachers come.

4. *The lower-middle class* (about 20–30 percent of the population). This is the group made up largely of small businessmen, white-collar workers, and a few of the most highly skilled tradesmen. It is characterized by conservatism, respectability, and similar virtues identified with the upper-middle class. It is also the social class from which most teachers come—unlike the bulk of their pupils, who derive mostly from the lower social classes.

5. *The upper-lower class* (about 30–40 percent of the population). This class is characterized by honest workmen, the clean poor people of the community, semiskilled workers, service workers, and small tradesmen. Unlike the middle classes, they are not career oriented or emotionally involved in their work and may change jobs frequently, looking for higher wages or more security.

6. *The lower-lower class* (about 15–25 percent of the population). This group generally depends for its income on odd jobs or seasonal work or may subsist on public-welfare money, pensions, and unemployment compensation. Often living in the ghettos and slums of the large cities, these people as a group are considered at best "poor but not respectable" members of society, and at worst as "ne'er-do-wells," "river rats," or "poor white trash." The children of this class are spoken of by the middle class as the "culturally deprived" or "culturally disadvantaged," for whom the schools should provide "compensatory education."

While the basic class composition has remained unchanged since these studies were conducted, there have been recent indications of shifts in the percentages of membership in the various strata. For example, there has been some redistribution of the nation's wealth from the upper to the middle classes; and, although the lower classes have not benefited proportionately to our nation's current prosperity, the percentage of the population who live below what has been defined as the "poverty threshold" has declined significantly.

SOCIAL MOBILITY—OPEN CLASS AND CASTE

Now that we have considered the more stable aspects of social stratification, let us see how individuals may alter their status either within strata (horizontal mobility) or between classes (vertical mobility). As we have suggested, certain societies, such as in medieval Europe or India, are stratified by ascribed criteria—characteristics with which one is born and over which one has little or no control. At the other extreme are societies that are stratified largely by means of achieved criteria—characteristics that the individual is able to control and change, as, for example, income, occupation, religion, and particularly education. A *caste* society in its pure form is composed of strata based entirely upon ascribed criteria. Unlike the caste society, the open-class society allows complete freedom of association among the members of all strata and permits vertical mobility from bottom to top. Of course, just as there has never been a pure caste society, neither has there ever been a completely open-class society. For example, in the United States, which has tended toward an open-class system, ascribed criteria are often applied—as in the case of the upper-upper class, whose

An Interview with Smith Brown
of Jonesville

"Since I made that crack about class to you the other day . . . I've done a lot of thinking about this class business. First thing, I want to say there's no use talking about people being in a certain class and in a certain portion of a class unless they are accepted by the people in that group as equals. If they are not accepted, they just don't belong. . . .

"The society class around here is the 400 class. In the main, it's rooted right over there in the Federated Church. It comes from the Federated Church. Now, Bill, a lot of these people are 398's, but they think they're 400's. With a few exceptions, no one who's not in the Federated Church is in this class. . . .

"The Volmers from top to bottom are in; the Friedricks from top to bottom are in; the Caldwells—all of them are in. Now, there's a case of two families getting together and keeping the money in the family. You know, Ted Caldwell married the Volmers girl. As far as I can figure out, that was pretty well arranged by the old folks. You know, here for years, the Caldwells and Volmers have been close business associates. They worked out a lot of deals together. . . .

"Now, here's an example of a big boost up, Mrs. A. B. Henderson. Now, Mrs. A. B. Henderson is in and her daughter's family is in. . . . I'm going to tell you some details on that just so you can get the picture. . . . Don't get the idea I am just gossiping for gossip's sake. I am giving you the facts so that you will be able to fit in the picture. Now, Mrs. A. B. Henderson was clerk in a store here in town before her marriage. She married A. B. Henderson. The Hendersons were in around here, and they have been in [the 400] for a long time. . . . Oh, yes, she was a Stillwell. She has some sisters around here and some brothers who were down there, and they stayed there. They have never done anything.

"Some of the Stocktons do and some of them don't [belong to the upper class]. You've always got to make a division in the Stocktons. . . . Here are the Stocktons who don't. . . . Mrs. Helen Cross, she doesn't. Now, she is Carl Stockton's sister, but she's not in. Now, there's the case of a girl who married down and stayed there. . . .

"I think that's just about all the society class. There may be one or two that I have overlooked, but that's all I can think of.

"The next class down is what we call the fringe of society around here. . . . The fringe of this thing has a lot of families on it who have had money and lost it.

"The Robert Claytons were former members of the 400, but they failed in business and he was dropped. Oh, hell, he got to owing everybody around town, and he just wasn't worth a damn, and they just got left out of things. Mrs. Tom Cooper and her sister, Mrs. Henry Gardner, are on the fringe, too. Mrs. Gardner is a nice person, but she had a cousin, Everett Roberts. He never was in. He was just a no-good-so-and-so. . . . They both inherited a lot of money. Hell, they both just ran through it. Just phlooey. Just threw it away. . . . Everett was no good from the beginning. . . . He was just never accepted. Just as I told you, the whole thing is based on money, but it isn't money alone. You've got to have the right family connections, and you've got to behave yourself, or you get popped out.

"Now, the Halls are another family who were never in. They never did move in that set, but they had a hell of a lot of money at one time. Old man Hall was never liked around here. I don't know just what it was, but he was just excluded. Oh, if they had big parties or something, they might invite him; but they were never accepted by the society class.

"Then, there was the Adams family. . . . Arthur was the black sheep of the Adams family. He was just a wastrel; he never amounted to anything. . . . Now, Henry was a nice fellow, but he was tighter than hell. He was too niggardly and pinch-penny to be in. He could have been in the fringe, but he just didn't spend on anything.

"The next stratum starts with the fringe and takes in certain other elements. This is what you'd better call the upper-middle class. This level is made up mainly of the women who dominate the Country Club, along with some other groups, especially the top and the fringe. The top dominates the Country Club; at least they are in, but they're not active. They're the ones who, you might say, are behind the scenes and really control things. The fringe is pretty active, and this group of women are active, too. The women in this group just seem to split a gut to do things right. It's amusing as hell. We used to belong to the Country Club, but we don't any more. This Country Club is, of course, quite cosmopolitan. It's got a lot of people in it and diverse elements. Anybody who thinks he can afford to get in and play golf, and so on. But it's this bunch of women who really dominate the club and keep the activities going, although I'm pretty damned sure they don't have as much say-so in it as they think they do. . . .

"Now, here is another group that's all about at this same level, and my wife and I are in this group some of the time. It's not in a different class from the others. Now, we don't have any money, and our being included in these groups is due wholly to my professional position and the fact that my wife and I belong to several good organizations. Hell, if it weren't for them we wouldn't be in anything. . . .

"Now, we come to the working class. The working class is made up of good, solid people who live right but they never get any place. They never get in real trouble. They are the ones who work down at The Mill and the other factories. They are the ones who work around as clerks in the stores, own little trucks and maybe little businesses. . . . These neighborhood grocers, and so on. . . .

"Well, while they're fixing supper for us I just want to mention one more class. Now, this one is really a lulu. These are the families that are just not worth a goddam. Now, they're not immoral—they're not unmoral—they're just plain amoral. They just simply don't have any morals. I'll tell you they just have animal urges, and they just respond to them. They're just like a bunch of rats or rabbits.

"There's the Jones family. My God, that Jones outfit! . . . All their kids . . . are tougher than hell. They never went any place in school, and they're always getting into jams. Another family that's in the making is that Kraig family. Those poor little kids are half-frozen and ragged all the time, and they come along one after the other. I've seen them go to the store with a nickel or a penny to buy some candy and that type of thing. Every morning they come down to the store and buy five or ten cents' worth of sweet rolls for breakfast.

"Now, another family that's in the same class is the Rain family. They're Kentuckians and, I'll tell you, they're really something. Then, there's the Jackson family that live down south of The River. Well, they're lulus, too. Then, there's that John Harding bunch that live in back of the tannery. Old John Harding and his family have been in more trouble around here than you can really think about. Then, there's the Kilgore family. Old Tom's got four or five girls. They've got into trouble. Some of them are about half-witted, and Harry himself is not any too bright. They aren't worth a damn." *

* Note that Smith Brown was only able to identify five social classes in the middle western city of Jonesville.

W. Lloyd Warner, Marchia Meeker, Kenneth Eells, *Social Class in America*, New York: Harper, Harper Torchbooks, 1960. Reprinted by permission.

membership is determined almost entirely on the basis of ascription rather than achievement.

Certain other factors, in addition, determine the mobility patterns in our country. Obviously one is the personal *aspirations* of individuals—in other

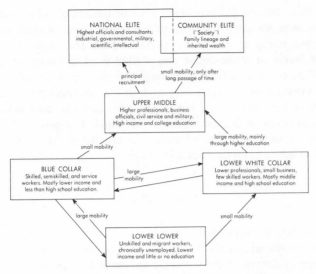

FIGURE 4. Stratification and Generational Mobility in the United States.

SOURCE: Leonard Broom and Philip Selznick, *Sociology*, 3d ed. (New York: Harper, 1963), Fig. VI:13, p. 214. Reprinted by permission.

words, whether or not, and how, people want to move. On the societal level is the question of *opportunities* for mobility—the opening of new vertical channels either through changes in the occupational and economic structure or, as is more common, through increased education. Enter here the schools: because American schools are supposedly free and open to all, a person from the lower-lower class can theoretically ride the social elevator from one class to another by means of acquiring an education.

Studies of mobility between generations, however, have shown that most people tend roughly to follow the social status of their parents.

It cannot be denied . . . that children tend to be cast in the image of their parents. They learn their manners, their morals, their attitudes, their values—and much more—from their parents and families. They also learn how to make a living from them. A child whose father is an unskilled worker is also likely to become an unskilled worker. A child whose father is in business for himself will probably enter the business world too. This is what we mean by "social class," then: the position which families occupy in society and the very strong tendency for children to be molded into the same position by influences in the home, the community, and the school.[2]

[2] Patricia Cayo Sexton, *Education and Income* (New York: Viking, 1961), pp. 10–11.

While this stability is particularly true of the middle-class occupational structures, it is not always so true of the upper levels of professionals and businessmen, many of whom are recruited from the lower classes, nor of the lower levels of white-collar and skilled workers, many of whom are victims of downward mobility. Although the movement of individuals during their work life is generally very high, it usually takes place between occupations at the same level; and when advancement does take place, it tends not to result in dramatic changes in status. The general paths of mobility and the importance of education in producing this upward flow are indicated in figure 4, on the preceding page.

Color Caste

As we have already suggested, there is a basic dilemma inherent in the existence of classes within the model of an open-class society. Classes function, by the evolution of their specific values and attitudes, to keep people apart, or segregate them, from one another and thus to inhibit mobility. Add to this the question of caste in what is predominantly an open society, and the problem becomes even more perplexing. In the United States, there are some characteristics of a caste society in the relations of whites to ethnic minorities such as Orientals, Indians, Mexican-Americans, and particularly black Americans, who comprise a substantial portion (12 per-

Every white man knows one thing: He would not like to be a black man. If he knows that, he knows everything he needs to know. He has no need to ask a black man what he wants.

James Baldwin, quoted in the *San Francisco Chronicle*, January 4, 1970, p. 16.

cent) of our population. Skin color happens to be an inalterably ascribed characteristic over which the individual has no control and which therefore limits his freedom to associate in various social, economic, and political ways with different "colored" members of the society. It should be noted, too, that this applies to whites as well as blacks, browns, and yellows and implies many of the same restrictions, albeit usually not to the disadvantage of the whites.

The extent of racial caste in the United States was demonstrated, to the fear and bewilderment of the nation, during the Watts riots in Los Angeles during the summer of 1965. Again in July, 1967, explosive racial disor-

We are men and women who have suffered and endured much and not only because of our abject poverty but because we have been kept poor. The colors of our skins, the languages of our cultural and native origins, the lack of formal education, the exclusion from the democratic process, the numbers of our slain in recent wars—all these burdens generation after generation have sought to demoralize us, to break our human spirit. But God knows that we are not beasts of burden, we are not agricultural implements or rented slaves, we are men. We are men locked in a death struggle against man's inhumanity to man.

Cesar Chavez, "Letter from Delano," a mimeographed general appeal for funds to support the strike of the Salinas lettuce pickers.

ders occurred in Newark, Detroit, and to a lesser degree in other American cities, causing extensive death and destruction. In order to understand why ghetto residents were resorting to riots and what could be done to prevent this from happening again, the National Commission on Civil Disorders was established that summer, and comprehensive investigations of these events were undertaken. In spite of its composition of "moderate" and "establishment" representatives, the commission's conclusions about caste and racism in our society were shockingly unmitigated, as is evident from the portions of the report summary reprinted on page 206.

Given the apparent magnitude of the color caste within our society, the implications for educational and economic opportunity are grim indeed. Such questions as the following will likely persist around this issue for years to come:

1. How do we account for the fact that the majority of the black and Third World populations exist below the official poverty level? Furthermore, in the presence of the "affluent society," the rise in average income, and the substantial rate of upward mobility for the majority, how can we eradicate these differences in the life chances of the impoverished minorities?

2. To what extent will racial integration within all spheres and all levels of society solve the problems of opportunity for all members of society? If integration is the answer, on whose terms? In bringing together culturally diverse people within a multiclass society, whose values are to be indoctrinated? Consider the following by two proponents of Black Power: is racial separatism the logical consequence of this point of view?

From the Report of the National Advisory Commission on Civil Disorders

This is our basic conclusion: Our nation is moving toward two societies, one black, one white—separate and unequal.

. . . This deepening racial division is not inevitable. The movement apart can be reversed. Choice is still possible. Our principal task is to define that choice and to press for a national resolution.

To pursue our present course will involve the continuing polarization of the American community and, ultimately, the destruction of basic democratic values.

The alternative is not blind repression or capitulation to lawlessness. It is the realization of common opportunities for all within a single society.

. . . Segregation and poverty have created in the racial ghetto a destructive environment totally unknown to most white Americans.

What white Americans have never fully understood—but what the Negro can never forget—is that white society is deeply implicated in the ghetto. White institutions created it, white institutions maintain it, and white society condones it.

Report of the National Advisory Commission on Civil Disorders (New York: Bantam Books, 1968), pp. 1–2.

The values of this society support a racist system; we find it incongruous to ask black people to adopt and support most of those values. We also reject the assumption that the basic institutions of this society must be preserved. The goal of black people must *not* be to assimilate into middle-class America, for that class—as a whole—is without a viable conscience as regards humanity. The values of the middle class permit the perpetuation of the ravages of the black community. The values of that class are based on material aggrandizement, not the expansion of humanity. The values of that class ultimately support cloistered little closed societies tucked away neatly in tree-lined suburbia. The values of that class do *not* lead to the creation of an open society. That class *mouths* its preference for a free, competitive society, while at the same time forcefully and even viciously denying to black people as a group the opportunity to compete.[3]

3. Of more than simply academic interest, too, is the question of ethnic

[3] Stokely Carmichael and Charles V. Hamilton, *Black Power: The Politics of Liberation in America* (New York: Random House, 1967), p. 40.

identification versus class identification. In other words, is the racial situation in America a matter of insuperable color issues, or is it a result of the lower-class positions that most ethnic minorities occupy? To what extent can these allegiances crosscut one another? In the two excerpts that follow, we will consider this problem in some depth, for the implications of each position are extremely pertinent to both social and educational-policy decisions. First, we have the position that racism is a function of class differences between the white middle class and lower-class blacks, that the former are not so much anti-Negro as pro–middle class:

Most racial antipathy in America is not "pure" racism but derives from the disdain of higher classes for those below them. The tragedy of race in this country (and many others) is that visible genetic differences, superficial in themselves, have become generally reliable clues to a person's class position— his education, his income, his manners. The present low position of black Americans is a legacy of centuries of living under a most extreme and brutal form of slavery and of strenuous efforts since legal emancipation to contain them socially as a subordinate caste. Events of the last 20 years have done much to modify the legal and political aspects of this subordination, but the more general social effects of the past remain: black Americans are disadvantaged and poor, and their culture—so much a "culture of poverty"—is offensive to more affluent classes.

Advocates of integration frequently note that interracial contacts in housing and schools are less strained when both racial groups are reasonably well educated and "middle class," and they suggest that this provides the key to successful integration. But the number of middle-class blacks, though growing, remains small, and . . . there just aren't enough of them to go around. Since the majority of whites today are broadly in the middle class, this means that most programs for quick integration by race must also involve integration by class. And the long-run problems of achieving genuine educational integration by class are vastly greater than those of genuine integration by race.[4]

Second, we have the position that the "common destiny shared by the Negro people," the sense of peoplehood that they have in common, will always supercede class interests:

Middle class Negro families, then, do share certain similarities with middle class white families. They share some, though not nearly all, the privileges, opportunities, resources, and amenities of their middle class white counterparts. When, rarely, they also share neighborhoods, schools, and other common ground on a basis of sustained interaction and equality, they are also likely to

[4] John Finley Scott and Lois Heyman Scott, "They Are Not So Much Anti-Negro as Pro–Middle Class," *New York Times Magazine*, March 24, 1968. Reprinted by permission.

share what [Milton] Gordon refers to as "participational identification." They are not as likely, however, to share a common sense of peoplehood. They have very different histories, very different statuses in society, and very different levels of economic security. They consequently do not share the "historical identification" which middle class Negroes share with other middle class Negro families, including those in the lower classes. It is with other middle class Negro families, however, that these two senses of identity are combined and fortified. They are, indeed, in the same boat.

While Negroes have always been aware of this historical connection with each other and with Negroes in other parts of the world, we have not always been free to recognize it, make it explicit, define it, and build on it. We have been brainwashed by the sea of whiteness which surrounds us and defines us. It was not until after World War II, when strides toward increasing freedom for Negroes were made both in this country and in Africa, that the Negro people again took up the theme, at one time advanced by Marcus Garvey, that black people have a common history, a common set of relations with the white world, and a common destiny. And it was not until twenty years later that the general society began to take note, mainly in negative terms, of this search for identity on the part of the Negro people. Now in every major community in the country, upper and middle class Negroes are turning in dozens of ways toward an explicit recognition of the common destiny shared by the Negro people. There is no important civil rights or protest activity that does not have substantial participation and leadership by the more privileged Negroes.[5]

To summarize what the problem of caste means on a less abstract level, take the following poem written by a high-school student, Frank Cleveland, aged 17, who uses the pen name "Clorox":

WHAT AM I?

I have no manhood—what am I?
You made my woman head of the house—what am I?
You have oriented me so that I hate and distrust
My brothers and sisters—what am I?
    You mispronounce my name and say I have no
    Self-respect—what am I?
    You give me a dilapidated education system and
    Expect me to compete with you—what am I?
    You say I have no dignity and then deprive me
    Of my culture—what am I?
    You call me a boy, dirty lowdown slut—
    What am I?

[5] Andrew Billingsley, *Black Families in White America* (Englewood Cliffs, N.J.: Prentice-Hall, 1968), pp. 10–11. Copyright © 1968. Reprinted by permission of Prentice-Hall, Inc.

Now I'm a victim of the welfare system—
What am I?
You tell me to wait for change to come, but 400
Years
Have passed and change ain't come—what am I?
I am all of your sins
I am the skeleton in your closets
I am the unwanted sons and daughters-in-law, and
Rejected babies
I may be your destruction, but above all I am, as
You so crudely put it, your nigger.[6]

Social-Class Differences in School

Keeping in mind that schools are basically white middle-class institutions, staffed and administered by middle-class persons but serving largely middle- and lower-class individuals, let us look at some of the generalizations —and remember that they are mere generalizations, with limited validity for describing individuals—regarding the apparent differences in the developmental experiences encountered by children with these class origins.

1. In their early socialization and child-rearing practices, middle-class families differ from lower-class families in that the former are generally child centered while the latter are adult centered. Because of the greater attention the middle-class child receives, he is urged to mature more quickly and to assume responsibility at an earlier age in such things as, for example, weaning, toilet training, walking, talking, and so forth. While the absence of this encouragement may somewhat retard the development of the lower-class child, needless to say, this kind of pressure can also be highly frustrating for the middle-class child.

2. Because of the uncertainty and unpredictability of slum existence, particularly in terms of such basic survival necessities as food and housing, lower-class people tend to focus their attention on present, immediate problems. In middle-class homes, on the other hand, thrift and planning can occur, since their present economic condition is sufficiently stable to allow concentration on the future. Unlike the lower-class child, then, the middle-class child is more geared toward deferment of gratification.

3. Concomitantly, since the lower-class child is not goal oriented, he tends to find his immediate pleasures in action-oriented activities with his

[6] Stephen M. Joseph, ed., *The Me Nobody Knows: Children's Voices from the Ghetto* (New York: Avon, 1969), p. 42. Copyright © 1969 by Stephen M. Joseph. Reprinted by permission of Stephen M. Joseph, Avon Books, and Henry Morrison, Inc.

peer group. His place in the "gang" becomes an important source of stability in his otherwise insecure existence. Since he is more dependent on his peer culture, and more distrustful of the outside world, he is less likely to adopt such school values as group competition and upward mobility because they may threaten to separate him from the people with whom and the milieu in which he feels comfortable.

4. The middle-class child, moreover, accustomed to curbing his impulses in order to accomplish something in the future, may be better able to accept the passive, impersonal role demanded of him at school. On the other hand, the slum child, who is often expected to assume adult responsibilities in the home, cannot as easily tolerate it when the school treats him like a child. This is particularly true for adolescent boys, who, in addition, are expected to assume a dominant, adult status within their peer group.

5. The reward and punishment structures of the lower and middle classes also differ. The rewards that school offers, such as grades and the teacher's verbal praise, are often less relevant to the more demonstrative lower-class child than to the middle-class child. Yet displays of physical or sexual aggressiveness, which may be highly rewarding to the lower-class child, are also highly discouraged at school.

6. Lower- and middle-class cultures have different value systems as a result of the experiences peculiar to their different environments. Often, however, we tend to think of middle-class morality as the norm, and anything else as a deviation from this norm. Lower-class values are, nevertheless, appropriate to the social conditions of that subsociety and are therefore functional for that environment, as middle-class values are for the middle-class environment. Teachers often make the mistake of automatically expecting their lower-class pupils to have such values as respect for material property and habits of thrift, not recognizing that the lack of these values is indeed appropriate within the context of their lives. Furthermore, as Frank Riessman, for one, has pointed out, there are many "positive" qualities of lower-class expressive behavior, such as directness, spontaneity, simplicity, and activity.[7]

Educational Discrimination and Compensation

Social-class differences affecting educational opportunity exist not only on the cultural level but on the institutional level as well. In other words, educational advantages are, in fact, differentially accessible relative to one's

[7] Frank Riessman, *The Culturally Deprived Child* (New York: Harper, 1962).

class background; and, of course, this operates in favor of the middle and upper classes and to the disadvantage of the lower class.

At the peak of the educational hierarchy, and controlling much of what goes on below it, are institutions of higher education. Yet despite the increasing requirement that persons in the "credential society" possess a higher degree in order to obtain a share of the society's wealth, status, and power, these institutions are, mainly because of their prohibitive cost and competitive admission standards, most discriminatory to lower-income individuals with demonstrated or latent abilities. As a result, secondary schools serving lower-class populations often do not even seriously bother to prepare their students for college entrance, offering neither the necessary courses nor encouragement to those who might have such "unrealistic" expectations.

While there have been efforts in recent years to expand educational opportunities for poor and minority-group students in colleges and universities (through increased scholarships, stipends, curricular modifications, and special counseling and remedial services), the overall picture, though changing, is still largely the same.

Although the public schools presumably provide universal compulsory education, still some studies have shown that the more money a pupil's parents make, the more will be spent on his education. For example, even within a single large city school system, it was found that the money spent and the quality of education offered varied from school to school in direct proportion to the incomes of the families in the school neighborhood. Inequalities were found in such factors as building maintenance; teacher-pupil ratio; quality of the teaching staff; methods of pupil evaluation; counseling facilities; health, recreation, and food services; and so on. All of these factors were also correlated with achievement—the poorer the neighborhood, the poorer the school, the poorer the student performance.[8]

As a result largely of pressure from civil-rights groups and the disadvantaged sector itself, however, the last decade has seen the beginnings of a reverse trend. Such federally funded programs as Head Start, Follow Through, Upward Bound, the Teacher Corps, VISTA, and particularly that of the Elementary and Secondary Education Act of 1965 have signaled increased support for poverty-area schools. Such national compensatory-education programs coupled with those on the state and local level have greatly diminished at least the financial gap between middle-class and lower-class schools. The added funds have enabled school districts to purchase a great deal of instructional material geared to the special needs of lower-class pupils, to hire additional specialized professional and paraprofes-

[8] Patricia Cayo Sexton, *Education and Income* (New York: Viking, 1961).

From *The Autobiography of Malcolm X*

EXCERPT FROM <u>MASCOT</u>

I kept close to the top of the class, though. The top-most scholastic standing, I remember, kept shifting between me, a girl named Audrey Slaugh, and a boy named Jimmy Cotton.

It went on that way, as I became increasingly restless and disturbed through the first semester. And then one day, just about when those of us who had passed were about to move up to 8-A, from which we would enter high school the next year, something happened which was to become the first major turning point of my life.

Somehow, I happened to be alone in the classroom with Mr. Ostrowski, my English teacher. He was a tall, rather reddish white man and he had a thick mustache. I had gotten some of my best marks under him, and he had always made me feel that he liked me. He was, as I have mentioned, a natural-born "advisor," about what you ought to read, to do, or think—about any and everything. We used to make unkind jokes about him: why was he teaching in Mason instead of somewhere else, getting for himself some of the "success in life" that he kept telling us how to get?

I know that he probably meant well in what he happened to advise me that day. I doubt that he meant any harm. It was just in his nature as an American white man. I was one of his top students, one of the school's top students—but all he could see for me was the kind of future "in your place" that almost all white people see for black people.

He told me, "Malcolm, you ought to be thinking about a career. Have you been giving it thought?"

The truth is, I hadn't. I never have figured out why I told him, "Well, yes sir, I've been thinking I'd like to be a lawyer." Lansing [Michigan] certainly had no Negro lawyers—or doctors either—in those days, to hold up an image I might have aspired to. All I really

sional personnel, and to extend education into the preschool, after-school, summer-school, and adult communities.

The success of these programs has fomented considerable debate between, on one side, the various critics who contend that the overall achievement levels of the affected pupils have not risen significantly under the programs and, on the other, those advocates who claim more subjective evidence of success like pupil's increased motivation to learn, their liking for school, and other less measurable growth factors. Part of the problem knew for certain was that a lawyer didn't wash dishes, as I was doing.

Mr. Ostrowski looked surprised, . . . and leaned back in his chair and clasped his hands behind his head. He kind of half-smiled and said, "Malcolm, one of life's first needs is for us to be realistic. Don't misunderstand me, now. We all here like you, you know that. But you've got to be realistic about being a nigger. A lawyer—that's no realistic goal for a nigger. You need to think about something you *can* be. You're good with your hands—making things. Everybody admires your carpentry shop work. Why don't you plan on carpentry? People like you as a person—you'd get all kinds of work."

The more I thought afterwards about what he said, the more uneasy it made me. It just kept treading around in my mind.

What made it really begin to disturb me was Mr. Ostrowski's advice to others in my class—all of them white. Most of them had told him they were planning to become farmers. But those who wanted to strike out on their own, to try something new, he had encouraged. Some, mostly girls, wanted to be teachers. A few wanted other professions, such as one boy who wanted to become a county agent; another, a veterinarian; and one girl wanted to be a nurse. They all reported that Mr. Ostrowski had encouraged what they had wanted. Yet nearly none of them had earned marks equal to mine.

It was a surprising thing that I had never thought of it that way before, but I realized that whatever I wasn't, I *was* smarter than nearly all of those white kids. But apparently I was still not intelligent enough, in their eyes, to become whatever *I* wanted to be.

It was then that I began to change—inside.

Malcolm X, with the assistance of Alex Haley, *The Autobiography of Malcolm X* (New York: Grove, 1964; Black Cat ed., 1966), pp. 35–37. Copyright © 1964 by Alex Haley and Malcolm X; copyright © 1965 by Alex Haley and Betty Shabazz. Reprinted by permission of Grove Press, Inc.

is certainly the inappropriate reliance on normative achievement and intelligence data, which are in general biased toward middle-class pupils and standardized curricula, to evaluate these programs. In fact, project assessment has not been the only discriminative application of these tests: traditionally they have also been instrumental in sorting and selecting students into various homogeneous groupings—the higher social strata usually entering the "higher-quality" groups while those from the lower strata enter the "lower-quality" ones. Not the least of the disadvantages of this practice is its tendency to generate self-fulfilling prophecies of success and failure both for the child and the teacher.[9] Cultural bias aside, this whole notion of formal and informal "tracking"—the static, statistical view of development—now current needs to be replaced by a more dynamic view of an individual's human potential for continuous growth.

These lower expectations of pupil performance no doubt may themselves be a factor in the dispute over the value of compensatory programs in the so-called target-area schools. After all, so the "cultural-deprivation" hypothesis goes, it's not the *school* that is to be held accountable for "failure" among low-income children; it's the "limited native intelligence," the family life and group culture of the disadvantaged, that are the sources of their "unteachability." While these may be contributing factors to lower scholastic achievement, nevertheless school personnel must not use this argument, as they sometimes do, to avoid their educative responsibilities. It *is* possible to regard I.Q. scores as only one indication of ability, and it *is* possible to enter into transactions with the students' "culture" by involving the community in school life and the school in community life.

Another argument against compensatory education has revolved around the ubiquitous Project Head Start, which attempts to intervene in the cognitive and social development of youngsters during their preschool, "formative" years. Some longitudinal studies on the effects of this program seem to indicate that while the "disadvantaged" child with Head Start experience enters kindergarten as the intellectual equal of other children, he tends to regress steadily as he continues in school, starting in about the third or fourth grade. While critics cite this as evidence of the program's ineffectiveness, the data would in fact seem to indicate that the locus of the problem is more in the school than in the home.

In essence, there seem to be two major reasons for the current disappointment with compensatory-education programs, once thought to be the educational panacea. First, they have too often been used in various parts of the country as a substitute for integration. Secondly, the whole concept of "compensation" implies that there is something wrong with the child, some grave deficiency in his makeup or development that needs repairing —not some failure with the schools, teachers, or educational institutions. The alternative to this very one-sided theory would seem to be somewhere

---

[9] In this regard see Robert Rosenthal and Lenore Jacobsen, *Pygmalion in the Classroom* (New York: Holt, Rinehart & Winston, 1968). Rosenthal relates the result of an experiment in which teachers were told that certain of their students through testing had revealed superior but hidden ability. Though the students were not in fact "special," at least by these standards, they began to perform better, apparently in response to their teachers' expectant treatment of them. See also Paul Lauter and Florence Howe, "How the School System Is Rigged for Failure," *New York Review of Books,* June 18, 1970, pp. 14–21.

in between the child and the school, taking into account the limitations and potentials of each.

Educators appear to be leaning toward this perspective, for they are beginning to turn from their previous emphasis on remedial services for failing pupils to "new solutions" such as in-service education for teachers; community control of schools; differentiated staffing patterns; experiments in school organization, from large educational parks to one-room mini-schools; the voucher system, which would permit open enrollment in a variety of accredited schools including private schools; and consideration of new models such as the British Infant Schools. One of the more widespread new solutions has been innovations in curricula, many of which are accommodating in their design not only to the differences in cultural heritage among pupils but to the differences in individual learning styles. Many new programs also tend to emphasize inquiry - and involvement rather than memorization of knowledge, a here-and-now orientation rather than a past orientation, and a stress on the affective aspects of learning equal to that on its cognitive content. Needless to say, this is what "relevancy" is all about.

Thomas C.'s Fable (Sixth Grade)

Once a boy was standing on a huge metal flattening machine. The flatterner was coming down slowly. Now this boy was a boy who loved insects and bugs. The boy could have stopped the machine from coming down but there were two ladie bugs on the button and in order to push the button he would kill the two ladie bugs. The flattener was about a half inch over his head now he made a decision he would have to kill the ladie bugs he quickly pressed the button. The machine stoped he was saved and the ladie bugs were dead.

Moral: smash or be smashed

Herbert Kohl, *36 Children* (New York: New American Library, Signet Books, 1967), p. 114.

Segregation and Integration

No discussion of class and caste would be complete without some reference to the issues of segregation and integration. While we do not intend to enter into the political fray in any depth, it might be helpful to review some of the sociological factors that ought to enter into one's thinking about the subject.

Pursuant to the provisions of the Civil Rights Act of 1964, a massive

The Coleman Report

Finally, it appears that a pupil's achievement is strongly related to the educational backgrounds and aspirations of the other students in the school. Only crude measures of these variables were used (principally the proportion of pupils with encyclopedias in the home and the proportion planning to go to college). Analysis indicates, however, that children from a given family background, when put in schools of different social composition, will achieve at quite different levels. This effect is again less for white pupils than for any minority group other than Orientals. Thus, if a white pupil from a home that is strongly and effectively supportive of education is put in a school where most pupils do not come from such homes, his achievement will be little different than if he were in a school composed of others like himself. But if a minority pupil from a home without much educational strength is put with schoolmates with strong educational backgrounds, his achievement is likely to increase.

This general result, taken together with the earlier examinations of school differences, has important implications for equality of educational opportunity. For the earlier tables show that the principal way in which the school environments of Negroes and whites differ is in the composition of their student bodies, and it turns out that the composition of the student bodies has a strong relationship to the achievement of Negro and other minority pupils. . . .

This analysis has concentrated on the educational opportunities

study was undertaken to investigate the extent and effects of de jure and de facto school segregation in the nation. About one million dollars and one million pupils later, the results of this comprehensive survey, comprising six thousand schools across the country, were published under the title *Equality of Educational Opportunity* (the Coleman Report, as it has come to be known, after the principal investigator, James Coleman). Some of its major findings follow:

1. "The great majority of American children attend schools that are largely segregated—that is, where almost all of their fellow students are of the same racial background as they are." Although it is most pronounced in the South, segregation exists in all regions of the country. Moreover, black pupils in black schools consistently score below white pupils on standardized tests, with the differences increasing as they grow older. For example, a typical black first-grader scores one year behind his white counterpart, yet is nearly three years behind by the end of high school.

offered by the schools in terms of their student body composition, facilities, curriculums, and teachers. This emphasis, while entirely appropriate as a response to the legislation calling for the survey, nevertheless neglects important factors in the variability between individual pupils within the same school; this variability is roughly four times as large as the variability between schools. For example, a pupil attitude factor, which appears to have a stronger relationship to achievement than do all the "school" factors together, is the extent to which an individual feels that he has some control over his own destiny. . . . The responses of pupils to questions in the survey show that minority pupils, except for Orientals, have far less conviction than whites that they can affect their own environments and futures. When they do, however, their achievement is higher than that of whites who lack that conviction.

Furthermore, while this characteristic shows little relationship to most school factors, it is related, for Negroes, to the proportion of whites in the schools. Those Negroes in schools with a higher proportion of whites have a greater sense of control. This finding suggests that the direction such an attitude takes may be associated with the pupil's school experience as well as his experience in the larger community.

U. S. Department of Health, Education, and Welfare, Office of Education, *Equality of Educational Opportunity* (Washington, D. C.: U.S. Government Printing Office, 1966).

2. Contrary to Sexton's findings, this survey did not indicate that there are significant differences in the facilities of white and nonwhite schools. In other words, it does not appear to be true that black schools spend less money per pupil, have larger classes, and get less qualified teachers and more antiquated facilities than white schools, although this seems to be partly because most white Americans live in smaller cities and towns, where the resources are often as limited as they are in ghetto areas.

3. Interesting, too, was the finding that high expenditures on facilities and materials seemed *not* to be correlated with school achievement— although experienced and articulate teachers did seem to make a slight difference.

4. The most surprising finding, however, was the dual relationship of the schools' social composition with individual achievement and with a pupil's belief that he can control his own destiny. It is this part of the report that has become most politically significant, since it has been cited

repeatedly by proponents of school integration and bussing plans as the only solution to quality and equality education.

A note of caution: the Coleman Report is by no means the last empirical word on integration and segregation. The study has been carefully analyzed and reanalyzed by numerous social scientists, many of whom have found it wanting not only in methodological elegance and purity but in its conclusions as well. After all, correlation coefficients are not necessarily evidence of causal relationships, especially given the highly complex variables that seem to affect the nature of learning and about which no one would claim complete understanding.

Some alternative perspectives on integration may need to be offered here in addition. First and most vociferous is the position taken by black and Third World separatists, who feel that integration is not only insulting to their capabilities as teachers of their own children but that it also represents an attempt by the white establishment to "assimilate" them (see the quotation from Carmichael and Hamilton above, page 206) and to deny them a unique identity.

Another point of view has been voiced by certain proponents of liberal or humanistic education who question the whole connection between education and economic opportunity. The more we see education as an instrument of upward mobility—and programs for the disadvantaged especially reinforce this concept—the less likely we are to appreciate the other known functions of education, such as its self-actualizing possibilities or its role in helping to understand the meaning of other people's lives. The

Members of social groups that are uncomfortable with one another, as lower-class and middle-class people often are, work out technics of avoidance and rituals for keeping unavoidable encounters smooth and superficial; they do not become intimate.

. . . The crucial lack of our society is not opportunity but intimacy. There is nothing it needs less at the present time, than another wave of status striving and a further alteration of its social institutions—especially the schools—to accommodate it. Already we have become a people at once casual and sly; searchers for angles who discard one another like old Kleenex after use. We must take time to settle down and learn to use our affluence and our leisure to redefine ourselves and reform our institutions—and, to some extent, the other way around.

Edgar Z. Friedenberg, *Coming of Age in America* (New York: Random House, Vintage Books, 1965), pp. 236, 240.

problem with integration, then, may be that schools will overfacilitate opportunity and underfacilitate good human relations.

Conclusion

Inhabitants of modern nations tend to fall into various vertically structured segments known as social classes. Although criteria for membership in

Let Us Be Dissatisfied

So I conclude by saying again today that we have a task and let us go out with a "divine dissatisfaction." Let us be dissatisfied until America will no longer have a high blood-pressure of creeds and an anemia of deeds. Let us be dissatisfied until the tragic walls that separate the outer city of wealth and comfort and the inner city of poverty and despair shall be crushed by the battering rams of the forces of justice. Let us be dissatisfied until those that live on the outskirts of hope are brought into the metropolis of daily security. Let us be dissatisfied until slums are cast into the junk heaps of history, and every family is living in a decent sanitary home. Let us be dissatisfied until the dark yesterdays of segregated schools will be transformed into bright tomorrows of quality, integrated education. Let us be dissatisfied until integration is not seen as a problem but as an opportunity to participate in the beauty of diversity. Let us be dissatisfied until men and women, however black they may be, will be judged on the basis of the content of their character and not on the basis of the color of their skin. Let us be dissatisfied. Let us be dissatisfied until every State capitol houses a Governor who will do justly, who will love mercy and who will walk humbly with his God. Let us be dissatisfied until from every city hall, justice will roll down like waters and righteousness like a mighty stream. Let us be dissatisfied until that day when the lion and lamb shall lie down together, and every man will sit under his own vine and fig tree and none shall be afraid. Let us be dissatisfied. And men will recognize that out of one blood God made all men to dwell upon the face of the earth. Let us be dissatisfied until that day when nobody will shout "White Power!"—when nobody will shout "Black Power!"—but everybody will talk about God's power and human power.

Martin Luther King, Jr., from "The President's Address to the Tenth Anniversary Convention of the Southern Christian Leadership Conference, Atlanta, Georgia, August 16, 1967." Copyright © 1967 by Martin Luther King, Jr., Estate. Reprinted by permission of Joan Daves.

these classes differ from society to society, generally factors such as family status, wealth, and occupational status are significant in determining one's place in the hierarchy of social classes. Education, too, is particularly important, since it is the primary variable in the movement from one social class to another. Teachers, then, need to be aware of their role in influencing the opportunities for social mobility among their pupils, especially in light of the schools' tendencies to reinforce social stratification. Given that the school's primary task is to maximize opportunities for self-fulfillment, then we as educators need to examine carefully how our schools and classrooms inhibit the potential development of each student by such class-ifying.

Questions for Discussion

1. In terms of your social origins, how do you see your upbringing as affecting your "natural abilities"? In your analysis make sure you are differentiating correctly between ascribed and achieved conditions.

2. How do you *personally* experience the existence of caste in our society? Have there been occasions when you have felt very separated from persons of another color? How do you see increased contact with these people as enriching *your* life, if at all?

3. Discuss your feelings about the quotation on page 206 from Carmichael and Hamilton. Do you think that black and ethnic identity will always be barriers to human relations? If not, how will this occur?

4. Discuss the poem "What Am I?" pages 208–9. How do you feel about the accusations it makes? What can be said about someone who expresses his anger in this way?

5. If we could recruit more teachers from the lower rather than the middle classes, would this solve the problem of providing understanding teachers for slum children? How might the recruitment be done? Can you think of some new paths that might be followed in establishing credentials for teachers?

6. Suppose your child had to spend forty-five minutes in the morning and forty-five minutes in the afternoon on a school bus in order to attend a racially integrated school. How would you feel about it? How might this affect his attitude?

7. Suppose you were the superintendent of a de facto–segregated school district. How far would you go toward providing racially integrated schools? What methods would you use? What problems do you foresee? Are there some other factors besides the "mix ratio" that need to be taken into consideration in developing your plan? What are they?

8. What strategies could you devise as a teacher to facilitate greater acceptance and intimacy among students of various socioeconomic backgrounds? If they were also of different colors, would you alter your strategy? How? Why?

9. If you were the president of the Ford Foundation or the Carnegie Foundation, what sorts of educational projects would you be interested in funding?

Activities and Projects

1. Devise a way in which to analyze and represent the social mobility of your family over the past three generations, keeping in mind such factors as the marriage, education, income, and occupation of yourself and of your relatives. Can you make any relevant projections about your own children?

2. Visit a school in the slums of your city. How closely do the neighborhood, school, curriculum, teachers, and pupils fit the patterns discussed in this chapter?

3. Choosing several social-class variables, prepare a study that would measure these factors comparatively in a suburban and an inner-city school system.

4. If you reside in or near an area comprised of various ethnic minorities, prepare a study that would compare and contrast their perceptions of how the school affects their chances.

5. Send for a copy of the Total Integration Program of the Berkeley, California, Unified School District, or of another recently integrated school district. Analyze and evaluate it. Are there procedures you would modify? Can you think of another method that would have accomplished these same goals?

6. Survey a variety of textbooks used at a particular grade level or for a particular course. In what ways do they reflect a cultural bias?

7. Make a study of several group intelligence and achievement tests that are commonly used in schools. In what ways are they culturally biased? See if you can devise what you think may be a brief culturally fair test, and try it out on some students.

References

Social Class

BROOM, LEONARD, and PHILIP SELZNICK. *Sociology*. 3d ed. New York: Harper, 1963.

CHILCOTT, JOHN H., NORMAN C. GREENBERG, and HERBERT B. WILSON, eds. *Readings in the Socio-Cultural Foundations of Education.* Belmont, Calif.: Wadsworth, 1968.

CORWIN, RONALD G. *A Sociology of Education: Emerging Patterns of Class, Status and Power in the Public Schools.* New York: Appleton, 1965.

DAVIS, ALLISON. *Social-Class Influences upon Learning.* Cambridge, Mass.: Harvard University Press, 1948.

DOBRINER, WILLIAM M. *Class in Suburbia.* Englewood Cliffs, N.J.: Prentice-Hall, 1963.

HOLLINGSHEAD, AUGUST B. *Elmstown's Youth.* New York: Wiley, 1949.

SEXTON, PATRICIA CAYO. *The American School: A Sociological Analysis.* Englewood Cliffs, N.J.: Prentice-Hall, 1967.

———. *Education and Income.* New York: Viking, 1961.

SOROKIN, PITIRIM A. *Social Mobility.* New York: Harper, 1927.

WARNER, W. LLOYD, MARCHIA MEEKER, and KENNETH EELLS. *Social Class in America.* New York: Harper, 1960.

Color Caste

BILLINGSLEY, ANDREW. *Black Families in White America.* Englewood Cliffs, N.J.: Prentice-Hall, 1968.

CARMICHAEL, STOKELY, and CHARLES V. HAMILTON. *Black Power.* New York: Random House, 1967.

CLARK, KENNETH B. *Dark Ghetto.* New York: Harper, 1965.

CLEAVER, ELDRIDGE. *Soul on Ice.* New York: McGraw-Hill, 1968.

CONANT, JAMES BRYANT. *Slums and Suburbs.* New York: McGraw-Hill, 1961.

DEUTSCH, MARTIN, IRWIN KATZ, and ARTHUR R. JENSEN, eds. *Social Class, Race, and Psychological Development.* New York: Holt, Rinehart & Winston, 1968.

HARRINGTON, MICHAEL. *The Other America.* New York: Macmillan, 1967.

McEVOY, JAMES, and ABRAHAM MILLER. *Black Power and Student Rebellion.* Belmont, Calif.: Wadsworth, 1969.

MALCOLM X. *The Autobiography of Malcolm X.* New York: Grove, 1964.

MEAD, MARGARET. *Science and the Concept of Race.* New York: Columbia University Press, 1968.

NATIONAL COMMISSION ON THE CAUSES AND PREVENTION OF VIOLENCE. *To Establish Justice, to Insure Domestic Tranquility.* Washington, D.C.: U. S. Government Printing Office, 1969.

UNITED STATES COMMISSION ON CIVIL RIGHTS. *Racial Isolation in the*

Public Schools. Washington, D.C.: U.S. Government Printing Office, 1967.

General

BLOOM, BENJAMIN S. *Compensatory Education for Cultural Deprivation.* New York: Holt, Rinehart & Winston, 1965.

DAWSON, HELAINE. *On the Outskirts of Hope.* New York: McGraw-Hill, 1967.

DENNISON, GEORGE. *The Lives of Children.* New York: Random House, 1969.

FANTINI, M., and G. WEINSTEIN. *Making Urban Schools Work.* New York: Holt, Rinehart & Winston, 1967.

————. *The Disadvantaged: Challenge to Education.* New York: Harper, 1968.

FRIEDENBERG, EDGAR Z. *Coming of Age in America.* New York: Random House, Vintage Books, 1965.

HENTOFF, NAT. *Our Children Are Dying.* New York: Viking, 1966.

HERNDON, JAMES. *The Way It Spozed to Be.* New York: Bantam Books, 1965.

HICKERSON, NATHANIEL. *Education for Alienation.* Englewood Cliffs, N.J.: Prentice-Hall, 1966.

JOSEPH, STEPHEN M., ed. *The Me Nobody Knows: Children's Voices from the Ghetto.* New York: Avon, 1969.

KOHL, HERBERT. *36 Children.* New York: New American Library, Signet Books, 1967.

KOZOL, JONATHAN. *Death at an Early Age.* Boston: Houghton Mifflin, 1967.

NATIONAL ADVISORY COMMISSION ON CIVIL DISORDERS. *Report of the National Advisory Commission on Civil Disorders.* New York: Bantam Books, 1968.

PASSOW, A. H., et al. *Education of the Disadvantaged.* New York: Holt, Rinehart & Winston, 1967.

RIESSMAN, FRANK. *The Culturally Deprived Child.* New York: Harper, 1962.

STONE, JAMES C. *Teachers for the Disadvantaged.* San Francisco: Jossey-Bass, 1969.

UNITED STATES DEPARTMENT OF HEALTH, EDUCATION, AND WELFARE, OFFICE OF EDUCATION. *Equality of Educational Opportunity.* Washington, D.C.: U.S. Government Printing Office, 1966.

Promote then, as an object of primary importance, institutions for the general diffusion of
knowledge. In proportion as the structure of a
government gives force to public opinion, it is essential that public opinion be enlightened.

GEORGE WASHINGTON

9

The Past

The growth of American education—which, in reality, begins before the
days of ancient Greece and Rome and continues through such important
eras as the Renaissance and the Reformation in Europe and the colonial
and Revolutionary periods in this country to the present—is without question one of the great epics of modern civilization. Teachers, as well as
physicians, lawyers, and ministers, can have but little real understanding
and appreciation of their chosen profession without some knowledge of the
historical development and significance of their profession. If education is
to move from its traditional conservative position toward one of improvement consistent with America's social, political, and governmental progress, teachers need constantly to evaluate and alter their philosophies and
procedures in the light of the events of the past.

In the few short years since this nation was born, there have been many
improvements in the status of teachers and their profession. A thumbnail
comparison of teachers in the early days of America's history with those
who are employed in twentieth-century schools may make some of these
improvements explicit:

	Colonial Teachers	*Twentieth-Century Teachers*
SEX	Predominantly male, except in "dame schools" and in certain Quaker schools and in some schools in the South.	Mixed, with women predominant in the elementary schools, though in recent years men have become much more in evidence. Men predominate in high schools, colleges, and universities.
EXPERIENCE	Teachers considered their work as temporary rather than a life's vocation, though some were permanent members of the profession with as many as fifty years' service.	The average teacher in the 1960's had taught for thirteen years. The greatest loss of professional personnel occurs within the first three years of teaching.
SALARIES	Varied greatly, ranging between £10 and £100 annually ($50 to $500), depending greatly upon the size of the community. Frequently salaries were paid in kind (wheat, corn, furs, etc.) on a semiannual or quarterly basis. Sometimes board and room was part of a teacher's compensation.	The typical salary for the American teacher of the late 1960's was more than $7,000 annually, paid usually in ten or twelve monthly paychecks. There is, however, a wide range in salaries, from about $4,500 to more than $16,000 annually.
EDUCATION	Varied greatly—from college graduates to those barely able to read and write, with the lesser-educated assigned to lower grades. College graduates were trained in the standard areas of Latin, Greek, and religion. There was no professional education until Franklin established his Academy—later to become the University of Pennsylvania—in 1750.	Teachers in America currently average 4.7 years of college education, and are rapidly approaching an average of 5 years of preparation for both elementary and secondary teaching. Their college work typically provides a fairly balanced array of general education, arts and sciences, and professional-education courses.
LICENSES	Licenses were not required of teachers in the colonies. There were, however, a few	All teachers have licenses issued by authorities in the states where they teach.

Colonial Teachers	Twentieth-Century Teachers
unsuccessful attempts at requiring licenses for schoolmasters.	There are various kinds of credentials or certificates, and the requirements for obtaining them are far from standardized.
WORK LOAD Many teachers held classes from 7 A.M. to 5 P.M. in the summer and from 8 A.M. to 4 P.M. in the winter, and then did the usual "homework" during the remaining waking hours. Teachers often were required or expected to serve in many capacities in the community and church, such as gravediggers, bell ringers, choir directors, church custodians, town criers, etc.	Mid-twentieth-century teachers work up to fifty hours a week in managing the classroom, grading papers, and planning lessons. They often participate in community and church activities of their own choice.

Historical Perspective of Education

The history of American education, as indicated previously, really begins with ancient Greece and Rome. Of course, education has been in existence since the beginning of man: in prehistoric times, parents taught their children; so do they also today. Education in prehistoric times and in ancient countries such as China and Japan, while important, contributed little, if anything, to education in America. This discussion, then, will be limited to the countries and leaders of Europe that have made direct contributions to our educational system; it will then proceed to an overview of the course that education has taken in the United States since the early days of our history.

The modern world's educational systems are indebted to the Greek city-states of Sparta and Athens for a number of their policies and practices. In Sparta, physical education was an important part of the training of men—and even of women, whose function was to bear children. Since the educational aim was the development of soldiers, after beginning their education at home boys received military training between the ages of seven and twenty; and they were taught military science or served in the army until they became full-fledged citizens of the city at the age of thirty.

The great Greek philosophers, poets, and artists came from democratic

Athens, where the educational aim was the preparation of citizens, not, as in Sparta, of soldiers. Children were educated in the home until the age of seven, at which time their formal training began. Then the girls remained at home under the guidance of their mothers and slave-nurses, while the boys attended various private schools until they attained the age of sixteen. The boy was accompanied to and from school by a slave called the *paidagogos*, hence the origin of the term *pedagogue* sometimes applied to teachers. Individualized instruction was a feature of Athenian schools; the subjects were music, literature, and physical education. At sixteen, boys attended the gymnasium, a state-supported school, where the principal subject studied was physical education. Eight- to sixteen-year-old students in Athens studied a wide range of subjects, including grammar, literature, poetry, rhetoric, drama, mathematics, and oratory. Athens produced such outstanding philosophers and teachers as Socrates, Plato, and Aristotle. The writings of the last two, particularly, give insight into the prevailing philosophies of education in Athens.

In Rome, the patterns of education were largely borrowed from the Greeks. Rome developed an intensive concentration in the field of oratory. With the spread of Christianity in the Roman Empire, the early church set up its own schools; finally, about A.D. 491, all except church schools were abolished by the emperor Justinian after Christianity had become the state religion. During the Dark Ages, when the Roman Empire was overthrown by invading barbaric tribes, the only learning activities took place in Christian centers, usually the monasteries. Here churchmen attempted to preserve the culture and learning that had been developed, but education generally was virtually at a standstill for several hundred years.

THE RENAISSANCE

What might be considered the beginning of modern education occurred in the last half of the fifteenth century with the period called the Renaissance. At that time a new interest in education accompanied new emphasis on such academic studies as literature, architecture, arts, and sciences. Beginning in Italy, the revival of learning spread north into central Europe and eventually to the British Isles. The most famous educational philosopher of the Renaissance period was Desiderius Erasmus (about 1469–1536), a Roman Catholic priest born in Rotterdam and educated in the Netherlands, at the University of Paris, and in schools in Italy. But it was his work in England at St. Paul's School and at Cambridge, where he instituted a humanistic curriculum emphasizing classical languages and literature, that had the most direct effect on American schools. His efforts in the English schools resulted in the establishment there of academies, and this type of institution, which stressed sciences and arts as well as the classics, eventually became the pattern of schools transplanted to some of the colonies. Erasmus's writings revealed that he believed in such modern educational practices as universal education, condemnation of corporal punishment, and the study of foreign languages (in his case, Greek and Latin), with the emphasis upon conversation rather than upon memorizing rules of grammar. It was during the Renaissance period that the humanities came into existence; these were the forerunners of such modern studies as political science, social studies, government, sociology, psychology, education, and languages.

THE REFORMATION

The Protestant Reformation, a movement in Europe during the fifteenth and sixteenth centuries, resulted from religious, political, economic, and social causes. Although it had many aspects and was not totally a progressive movement, it nevertheless produced the real pattern for education in a number of the American colonies. The actual break with the Roman Catholic Church came in 1517 when Martin Luther (1483–1546), a German monk, nailed his famous theses questioning certain religious practices to the church door in Wittenberg.

Luther's translation of the Bible into the German language provided a very strong incentive for the people to learn to read. Indeed, the Bible became the most-used textbook in the German nation, and Luther considered it the core of the university curriculum. Luther encouraged the teaching of religion in the schools and translated the catechism into the vernacular language so that it could be taught to children. He also believed that sacred music should be included in the school's curriculum, because it would inspire moral sentiments in pupils. And very significantly for American schools, he proposed that control of the schools be in the hands of civil authorities rather than of church leaders.

Three important aspects of modern American education are the direct result of the Protestant Reformation: (1) the growth of civil control of education as opposed to religious and private control (the so-called doctrine of separation of church and state); (2) the idea that each state should control education within its boundaries; and (3) the dominance of the subject of reading in the elementary schools.

Among the important educational leaders in Europe during the Reformation period, in addition to Luther, were Melancthon, Bugenhagen, Sturm, Calvin, Knox, and Comenius. As the student progresses in his professional-education program, perhaps he will take a course in the history of education and pursue in detail the study of these men and their educational contributions. In this volume, space allows for a cursory discussion of only one, the last.

COMENIUS

John Amos Comenius (1592–1670), member of a small religious sect that grew out of the Reformation in Moravia, a part of Czechoslovakia, was one of the greatest educational leaders of the post-Reformation era. He was a bishop in his church, but because his religious group was despised in his native Moravia, he had to go to Poland and Sweden before his educational ideas bore fruit. He was the first European to make use of pictures in his teaching—the result of attending school at the age of sixteen and observing young boys nine and ten years old struggling with their study of Latin. His illustrated book *Orbis Pictus* (*The Pictured World*) was a primer for teaching Latin. Comenius's educational principles, contained in his book *The Great Didactic,* resemble the objectives of schools

Nature Is Our Guide

Let us then commence to seek out, in God's name, the principles on which, as on an immovable rock, the method of teaching and learning can be grounded. If we wish to find a remedy for the defects of nature, it is in nature herself that we must look for it, since it is certain that art can do nothing unless it imitate nature.

· · · · ·

We find on investigation that the principle which really holds together the fabric of this world of ours, down to the smallest detail, is none other than order; that is to say, the proper division of what comes before and what comes after, of the superior and the subordinate, of the large and the small, of the similar and dissimilar, according to place, time, number, size, and weight, so that each may fulfill its function well.

· · · · ·

. . . Very aptly does Cicero say: "If we take nature as our guide, she will never lead us astray."

· · · · ·

The art of teaching, therefore, demands nothing more than the skillful arrangement of time, of the subjects taught, and of the method.

M. W. Keatinge, *The Great Didactic of John Amos Comenius* (London: A. & C. Black, 1896), pp. 250, 245, 252, 248.

in twentieth-century America. He advocated that *all* children—boys and girls alike—should be educated and that each should have his own textbook. Believing that universal education is impossible unless there is simultaneous instruction of numbers of pupils, Comenius was the first to advance the idea of teaching large groups of children together at the same time. He also recommended that the school year begin on a specific date and that lessons be divided into daily, weekly, and monthly plans. Humor has a place in education, avowed Comenius, and he made great use of fairy tales, play, music, and manual instruction in his teaching. His method was teaching from the known to the unknown, and he made extensive use of sensory learning in his classrooms.

OTHER EARLY EUROPEAN EDUCATORS

Following the era of Comenius were four European leaders in the field of education who are worthy of some note. Jean Jacques Rousseau (1712–78) was an extreme critic of the conditions to be found in France in areas of religion and government as well as in the field of education. He protested against the humanist, formal-discipline educational theories that were in vogue in his time and against the treatment of children as "little adults." Rousseau's theory, explained in his famous book *Emile,* was that children should develop naturally, instead of in accordance with stiff, unnatural, meaningless situations. Among Rousseau's ideas held in high repute in education today are that the school's curriculum should be planned according to the needs and interests of boys and girls, and that reason and experimentation should replace authority. Rousseau's philosophy of education spread throughout France, into Germany and other European countries, and eventually to the United States.

One of Rousseau's disciples was Johann Heinrich Pestalozzi (1746–1827), a Swiss educator who was greatly inspired by reading *Emile* and by the teachings of the French reformer. Pestalozzi experimented with Rousseau's methods on his own children and on children in five different schools in Switzerland, the most famous being that at Yverdon, which he directed for twenty years. Like Rousseau, he believed in the natural development of children and in the doctrine of interest as a means of motivation for learning. Pestalozzi made great use of "object lessons," in which real articles—such as oranges, tools, and so on—were used as teaching aids. His most famous book, *Leonard and Gertrude,* is a novel dealing with peasant life in his native country and with functional home education; his book on educational philosophy and method is *How Gertrude Teaches Her Children.* Many of Pestalozzi's ideas were transplanted directly to American schools.

A pupil of Pestalozzi was the German educator Friedrich Froebel (1782–1852), who conceived the idea of the kindergarten and who opened the first school of this type in 1837 in Blankenburg. Froebel's educational philosophy quite naturally fell in line with that held by his teacher in Switzerland as well as those held by his predecessors, Comenius and Rousseau: he believed in the natural development of children. Teachers from all over the world attended Froebel's school for kindergarten teachers, and the rapid growth in the establishment of kindergartens throughout the world is attributed to the zeal of the graduates of Froebel's school. His philosophy of education is expressed in his book *The Education of Man*.

The Evils of Education

Nature requires children to be children before they are men. By endeavoring to pervert this order, we produce forward fruits, that have neither maturity nor taste, and will not fail soon to wither or corrupt. Hence it is we have so many young professors and old children. Childhood hath its manner of seeing, perceiving, and thinking, peculiar to itself; nor is there anything more absurd than our being anxious to substitute our own in its stead. I would as soon require an infant to be five feet high, as a boy to have judgment at ten years of age. In fact, of what use would reason be to him at that age? Reason is given us as a check upon our power; a child has no need of such restraint.

Jean Jacques Rousseau, *Emile* (1762).

In 1831, Johann Friedrich Herbart (1776–1841), a German professor of philosophy and education, published a book entitled *Letters Dealing with the Application of Psychology to the Art of Teaching*, and thus was planted the seed that eventually became the foundation for modern empirical psychology. Herbart's work was principally in the areas of psychology and method; his thesis with respect to the purpose of education was that it should help children develop moral character. Educational and psychological innovations by this German scholar included the establishment of the first demonstration school connected with a university and the replacement of the old "faculties of the mind" theory—which held that the mind is divided up into such compartments as memory, reasoning, and will, each operating as a separate entity—with the currently accepted idea that the mind functions as a unit. Herbart and his disciples viewed educational method as a science and devised five formal steps in teaching: (1) preparation, (2) presentation, (3) comparison, (4) conclusion, and (5) application. The National Society for the Study of Education, currently an important professional organization in the United States, had its beginning as the National Herbartian Society, organized in America in 1895 by educators who had studied under Herbart's followers in Germany.

Development of American Education

The settlers of the early American colonies brought with them the languages, religions, customs, and educational systems they had known in their homelands. As a result, many different types of schools, most of them largely unsatisfactory, were established on the new continent. Most authorities, however, have defined three important patterns of education in the colonies: that of New England, that of the Middle Atlantic region, and that of the South.

NEW ENGLAND COLONIES

Since religious freedom was one of the strong motives of the English colonists for settling in the New World, it was natural for the early settlers, following as they did the concepts of the European reformers in believing that the only way to salvation was through individual interpretation of the Scriptures, to establish schools so that their children might be able to read. In 1635, fifteen years after the Pilgrims landed at Plymouth Rock, they established the Boston Latin School, the first organized school in New England to be successful. While the educational policy of the New England colonists was different from the European system, the schools themselves were simply transplants of similar schools in the mother country.

Latin grammar schools, the predominant type of educational institution prior to the Revolutionary War, had as their objective the preparation of boys for college, where the emphasis was upon preparation for the ministry. The curriculum of these forerunners of secondary schools in America thus consisted primarily of Latin, Greek, and theology. The Latin grammar school was a seven-year institution, which boys usually entered at the age of seven. Although some money for the support of the Latin grammar schools was raised through taxation, they were chiefly private schools charging tuition, and thus were attended principally by children of the elite in the New England colonies. Remnants of the grammar schools remaining in today's public schools include the emphasis upon a classical education, the rigid graduation requirements channeled toward admission to college, and the emphasis upon a logical rather than a psychological approach to learning.

Some children of both sexes attended "dame schools" in New England. Here they received their elementary education from housewives or mothers, who taught the rudiments of reading and arithmetic and the catechism and who usually charged a small tuition fee. Other children studied under private tutors when their parents could afford them.

The first legislation affecting education in the New England colonies, the Massachusetts School Law of 1642, passed by the Massachusetts Bay Colony, encouraged the education of children. It provided that town magistrates periodically check up on the education of children, and, if it was found wanting, the town officials could attempt to force parents to see that their children learned to read. This law was not strictly enforced, however, so the Massachusetts Law of 1647, better known as the "Old Deluder Satan Law," was passed. With its requirement that each town of fifty householders provide a teacher for its children and that each town of one hundred families provide a Latin grammar school came the first "compulsory" school legislation.

MIDDLE ATLANTIC COLONIES

In the Middle Atlantic colonies, the schools were organized by churches instead of by civil authorities, but, of course, the motive remained the same: that children learn to read so that they might read the Bible. Whereas the Puritan-Calvinist influence was felt in church and civil organizations in New England, such a single influence was not possible in the Middle Atlantic colonies, with their mixture of Protestant denominations. The result was the establishment of private schools by each denomination to teach its own specific beliefs. Civil authorities had little, if any, responsibility for the support of education.

Teachers were usually clergymen until regular instructors were obtainable. Children, both boys and girls, were taught in their native tongues— Dutch in New York, English in Pennsylvania, and Swedish in Delaware—and the emphasis was upon reading, writing, arithmetic, and catechism.

SOUTHERN COLONIES

Virginia and the other southern colonies were principally settled by Englishmen of some means who became the aristocracy and who operated large plantations. These colonists hired private tutors for their own children, but they provided no education for the children of slaves they had imported to work on the plantations. When their children reached a certain age, they were usually sent back to England to finish their education. Since the colonists in the South came to America primarily to improve their economic condition, their government took little interest in education.

A few free schools, however, were established in the southern colonies, principally through contributions of individuals interested in schools. These became known as "pauper schools," because parents whose children attended were required to declare publicly that they were paupers.

EARLY AMERICAN SCHOOLS

Elementary education in the early days of our country's history was, to say the least, hard and crude. The school buildings themselves contained one room with the barest of furniture and educational equipment. Reading, writing, arithmetic, and religion were the principal subjects taught, and these in a way that today seems crude and wasteful. Textbooks were practically nonexistent, the earliest ones being hornbooks consisting of a sheet of paper attached to a wooden paddle and protected by a thin, transparent sheet of horn. These books usually bore the alphabet, a set of syllables, and the Lord's Prayer. *The New England Primer,* which made its debut in the colonies in 1691, was the predominant textbook for 150 years.

Teachers in colonial schools, except in dame schools, were usually men not particularly prepared for their work. None was licensed for teaching. There were no actual grades in the early schools; all children were placed in one large room, and each progressed at his own rate.

While the colonial period in America produced no really great leaders in the field of education, the early national era immediately following the Revolutionary War and leading up to the Civil War saw a few luminaries come forward as statesmen, philosophers, and educators.

Benjamin Franklin (1706–90), born and educated in Boston, believed that education was an individual, not a state function, that schools should be established by individual contributions, and that public monies should be used only for the education of the poor. Convinced that children should be taught practical instead of classical subjects and that they should be taught in English, Franklin established in 1751 in Philadelphia the first public academy, a secondary school that eventually became the University of Pennsylvania.

Thomas Jefferson (1743–1826), one of the nation's earliest and greatest statesmen, had considerable effect on the development of education in America, particularly in his native state of Virginia. He believed in universal education, so that enlightened human beings could govern themselves, and his suggestions led the way for the establishment of the first state school system. The education bill that Jefferson introduced in 1779 in the Virginia legislature proposed a democratic school system in which the state would be divided into sections corresponding to school districts; the bill would also provide for the education of both boys and girls—free for the first three years of primary school—and set up the provisions for electing a superintendent of schools and for secondary education. Worthy graduates of Virginia's high schools would be sent at public expense to the College of William and Mary. Because of the plantation owners' opposi-

The Common School

Without undervaluing any other human agency, it may be safely affirmed that the common school, improved and energized as it can easily be, may become the most effective and benignant of all the forces of civilization. Two reasons sustain this position. In the first place, there is a universality in its operation, which can be affirmed of no other institution whatever. If administered in the spirit of justice and conciliation, all the rising generation may be brought within the circle of its reformatory and elevating influences. And, in the second place, the materials upon which it operates are so pliant and ductile as to be susceptible of assuming a greater variety of forms than any other earthly work of the Creator. The inflexibility and ruggedness of the oak, when compared with the lithe sapling or the tender germ, are but feeble emblems to typify the docility of childhood when contrasted with the obduracy and intractableness of man. It is these inherent advantages of the common school, which, in our own state, have produced results so striking, from a system so imperfect, and an administration so feeble. In teaching the blind and the deaf and dumb, in kindling the latent spark of intelligence that lurks in an idiot's mind, and in the more holy work of reforming abandoned and outcast children, education has proved what it can do by glorious experiments. These wonders it has done in its infancy, and with the lights of a limited experience; but when its faculties shall be fully developed, when it shall be trained to wield its mighty energies for the protection of society against the giant vices which now invade and torment it—against intemperance, avarice, war, slavery, bigotry, the woes of want, and the wickedness of waste—then there will not be a height to which these enemies of the race can escape which it will not scale.

Horace Mann, *Twelfth Annual Report.*

tion, Jefferson's bill did not pass the Virginia legislature, but a great deal of credit is due him for implanting the idea of a complete state system of education into the minds of leaders of other states and eventually of the entire country.

The "Father of American Public Education," Horace Mann (1796–1859), was a lawyer who served his state of Massachusetts in the House of Representatives and in the Senate prior to his appointment in 1837 as first secretary of the newly created Massachusetts State Board of Education, a position he held for twelve years. At the end of each of these years Mann published a report on the accomplishments and needs of the state schools; his most famous report is the seventh, made following five months' study of various schools in Europe. A forerunner of modern teachers' colleges and schools of education was the normal school established by Mann in 1839 in Lexington, Massachusetts. Among the innovations and reforms Mann instigated in his own and other states were the following: improvement of buildings and physical equipment; higher standards for the training of teachers and greater care in the selection of trainees for the profession; higher standards in supervision of instruction; encouragement of the establishment of libraries in schools and towns; improvement of classroom instruction; consolidation of small school districts into larger ones; introduction of vocal music, history, geography, physiology, and hygiene into the public-school curriculum; insistence upon regular attendance; higher teachers' salaries; inauguration of uniform textbooks; and abandonment of corporal punishment.

Henry Barnard (1811–1900), a scholar who graduated from Yale at the early age of nineteen, did for education in Connecticut and Rhode Island what Horace Mann had done in Massachusetts. Barnard's writings are valuable as a comprehensive story of the field of education. He started the *American Journal of Education* in 1855, and in 1867 he was appointed the first United States Commissioner of Education, a position he held for three years.

THE ACADEMY

The school that replaced the Latin grammar school in the early days of our republic was the academy. After Franklin sparked the establishment in 1751 of the first academy in Philadelphia, many schools of this type were initiated throughout the country. They were patterned after the academies in England, with a curricular emphasis upon "everything that is useful and everything that is ornamental." The curriculum of the academy represented a radical departure from that of the Latin grammar school, which was strictly classical in nature. Classes in the academy were conducted in English, and the courses included grammar, arithmetic, accounting, geometry, astronomy, public speaking, writing, history, penmanship, composition, English literature, drawing, science, modern foreign languages, bookkeeping, and navigation. Boys and girls alike attended. While the academies served a need in the eighteenth century and provided schooling for more children than ever before, still, since they were private schools and charged tuition, they did not provide education for all children of secondary-school age. It was not until the first quarter of the nineteenth century that the dream of making secondary education available to all children in our country was realized.

FIRST PUBLIC HIGH SCHOOL

Pressures from citizens for free public secondary schools for their children after they had completed the common schools resulted in the establishment of the Boston English Classical School in 1821; three years later the name was changed to English High School. College-entrance subjects were omitted from the high-school curriculum, but otherwise the new school's program resembled that of the academy. English, mathematics, science, logic, and history were stressed in the school, which at first admitted only boys. In 1826, a girls' high school was opened in Boston, but not until thirty years later did the first coeducational public high school open, in Chicago. The new secondary-school movement spread slowly at first: by 1840, only fourteen towns and cities in Massachusetts had public high schools, and by 1860 about three hundred such schools existed, chiefly in Massachusetts, New York, and Ohio; but by the turn of the century the number had increased to about six thousand, enrolling 80 percent of the nation's youth. In 1827, the Massachusetts legislature passed a law requiring every town of five hundred or more families to maintain a high school that would teach American history, bookkeeping, algebra, geometry, and surveying, and in towns of four thousand or more, Greek, Latin, history, logic, and rhetoric were to be included.

A number of people in the nineteenth century protested against the free public high schools, principally because of the taxation necessary for their maintenance. The famous Kalamazoo case, a test case of public-supported schools tried in 1874 before the Michigan Supreme Court, resulted in the ruling that the city of Kalamazoo could levy taxes to support free public secondary schools. The case, and others that followed, settled the question in America of a community's right to tax its citizens for the support of free public high schools.

EARLY COLLEGES

Several colleges and universities were established in the colonial and early national eras of our country's history. Harvard College, founded in 1636 "to advance learning, and perpetuate it to Posterity, dreading to leave an illiterate Ministery to the Churches, when our present Ministers shall lie in the Dust," was the first institution of higher learning in America. Others—like Harvard open only to young men aspiring to the ministry—included William and Mary in Virginia, 1693; Yale in Connecticut, 1701; Princeton in New Jersey, 1746; Columbia in New York City, 1754; University of Pennsylvania in Philadelphia, 1755; Brown in Rhode Island, 1764; Rutgers in New Jersey, 1766; and Dartmouth in New Hampshire, 1769.

EDUCATION OF WOMEN

Higher education for women was unthought-of for a half-century after the Revolution. But through the untiring efforts of women like Emma Willard (1787–1870), Catherine Beecher (1800–1878), and Mary Lyon (1797–1849), the education of women in secondary school and college became an established reality in the United States. In 1821 Mrs. Willard established the Troy (New York) Female Seminary, in which many teachers of the time were educated. Seven years later, Miss Beecher opened the Hartford (Connecticut) Female Seminary for the training of teachers, nurses, and homemakers, and after she moved in 1838 to Cincinnati, Ohio, she founded the Western Female Institute. At the college level of education, Mary Lyon established Mount Holyoke Seminary in 1836.

EDUCATION OF NEGROES

Education for Negroes in the early days of this nation was, to all intents and purposes, nonexistent, except for that which benevolent plantation owners provided for their slaves' children. In the South it was a serious crime to teach black men to read; in eighteenth-century South Carolina, a hundred-pound fine could be levied against a person who was convicted of teaching Negroes. It was only after the Civil War that educational opportunities began to open up for Negroes, centered around providing basic literacy and training in skilled occupations, in such schools as the institute established by Booker T. Washington. A few institutions, such as Howard, Tufts, and Dillard, offered higher education to Negro students.

THE EDUCATION OF AMERICAN INDIANS

When Lyndon B. Johnson was president of the United States, he said it was a "shameful fact" that the poorest group economically in the nation was the American Indian. Evidence indicating that the American Indians are on the bottom rung of the economic ladder is the fact that they have the highest rate of unemployment and of school dropouts, that they live in the poorest housing, and that in some areas of the nation they are accorded the lowest social status. The deplorable truth is that, here in the last quarter of the twentieth century, many Indians are disinherited, are deprived of their birthright of freedom, and are denied equality of opportunity for an adequate education. Increasing alcoholism, juvenile delinquency, and crime among adult Indians point to the psychological weakening of Indian men, the lowered morale of Indian women, and the alienation of Indian children. These are all symptoms of the white man's inhumanity to his Indian brother.

Most Indian children are disadvantaged because, like their Negro, Mexican-American, and Puerto Rican brothers and sisters, they have been denied the psychological, social, economic, and cultural advantages enjoyed by other American children. Unlike the children in other minority groups, however, the Indian children, along with their fathers and mothers, have been under the jurisdiction of the federal government's Bureau of Indian Affairs in the Department of the Interior. That bureau, having the responsibility of overseeing the general welfare of American Indians and Eskimos, including the education of Indian youths, has established a number of different types of schools, including government reservation and nonreservation boarding schools and government day schools. All too often, these schools have been ill-fated efforts to Americanize the Indians. It is estimated that about one-third of the 150,000 Indian children in schools attend the federally operated institutions. Though some Indian children go to mission and private schools, the majority are enrolled in regular public schools, with the federal government paying the tuition if the children are not residents of the district in which they attend. The fact that the federally operated schools have not been in the hands of the people they serve has produced some disappointing consequences: it is difficult for the most well-meaning of outsiders to know the genuine educational needs of Indian children, and consequently they cannot see the academic retardation and the deplorable social, psychological, and physical deprivations that exist.

During colonial days, prior to the government's assumption of responsibility for the welfare of the Indian population, the Society for the Propagation of the Gospel in Foreign Parts (SPG), established at the turn of the eighteenth century in London by the Church of England, set up many elementary schools and over 340 missions in the American colonies. The SPG provided a type of pauper education in New York from 1704 to 1782; in New Jersey from 1712 to 1777; in Pennsylvania from 1712 to 1778; in Boston and Salem from 1707 to 1773, with three schools operating in Boston in 1709; and in South Carolina from 1707 to 1773. About two-thirds of all SPG's funds were expended in the colonies until its work was terminated by the Revolution. American Indians and Negro slaves received special attention: a missionary would teach children their letters and some hymns and prayers in a building, usually abandoned, on a worn-out piece of land; hence reference is often made to "old field schools."

The first government appropriation for Indian schools was made in the early 1800's. Treaties between the United States and various Indian tribes occasionally promised that the government would provide schools for the Indians. Private funds also went to Indian education. In 1819 Congress passed a law providing for ten thousand dollars a year for the education of American Indians, this money to be assigned to missionary groups as federal aid for the support of church schools for Indians. It was not until June 2, 1924, that Congress passed a law providing that every American Indian now born in the United States is a citizen of this country. With this law now in effect, the federal government's responsibility for Indian education is shifting to the individual states, which continue to have the obligation to provide educational facilities for citizens within their boundaries; hence, most Indian children now attend state-operated public schools. A few federally operated schools for Indians remain for children with special educational needs. For example, the Chemawa Indian School, near Salem, Oregon, provides a specialized curriculum for Navajo and Alaskan Indian adolescents who have never attended school before and thus cannot read, write, or, often, speak English. The Bureau of Indian Affairs also operates three postsecondary schools: Haskell Institute in Lawrence, Kansas; Chiloco Institute in Chiloco, Kansas; and the Institute of American Indian Arts, which opened in 1962 at Santa Fe, New Mexico, to develop artistic and creative talents of Indian pupils.

Funds for the education of Indians have traditionally been very limited, and coverage has consequently been poor. At mid-century, about half of the Navajo children of school age were not in school; today the average amount of formal education that adult Indians have had is about half that of adults in general. Achievement-test scores of Indian children are far below those of other students, and generally the longer the Indian pupil remains in school, the farther behind he gets. All of this results in the Indian graduate's earning about 75 percent less than the national average.

The Indian, the first American, is indeed entitled to the best in education, but traditionally he has not gotten, and does not get, the best. Most government programs in the past have apparently not been successful in assisting Indians in their efforts to maintain individual dignity and culture identity while attaining success in the larger society. The deficiencies in Indian education reflect a growing need for school personnel and literature that will more adequately reflect a multiethnic society.

EDUCATION OF OTHER MINORITIES

In the southwestern states of Texas, New Mexico, Arizona, California, and Colorado, more than two million Mexican-American children attend public schools. Many of them will experience failure in academic achievement, because the schools, for one reason or another, have not provided a curriculum around their Spanish-speaking background. Many Mexican-American boys and girls find it extremely difficult to identify with the more affluent boys and girls pictured in typical textbooks; most disadvantaged Mexican-American children have been no farther than a few blocks away from their homes, and many have not seen a motion picture, nor ridden in a beautiful automobile or boat, nor even seen a house as spacious as the ones pictured in many of the textbooks at school. The pupils reflect a variety of cultural patterns, depending upon parental heritage and the length of time the parents have been American citizens. Some—descendants of early Spanish settlers—have achieved considerable affluence, while others —second- and third-generation descendants of agricultural workers—tend to be very poor. All of these, however, have become pretty well Americanized and have been assimilated into the white society, especially since Mexican-Americans are officially listed as "Caucasian." A third group, however, are first-generation descendants of *braceros*—migrant farm workers who have recently come to this country from Mexico—and they hold tenaciously to Mexican mores and to speaking the Spanish language. It is possible that the Mexican-American children have suffered more from belonging to a family of itinerant farm laborers than they have from segregation. Mexican-Americans who live in cities are often congregated into *barrios,* similar to Negro ghettos, with large families, frequent unemployment, and low-level education.

In improving the school situation for Mexican-Americans, curricula will need to be implemented that more accurately and effectively reflect the real Spanish-speaking backgrounds. Mexican-American pupils can achieve on a par with other youngsters in the various subject areas provided they are taught first in the Spanish language; many more schools in areas where Mexican-American pupils are concentrated will have to provide additional bilingual classroom instruction. They are not inferior to Anglo-Saxon children just because they are culturally different.

In New York and other large cities of the East, many Puerto Rican pupils are experiencing difficulties centering around acculturation, economics, and language, as they try to become assimilated into the regular public-school classes. Teachers there must concentrate on learning and appreciating cultural differences and become more sensitive to the economic and language barriers that the Puerto Rican children in their classes have to surmount. The same could be said for the large numbers of Oriental children in our public-school classrooms, most of whom are concentrated on the West Coast and in Hawaii.

THE EARLY NATIONAL PERIOD

It may be seen from the foregoing paragraphs that from the time of the Revolution to the Civil War (1776 to 1860), education saw some forward-looking advancements. The curriculum of the secondary schools was broadened in the academies and the public high schools; the schools became tax supported and free; and the education of women at secondary and college levels began to receive attention. In 1829, Samuel R. Hall wrote and published the first professional book in education, *Lectures on School Keeping.*

THE POST–CIVIL WAR PERIOD

The years between 1860 and 1918 were marked by some great strides in the development of education in this country. Three emerging philosophies influenced education: idealism, with its emphasis upon the spiritual rather than the material; classical humanism, with its advocation of hard, unpleasant tasks for pupils; and pragmatism, with its practical application of learning and its insistence upon experimentation and research. The ideas and methods of such European educators as Pestalozzi, Herbart, and Froebel began to be adopted in the schools during this period, and several Americans who appeared on the scene profoundly affected education in the United States. Elementary education was greatly expanded during the period, partly because of the rapid growth of urban areas, and the kindergarten became a part of the public-school system in several communities, beginning in St. Louis, Missouri.

America's first real titans in the promotion of educational philosophy, psychology, and methodology made their influence felt in schools throughout the nation during this period. Francis W. Parker (1837–1902), after serving as superintendent of schools in Quincy, Massachusetts, went to the Department of Education at the University of Chicago in its early days and there established some innovations in teaching methods that led to less artificiality in the classroom. William T. Harris (1835–1909) was superintendent of St. Louis schools when Froebel's kindergarten plans were introduced there for the first time in American public schools. G. Stanley Hall (1844–1924) contributed the theory of genetic psychology, concerned with developmental aspects of psychology—tracing processes whereby individual and racial behavior modes are developed—and stressed the idea that methodology needs to be related to the subject being studied, the age of the learner, and the predominant psychology of the era.

William James (1842–1910), America's first great psychologist, published in 1890 a two-volume work entitled *Principles of Psychology,* which forcefully pointed up the relationship between psychology and education. In collaboration with John Dewey and C. S. Peirce, he successfully developed the philosophy of pragmatism, the only American educational ideology. James's writings, including his *Talks to Teachers,* provided the basis for many of the theories and practices of progressive education in this country.

John Dewey (1859–1952), the first great American educator who was educated entirely in the United States, came to pragmatism from idealism. The most important part of his life was the period 1895–1905, when he was a professor of philosophy at the University of Chicago. There, in 1896, he opened his famous experimental school, where, in an ideal school environment, the children studied the great social needs of mankind through an interest approach.

To Dewey, every problem was different, requiring a fresh approach and a fresh solution. The basis of his educational philosophy was change, and the learner, rather than the subject matter, was the important concern in the learning process. Dewey promoted the method of scientific problem solving in the teaching-learning situation, and he had real concern for the use of critical inquiry in all problematic arrangements.

Dewey was a voluminous writer in the fields of both philosophy and education. His outstanding contributions in the latter area are *School and Society, Democracy and Education,* and *Experience and Education.* Among the organizations inspired by this foremost American educational thinker are the Progressive Education Association and the John Dewey Society, which has been in continuous existence since it was founded in 1927.

Among the disciples of Dewey who made an impact upon education in this country are William Heard Kilpatrick, the leading exponent of the concept that the curriculum should be the total range of experiences involved in the school's activities, and Boyd Henry Bode, a progressive-edu-

Definition of Education

We reach a technical definition of education: it is that reconstruction or reorganization of experience which adds to the meaning of experience, and which increases ability to direct the course of subsequent experience. (i.) The increment of meaning corresponds to the increased perception of the connections and continuities of the activities in which we are engaged. The activity begins in an impulsive form; that is, it is blind. It does not know what it is about; that is to say, what are its interactions with other activities. An activity which brings education or instruction with it makes one aware of some of the connections which had been imperceptible. To recur to our simple example, a child who reaches for a bright light gets burned. Henceforth he *knows* that a certain act of touching in connection with a certain act of vision (and *vice-versa*) means heat or pain; or, a certain light means a source of heat. The acts by which a scientific man in his laboratory learns more about flame differ no whit in principle. By doing certain things, he makes perceptible certain connections of heat with other things, which had been previously ignored. Thus his acts in relation to these things get more meaning; he knows better what he is doing or "is about" when he has to do with them; he can *intend* consequences instead of just letting them happen—all synonymous ways of saying the same thing. At the same stroke, the flame has gained in meaning; all that is known about combustion, oxidation, about light and temperature, may become an intrinsic part of his intellectual content.

The other side of an educative experience is an added power of subsequent direction or control. To say that one knows what he is about, or can intend certain consequences, is to say, of course, that he can better anticipate what is going to happen.

John Dewey, *Democracy and Education* (New York: Macmillan, 1916), pp. 89–90. Copyright 1916 by The Macmillan Company, renewed 1944 by John Dewey. Reprinted by permission of The Macmillan Company.

cation exponent, who emphasized a methodology based on the students' interests as well as the democratic approach to learning.

During the post–Civil War period, the government became more active in educational affairs. In 1862, Lincoln signed the Morrill Act establishing a federal fund for vocational education and providing for the education of larger numbers of students. The Supreme Court of Michigan in 1874 handed down the famous decision in the Kalamazoo case, which made it legal for communities to tax themselves for the support of secondary schools. The Committee of Ten on Secondary School Studies of 1893 and the Committee of Thirteen on College Entrance Requirements of 1895 were charged by the National Education Association to study and define the college-preparatory curriculum.

MODERN EDUCATION IN THE UNITED STATES

Since the end of World War I, education in this country has been marked by further important changes. Beginning with the Seven Cardinal Objectives proposed in 1918 by the Commission on Reorganization of Secondary Education, several efforts have been made by various groups to define specifically the purposes of public education in the United States. Interest in education has been at a peak; this, in addition to a population explosion, has resulted in increased enrollments at all school levels as well as in experimentation and research in the techniques of teaching.

Since 1918 there has been an increased emphasis upon the scientific education of pupils; the concern of teachers has been the education of the whole child and providing for the individual differences of children. The federal government has taken an increased interest in education and has provided federal funds for programs in vocational education, through the Smith-Lever Act of 1914, the Smith-Hughes Act of 1917, and the Civilian Conservation Corps Act of 1933; for aid to students in higher education through the National Youth Authority of 1935; for assistance to veterans through the Servicemen's Readjustment Act of 1944 (the GI Bill of Rights); and for programs in foreign languages, science, and guidance through the National Defense Education Act of 1958. The thrust of the federal government in education at all levels in future years will be toward garnering greater resources and stronger tools with which to capitalize fully on already existing programs. Adequate funding of United States Office of Education (USOE) programs, better coordination and more effective use of current USOE programs, and increased participation of schools and colleges and parents and students in the programs that are for their benefit—these are top priorities of the federal activities in education. The USOE will, of course, be active in promoting educational programs and buildings for inner-city schools and the areas of disadvantaged population. Philanthropic foundations, such as the W. K. Kellogg Foundation and the Ford Foundation, have provided funds to public schools and institutions of higher education for the purpose of promoting research and experimentation to improve education.

The Federal Government and Education

While the United States Constitution does not mention education, since the early days of our history the federal government has been friendly toward public education and has, in fact, encouraged its promulgation by a number of actions. Following is a chronology indicating its most important activities and their dates:

1787   Northwest Ordinance. This act provided for one section of each township in the Ohio Territory to be given for maintaining public schools in that township.

1791   Tenth Amendment included in Constitution. Control of education left to the states.

1802   Establishment of the United States Military Academy at West Point, New York.

1803   Policy stated in Northwest Ordinance extended by Congress to other states when Ohio was admitted to the Union.

1818   First federal financial aid to states for education.

1819   Dartmouth College case. New Hampshire legislature attempted to change Dartmouth College from a private to a public college. United States Supreme Court ruled that a college charter is a charter that legislatures may not impair; higher education in this country cannot be entirely a state activity.

1845   Establishment of the United States Naval Academy at Annapolis, Maryland.

1862   Morrill Act, which provided that each state should receive 30,000 acres for each senator and representative in Congress. Money received from the sale of this land was to be invested, and the interest to be used for agricultural- and mechanical-arts colleges. Such colleges continue to receive federal money for their maintenance.

1865   Establishment of Freedmen's Bureau to assist schools for Negro children.

1867   Creation of the United States Office of Education in the Department of the Interior. In 1939, the office was moved to the Federal Security Agency; in 1953, it came under the Department of Health, Education, and Welfare. The United States Commissioner of Education, the chief executive officer in the office, is appointed for an indefinite

246

tenure by the president of the United States. The office is maintained to promote the cause of education in the country and to diffuse information about the condition of education.

1874 Kalamazoo case. The Michigan Supreme Court ruled that it was legal for the public to be taxed to support public secondary schools.

1887 Hatch Act. The federal government appropriated $15,000 annually to each state maintaining an agricultural college, and established agricultural experimental stations.

1909 First White House Conference. Called by President Theodore Roosevelt, the meeting was held in Washington, D.C. Other meetings were held in 1919, 1931, 1940, 1950, 1955, and 1960.

1914 Smith-Lever Act. Provided for matching federal funds with state monies for the promotion of extension work in agriculture and home economics at the college level.

1917 Smith-Hughes Act. Provided for matching federal and state funds to promote agricultural education, manual arts, and home economics at the high-school level.

1918 Compulsory education effective in all states.

1920 Vocational Rehabilitation Act. Federal money provided to states for educating handicapped persons.

1920 Reserve Officers' Training Corps program initiated. Personnel and equipment for training programs in secondary schools and colleges provided by federal government.

1925 Oregon case. United States Supreme Court ruled unconstitutional a law passed by the Oregon legislature in 1922, which required every child in the state to attend public schools. Private and parochial schools can exist in the states, in addition to public schools. The state, however, supervises and inspects all schools.

1933 Federal Emergency Relief Act provided for nursery-school program.

1933 Civilian Conservation Corps. Among other things, this program provided for education and employment of young people.

1937 George-Deen Act. Provided further federal funds for vocational education.

1944 Servicemen's Readjustment Act. The GI Bill of Rights

supplied federal monies for veterans' education. A second act was passed in 1952.

1946   Congressional approval of this country's membership in the United Nations Educational, Scientific and Cultural Organization (UNESCO).

1946   Congressional approval of Fulbright program for international exchanges.

1947   National School Lunch Act. Public and parochial schools were provided federal funds on a permanent basis for school hot-lunch programs.

1948   Congressional approval of Smith-Mundt Act for global program "in information and educational exchanges."

1948, 1949   McCollum and Zorach decisions of United States Supreme Court rendered on religious instruction in public schools.

1950   National Science Foundation created by Congress "for the promotion of basic research and education in the sciences."

1952   More than two hundred channels for noncommercial television reserved by Federal Communications Commission, thus giving birth to educational television with a national potential.

1952   Zorach case. United States Supreme Court ruled that released time for religious instruction off school property was constitutional, thus reversing the 1948 decision.

1953   United States Office of Education made part of the federal Department of Health, Education, and Welfare.

1954   Segregation in public schools ruled unconstitutional by Supreme Court.

1955   White House Conference on Education called by President Eisenhower in Washington, D.C. About 2,000 educators and laymen representing all states and territories discussed aims of education; teacher supply; and school organization, building needs, and finances.

1958   National Defense Education Act. Provided federal funds for the promotion of science, foreign languages, guidance, and audiovisual aids in the schools; also funds for student loans and fellowships.

1961   Peace Corps launched by United States. This program sends volunteers abroad to work in education and other fields.

1962	Schools' use of prayer approved by New York Board of Regents ruled unconstitutional by the United States Supreme Court.
1963	Bible reading in public schools declared unconstitutional by the United States Supreme Court.
1964	Congressional passage of Civil Rights Bill, with provisions for withdrawal of federal financial assistance from any school district practicing segregation.
1964	Federal antipoverty legislation, including some provisions for education, initiated through Economic Opportunity Act.
1965	Congressional approval of National Teacher Corps to serve in local poverty-stricken areas.
1965	Head Start changed to a year-round project of the Office of Economic Opportunity. Formerly it was a summer-only program.
1965	Elementary and Secondary Education Act passed by Congress, authorizing educational benefits directed principally toward pupils from low-income families. Private-school pupils were permitted to share in some services.
1966	Permanent GI Bill passed by Congress. Provided for additional educational benefits for veterans.
1966	Regional educational laboratories and educational research-and-development centers established by United States Office of Education.
1966	Congressional approval of proposal for Internal Education Act.
1967	Head Start program extended upward experimentally by Follow Through for disadvantaged pupils.
1967	Congressional passage of Federal Broadcast Act, creating a public television corporation to promote educational, cultural, and public-affairs programming.
1967	Congressional adoption of Education Professions Development Act, which funds various programs of teacher training, especially for those who will work with disadvantaged or handicapped children but also for certain high-priority programs in the ongoing school functions.
1967	Special research centers established by United States Office of Education to study future educational needs and resources.

1967	Amendments added to, and time extended for, several federal acts, including National Defense Education Act and Elementary and Secondary Education Act.
1968	United States Supreme Court decision that may require teachers to take oaths of allegiance to state and federal constitutions.
1969	Target date for school-district compliance with desegregation provisions of Civil Rights Act of 1964.
1970	White House Conference on Children and Youth, Washington, D.C.

Are the Questions Asked about Education Today New?

Although the preceding broad overview of the history of education, with special emphasis upon the development of schools in America, has not precisely pointed up that specific questions existed in the minds of citizens of the various eras with respect to the schools and their effect on children, such questions are quite readily implied. There is little doubt that since the dawn of civilization people have questioned schools and what they are trying to accomplish and how they are going about it.

Over the past few years the authors have collected several references to people's questions relative to schools and the schooling of their children. Among them is the following, attributed to Socrates, some 2,500 years ago:

The children now love luxury, they have bad manners, contempt for authority, they show disrespect for elders, and love chatter in place of exercise. Children are now tyrants, not servants of their households. They no longer rise when elders enter the room. They contradict their parents, chatter before company, gobble up dainties at the table, cross their legs, and tyrannize over their teachers.

Another reference is the following statement, attributed to Confucius (551–478 B.C.):

The teachers of today just go on repeating things in a rigmarole fashion, annoy the students with constant questions, and repeat the same things over and over again. They do not try to find out what the students' natural inclinations are, so that the students are forced to pretend to like their studies, nor do they try to bring out the best in their talents. What they give the students is wrong in the first place and what they expect of the students is just as wrong. As a result, the students hide their favorite readings and hate their teachers, are exasperated at the difficulty of their studies and do not know what good it does them. Although they go through the regular courses of instruction, they are quick to leave them when they are through. This is the reason for the failure of education today.

Some persons in Aristotle's day complained that children preferred sitting and chatting to participation in physical-education activities and that they had unsavory manners. Complaints were so numerous that the famous Greek philosopher wrote, in 384 B.C., "There are doubts concerning the business of education, since all people do not agree in those things they would have a child taught."

Every generation has had its critics of the schools; the literature abounds with indications of profuse criticism of schools in the United States from colonial times through the present era. In the 1960's we had the Rickovers, Bestors, and Conants. The nature of their criticisms has been that schools are not as good as they once were, that they do not teach the fundamentals, that progressive education has taken over the schools. Today's critics say schools are obsolete and the content of education is irrelevant, especially for the poor, for nonwhites, and for non-college-preparatory suburbanites.

Are the Questions the Result of Misunderstandings?

There can be little question that a great deal of the criticism has merit. Some teachers are not properly prepared—just as some practitioners in any profession or vocation are not properly prepared. Progressive education (whatever that means!) is something that almost everyone opposes— for different and often contradictory reasons. This educational ideology has been held responsible for almost every social evil of the twentieth century. When John Dewey, who formulated the basic principles of progressive education, stated that education should concern itself with the whole child, he meant that development of the child's physical, intellectual, emotional, social, and spiritual being must take place simultaneously; one aspect of a child's being, such as the intellectual, is not isolated from another. Teachers, thought Dewey, must take advantage of the natural interests of children and place as few artificial restraints upon these interests as possible. Some followers of Dewey, however, interpreted this idea to mean that children's interests should reign supreme—a theory Dewey himself violently opposed, accusing these followers of carrying freedom to a point of near anarchy.

When Dewey and the original progressives proposed that education is life itself, not a preparation for life, some disciples assumed that the curriculum should be based on real needs of children at present. Others, however, carried this idea to the point of asserting that such subjects as social dancing and driver training were more important that the more "solid" academic subjects. To this Dewey strongly objected, indicating that the absence of intellectual control through significant subject matter was deplorable.

Currently, the term *progressive education* has no specific meaning. Critics seem to have taken it to mean almost anything that they wish it to mean.

So it is with many of the other questions that are being raised today concerning public education. There can be little question but that today's schools are superior to those of earlier days; children are receiving a better education now than they did formerly, as a number of studies bear out. There has never been a time when teachers failed to accept as a major part of their responsibility the teaching of the fundamental subjects. But the present emphasis upon teaching these fundamental subjects in a meaningful manner sometimes leads people to suspect what the teachers are doing, because this methodology contrasts so sharply with that of the first quarter of this century.

Are the Questions Unhealthy?

A school system is only as good as the teachers and administrative and supervisory officials who make up its personnel. It is natural for professional people to tend to counterattack when numerous emotional charges, especially those having little or no foundation, are hurled in their direction. Such actions and reactions usually generate more heat than light, however, more confusion and discontent than enlightenment and improvement. Actually, it is during a time of dynamic social change, when questions are raised about everything, that educators have their greatest opportunity to improve the schools.

The findings of a recently conducted survey by the Gallup organization, said to be the most comprehensive poll ever taken on opinions of the American people about schools and teachers, indicated that the teaching profession currently is held in higher esteem than ever before. Though laymen do not agree on what is meant by a "qualified teacher," the poll indicated that Americans believe qualified teachers are the most important element in building good schools. Of those Americans polled, 75 percent indicated they would like to have a child of theirs become a public-school teacher.

Criticisms of and questions about the education of children indicate a real concern for and interest in the schools and what they are trying to accomplish. Throughout the length and breadth of this land there is ample evidence that concern and interest are at a peak now: newspapers and magazines publish countless reports concerning education in America; statewide conferences and national White House conferences on education are further indications of the heights to which concern and interest have ascended.

Such times present excellent opportunities for professional educators to evaluate what they are actually accomplishing in the schools and to make improvements where the need is indicated. Generally speaking, the American people are interested in having for their children education that is second to none in the world, and they are willing to pay for it. And as long as there are schools, there will always be room for improvement in their programs.

Will These and Other Questions Continue?

Since there will always be room for improvement in the school programs in the United States, there is no reason to assume that the time will come when people will no longer question and criticize their schools. In the foreseeable future, with dynamic social changes in our culture almost inevitable, there is little to indicate that pressures on schools to provide new and more relevant programs will abate.

It is reasonable to expect the questions and criticisms regarding education to continue as long as the concern and interest remain at their peak, as long as certain inadequacies actually do exist, as long as a certain portion of the country's population questions the advisability of operating public schools at public expense, and as long as there are some individuals in whose minds exists a nostalgic, reactionary belief, on the one hand, and activists bent on revolution, on the other. A needed innovation in most public school systems is the establishment of an objective scheme to audit the school's program in order to determine the extent to which it is meeting its goals and objectives.

The Adequacy of
American Education

By now, it should be evident to the future teachers of the United States that the professional educator's great dream of the attainment of excellence has not been realized. Nor is there evidence at hand that the pursuit of excellence is near its end. In education, as in most of the physical and life sciences, each advancement serves only to open up wide new vistas of what might be tried in the future to provide better school programs for America's most precious natural resources—its boys and girls.

Although there is no general agreement as to the kinds of schools needed in America, parents, taxpayers, and voters all seem to agree that schools are not all they should be, that they should be much more effective than they are, that they do not respond as they should to modern society's problems. In the ghettos, students strike or become dropouts from what they call "the phony school"—one that they see as completely out of touch with the clients and the community it was designed to serve. In suburbia, students mount protests, sit-ins, and lock-outs to call attention to educational practices that are irrelevant to growing up in the McLuhan "the medium is the message" age. Analyses of compensatory-education programs indicate that precious little has been accomplished in raising the achievement levels of minority-group pupils, despite special programs and special funds.

One explanation for these school failures is that many teachers do not put forth the effort to teach as they know how to, that in many schools, unfortunately, they are able to get by without making the effort to reach or touch their students. One of the two coauthors of this volume holds this point of view. The other harbors the gnawing suspicion that for an increasing number of children (the poor, obviously, and perhaps all others with the exception of the college-preparatory types) education is failing. We also disagree on the remedy. One believes that if we were to provide the incentives, freedoms, and supporting structure so that most teachers can teach as they were trained to teach, with the courage to do what they believe ought to be done, regardless of consequences to themselves from the "educational establishment" and the community, this would help solve the problem. The other believes that the problem goes beyond what teachers, individually or collectively, can do and that only radical reforms in the present establishment and the development of some entirely new (and competing) educational agencies will solve the problem.

One of the more recent radical suggestions is to eliminate the public schools entirely. Alternative schools of various types are being established —and supported—by many parents; middle-class children are being removed from public schools and placed in private ones; ghetto parents are fighting for control of schools in their own neighborhoods; storefront schools are being organized by minority groups so that their children may have a better chance than they now do. Whether or not these innovations will, in fact, solve the problems is not known on the basis of any objective evidence to date; still it is clear that a growing number of people are becoming convinced that schools are not giving the proper results for the amount of tax money going into them.

One innovative procedure currently gaining widespread attention is the "voucher plan," whereby each child could attend whatever school his parents chose for him. The child would take to the chosen school a voucher that would entitle the school to the amount of money appropriated per pupil in the local school budget. Proponents of the plan believe that the expanded options offered parents would stimulate the creation of new independent schools, which would be free of the bureaucratic public-school inertia and uninhibited by the traditional constraints of existing private schools. Opponents of the plan believe it to be a scheme to juggle children as a means of satisfying adults' latest political whim. They fear that the voucher-plan advocates have no design for the experiment, that controls are not adequate, and that criteria for assessing results have not evolved.

So, despite the past accomplishments of America's public schools, which shine out so brightly and clearly in many respects, the challenge they currently face is to reform in such a way as to recognize the problems of the society and to help in their solution, thereby strengthening and preserving themselves so that they may in future better serve pupils of all racial, religious, and political backgrounds.

What Is Meant by "Progress"

At one time in the history of American education, progress in the education of students referred to their increasing ability to memorize and verbalize; this was measured by tests that placed a premium on pupils' ability in these two types of activities. Today, progress is considered to be multidimensional. With greater emphasis on quality than on quantity in our education, the feeling is that efforts toward progress should focus on trying to stimulate each child to achieve his fullest potential, to develop the creative powers of children and youth, and to help prepare them to meet the changes and challenges of our society. Progress is to be measured now by our success in teaching children how to think rather than what to think.

For the sake of convenience, most studies and textbooks on child growth and development utilize case studies and other techniques to indicate children's progress in physical, mental, social, personality, and language development, among other areas, and they present frequency distributions and other statistical data resulting in the establishment of norms at certain chronological ages. Few studies have dealt with individual children and their unique total-growth patterns. Most teachers can attest to the fact that no one child in the classroom conforms to the average performances reported in these studies as norms.

What statistical techniques and procedures do not show is what is most significant: what is happening in the intact, functioning child. In attempting to pinpoint a child's makeup and functioning, one must attempt to assess his efforts to encompass a number of divergencies and incongruities that evolve as he grows and develops. As he matures, the growing child is constantly trying to relinquish and reject what he has laboriously achieved in the past and replace it with new means of coping with transitions and of perceiving his world.

Progress, then, takes place in each of several behavior dimensions simultaneously, and it is the responsibility of the teacher to try to encourage this process. To determine the amount of progress made by pupils in the several behavior dimensions, it is necessary for the teacher to evaluate gains made in each dimension for which he has responsibility. In some areas—primarily those in which information is learned—it is relatively simple to assess pupil progress through the use of standardized or teacher-made tests. In other areas, however, measuring pupil progress is not so easy; these involve measuring the pupil's real understanding and his ability to use the information he has presumably learned, and also how he feels about what he has learned and his attitude toward continued learning. It is clear that teachers must learn to use a wide variety of evaluative techniques and also must attain an understanding of instruments used by specialists in testing, guidance, and diagnosis. Most important, teachers need to consider values held by the culture and by children and to translate these into aspects of desirable behavior.

ARE OUR STUDENTS MORE POORLY EDUCATED THAN THEIR FOREBEARS?

There has always been, in the United States, a sentimentality toward the schools that is perfectly normal and understandable. Almost everyone in our communities was at one time or another a pupil in the public schools; in earlier days, and even in the present era in many parts of our country, the school was the center of community social life. Pleasant memories are usually the only ones recalled when present-day pupils' parents and grand-parents reminisce about the "good old days" and the activities that took place in the school they attended. It is quite natural for an adult to feel that his education was superior and that a similar education should be good enough for his offspring.

Some documented studies in existence reveal that modern schools are doing a better job of educating the boys and girls of the land than did the schools of the past. A recent study in the area of reading, for example, indicates that, because of better instruction, today's schoolchildren show reading ability about one-half year higher than any previous generation's.

Present-day quality education reflects a number of variables bearing on the current status of the profession. One conspicuous element in the picture is the fact that teachers are better prepared to teach than ever before: more than 93 percent of today's public-school teachers have the bachelor's degree, and about 25 percent have the master's degree. A second element is the fact that children now attend school longer than in years past: about forty years ago, 400 of every 1,000 fifth-grade pupils stayed long enough to graduate from high school, whereas the figure today is nearer 750 of every 1,000. Reflecting these two elements is a third: expenditures have risen, especially in the past few years. According to the United States Office of Education, the annual expenditure now is five times what it was in 1949–50 (not allowing for changes in the purchasing power of the dollar), and further increases are projected for the next several years. Educational expenditures at all levels were just under 4 percent of the gross national product in 1930, whereas in 1966 they had increased to 6.6 percent of a much larger GNP. A further indication of quality education in the United States today is the provision of essentially universal schooling—or the opportunity available to all citizens in this nation for free public education, from nursery school through adult education.

Despite the fact that there is always room for improvement in American schools, the facts just cited would seem to indicate that, in general, teachers are doing a better job of teaching boys and girls than did their predecessors of some years ago. The demands of the present and future, however, make increasingly better teaching and school programs an absolute necessity.

Are We Losing the Educational Race in the World?

One of the favorite pastimes of critics of American education is to compare our schools unfavorably with those of European nations. Admiral Hyman G. Rickover, USN, one of the most vociferous of the critics, for example, recently made such statements as, "It is time we look around and see what is being done in other countries," and, "Rightly, Sputnik has been seen as a triumph of Russian education." But on the worldwide educational scene, a great paradox seems to exist: while many educators and lay persons in the United States are rushing madly to make changes in our educational pattern so that it will resemble that of certain of the European countries, leaders in those nations are fashioning their education systems to correspond to that of the United States. This paradox was recently expressed eloquently by Stanley Elam, editor of the *Phi Delta Kappan,* in an editorial in that journal:

It is one of the ironies of our time that in the decade of the Fifties, while domestic critics were castigating American schools for "anti-intellectualism" and comparing them unfavorably with those of Europe, the liberal democracies of that continent were abandoning their rigid caste system, with its emphasis on advanced education for the élite only, and beginning to adopt the kind of free, universal, public, unitary, comprehenseive school we take so much for granted.[1]

Countless articles and speeches made by firsthand observers of school systems in other countries bear out the truth that this paradox does, in fact, exist.

To compare objectively the educational systems of foreign countries and the United States is a task of no small proportion. If such a comparison were to be made accurately, it would require, in the words of Medlin, Lindquist, and Schmitt,

. . . *first,* an extensive and intensive investigation into every subject area at every level of the education structure, in order to establish an inventory of quantity and quality, and, *second,* research into the historical, philosophical, social, and economic foundation of the . . . societies from which the schools are created and which they must serve.[2]

Cornell psychologist Urie Bronfenbrenner has visited the Soviet Union nine times since 1960 and has written a book, *Two Worlds of Childhood,* about child-rearing practices in the United States and in Russia. He blames increasing alienation, indifference, antagonism, and violence on the part of the younger generation on a perilously deficient United States system. While admitting that the two nations' child-raising goals are obviously different, Bronfenbrenner believes we could do worse than to borrow

[1] Stanley Elam, Editorial, *Phi Delta Kappan,* November 1961, p. 49.

[2] William K. Medlin, Clarence B. Lindquist, and Marshall L. Schmitt, *Soviet Education Programs* (Washington, D.C.: U.S. Department of Health, Education, and Welfare), pp. 201–10.

selectively from Soviet techniques. He describes Soviet children as members of collectives, like nurseries, schools, camps, and youth programs, that emphasize obedience, self-discipline, and, most important, subordination of self to the group. After admonishing parents to become increasingly "reinvolved" in the lives of their children, Bronfenbrenner points up what he believes to be the responsibility of the schools in the present time: teachers need to renew their interest in the development of their pupils; classrooms should encourage "healthy group competition and organized patterns of mutual help"; and older classes should adopt the Soviet plan of taking on younger grades as "ward classes." Bronfenbrenner, one of the founders of Head Start, is a firm believer in neighborhood programs involving parents and other adult models to help form, or re-form, proper behavioral modes.

When all is said and done, the function of comparative education is not to determine whether one system is better than another (and, as a matter of fact, standards for such a determination have not yet been developed except, perhaps, in the area of educational philosophy), but rather to enrich and fructify ideas and thinking.

We are not losing the educational race in the world today. The educational system we have has played a large part in making this nation the leading one in the world in any aspect one could mention.

Are We Sacrificing Quantity for Quality?

Earlier in this chapter mention was made of the pursuit of excellence in education and of the fact that educators, above all people, realize that the goal of excellence is far from attainment. The publication of *The Pursuit of Excellence* by the Rockefeller Brothers Foundation has challenged the thinking of educators with respect to the responsibilities of the schools and their personnel to students and to the general public.

Having been much used in the literature and in speeches since the publication of the Rockefeller report, the term *excellence* has taken on several different meanings. To certain individuals, the term means that the quantity of work required of students should be increased; to these persons, excellence would be achieved if students spent a greater amount of time and effort on their schoolwork. To others, it means a greater emphasis in school upon the teaching of foreign languages, sciences, and mathematics, and consequently a radical alteration of existing curricular patterns. Still other proponents of excellence in education advocate leaving the responsibility for character development and for citizenship training to the home and church, with the school concentrating exclusively upon the intellectual development of children and youth.

Excellence in education is a complex concept involving much more than simply the instigation of a "get tough" policy on the part of teachers. Quantity of work must not be confused with quality of work; the increase in academic efforts must not result simply in increased busywork, and no stone should be left unturned in an attempt to help students develop their abilities in such areas as creative and critical thinking.

Excellence in education, while undeniably a meritorious goal, poses many problems in the course of its pursuit. It cannot be denied that learning really is an individual matter, and since education is involved in the business of learning, excellence in education can be attained only to the degree that schools provide for experiences that will result in the optimum development of each student. In a democratic society, excellence in education cannot be attained by educating the elite only; schools must provide worthwhile learning experiences for "all the children of all the people." The future of our nation and our way of life depends upon the ability of our people to think independently, critically, and creatively.

Conclusion

To trace the history of education from ancient times to modern twentieth-century schools is to relate an inspiring story of progress and achievement. Through study of the contributions of the great leaders in education and philosophy, present-day American educators can profit from the accomplishments, as well as the errors, of their predecessors, so that education in the world's greatest nation may continue to progress unabatedly toward the ever-elusive goal of excellence.

The years since World War II have seen the rise of many critics of public education in America. They have raised many questions about the programs being offered to children and youth in this country, and in so doing, they have perhaps rendered public education a very real service.

Questions for Discussion

1. In what ways are teachers' situations in modern schools like those of teachers in colonial schools? In what ways are they different? In which aspects of the profession have we apparently made the most progress as far as the teaching situation is concerned?

2. What has the modern American school system inherited from ancient Greece and Rome? the Renaissance period? the Reformation?

3. Which of the early European educators do you think contributed most

to the development of America's educational system? What was his contribution?

4. American colonists were "on fire" in favor of freedom of religion, speech, and assembly. Do you think they also were "on fire" to establish democratic schools? What evidence do you have to substantiate your answer?

5. What remnants of the early schools in this country are still in evidence in modern schools? Do you think that schools of the future are likely to retain these remnants? Why?

6. In what ways do you think recent criticisms of the public schools have resulted in changes in their curricula, methods, organization, and administration?

7. What implications for today's teachers are contained in John Dewey's definition of education?

8. To what extent have the goals that Horace Mann envisioned for the common school been accomplished? Why do you think they have not all been accomplished in the more than a hundred years since Mann presented them?

9. What is the importance of the Kalamazoo case?

10. What is your attitude toward federal activity in the field of education?

Activities and Projects

1. Consulting history books, state departments of education, and "old-timers" in your community, write a paper on the historical development of education in your state.

2. After consulting current periodicals and textbooks containing information on comparative education, prepare a chart on education in the United States and in two countries of your choice. Arrange your paper in three columns, each headed by the countries, and cover items such as elementary- or common-school program, secondary-school program, number of years included, predominant philosophy, method of financing, primary control (national, state, local, etc.), education of teachers, salaries of teachers, types of local administration, and others you may wish to pursue. The arrangement of your page might be as follows:

	Soviet Union	*France*	*United States*
ELEMENTARY PROGRAM			
SECONDARY PROGRAM			

3. Prepare a time chart of the part the federal government has played in the development of education in the United States.

4. Choose one of the European educational leaders mentioned in this chapter and write a biographical paper emphasizing his contributions to American education. Use the term-paper format acceptable in your college's education department.

5. Do the same thing with one of the current leaders in American education.

6. If possible, secure copies of textbooks used in early American schools (or those in use when your grandparents or parents were in school). Compare them with books currently in use, noting differences and what the changes are intended to accomplish.

References

European Influences and the History of American Education

BARNARD, HENRY. *Henry Barnard on Education.* Edited by John Brubacher. New York: Russell & Russell, 1965.

BAYLES, E. E., and B. L. HOOD. *Growth of American Educational Thought and Practice.* New York: Harper, 1966.

BUTTS, R. FREEMAN. *A Cultural History of Western Education.* 2d ed. New York: McGraw-Hill, 1955.

CALLAHAN, RAYMOND E. *An Introduction to Education in American Society.* 2d ed. New York: Knopf, 1960.

COLE, LUELLA. *A History of Education—Socrates to Montessori.* New York: Holt, Rinehart & Winston, 1950.

COMMAGER, HENRY STEELE. *Our Schools Have Kept Us Free.* Washington, D.C.: National School Public Relations Association of the National Education Association, 1963.

DEYOUNG, CHRIS A., and RICHARD WYNN. *American Education.* 6th ed. New York: McGraw-Hill, 1968. Pp. 5–13.

FRENCH, WILLIAM M. *America's Educational Tradition.* Boston: Heath, 1964.

HASKEW, LAURENCE D., and JONATHON C. McLENDON. *This is Teaching.* 3d ed. Glenview, Ill.: Scott, Foresman, 1968. Chaps. 12, 13.

HUGHES, JAMES MONROE. *Education in America.* 2d ed. New York: Harper, 1965.

JOHNSON, JAMES A., HAROLD W. COLLINS, VICTOR L. DUPUIS, and JOHN H. JOHANSEN. *Introduction to the Foundations of American Education.* Boston: Allyn & Bacon, 1969. Sec. 3, chap. 1.

KRUG, EDWARD A. *The Shaping of the American High School.* New York: Harper, 1964.

MAYER, FREDERICK. *A History of Educational Thought.* Columbus, Ohio: C. E. Merrill, 1960.

ORLICH, DONALD C., and S. SAMUEL SHERMIS, eds. *The Pursuit of Excellence: Introductory Readings in Education.* New York: American Book, 1965. Chap. 1.

RICHEY, ROBERT W. *Planning for Teaching.* 4th ed. New York: McGraw-Hill, 1968. Chap. 13.

RYAN, PATRICK J. *Historical Foundations of Public Education in America.* Dubuque, Iowa: Brown, 1965. Chaps. 1–6.

THAYER, V. T. *Formative Ideas in American Education: From Colonial Period to the Present.* New York: Dodd, Mead, 1965.

THUT, I. N. *The Story of Education.* New York: McGraw-Hill, 1957.

WILDS, ELMER H., and KENNETH V. LOTTICH. *The Foundations of Modern Education.* New York: Holt, Rinehart & Winston, 1961.

Criticisms, Questions, Issues, and Trends

"De Facto Segregation." *NEA Research Bulletin,* May 1965, pp. 35–37.

DUKER, SAM. *The Public Schools and Religion: The Legal Context.* New York: Harper, 1966.

"Education and Automation: The Coming World of Work and Leisure." *National Association of Secondary School Principals Bulletin,* vol. 48, no. 295, pp. 56–72, 99–110.

EHLERS, HENRY, and GORDON C. LEE, eds. *Crucial Issues in Education.* New York: Holt, Rinehart & Winston, 1964.

FINN, JAMES D. "A Revolutionary Season." *Phi Delta Kappan,* April 1964, pp. 348–54.

FIORINO, JOHN. "A Question of Values." *Kappa Delta Pi Record,* April 1967.

GRAMBS, JEAN D. *Schools, Scholars, and Society.* Englewood Cliffs, N.J.: Prentice-Hall, 1965.

HAND, HAROLD C. "National Assessment Viewed as the Camel's Nose." *Phi Delta Kappan,* September 1965, pp. 8–13.

HASKEW, LAURENCE D., and JONATHON C. McLENDON. *This Is Teaching.* 3d ed. Glenview, Ill.: Scott, Foresman, 1968. Pp. 301–6.

HAVIGHURST, ROBERT J., and BERNICE L. NEUGARTEN. *Society and Education.* 3d ed. Boston: Allyn & Bacon, 1967.

HICKERSON, NATHANIEL. *Education for Alienation.* Englewood Cliffs, N.J.: Prentice-Hall, 1966.

JOHNSON, JAMES A., HAROLD W. COLLINS, VICTOR L. DUPUIS, and JOHN

H. JOHANSEN. *Introduction to the Foundations of American Education.* Boston: Allyn & Bacon, 1969. Sec. 1, chaps. 4, 5.

JOHNSTON, BERNARD, ed. *Issues in Education: An Anthology of Controversy.* Boston: Houghton Mifflin, 1964.

KALLENBACH, WARREN W., and HAROLD M. HODGES, eds. *Education and Society.* Columbus, Ohio: C. E. Merrill, 1963. Chap. 9.

MISNER, PAUL J., FREDERICK W. SCHNEIDER, and LOWELL G. KEITH. *Elementary School Administration.* Columbus, Ohio: C. E. Merrill, 1963. Chap. 17.

NATIONAL EDUCATION ASSOCIATION. *Freedom to Teach; Freedom to Learn.* Washington, D.C.: Commission on Professional Rights and Responsibilities of the National Education Association, 1964.

————. *School Programs for the Disadvantaged.* Educational Research Service Circular no. 1. Washington, D.C.: Research Division of the National Education Association, 1965.

————. *State of the Nation in Regard to Criticisms of the Schools and Problems of Concern to Teachers.* Washington, D.C.: Commission on Professional Rights and Responsibilities of the National Education Association, 1966.

————. *What Teachers Think: A Summary of Teacher Opinion Poll Findings, 1960–65.* Research Report 1965R-13. Washington, D.C.: Research Division of the National Education Association, 1965.

————, and AMERICAN LEGION. *Teaching about Communism.* Indianapolis: American Legion, 1962.

OLSEN, JAMES. "Challenge of the Poor to the Schools." *Phi Delta Kappan,* October 1965, pp. 79–84.

Problems and Issues in Contemporary Education. An anthology from the *Harvard Educational Review* and the *Teachers College Record.* Glenview, Ill.: Scott, Foresman, 1968.

RICHEY, ROBERT W. *Planning for Teaching.* 4th ed. New York: McGraw-Hill, 1968. Chap. 17.

STINNETT, T. M., and ALBERT J. HUGGETT. *Professional Problems of Teachers.* New York: Macmillan, 1963. Chap. 2.

THAYER, V. T., and MARTIN LEVIT. *The Role of the School in American Society.* 2d ed. New York: Dodd, Mead, 1966. Pt. 4.

UNITED STATES DEPARTMENT OF HEALTH, EDUCATION, AND WELFARE, OFFICE OF EDUCATION. *Contemporary Issues in American Education.* Washington, D.C.: U.S. Government Printing Office, 1965. See especially "School Desegregation," pp. 97–105.

Any man more right than his neighbors constitutes a majority of one. . . .

HENRY DAVID THOREAU

10

The Philosophies

In speaking of the scope of educational philosophy, Adler says, "It addresses itself only to professional educators; it is even written in a peculiar
technical language, which is called 'pedaguese' and is almost totally unin-
telligible to anyone who has not 'done time' in a school of education." [1]
But even many of these who have "done time" in a school of education
find difficulty in working out a specific philosophy that is workable within
a classroom and that can be described in down-to-earth terms in answer to
that favorite question of school-district panels interviewing applicants:
"What is your philosophy of education?" It would be interesting if the applicant were to turn the tables on his interrogators!

A philosophy may be drawn from several schools, not just one. It may
be of the teacher's own making and hence couched in a language all its
own. Furthermore, it may vary from situation to situation, depending on *la
race, le milieu,* and *le moment.*[2]

Passion for Life, a French educational film of 1920 vintage, presents a
good example of the quest for an applicable philosophy of education. As a
fledgling, the new teacher standing before his motley crew of boys in-

[1] Mortimer J. Adler, "In Defense of Philosophy of Education," in *Philosophies of
Education,* Forty-first Yearbook, National Society for the Study of Education
(Bloomington, Ill.: Public School Publishing Co., 1942), p. 218.

[2] The French philosopher Hippolyte Taine used these terms in his literary works to
explain mechanical action. Their use here is in a different context to point out
three factors: the sociological, *la race;* the philosophical, *le milieu;* the psychological, *le moment.*

wardly soliloquizes: "How does one reach the educational soul of each youth; how does one put the element of inquiry into the mind of this one or that one; how does one kindle the spark that unlocks enthusiasm for learning? Look at ———, his pastime is chasing flies on the ceiling; and ———, he is still fishing by the stream where I first met him; and ———, his bewildered look bespeaks what is in his mind; and ———, already a man and still here; and ———, so shy that the slightest motion on the part of the teacher unnerves him."

This new teacher has the very essence of a philosophy of education, "to take a student where he is and bring him where he ought to be and could be, and to make it possible for him, in every way, to open the door to knowledge." But how would this teacher answer the question "What is your philosophy of education?"

To provide for a more meaningful overview of the philosophies of education, two questions must be resolved: first, "What is a philosophy of education?" and second, "Who has a philosophy of education?" A philosophy of education is any reasonably coherent set of values and fundamental assumptions used as a basis for evaluating and guiding educational practice. And every person who has a reflectively held point of view about basic values and assumptions in education has a philosophy of education.

Before any attempt can be made to determine the applicability of a philosophy of education to the classroom, account must be taken of the fact that the writers of philosophies of education did not expound their concepts with a clear-cut picture of the public-school teacher or his student. They were in a sense issuing learned statements from the podium of wisdom for the intellectual consumption of other philosophers.

To develop this thought further and to justify the philosopher's point of view, let us consider the following observation:

> But when the philosopher, for example, tries to answer the question of what education is, he does not set out to observe something called education. This question . . . cannot be answered by observation. Rather, the philosopher seeks to answer his questions by construing definitions and making conceptual and linguistic analyses, by arguments that involve cases and counter-examples, by the use of particular facts and cases, as well as by other logical and linguistic techniques. Educational questions answered in these ways come within the scope of educational philosophy.[3]

Applicability of a philosophy of education is relative to the situation within which application can be found. That is to say, the philosophy—or

[3] Chester W. Harris, ed., *Encyclopedia of Educational Research,* 3d ed. (New York: Macmillan, 1960), p. 957.

offshoots of it—must be shaped to the situation, not the situation to the philosophy. It would seem, then, that when the advocate of a particular philosophy of education states that he unflinchingly adheres, without deviation, to the tenets of *his* philosophy of education, his contention may lack credibility. On the other hand, to be more practical, a teacher who subscribes to any one of the statements of objectives presented in chapter 2 above, "The Goals," is embracing a philosophy of education!

The question of how to classify the various philosophies of education is difficult to answer, because there are no clear-cut schools of educational philosophy. One of the more widely used classifications is based upon the principles distinguishing the various schools of general philosophy. Thus, as "schools" of educational thought are to be found idealism, scholasticism, realism, experimentalism, and existentialism.

But even schools of general philosophy are not themselves mutually exclusive. Only when each school is considered in bold outline and its principles taken in their totality as a system of thought can one school be set apart from another. Even so, in their details, there are still similarities among these schools.

Different philosophical positions bring about differing answers as to what a philosophy of education ought to be and ought to do. We will now consider in the light of this statement the educational philosophies of (1) idealism, (2) scholasticism, (3) realism, (4) experimentalism, and (5) existentialism.

Traditional versus Modern

Idealism, scholasticism, and realism are known as the *traditional* philosophies. They have a common point of view: the end is fixed, established by authority outside and above the individual; within this framework, the individual is free to choose the means of achieving the end.

Experimentalism and existentialism—the *modern* philosophies—also have a common focus, and one that is the antithesis of the traditionalist point of view. Modernists hold that means and ends are of the same dimension—of equal worth—and that the individual is free to select both his ends and the means of achieving them.

Within this wide dichotomy between traditionalists and modernists, there are subtle and interesting differences among the traditionalist philosophies themselves and among individual traditionalists, and between the modernist philosophies and among individual modernists.

In this section, we shall proceed first to examine each of the five "schools"—their tenets and the implications of these for education and teaching—and then return to the traditionalist versus the modernist in terms of the real world of the classroom. (Before going farther, the reader might wish to review the various statements of objectives in chapter 2 above, "The Goals." He will find that most of the earlier statements of goals—earlier in a historical sense—are based on traditional philosophies, while the later ones embrace modern philosophies, at least in part.)

The Philosophy of Idealism

ITS TENETS

Idealism has come to be used for all philosophic theories that give priority to the mind. There is no single meaning for idealism, but a family of meanings, and therefore no single inclusive definition, but a family of definitions. There are different kinds of idealism, but they all stress the reality of personality, though in unequal degrees.

Plato's expression "to see with the eye of the mind" adapts itself well to the main concept of idealism when added to it is the meaning of the word *idea:* of Greek origin, "things clearly seen." Seeing clearly with the mind's eye means to see in a very personal manner. Thus, the idealist can conceive of nothing higher or more valuable than personality. Personality is defined as "that which has value in itself, that for which other values exist, and that which is deserving of respect above all things." [4] In point of origin personality is conceived as descending from the superpersonal, or the original Person. The personality of man is a part of the infinite mind that comprehends the entire universe in personal terms. As Horne has defined the term, "To think of the universe in terms of an original Person expressing himself in finite persons is idealism as a philosophy." [5]

The idealist's world is thus a world in which personality is not only supreme but enjoys freedom, a world of the nature of the mind. In this world mind explains matter, and personality counts for most as it shapes the world to suit its own cosmic purposes. In such a world the destruction of selfhood is unthinkable, and lack of consideration for the personalities of other racial, religious, and ethnic groups is inconsistent with the ideal of the immortality of human personality. To the idealist, the individual must always be considered an end and can never be treated as a means.

[4] Herman H. Horne, "An Idealistic Philosophy of Education," in *Philosophies of Education*, Forty-first Yearbook, National Society for the Study of Education (Bloomington, Ill.: Public School Publishing Co., 1942), p. 152.

[5] Ibid., p. 147.

Idealists claim that ultimate reality is spiritual or ideal. But idealists, like realists, exhibit wide variations in beliefs about philosophical and educational questions. Even so, idealists subscribe in one way or another to the view that consistency and correspondence to reality, as they see reality, are the primary criteria of true ideas.

Mind is the principle of explanation. We live, and move, and have our intellectual being in a world of mind. There is no denying this fact. Mind, subjectively used and objectively applied, is the sole principle of explanation.

IMPLICATIONS FOR EDUCATION

To idealists the chief purpose of education is to develop the individual as a finite personality, and to do so in such a way as to bring him into harmony with a superior life. Only if the person is so developed can he enjoy the basic well-being of which he is capable. This aim is to be achieved partly through positive expression of the self, partly by use of dialectic methods to develop judgment and reasoning, and partly by teaching those skills, knowledges, and ways of thinking essential to responsible citizenship.

Applied to the educational process, this philosophy of personality means that *the learner is an individual who counts for something in the creation of values in the world.* But more than this, the idealist sees the learner not only as an individual but also as a person. The distinction here is one of socialization.

For the idealist, the method (or means) of education is relatively unimportant in the light of the end, i.e., the cultivation of the personality of the pupil. *The idealist teaches pupils, not subjects.*

To summarize the idealist's position, the individual is a finite person capable of growth, under guidance, into the image of the infinite Person, and nothing is higher or more valued than personality. Respect for personality in feeling and behavior is the highest virtue and, if practiced, would solve all human problems.

IMPLICATIONS FOR TEACHING

"I want to see you think," said the seventh-grade teacher to her pupils. The teacher uses this expression as an attention-getting device to impress upon her charges at the beginning of the school year and many times throughout it just what she expects of them. She wants to see all eyes, ears, and minds open. She does not want to sense that some of her students are out of the learning situation.

Idealism: An Example for Illustration and Comment

(The director of a private summer military camp for boys is talking to a group of parents who have expressed an interest in sending their sons to the camp.)

"Our camp, as you know, is known as 'the character camp for boys.' This phrase epitomizes our major objective—to develop the moral fiber of each boy so that he can stand alone against the wind, knowing he is right and armed with the willingness to enforce it. Thus, through participation in sports and games, he learns to work with others and acquire such characteristics as courage, self-reliance, and respect for others, for authority, for God, and the ideals that go with the making of a strong character. We stress involvement in competitive sports and games, so each individual can test and develop his strength against those of his peers. We believe in discipline. Our boys drill for an hour each day as a part of their development of a disciplined mind in a disciplined body. The rationale for military discipline as an integral part of our summer-camp program is the conviction that ready obedience to properly constituted authority is the significant element in the development of mature manhood.

"We begin each day with chapel and end each day with vesper prayers. Every afternoon just after the noon rest period we have a reflection hour when each boy alone or with his counselor can contemplate his own nature, the nature of the universe, and God's nature, to the end that each boy will find strength and inspiration in his own personal self-development and toward the ideal of the well-trained military man, as exemplified in the traditions of West Point: 'Duty, honor, country.' "

In talking with the above teacher (who is not letting the approach of retirement diminish two of the marks of good teaching, namely, youthful zest and unlimited enthusiasm), one is not aware that she espouses a particular philosophy of education or that she works toward putting into practice the tenets of more than one philosophy. As a matter of fact, she leaves the impression that her answer to "What is your philosophy of education?" would probably be, "Let the 'pedaguesists' express their concern for philosophies of education; my job is teaching pupils." Yet this teacher has adopted and put into use two of the basic principles of idealism, to wit, priority of the mind and priority of the individual. She is in effect bringing about the positive expression of self.

Many conversations with her over a period of years indicate that she adapts herself to the situation (culturally disadvantaged students), that she uses well the method she has adopted, that she gets both her subject and herself liked. And as Horne says, continuing along this line of thought, "It is not enough to know method. We must know our pupils and our subjects, and we must be likable people. The objective of all method in teaching is the cultivation of the personality of the pupil." [6] The main thing to remember is that we are teaching students, not subjects.

There is perhaps no other philosophy of education that has a greater impact on the beginning teacher, yet the neophyte is frequently not aware of it. A number of first-year teachers were asked which of the five philosophies of education was likely to exert the greatest influence on their teaching. Although eclecticism was apparent in their answers, the mode of expression, such as "concern for my students," "raise their level of thinking," "reach the individual," and so on, indicated tendencies toward idealism.

Some teachers confuse ideals with idealism. "My most serious setback," remarked one, "was to find that the high ideals which I brought to the classroom could find no applicability with some of my classes." In her case, it turned out that she was assigned to two kinds of students, the academically oriented or college-preparatory, and the nonacademically oriented or non-college-preparatory. This teacher, who had excelled throughout her own scholastic years, could not find continuous application for the high standards under which she herself had worked.

While there is some affinity, in a broader sense, between ideals and idealism, the ideal defined as something in its most perfect or excellent form is not compatible with idealism, which can make allowance for the less than perfect and the less than excellent.

The Philosophy of Scholasticism

ITS TENETS

Scholastic philosophy is theocentric; it has God as its basis. This cornerstone of scholasticism is likely to prove irritating to the modern secularist, who either ignores God or relegates Him to lower case. Secularism and naturalism, so characteristic of other schools of educational philosophy,

[6] Horne, op. cit., pp. 156–71.

make it exceedingly difficult for the modern mind trained in these philosophies to understand the Catholic position on this important matter. Without God, the Catholic maintains, there is no ultimate purpose in life, no ultimate purpose in education.

Like the idealist, to whom he is closely allied, the scholastic also believes in a hierarchy of values. But the supreme value in this instance is union with the church rather than respect for personality per se. "Supernatural values are obviously more important than the natural; spiritual values of greater import than the bodily and eternal of more significance than temporal." [7] Although personal identity is fused in a unity of thought, this still leaves freedom of will and freedom of choice unimpaired.

Scholastic philosophy teaches that there is a yardstick with which to measure the good and the bad. This yardstick deals with the formation of the whole man, body and soul, intellect and will. It is fixed and unchanging, suitable for all ages and all countries. Scholastic philosophy teaches that there is such a yardstick, such a norm of morality, one eminently usable, namely, man's rational nature taken in its entirety.

The scholastic holds the firm belief that man was not placed by happenstance on the face of this earth. His goal is clear-cut: to be saved. Thus his educational goal must be fused with his spiritual; the two must be one, inseparable.

On this point a first-year teacher says: "We are called, in fact admonished, to be perfect as our heavenly Father is perfect (Matt. 5:48). Moreover, experience has shown that the pursuit of perfection, if properly controlled both exteriorly by those concerned with the life of an individual, and interiorly by the individual himself, can be made a source of enduring happiness and fulfillment. Of course, there are various levels of perfection, i.e., religious, social, moral, political, physical, mechanical, intellectual, etc." Since education encompasses all these levels, it would seem that its goals should be the perfecting of the individual on as many levels as possible with proper respect for the person's ability, obligations and— by no means least—freedom to choose whether he will be perfect or not.

To reaffirm what has been previously stated, the philosophy of education most akin to scholasticism is idealism. The most striking thing to the idealist is his own ideas, his mind. Mind, however, is not just composed of ideas; it is the thinking, feeling, purposing self which everyone introspectively knows himself to be. As such it is the strongest conviction of reality that he has. Both the Catholic and the idealist are concerned to explain the origin of mind.

[7] William J. McGucken, "The Philosophy of Catholic Education," in *Philosophies of Education,* Forty-first Yearbook, National Society for the Study of Education (Bloomington, Ill.: Public School Publishing Co., 1942), p. 267.

To summarize, the whole educational aim of scholasticism is to give new life to all persons, restoring them to their place as citizens of the kingdom of God.

IMPLICATIONS FOR EDUCATION

It is the function of education to aid and guide the individual in attainment of the true, the beautiful, and the good, which possess an inherent value. Knowledge is not considered the final end of education. Rather, the aim of education is a gestalt—the formation of the whole man into the likeness of God, better still, transformation of Christians into other Christs.

Quite independently of any dogmas of faith, or any calling on truths known through revelation, the scholastic can formulate a definition of education: "Education is the organized development and equipment of all the powers of a human being, moral, intellectual, and physical, by and for their individual and social uses, directed towards the union of these activities with their Creator as their final end." [8]

Such an end justifies any method of learning based on the theory that all education is ultimately self-education and should eventuate in a self-disciplined individual. Thus are included the full range of teaching methods, from the most traditional to the most progressive.

There has been acrimonious debate within the Catholic church at various periods of history as to what the child should be taught, but the attitude of the church in the matter of the child's nature has never changed. Every child born into this world is regarded as a child of Adam. And the church's whole educational aim is to restore the sons of Adam to their high position as children of God.

Hutchins, in *Higher Learning in America*,[9] points out that modern man is obliged to go to metaphysics to draw education out of its disorder and chaos. He says that in the modern world theology, the principle of order in the medieval university, cannot be an integrating force in education. This is in contradiction to the Catholic viewpoint, which holds that metaphysics necessarily deals with the existence and nature of God. The dispute over the definition of metaphysics is typical of the secularism of this period, which threatens to become so dominant that scholasticism will no longer find any expression in the public schools.

[8] T. Corcoran, S.J., *Private Notes,* quoted in McGucken, op. cit., p. 255.

[9] Robert Maynard Hutchins, *Higher Learning in America* (New Haven: Yale University Press, 1936), pp. 33–58.

Scholasticism: An Example for Illustration and Comment

(A Sister, in garb, is teaching a class in a Roman Catholic school. The room is adorned with a crucifix and pictures of Christ, as well as the usual maps, blackboard, etc.)

Sister: Children, we have been discussing what will happen to us when we receive Confirmation. We said that Confirmation does these things for us: It makes us stronger Christians, more perfect Christians, and soldiers of Christ. Today we have been discussing this third point—being soldiers of Christ. The first two we said have to do only with ourselves. You children know that Christ did not just say, "Be strong Christians, be perfect Christians," but He gave us, first of all, His example, secondly, His Commandments and directions, and thirdly, some special helps. What did we say those special helps were, Jean?

Jean: The seven gifts of the Holy Ghost.

Sister: Good, Jean. The first of these two points have to do only with ourselves, to be strong Christians, perfect Christians. Today we talked about that third point: a soldier of Christ. The first quality of a soldier must always be what?

Sam: Courage.

Sister: Yes, now let's look at that last point. A soldier of Christ is responsible for others. Let's take that idea and apply it to our social studies. Look at the map for a moment. We have been studying the Eastern States, and we have noticed how these people depend on

IMPLICATIONS FOR TEACHING

Two questions about values and ethical ideals have claimed the interest of educational philosophers: (1) What values and rules of conduct are to be taught in the public schools? and (2) How are these values and rules to be taught? Answers to each of these questions have tended to follow differences among philosophers as to the source of values. Those who hold that spiritual values are rooted in the supernatural maintain that moral and spiritual education divorced from religion and religious instruction is inadequate if not impossible. The position of the scholastic is clear: secular education cannot meet the values and rules of scholasticism. These views are exemplified in the American Catholic elementary and secondary schools.

On the other hand, some—those who believe in a naturalistic theory of value, for example—insist upon the view that the secular school can and does develop the highest type of moral as well as spiritual character. "All education is moral, for the end of all teaching is to complete the moral each other and need each other. All year in our various units we have discovered how interdependent the sections of the United States are. Now children, can you see what the attitude of a Catholic should be toward these interdependent people? Interdependence is not just being a good American. Realizing our interdependence, the need for justice and charity, is part of our Confirmation, part of being a good soldier of Christ. Can you think of some special ways in which these people of the Eastern States depend on each other and depend on other parts of our country?

First, it should be pointed out that this example is taken from a catechism class. It illustrates the teaching of doctrine, which is done formally in classes of this sort. This is not a class in arithmetic or social studies as such, which would probably be taught in a more formal fashion. The presence of various religious symbols in the classroom helps to remind everyone of the religious beliefs which permeate the school. The example also illustrates the effort of the Catholic educator to put Catholic faith and principles into all of the child's obligations, his civic as well as his religious ones.

Finally, I would mention that while the classroom technique suggested in this example is typical of many Catholic schools, as well as of others, further examples would show that a great variety of techniques are used in the Catholic schools.

Robert J. Henle, "A Roman Catholic View of Education," in *Philosophies of Education*, ed. Philip H. Phenix (New York: Wiley, 1961), pp. 81–82. Reprinted by permission.

growth of the child, and to impart to him the moral ideals of the race. No knowledge is merely for its own sake, but all must in some way affect conduct. Children act as they have been taught, or as society has let them teach themselves. Honesty, truthfulness, industry, and the other essential virtues of the moral life can be taught. Moreover, the ethical end is not a far-off culmination of one's education, but an idea that is to be realized in every step of the educational process. The child is to grow continuously in the moral as in the intellectual life, and these two aspects of life are inseparable. The contentions of both sides are clear. But the Catholics have a better chance of achieving their aims, because they have their own school system dedicated to their one purpose in education.

That the yardstick of the scholastic has breadth and depth is reaffirmed by Pope Paul VI. Holding that young people tend to be conformists, he said that teachers ought to try to develop their individual personalities and self-affirmation. He remarked to a delegation of teachers active in the youth movement of Italian Catholic Action that an educator should not be "a passive observer of the phenomena of the life of young people." "There is nothing like young people—impatient and rebellious toward principles of the past, and particularly the recent past—for acquiescing to fashion, for fearing being different from others, and for being prone to imitation." The pope warned the educators against mistaking action for thought and "of making experience the fount of truth." The teacher's goal, he said, must be to train a man to act as he thinks.[10]

A first-year teacher, although espousing idealistic naturalism, seemed, by her own admission, to be groping for something more: "My broader goal as a functioning teacher is an attempt to develop in each student an awareness of self as an individual, *but* an individual who can attempt responsibility for himself and his actions within the society of which he is a member—thus necessitating a keen awareness of self-control for successful interaction within the society. The future of the world lies with those we educate today who will become the ministers, the lodge leaders, the corporation presidents, the parents, the professors—the educators of tomorrow!"

The Philosophy of Realism

ITS TENETS

Modern realists hold ultimate reality to be the objective world, a world independent of any and all human experience. Although realists disagree among themselves on many important points, they all seem to agree that not only the true but also the desirable educational ideas and doctrines are those corresponding to the structure of the objective world. In the realistic view of education, theory and reason play a central role. Since right conduct as well as knowledge is grounded in reality, the chief purpose of education is to enable the student to understand the world as it really is. Hence the basic ideas that make up our knowledge of all forms of reality, including the common purposes and points of view that characterize society, should constitute the content of the educational program. Logic, grammar, and mathematics are to be taught, not only as tools of communication but also as instruments for the apprehension of reality.

Thus, in the pursuit of education, the modern realist makes no allowance for the supernatural. His objectivism is purely external. This externalism has for its credo the central role of theory and reason.

[10] *The Catholic Voice*, April 3, 1964, p. 18.

In realism, a familiar as well as useful starting point is the nature of experience. The realist holds that experience is a secondary notion, that a subject and an object must exist in reality before an experience can take place between them. Experiencing, in the realist's view, is the process by which these two independent, antecedent entities come together into a knowing relationship. Thus, the purpose of experiencing is to gain knowledge of what is. In contrast, the experimentalist regards experience as much broader than conscious awareness.

Realism is a gospel not devoid of discipline in the sense of external pressure—even accepting the idea of compulsion from without, a factor in method derided by experimentalists. The teacher operates not only *in loco parentis;* more fundamentally still, he operates *in loco naturae.* The laws of nature provide the basis for discipline in life. A teacher guilty of arbitrary compulsion would be looked down upon by many of his colleagues, but not a parent using rational compulsion in keeping Junior from jumping out of the moving family car.

Realism is more realistic than idealistic, that is, more occupied with things as they *are* than with things as they *should be,* and the realist is frank to admit that if anything is unknown, it cannot at the same time be known; and hence, on the basis of direct knowledge, the truth of the principle of independence—the principle above all others that unifies the realists—cannot be asserted. But the realist does not claim to prove his truth in this impossible way. The principle is not an established generalization from fact. Indeed, realism in its totality is an hypothesis. This theory can be exemplified by examining generic traits of reality as in the following example.

In searching for the reasons to support his practices, the teacher seems ultimately to come to reasons that are basic, beyond which he cannot go or does not care to go. He finally comes to "The world just is that way" or "That is just the nature of things." In other words, there are generic traits of reality that constitute the data, the "givens," of the educative process. If the course of education is set in accordance with them, it can have reasonable assurance of succeeding.

To accept something the way it really is, at face value, that is, to accept it with the finality of reasoning, is the prerogative of the realist. The realist is a fellow close to common sense and to the common man in his attitude toward knowledge. He observes things coming into his ken, then going out, or seeming to, without suffering any significant modification as a result of such experiencing.

To the writer pounding away at the typewriter in his study, the typewriter does not become less real—does not seem to vanish from the world —when he leaves his study to answer the front doorbell. The configuration of the typewriter—its keys, space bar, ribbon, and so forth—can form an instant picture in the mind of the realist, the observer.

To summarize, realism confines itself to the realm of the natural, to the act of knowing—a form of reaction of the organism to a problem situation. To the realist, the problem method in teaching is the one demanded by the nature of the situation.

Respect for the individual is central in the realist's point of view—an individual whose growth is bidirectional in origin, resulting from both the demands of society from without and the needs and pressures from within the individual.

IMPLICATIONS FOR EDUCATION

The realist finds educational value in everything that contributes to his intellectual development. The philosopher's term for "theory of knowledge" is *epistemology;* whatever else education deals with, knowledge certainly has been its central interest through the centuries. For the curriculum of the schools, sound knowledge provides a most important objective.

The realist believes in an educational program conceived as a middle-of-the-road pattern between the point of view of the experimentalist on the one hand and the idealist on the other. The one emphasizes the method of education; the other, the materials of knowledge.

The realist accepts as an equal aim of education—along with individual development—the acquisition of and adjustment to the group culture. The individual develops through adapting to social pressures so that in the final outcome the demands of the individual and the demands of society have been blended into one.

. . . the aim of education, as the realist sees it, is fourfold: to discern the truth about things as they really are and to extend and integrate such truth as is known; to gain such practical knowledge of life in general and of professional functions in particular as can be theoretically grounded and justified; and finally, to transmit this in a coherent and convincing way both to young and old throughout the human community. . . .

Education is the art of communicating truth. It has not been fully achieved until this truth not only lies within but actually possesses the mind and heart of the student. . . . this process of communication is both theoretical and practical, but the theoretical is prior. . . . The child, of course, should be interested in what he is learning. But it does not follow that whatever the child is interested in is, therefore, valuable. This is absurd. The skill of the . . . teacher lies in eliciting the interests of the child in the right things, especially in grasping the truth for its own sake.[11]

[11] John Wild, "Education and Human Society: A Realistic View?" in *Modern Philosophies and Education,* Fifty-fourth Yearbook, National Society for the Study of Education (Chicago: University of Chicago Press, 1955), p. 31.

The accidental interests of children should not determine the direction of education. These interests furnish only the point of departure. The teacher who said, in reply to a visitor's question about the program for the morning, "I don't know what it will be; the children haven't come in yet," does not meet the requirements of the realist's theory of education. For the realist, the function of the teacher is not that of an impartial or inert observer, but that of an intelligent guide who directs the process of learning in the light of both the present status of the learner and the important ends to be achieved.

IMPLICATIONS FOR TEACHING

The "Spare the rod and spoil the child" adage does not hold true for the realist, since he substitutes reason for the rattan. The student is given a glimpse of higher wisdom.

The general assumption is that if a thing is worth doing, a good teacher can prove it; and if so, an intelligent class, like an intelligent community, will approve it. This is the doctrine of consent.

The student who enrolls in a foreign-language class just to study, to provide mental challenge, or—in the common vernacular—to fulfill a requirement, will not do nearly so well as the one who is keenly motivated by the fascinatingly exciting appeal of communicating with someone from another culture, or of serving his country as a career diplomat, or of becoming a teacher of the foreign language.

"L'art pour l'art," Théophile Gautier's poetic doctrine of art for the sake of art, although realistic in art, finds little applicability in the central philosophy of realism. How much interest holds "math for the sake of math," "chemistry for the sake of chemistry," "biology for the sake of biology"? However, to the magnitudes of the operation of mathematics, the formulas of chemistry, and the language of biology, add the proper ingredients of interest on the part of the student (for career or professional attainment) and knowledge of subject matter, suitable methodology, and creativity on the part of the teacher, and there evolves a recipe conducive to separating the known from the unknown.

The Philosophy of Experimentalism

ITS TENETS

Experimentalism as an explicit and systematic theory of education stems primarily from the work of John Dewey. It belongs to the twentieth century, and, like Dewey, it is characteristically American in its temper and

Realism: An Example for Illustration and Comment

(This is a portion of the discussion in a high school physics class.)

Teacher: Today in physics lab we are going to devote our time to a preliminary study of Sir Isaac Newton's three laws of motion. If you have read your homework carefully you will be able to tell me which law I shall be illustrating as I roll this ball across the table. Mary Ann?

Mary Ann: The law of inertia. This means that when something is moving it does nothing itself to change its motion.

Teacher: That is half of it. Can you tell me the other half?

Mary Ann: Yes. When something is at rest it remains that way until something moves it.

Teacher: Good. This ball will continue to roll until it is stopped by me or by some other force. This brings us to Newton's second law of motion. Arnold, will you state it for us?

Arnold: When anything is made to move, its motion is in strict proportion to the force acting on it.

Teacher: Exactly. You boys on the baseball team will know what I mean when I explain the theory of the fast ball and the slow ball. That brings us to the third law of motion. Mary Ann?

Mary Ann: I don't really understand this one. But it says that the action and reaction are equal and opposite.

Teacher: Let me illustrate it for you. It has to do with the truth that rest is a balance of forces. For instance, this book as it stands on the table is attracted by the force of gravitation, but the strength of the table resists this force, so the book remains at rest. Arnold?

Arnold: May I ask a question?

Teacher: Yes.

outlook. The full realization of experimentalism as a comprehensive philosophy came with the advent of industrialism, modern science, and technology.

According to some educational philosophies, the doctrines and practices of education find their ultimate vindication in the analysis, criticism, and organization of human experience. Other philosophies hold that some of these doctrines are rooted in a conception of an ultimate reality that transcends ordinary experience. A general view that finds acceptance by experimentalists is that philosophers who stress experience as the final court of appeal in the justification of educational ideas look to practical conse-

Arnold: Well, Sir Isaac Newton lived a long time ago. Why are we studying about him today?

Teacher: That is a good question, Arnold. In any field of learning, whether it is mathematics, science, or even music, there are certain basic fundamentals and truths. Sir Isaac Newton, though more of a mathematician than an astronomer, discovered the laws that explain why the moon goes around the earth and the planets revolve around the sun. Now, our whole modern machine world also exemplifies the same Newtonian principles. For instance, modern rocketry is an application of Newtonian physics. So Newton is really very modern after all.

In this example we have a teacher trying to induct the class into a field of knowledge, an organized, systematic body of knowledge, physics in this case. They are discussing the laws of Sir Isaac Newton, who illustrates one of the peaks of excellence in the development of physics. This is certainly compatible with the emphasis of classical realism. Notice also the concern for the theoretical, for understanding general laws, which is also characteristic of the classical realist approach.

What the example does not and really could not show, because of its brevity, are the arts of learning: the forming of habits of acquiring, using, and enjoying knowledge through engaging in these acts day after day until the student becomes adept at them. Among these are the arts of reading, of studying, of research, of deliberation, and of discussion. Nor does the example show the arts of imagination being developed. For that we might use a different kind of lesson, such as one in the fine arts, in literature, or even in history.

Harry S. Broudy, "A Classical Realist View of Education," in *Philosophies of Education,* ed. Philip H. Phenix (New York: Wiley, 1961), pp. 22–23. Reprinted by permission.

quences. For experimentalists the test of educational doctrines is to be found in how they work out at the level of observation and practice.

In further substantiation of this approach is a statement of the viewpoint of the experimentalist Hullfish:

The experimentalist turns *to* experience rather than *away* from it in order to find values that are to direct this experience. Experimentalists . . . turn to experience, believing that values emerge in the stresses and strains and in the hopes and aspirations of daily life and that these, when further reflected upon and refined, are then set up as ideals to serve until such time as it seems necessary for them to undergo reconstruction in order that they may guide human activities more effectively.[12]

Knowledge for the experimentalist does not exist objectively as it does for the idealist. Knowledge exists only within experience—as a process of interaction between the individual and his environment. "We always live at the time we live and not at some other time, and only by extracting at each present time the full meaning of each present experience are we prepared for doing the same thing in the future. This is the only preparation which in the long run amounts to anything." [13] It is by and through this process of interaction between a person and the social group of which he is a part that personality of selfhood is formed—"a being able to think itself of what it knows of itself." [14]

It is certain, then, that for the experimentalist, experience assumes both an organism and an environment and is the outcome of their continual interaction. Furthermore, experience is not just something privy to the person who has it. Experience is what it is largely because of the social context in which it takes place. Indeed, if experience did not occur in a common culture, it would have far less meaning than it does. One's knowledge of himself is enhanced by his knowledge of others and his knowledge of others by knowledge of himself. Since the breadth and depth of experience depend on the culture context in which it occurs, preparing the individual to participate in that culture is the main objective of education. Only as it is lived does this culture enter into experience, and it can be lived only as the school enters into community activities, takes field excursions, has shops, and the like.

To the experimentalist the sum total of experience, its aggregate, can find realization within the individual always as an end and never merely as a means. In this regard the experimentalist outlook is interwoven with the following three conceptions from Kilpatrick:

1. Ideas mean only their consequence in experience.

2. Experience is essentially social in origin and predominantly social in purpose.

3. We find out what to expect in life by studying experimentally the uniformities within experience.[15]

[12] Philip H. Phenix, ed., *Philosophies of Education* (New York: Wiley, 1961), p. 11.

[13] John Dewey, *Intelligence in the Modern World* (New York: Random House, 1939), p. 673.

[14] William H. Kilpatrick, "Philosophy of Education from the Experimentalist Outlook," in *Philosophies of Education,* Forty-first Yearbook, National Society for the Study of Education (Bloomington, Ill.: Public School Publishing Co., 1942), p. 41.

[15] Ibid., p. 44.

To summarize, the experimentalist stresses both the experience of the individual and the experience of the group, but sees the growth of the individual as the end and the social order as the instrument for achieving the development of personality.

IMPLICATIONS FOR EDUCATION

On the strictly pedagogical side, experimentalism holds the view that the method of problem solving, by which science has progressed in its conquest of nature, is the best method of learning. It claims that the standards of intellectual discipline to be developed through education are determined by the demands of the problematic situation and the process of its resolution. Pragmatism holds that the end of education is growth, and that the optimum conditions of growth consist of freedom to investigate, together with an absolutely free sharing and exchange of ideas. The most widespread objection to the pragmatic theory of inquiry is that voiced by philosophers who insist upon absolute standards of conduct and upon some conception of knowledge as *transcending* ordinary experience. Other critics, holding man's fundamental knowledge to be metaphysical, insist that scientific knowledge is secondary.

We may see both how the child learns the culture and how to state the correlative aim of education. The child shares in the life of the family and neighborhood; he must do so: his existence depends upon it. This surrounding life goes on, as we saw, in terms of the culture. The child in living this life lives it as shaped and permeated by the cultural distribution. What is thus lived is not lost, as Clifford says, but retained, built at once into the child's organism, into the very structure of his being, to serve as the foundation for future action.[16]

In brief, any adequate educational program will thus be concerned to help each individual child grow up from his state of initial dependence into full participation in the richest available group life, which, in a democratic country, includes a full share in the active management of group affairs. Such an educational program will go on further in an active effort to improve the group culture.

The social concept of experimentalism was nurtured by new interpretations of the school as a social institution, which in turn gave birth to the term *progressive education*. Most of the educational reforms of the first half of the twentieth century were loosely grouped under this term, as the movement had its greatest influence between 1918 and 1935. Progressivism in education rested in part upon new psychological evidence about the

[16] W. K. Clifford, *Lectures and Essays,* quoted in Kilpatrick, op. cit., p. 62.

nature of the learner and the learning process and in part upon new interpretations of the school as a social institution.

IMPLICATIONS FOR TEACHING

It is not the business of the school to transport young people from an environment of activity into one of cramped study of the records of other men's learning, but to transport them from an environment of relatively chance activities into one of activities selected with reference to guidance of learning. The most direct blow to the traditional separation of doing and knowing and to the traditional prestige of purely "intellectual" studies has been given by the progress of experimental science. If this progress has demonstrated anything, it is that there is no such thing as genuine knowledge and fruitful understanding except as the offspring of doing. Men have to do something to things when they wish to find out something; they have to alter conditions. This is the rule of the laboratory method, and the lesson all education has to learn.

In short, "You live what you learn, and you learn what you live," as Dewey pragmatically put it!

In an experimentalist classroom, two things would be expected to predominate. The first of these may be called the continuity of a reflective atmosphere, where students are not merely engaged in fruitless memorization but are thinking through problems of concern and are being helped to do so by the knowledge they bring to bear on them. The second, if we take seriously the development of the quality of human relationships, may be called the continuity of a democratic atmosphere.

There are problems which may easily become too personal for free study, for example, local political problems. But the deeper problems of civilization have to be studied, and our citizens must become intelligent about them. Thinking through problems, or the continuity of a reflective atmosphere, and developing human relationships, or the continuity of a democratic atmosphere, are basic to the "Seek and you shall find" theory of experimentalism.

To the above implications for classroom teaching, a teacher's reaction may well be, "How can I put all this theory into practice? How can I—a kindergarten teacher, an elementary-grade teacher, a junior- or senior-high-school teacher—practice what the experimentalist preaches?" And the experimentalist will answer, "Go to the butcher, the baker, the kilowatt maker. Visit the courtroom, the city hall, the auto factory, the marina, the propulsion plant, the jet runway, etc., etc., etc., and take back to the classroom for exploration and experimentation the substance of your sorties." In addition, the experimentalist is bound to say, "Remember, the experience of children is the curriculum of the classroom."

Experimentalism: An Example for Illustration and Comment

The course of study for fifth-grade social studies in the Bluegrass public schools requires a unit on the community. To introduce it, the teacher has taken the class on a field trip. The class has spent part of a day bussing about the city, observing its geographic features and its industrial complex, and hearing about such things as its unique form of city government.

Now the class has divided into interest groups at work on various projects. One group is concerned with the historical development of the city, another with its economy, another with its cultural features. Each group is responsible for making a detailed study of its topic and for devising a means of writing it up and presenting it to the entire class. Some of the students are working with reference books; others have gone to the library or to interview resource persons; still others are making charts, exhibits, or posters, or are writing up materials.

The teacher moves from group to group, assisting, suggesting, encouraging. The students move about freely. Some work at committee tables in groups; some work individually, then consult and talk with each other.

In the illustration, several features are apparent:

1. The pupils are learning from direct experiences as a prelude to or in conjunction with indirect or vicarious experiences.

2. They are working on problems they have chosen—problems that are therefore real to them ("lifelike") and for which they have considerable inherent motivation.

3. Their intellectual skills are developing, as are their skills of cooperation and deportment.

4. The role of the teacher is that of stimulator, activator, group leader, always in control, but usually from behind the scenes.

The Philosophy of Existentialism

ITS TENETS

The philosophy of existentialism springs from the works of such ideologically varied thinkers as Sören Kierkegaard, Jean-Paul Sartre, Karl Jaspers, Martin Heidegger, and Gabriel Marcel. What these philosophers have in common is their acceptance of the need for introspective examination of *one's own experience* in order to arrive at an answer to the question "What gives meaning to man's existence?"

To some, existentialism represents a philosophy of despair in its stress on the "aloneness" of man, for its philosophical basis lies in *experiential* rather than intellectual knowledge. The source of this experiential knowledge does not lie in empirical life or in the social world, but in the *Angst* or *angoisse* or dread with which man becomes aware of his own situation.

However, those who view existentialism in a positive manner see this very awareness of one's individual situation as a source of complete freedom for man. To the existentialist, man is completely free to determine his own nature by the choices he makes. Values do not exist apart from the freely chosen acts of man. This position differs from that of traditional philosophies, which see choices or decisions as the results of a preexisting "essence"—the essentials of human nature. The existentialist reverses this position by saying that "existence preceded essence."

Kneller explains that essence refers to what a thing or being is intrinsically made of, while existence refers to the act by which it comes about and *is*.[17] For the existentialist, reality is the world of the existing. There is no difference between the external world and the internal world of the mind. Truth has to be sought in one's individual feelings, one's own situation, one's own soul. For example, a man may carefully describe a particular object or living thing, seeking to explain that "certain something" that constitutes its essence, but in order to know if it is genuinely alive, or real, we must personally have an experience with it, become authentically involved in it.[18]

It follows, then, that the individual is thrown on his own resources and that he has great personal freedom. He can rely neither on the past, the lessons of history, nor on the wisdom of others; for although he may find these somewhat helpful in seeking answers, his own situation is particular and unique. As he is confronted by one situation after another, the manner in which he chooses always entails a crucial consequence, because he is creating by his choices the kind of being that he becomes. Along with his personal freedom, therefore, he alone bears the burden of responsibility for his choices.

The existentialist is then committed to developing the choice-making power in the individual. Since there is no established body of knowledge or set of values that the existentialist sees as being handed down to each

[17] George F. Kneller, *Existentialism and Education* (New York: Wiley, 1958), p. 26.
[18] Ibid., p. 3.

individual, emphasis must be placed on the individual's interaction with and evaluation of his own experience, so that he can arrive at his own value judgments and pursue his personal version of the truth. Only by doing this can he become a free agent, a self-actualizing person who knows "when and why he is conforming with or dissenting from the rest of society." [19]

IMPLICATIONS FOR EDUCATION

Immediately one can see the crisis that acceptance of the existentialist position poses for education. One of the values that has been historically a part of education is the desire of an organized society to develop and perpetuate the kind of culture that it has established. How can these demands of social conformity be reconciled to the intrinsic natural diversity in human beings and the desire of the individual to control his own actions in the light of personal motives and preferences? Unlike experimentalism, which also values individualism but stresses a type of education enabling the individual to get along with others and function in groups according to accepted social or psychological norms, existentialism seeks absolute and authentic freedom for the individual. The ideal school system would be one that gives the widest scope for individual expression. It follows, then, that anything "required" or "demanded," such as time schedules, majors, minors, grading systems, or specific courses, would be out. Since the existentialist is committed to developing choice-making powers in the individual, he must provide an environment in which freedom is allowed.

Under the existentialists there would be an emphasis on active participation or involvement in life, as opposed to reflection on life. Experimental-action learning, which might include projects, and tutorial methods and disciplinary devices *chosen by the learner* would replace traditional methods. This does not mean that the existentialist would reject evaluation, books, or group discussions as being worthless, but only that he would have them seen in proper perspective to learning that allows for active personal involvement. As an illustration, the man who has spent his life in practical politics "knows" politics in one way, the way of engagement; the social scientist "knows" politics in another way, the way of rational reflection. [20]

In keeping with this stress on personal engagement, the educational environment might be a home, a street corner, a factory, a hospital, a cafe, or a natural setting, rather than the physical setup of the schools as they

[19] C. A. Bowers, "Existentialism and Educational Theory," *Educational Theory*, July 1965, p. 222.
[20] John Macdonald, *A Philosophy of Education* (Toronto: W. J. Gage, 1965), p. 270.

Existentialism: An Example
for Illustration and Comment

. . . in one class each day for several weeks time was spent in reading current newspapers and listening to news reports on television. Discussion was encouraged concerning different ways in which the news is presented; points of view were identified; and each student was encouraged to read in the papers what was of personal interest and to express personal opinions during discussions. As new or novel ideas of the news were expressed, questions were asked and additional materials on those aspects were made available. Debates were encouraged, and the teacher aided individuals in relating ideas and group behavior in the news to personal behavior. Gradually the individual began to identify areas of personal concern about news items, such as poverty legislation, the peace movement, and the like. With the guidance of the teacher, he made plans for the study and development of his ideas and centers of interest in the news. Specific needs and plans for study were developed. Skills in comprehension and reading, the subject matter to be considered, and the news materials to study and evaluate were selected according to individual recognition of needs and a personal sense of responsibility and commitment. Each student became involved directly and personally with subject matter of the news and news reports and news reporting. In class, students worked at different levels of achievement and at different rates of speed. The teacher assisted in learning; appealed to the individual, provided ample materials, aided in skill development and the stimulation of thought, assisted in evaluation, and facilitated the analysis of behavior.

J. Minor Gwynn and John B. Chase, Jr., *Curriculum Principles and Social Trends* (New York: Macmillan, 1969), p. 45. Copyright © 1969 by The Macmillan Company. Reprinted by permission of The Macmillan Company.

now exist. Since the nonrational side of man, his moral and emotional self, will be developed as well as his rational self, there will be a shift in emphasis from the physical sciences to the humanities and the arts and to the social sciences. Whether a man can build an SST plane or an IBM system on another planet will not matter as much in an existentialistic school system as whether that person has the ability to love, to appreciate, and to respond to the world around him.

IMPLICATIONS FOR TEACHING

For the existentialist, education must become a fundamental "I-thou" relationship. A communion must exist between the teacher and the student, because the development of the pupil as a person rests on the impact or interaction of one human being on or with another. In Martin Buber's words, "The relation in education is one of pure dialogue." [21]

This presupposes that the teacher is aware of his own freedom and possesses both self-commitment and self-identity. In an existentialist role the teacher is no longer in a hierarchical relationship with the pupil; his job is, not to impart information or to discipline, but rather to be a facilitator, a diagnostician, a helper, a genuinely concerned person who sees each individual as unique. Consequently the teacher can no longer rely on group methods to make group decisions or on lecturing, but must present opportunities for individual work and individual decision. Often he might use the Socratic method to draw information actively from the student, and he would value not only objective answers but also subjective responses to subject matter. For example, an honest personal reaction to a piece of literature would be valued as much as a cogent literary analysis of the same work. What is important to the existentialist teacher is not abstract objective reality alone but also personally meaningful reality.

His tasks include bringing the student to a realization of personal freedom and to an acceptance of personal responsibility for the implications of his decisions. The student must not be sheltered from the consequences of his choices. In addition, by his own relationship with each of the students the teacher should lead the student to value the right of others to choice as well as his own. Ideally he aids the student to transcend his present self, to become something more, to realize to the fullest extent his possibilities.

Conclusion

The irreducibles in the teaching process are the teacher, the learner, the thing taught and learned, the method used, the locale (where), and the time (when). Of these, the teacher and the learner are the most important. And of these two, the teacher is engaged only for the sake of the learner.

Whether or not the teacher is aware of this "ultimate irreducible," he must have a philosophy of education—a series of beliefs on the basis of which he makes educational decisions and that guide his actions. Similarly,

[21] Martin Buber, *Between Man and Man*, trans. Ronald Gregor Smith (Boston: Beacon, 1955), p. 58.

MAJOR PHILOSOPHICAL DIFFERENCES

Basic Philosophies	Subject-Matter Emphasis	Preferred Methods	Approaches to Behavior	Scope of the Curriculum
Idealism	Subject matter of the mind: literature, religion, intellectual history	Recitation; lecture; discussion; "seeing" ideas	Imitation of the ideal	Emphasis upon the past: stable and predetermined by authority
Realism	Physical world of things: precise, definite, and measurable answers— mathematics, science	Demonstration; factual recitation; lectures and drill for precision	Rules and laws of conduct for objective recall	Emphasis upon the past: stable, and quantitative structure
Scholasticism and classical humanism	Subject matter for the intellect and spirit: language, mathematics, doctrine	Formal drill; catechism; recitation; lecture	Discipline the mind; discipline to reason	Emphasis upon the past: stable and unchanging
Experimentalism	Human experiences: social problems, scientific problems	Problem solving: analysis; criticism; organization; try out ideas; discovery	Cooperative decisions relative to consequences	Emphasis upon the present: changing; relating to past and future
Existentialism	Individual choice: art, music, literature, religion, moral ethics	Appeal to the total: commitment; personal responsibility	Caring, self-responsibility	Changing individually from present and past toward the future

SOURCE: J. Minor Gwynn and John B. Chase, Jr., *Curriculum Principles and Social Trends* (New York: Macmillan, 1969), p. 46. Copyright © 1969 by The Macmillan Company. Reprinted by permission of The Macmillan Company.

every school faculty and every school district has a philosophy of education.

The five philosophical "schools" reviewed in this chapter agree on (1) the importance of the individual or respect for personality as a basic value; (2) the need for an understanding of the social and cultural development of our civilization as well as the development of the intellectual powers of the child; (3) the necessity to prepare the student for his future role in life; and (4) the necessity to educate for character development and ethical behavior.

The traditionalist schools (idealism, scholasticism, realism) are at opposite poles from the experimentalist and existentialist schools on such points as (1) the place of fixed standards in guiding behavior; (2) the importance of knowledge as end rather than means; (3) the contribution of the present to the process of learning; and (4) the responsibility of the individual for his own behavior. Applied to teaching, the traditionalist philosophies place top priority on the student's knowledge of the cultural heritage and on a curriculum aimed at preparing students for the future by gaining an understanding of the accumulated wisdom of the past. Modern philosophy applied to teaching places top priority on the student's studying his own problems, growing out of his own experience, and mastering the understandings and skills necessary to work cooperatively with his peers or completely on his own toward the solution of these problems.

Similarities and differences between the schools, for *teaching* purposes, are shown in the table opposite, with respect to (1) subject-matter emphasis, (2) preferred methods, (3) approaches to behavior, and (4) scope of the curriculum.

By both direct and implicit statements, this chapter has emphasized that few teachers have a philosophy of education that can be tied directly to one school or to the single label *traditional* or *modern;* most are *eclectic* in their point of view. But all have one, usually unexpressed or implied, to guide them.

Questions for Discussion

1. Look over the various statements of goals in chapter 2. Can you classify each as traditional or modern? To what school of philosophy would you assign each one?

2. How would you classify the educational philosophy of the instructor of this course? Why?

3. What are the chief sources of one's philosophy? Home? School? Religious affiliation? College? Or what?

4. Can a strict adherent of scholasticism be a satisfactory public-school teacher? Do you know of any? What adjustments or concessions might such a person have to make?

5. To what extent do your local newspapers reflect a school of philosophy in their editorials on educational matters?

6. What about the curriculum of the college or university you are now attending? What philosophy of education does it reflect?

7. What parts of the local school curriculum reflect traditional and modern philosophies? Begin by examining the objectives listed for the course you are (or are expected) to teach.

8. Examine the list of activities and projects in an elementary or secondary-school textbook. To what extent do they reflect the influence of progressive education?

9. Recall the quotation from Thoreau at the beginning of this chapter. To what school of philosophy does he belong? Why?

10. Should the schools teach democratic values? How is your answer a reflection of a particular school of philosophy?

11. To what extent should a teacher try to get his students to adapt to his own philosophy?

12. If the goal is "the quest for questions," or "self-actualization," or "tolerance for ambiguity," who decides what and how?

Activities and Projects

1. Write to a school district of your choice and obtain a statement of its philosophy of education. To what extent would you say it is eclectic?

2. Prepare a report on the life and times of John Dewey, showing in particular how his philosophy was a reaction to the social milieu of his times.

3. Visit a kindergarten and spend a day observing the program. How does it reflect the concepts of progressive education?

4. Observe a class in vocational education in a nearby secondary school. To what extent is the program a reflection of the influence of John Dewey and company?

5. Observe some college-preparatory junior-high-school classes of English. To what extent is the teaching a reflection of the traditionalist philosophies?

6. Visit a Catholic school in a nearby community. To what extent are what is taught and how it is taught a reflection of scholasticism?

7. Interview the superintendent or principal of a public school. Inquire about his philosophy of education, and then try to classify it.

8. Interview the mother superior of a Catholic school and ask her for a brief statement of her philosophy of education. How does it differ from that of a realist?

9. Interview the headmaster of an independent elementary or secondary

school. Ask about his philosophy of education. How does it fit into this chapter's classification of schools?

10. Write an essay on current philosophies of education, in which you compare the writings of various exponents of existentialism. Include how teaching would be carried on by each.

References

Idealism

ADLER, MORTIMER J. "In Defense of Philosophy of Education." In *Philosophies of Education*. Forty-first Yearbook, National Society for the Study of Education. Bloomington, Ill.: Public School Publishing Co., 1942. Chap. 5.

BARRET, CLIFFORD, ed. *Contemporary Idealism in America*. New York: Macmillan, 1932.

BRAMELD, THEODORE. *Philosophies of Education in Cultural Perspective*. New York: Dryden, 1955. Pt. 3, "Education as Cultural Conservatism."

BUTLER, J. DONALD. *Four Philosophies and Their Practice in Education and Religion*. New York: Harper, 1957.

———. *Idealism in Education*. New York: Harper, 1969.

HORNE, HERMAN H. "An Idealistic Philosophy of Education." In *Philosophies of Education*. Forty-first Yearbook, National Society for the Study of Education. Bloomington, Ill.: Public School Publishing Co., 1942. Chap. 4.

KIRK, RUSSELL. "A Conservative View of Education." In *Philosophies of Education,* ed. Philip H. Phenix. New York: Wiley, 1961. Chap. 10.

LIGON, ERNEST M. "Education for Moral Character." In *Philosophies of Education,* ed. Philip H. Phenix. New York: Wiley, 1961. Chap. 6.

PARK, J. *Selected Readings in the Philosophy of Education*. 3d ed. New York: Macmillan, 1968.

ROYCE, JOSIAH. *Lectures on Modern Idealism*. New Haven: Yale University Press, 1919.

Scholasticism

BUTLER, J. DONALD. *Four Philosophies and Their Practice in Education and Religion*. New York: Harper, 1957. Chap. 6.

HENLE, ROBERT J. "A Roman Catholic View of Education." In *Philosophies of Education,* ed. Philip H. Phenix. New York: Wiley, 1961. Chap. 8.

McGUCKEN, WILLIAM J. "The Philosophy of Catholic Education." In *Philosophies of Education*. Forty-first Yearbook, National Society for the Study of Education. Bloomington, Ill.: Public School Publishing Co., 1942. Chap. 6.

MARITAIN, JACQUES. *Education at the Crossroads*. New Haven: Yale University Press, 1943.

OUTLER, ALBERT C. "Quid Est Veritas." *Christian Century*, March 9, 1959, pp. 258–60.

PARTRIDGE, GEORGE E. *Genetic Philosophy of Education*. New York: Macmillan, 1912.

WILDS, ELMER H., and KENNETH V. LOTTICH. *The Foundations of Modern Education*. 3d ed. New York: Holt, Rinehart & Winston, 1961. Chap. 7, "Spiritual Discipline for the Soul's Salvation."

Realism

BANDMAN, B. *The Place of Reason in Education*. Columbus, Ohio: Ohio State University Press, 1967.

BRAMELD, THEODORE. *Philosophies of Education in Cultural Perspective*. New York: Dryden, 1955. Pt. 4, "Philosophic Foundations of Perennialism."

BREED, FREDERICK S. *Education and the New Realism*. New York: Macmillian, 1939. Chaps. 1, 10.

———. "Education and the Realistic Outlook." *Philosophies of Education*. Forty-first Yearbook, National Society for the Study of Education. Bloomington, Ill.: Public School Publishing Co., 1942. Chap. 3.

BROUDY, HARRY S. *Building a Philosophy of Education*. Englewood Cliffs, N.J.: Prentice- Hall, 1954. Chaps. 1, 2.

———. "A Classical Realist View of Education." In *Philosophies of Education*, ed. Philip H. Phenix. New York: Wiley, 1961. Chap. 2.

———. "Realism in American Education." *School and Society*, January 17, 1959, pp. 11–14.

BUTLER, J. DONALD. *Four Philosophies and Their Practice in Education and Religion*. New York: Harper, 1957. Chap. 3.

MARTIN, WILLIAM OLIVER. *Realism in Education*. New York: Harper, 1969.

THUT, I. N. *The Story of Education*. New York: McGraw-Hill, 1957.

Experimentalism

BAYLES, ERNEST E. *Pragmaticism in Education*. New York: Harper, 1969.

BODE, BOYD. *Modern Educational Theories*. New York: Macmillan, 1927. Chaps. 4–6.

CHILDS, JOHN L. *American Pragmatism and Education.* New York: Holt, Rinehart & Winston, 1956. Chap. 11.

———. *Education and Morals: An Experimentalist Philosophy of Education.* New York: Appleton, 1950.

———. *Education and the Philosophy of Experimentalism.* New York: Century, 1931.

CREMIN, L. A. *The Transformation of the School: Progressivism in American Education, 1876–1957.* New York: Knopf, 1961.

DEWEY, JOHN. *The Child and the Curriculum.* New York: Macmillan, 1920.

———. *Democracy and Education.* New York: Macmillan, 1916.

———. *Intelligence in the Modern World.* New York: Random House, 1939.

———. *The School and Society.* New York: Macmillan, 1915.

HANDLIN, OSCAR. *John Dewey's Challenge to Education.* New York: Harper, 1959.

KILPATRICK, WILLIAM H. "Philosophy of Education from the Experimentalist Outlook." In *Philosophies of Education.* Forty-first Yearbook, National Society for the Study of Education. Bloomington, Ill.: Public School Publishing Co., 1942. Chap. 2.

SMITH, B. OTHANEL. "Philosophy of Education." In *Encyclopedia of Educational Research,* ed. Chester W. Harris. 3d ed. New York: Macmillan, 1960. Pp. 957–63.

STRATEMEYER, FLORENCE B. "Education for Life Adjustment." In *Philosophies of Education,* ed. Philip H. Phenix. New York: Wiley, 1961. Chap. 3.

WILHELMS, F. T. "A New Progressive Education." *National Elementary Principal,* September 1968, pp. 30–37.

Existentialism

BAKER, BRUCE F. "Existential Philosophies of Education." *Educational Theory,* July 1966, pp. 216–24.

HEIDEGGER, MARTIN. *Existence and Being.* London: Vision Press, 1949.

KAUFMAN, WALTER. *Existentialism from Dostoevsky to Sartre.* New York: Meridian, 1956.

KNELLER, GEORGE F. *Existentialism and Education.* New York: Wiley, 1958.

MORRIS, VAN CLEVE. "Existentialism and Education." *Educational Theory,* October 1954, pp. 247–58.

———. *Existentialism in Education.* New York: Harper, 1969.

PATTY, AUSTIN. "Existential Teaching." *Educational Theory,* October 1967, pp. 329–34.

WORTH, ARTHUR G. "On Existentialism, the Emperor's New Clothes, and Education." *Educational Theory,* July 1955, pp. 152–57.

Eclecticism and Getting into the Classroom

BRACKENBURY, ROBERT L. *Getting Down to Cases.* New York: Putnam, 1959.

BRUBACHER, JOHN S., ed. *Philosophy of Education.* Englewood Cliffs, N.J.: Prentice-Hall, 1951.

BUTLER, J. DONALD. *Four Philosophies and Their Practice in Education and Religion.* New York: Harper, 1968. Chap. 7.

GWYNN, J. MINOR, and JOHN B. CHASE, JR. *Curriculum Principles and Social Trends.* New York: Macmillan, 1969. Chap. 2.

If society clearly defines the new duties it wishes
our schools to fulfill and if it steadfastly supports
them not only with money but also with faith,
they will surely justify that faith in the future as
they have in the past.

HENRY STEELE COMMAGER

11

The System

Organization of the Schools

As indicated previously, there are fifty separate systems of education in
the United States—one for each state—instead of one system for the entire country. Since the nation's Constitution makes no mention of education and its control, this aspect of the culture has been considered an implied power of the states and falls under the provisions of the Tenth
Amendment. Thus, education is legally a function of each state, and each
has made provisions in its constitution for the establishment of public
schools. The states, in turn, have delegated a large part of their responsibility in education to local school districts, which elect directors who are
state officials. The federal government, too, has, since the earliest days of
this nation's history, played an important role in the development and operation of public schools. Thus, public education in the United States is, in
reality, a function shared by the federal and state governments and the
local districts. Legally, however, it is a function of the states, and the state
legislatures have complete control over public education within their
boundaries, subject, of course, to limitations of the federal and state con-
stitutions.

The number of local districts within each state varies considerably; for example, whereas in 1962 the state of Nevada had only 17 districts, the state of Nebraska had more than 3,500. The number of districts in all states has been reduced to a great extent since 1962: the total number for all the states was reduced from 35,330 in that year to 20,440 in the 1969–70 academic year—a figure still considerably below the 10,000 by 1970 recommended in 1960 by the President's Commission on National Goals.

Most school districts provide for a program of instruction from kindergarten or grade one through at least grade twelve, with many districts extending to grades thirteen and fourteen. Though many other organizational schemes are in operation, typically the elementary school includes grades kindergarten or one through six; the junior high school, grades seven through nine; and the senior high school, grades ten through twelve. Some districts employ an 8–4 structure, others use a 6–6 or a 6–2–5 plan; newer experimental plans use arrangements different from these, or none at all, as in the nongraded schools.

Elementary and secondary schools provide programs that meet the minimum standards prescribed by state codes, and they embellish their curricula in accord with their financial abilities. Thus, the offerings of these two school levels ordinarily provide for rather complete educational programs and services, including special classes at various age levels for physically and mentally handicapped and mentally superior students, guidance and counseling services, health services, and remedial programs commensurate with the district's initiative and capabilities. Though some secondary schools specialize in vocational training, most operate as comprehensive high schools, offering a complete program of studies suitable for all students—those going to college, those undecided about college, and those going to work after high school. Of the comprehensive high schools' programs, Conant suggests that they

. . . have three main objectives: first, to provide a general education for all the future citizens; second, to provide good elective programs for those who wish to use their acquired skills immediately upon graduation; and third, to provide satisfactory programs for those whose vocations will depend on their subsequent education in a college or university. . . . This high school should have no less than 100 students in its graduation class.[1]

It is recommended that each elementary and secondary attendance unit employ a full-time principal and sufficient supervisory personnel to care for its needs in this area. If the staff of a building exceeds twenty-five per-

[1] James Bryant Conant, *The American High School Today* (New York: McGraw-Hill, 1959), pp. 14, 17.

sons, the principal should have additional administrative personnel to assist with his work. To be self-sufficient—that is, to be economically able to offer a wide range of special services, including health personnel, a psychological consultant, and so on—it has been suggested that school districts should have at least ten thousand students, or two thousand pupils if the district can obtain certain special services from such other sources as a county or an intermediate unit.

Financing and Control

School finance is one of the most important and, generally, one of the most complex aspects of public education. While financial matters are usually considered principally the concern of the superintendent or one of his assistants or the business manager, in reality they directly affect each teacher and each lay person in the community. Teachers are, of course, vitally interested in such financial aspects as salaries; amounts allocated for teaching-learning materials and equipment, including textbooks; and adequate physical facilities in which to work. Lay citizens, while normally interested in providing a good education for children in the community, are, at the same time, concerned with the costs of the school system's programs. In most communities in the United States, the public school is the largest of all business enterprises.

Although a great sum of money goes into the public schools each year —currently about $38.4 billion annually—it is still doubtful that enough is being spent for the education of America's most important natural resources—its children and youth. That figure, up considerably from the $18 billion per year spent in the early 1960's, reflects the major change in the past few years, namely, a decided increase in the federal contribution. Federal spending, however, amounted to $26 million less in 1969–70 than in 1968–69; in the latter academic year the federal government's effort in funding schools dropped for the first time in twenty-six years to 7.4 percent of total school financing. Federal expenditures for schools reached a high of 8 percent in 1967–68. It has been estimated that by the year 1982 the cost of maintaining and operating all schools and colleges in the nation will exceed $50 billion.

Currently across the country, the local community pays about 52 percent of the total cost of public-school education, about 90 percent of that amount being derived from taxes on local real estate and personal property. The states' share, nationally, approximates 40.3 percent of the total school costs, though the proportion of support provided at that level varies widely, from about 3.9 percent in Nebraska to 84.5 percent in Hawaii.

There is a need for action that will widen the local tax base to relieve real property of a disproportionate share of financing schools, and since most school districts are not empowered to devise new tax revenues, there is a need for increased state and federal support of education. In one way or another, however, there is no way to support public schools other than by taxation.

Many problems of the schools relate to the matter of their finances, or, rather, their lack of finances. The problems have become more numerous and critical in recent years with the trend toward extending school systems upward to include the junior college and downward to include the kindergarten and nursery school, the trend toward equalizing educational opportunity for all boys and girls in the country, colossal increases in enrollment, the attempt to provide more quality in the educational program, tremendous increases in school-building construction, and inflation.

The school budget is the instrument whereby the school systems cope with financial problems. Generally, the budget is prepared by the superintendent or his assistant in charge of finance and is presented to the board of education for approval. There is a current trend in budget preparation toward the cooperative involvement of representatives of all groups of school personnel and, in many instances, of lay people in the school community. A good budget includes not only an annual financial plan of educational program, receipts, and expenditures but also a projection of these budgetary areas on a long-term basis, sometimes extending up to twenty years into the future. The educational-program portion of the plan includes such factors as the curriculum, pupil population, teacher-pupil ratios, and scope of offerings. The plan for receipts involves listing the sources of funds other than those to be raised by local taxes and the amounts estimated to be received from each source. Included in the expenditures section of the budget are the classifications of instruction (which generally accounts for an average of 66.7 percent of the total expenditures), administration (4.5 percent), fixed charges such as rent and insurance (6.4 percent), operation and maintenance of the physical plant (13 percent), and special services such as health and school lunch, summer school, capital outlay, and debt services (9.4 percent).

The American people are zealous in their desire to maintain the operation of their schools at a local level. As a result, people living in school districts establish their schools and provide buildings, materials, personnel, and programs for their operation and maintenance. The districts originally were formed by a vote of the people with approval of the state legislature. The boundaries of the districts vary to a great extent; sometimes they follow city, township, or county lines, sometimes not. Generally, counties are broken up into school districts, though in a number of southern states the local school district's boundaries are the same as those of the county. As indicated previously, there is a national trend toward consolidation of two or more local districts into one so that small, inefficient units may be replaced by larger ones that can provide improved educational programs. Some states have established intermediate units. In previous years these consisted of administrative units operating within county lines with a primary concern for schools in rural areas and small towns. Currently, the intermediate units assist the state office in supervising local schools, provide for special supplementary services to local districts that for some reason cannot provide these services for themselves, assume the responsibility of providing a special educational program for such areas as vocational training and handicapped youngsters, and provide an educational program for post-high-school students who do not intend to go to college.

BOARDS OF EDUCATION

The governing board for each school district is a four- to nine-member lay group known as the board of education. The board is usually elected by the citizens of the district and derives its powers from the state. Approving the system's annual budget and employing a district superintendent are the two primary responsibilities of the board of education, though it is usually charged also with hiring all school-district personnel, levying taxes, contracting for school-building construction, approving salary schedules, and generally setting school-system policy. A board of education is a policy-making group, and its functions do not include administering the schools, though it does have the power to make and enforce reasonable rules and regulations. To carry out its policies, it names a chief executive officer, the superintendent of schools.

SUPERINTENDENT OF SCHOOLS

The superintendent of schools serves not only as the executive officer of the board of education but also as the school system's chief administrator. Since the first professional superintendent was appointed in 1837 in Buffalo, New York, the person in this office generally has been charged with carrying out policies of the board and serving as educational leader of the community and of the professional staff.

THE BUILDING PRINCIPAL

As the superintendent is the professional leader for the system, so the principal is the educational leader of an individual elementary- or secondary-school building. The principalship no longer is a teaching position from which a little time is released for care of administrative details; ideally, it is a full-time professional position, the holder of which is considered an educational statesman in his school community.

Today's principal is an instructional leader; national administrators' organizations are advocating that elementary and secondary principals spend at least 50 per cent of their time in supervisory activities. In addition to helping teachers through various supervisory activities, principals maintain records on pupils and staff, prepare schedules, employ substitute teachers, prepare various kinds of reports, provide teachers with teaching materials, spark curriculum improvement, and assist with hiring teachers.

STATE DEPARTMENTS OF EDUCATION

The state-government agency that licenses public-school teachers and issues their teaching credentials is the state department of education. Of course this agency also carries out a number of other important functions besides that of licensing: these include providing adequate, balanced, comprehensive plans for the state's public-school programs; proposing educational measures for legislative consideration and executing school laws that have been passed by the legislature; distributing monies from the state for support of local schools; and establishing certain minimum regulations governing curricula, building construction, and health and safety measures. In most states, the state department provides certain supervisory assistance, such as consultants and materials in various fields of knowledge, for the use of teachers in the state; also, professional information of all kinds is accessible in state-department offices.

CHIEF STATE SCHOOL OFFICER

The executive officer of the state department of education is called variously the state superintendent of schools, the state superintendent of public instruction, the commissioner of education, or the state director of education. He is generally elected by the people or appointed by the governor, although there is a trend toward appointment by the state board of education. His tenure is generally for four years, though some states provide an indefinite term of office.

Among the duties of the chief state school officer are to have general supervision of the public schools; to act as the executive officer of the state department of education and the state board of education; to nominate (and remove from office) personnel for his professional and clerical staff; to organize the state department of education, subject to the state board of education's approval; to prepare outlines for state courses of study; to prepare and submit to proper state officials a budget for current expenses of the state department and for amounts of money to be appropriated to public schools and to institutions under control of the state department; to interpret school laws; to prepare forms for reports from school districts and state educational institutions; to evaluate credentials and issue licenses to certificated school personnel; to approve school sites and plans; to review proposals for school consolidations; to report state school status and needs to the legislature and the governor; and to approve teacher-education curricula.

STATE BOARDS OF EDUCATION

All states except Illinois, Michigan, North Dakota, and Wisconsin have state boards of education whose chief responsibility consists of interpreting the educational needs, practices, and trends of the schools to the people in the state, and of developing the educational policies desired by the people. In the four states mentioned, these responsibilities are carried out by the chief state school officials. Most members of the state boards are appointed by the governor or other state officials, but there seems to be a trend toward having the members elected by the people. The number on the boards and the tenure of the members vary widely among the states.

State Certification

Enormous differences exist among the fifty states in the certification of teachers and other school personnel such as principals, guidance workers, and superintendents. So great is the variation in requirements that about all one can say the various states have in common is the requirement that the teacher be issued some type of license before he can commence to practice his profession.

In some states a person may be issued a regular teaching certificate even if he does not possess a bachelor's degree. At the other extreme are states in which a regular certificate is issued only after the completion of five years of preparation. There also are wide variations in the specific requirements for a teaching certificate. For example, no two states have the same requirements for an elementary-school certificate. To add to the lack of agreement on what constitutes essential minimum preparation for a teacher, even the high-standard states have loopholes and "escape hatches" that permit teaching on less than the regular fifth-year standard. Sometimes these forms of substandard certification are called "provisional" or "emergency," and in other cases a so-called "standard" certificate is issued with the fifth-year requirement "postponed," that is, to be completed during the ensuing five years of teaching service.

While the wide variation in practices and requirements leads to the conclusion that licensing by the states can best be described as in a state of confusion, there is an important concept that should not be overlooked, the one requirement that all states have: that teachers be licensed. States do this to assure the public that only properly qualified and properly educated persons will teach their children. Some states, like New York, even require teachers in private schools to be licensed.

Fortunately, there are statewide and national movements working for reform in certification. Let us look briefly at four developments that seem to be having the greatest influence. These are (1) reciprocity, (2) political action, (3) recommendations of scholars, and (4) experimental programs of teacher preparation.

RECIPROCITY

It seems ludicrous that a person who is certifiable in one state and thus considered a competent practitioner of his art and craft turns out to be a substandard and noncertifiable teacher in a neighboring state. But each state sets up its own qualifications for teachers' certificates just as it does for drivers' licenses. Teachers, like all other Americans, are an increasingly mobile group, but the variety in state-certification requirements has become a serious obstacle in their movement from state to state. Reciprocity—the acceptance by a state of a teacher licensed by another state—is an effort to resolve the problem. Some states have achieved reciprocity by developing "compacts" in which the certifying authorities of a group of neighboring states with somewhat comparable standards have agreed to accept any teacher certified by a member of the group. If there are minor differences in requirements, these are worked out during the initial teaching service.

A bolder step to achieve the goal of reciprocity is national accreditation of the colleges and universities that prepare teachers. The rationale of this approach is that a graduate of an approved institution, with its approved program, should *ipso facto* be certifiable in any state of the union. This means that state boards of education must accept the stamp of the teaching profession's accreditation as meeting their own legal definitions of minimum teaching qualifications.

Twenty years ago, a national agency known as the National Council for Accreditation of Teacher Education was established. It has approved the institutions in the United States in which approximately 75 percent of the nation's teachers are educated. For an illustration of the colleges and programs approved by NCATE, see the table following, which shows acceptable institutions in the representative states of Florida, New York, Ohio, Oregon, and Texas.

Institutions	Elementary	Secondary	School Service Personnel	Highest Degree
FLORIDA				
Florida Agricultural and Mechanical University, Tallahassee	X	X		B
Florida State University, Tallahassee	X	X	X[18]	D
Stetson University, DeLand	X	X	X[18]	M
University of Florida, Gainesville	X	X	X[18]	D
University of Miami, Coral Gables	X	X	X[18]	D
NEW YORK				
Canisius College, Buffalo		X	X[2]	M
City University of New York:				
Brooklyn College, Brooklyn	X	X	X[2]	S
City College, New York	X	X	X[2]	S
Hunter College, New York	X	X	X[2]	S
Queens College, Flushing, Long Island	X	X	X[2]	S
Hofstra University, Hempstead, Long Island	X	X	X[2]	M
Ithaca College, Ithaca		X		M
New York University, New York	X	X	X[18]	D
State University of New York				
State University at Albany		X	X[18]	D
State University at Buffalo	X	X	X[18]	D
State University College at:				
Brockport	X	X		M
Buffalo	X	X		M

Institutions	Elementary	Secondary	School Service Personnel	Highest Degree
Cortland	X	X		M
Fredonia	X	X		M
Geneseo	X	X		M
New Paltz	X	X		M
Oneonta	X	X		M
Oswego	X	X		M
Plattsburgh	X	X		M
Potsdam	X	X		M
Syracuse University, Syracuse	X	X	X^{18}	D
Teachers College, Columbia University, New York	X	X	X^{18}	D
University of Rochester, Rochester	X	X	X^{18}	D
OHIO				
Baldwin-Wallace College, Berea	X	X		B
Bowling Green State University, Bowling Green	X	X	X^{18}	M
Capital University, Columbus	X	X		B
Central State University, Wilberforce	X	X		B
Hiram College, Hiram	X	X		B
John Carroll University, Cleveland		X	X^2	M
Kent State University, Kent	X	X	X^{18}	D
Miami University, Oxford	X	X	X^{18}	S
Ohio State University, Columbus	X	X	X^{18}	D
Ohio University, Athens	X	X	X^{18}	D
Otterbein College, Westerville	X	X		B
Saint John College of Cleveland, Cleveland	X			B
University of Akron, Akron	X	X	X^2	M

University of Cincinnati, Cincinnati	X	X	X^{18}	D
University of Dayton, Dayton	X	X	X^2	M
University of Toledo, Toledo	X	X	X^{18}	D
Wilmington College, Wilmington	X	X		B
Wittenberg University, Springfield	X	X		B
Youngstown State University, Youngstown	X	X		B

OREGON

Eastern Oregon College, La Grande	X	X		M
Lewis and Clark College, Portland	X	X		B
Marylhurst College, Marylhurst	X	X		B
Oregon College of Education, Monmouth	X	X		M
Oregon State University, Corvallis	X	X	X^7	D
Portland State University, Portland	X	X		B
Reed College, Portland		X		M
Southern Oregon College, Ashland	X	X		M
University of Oregon, Eugene	X	X	X^{18}	D

TEXAS

Abilene Christian College, Abilene	X	X		B
East Texas State University, Commerce	X	X	X^2	M
Hardin-Simmons University, Abilene	X	X		B
Incarnate Word College, San Antonio	X	X		M
North Texas State University, Denton	X	X	X^{18}	D

Institutions	Elementary	Secondary	School Service Personnel	Highest Degree
Our Lady of the Lake College, San Antonio	X	X	X[7]	M
Prairie View Agricultural and Mechanical College, Prairie View	X	X		B
Sam Houston State College, Huntsville	X	X		M
Southern Methodist University, Dallas	X	X	X[2]	M
Southwest Texas State College, San Marcos	X	X	X[2]	M
Stephen F. Austin State College, Nacogdoches	X	X	X[2]	M
Texas A&I University, Kingsville	X	X	X[2]	M
Texas Christian University, Fort Worth	X	X	X[2]	M
Texas Southern University, Houston	X	X	X[2]	M
Texas Technological College, Lubbock	X	X	X[18]	D
Texas Wesleyan College, Fort Worth	X	X		B
Texas Woman's University, Denton	X	X		M
Trinity University, San Antonio	X	X	X[2]	M
University of Houston, Houston	X	X	X[1]	M
University of Texas, Austin	X	X	X[18]	D
West Texas State University, Canyon	X	X	X[2]	M

B   Baccalaureate degree
M   Master's degree
S   Sixth-year or specialist certificate
[1]   Elementary and secondary principals
[2]   Elementary and secondary principals; guidance counselors
[7]   Guidance counselors
[18]   Elementary and secondary principals; school psychological personnel; superintendents.

SOURCE: *Annual List Number Sixteen* (Washington, D.C.: National Council for Accreditation of Teacher Education, 1969–70). Reprinted by permission.

Although fewer than one-fourth of state certifying boards or commissions accept this form of accreditation, it is nevertheless both an important and a controversial development in the professional-standards movement and represents a significant breakthrough in the certification confusion.

POLITICAL ACTION

The increasing importance of education in America's technological development and the sudden surge in the sheer number of bodies to be educated, coupled with the increased cost of education, have brought public education, kindergarten to university, into the center of the political arena in a number of states.

As a consequence of the people's interest and legitimate concern, reflected in the behavior of their elected representatives, a number of states have sought to bring greater flexibility to certification standards by taking direct legislative action to minimize the minutiae of state credential requirements. By so doing, laymen have sought to make teaching more available to an increasing number of applicants, with varying but acceptable qualifications. Reducing the specificity of state requirements through such means helps bring state licensing closer to the purpose for which it is basically intended—to assure the public that the holder of the license has the minimum qualifications to be a teacher.

RECOMMENDATIONS OF SCHOLARS

In the 1960's outstanding scholars devoted major attention to the need for certification reform. James B. Conant, former president of Harvard University, in his book *The Education of American Teachers,* proposed some radical alterations. He raised certain basic questions and then proceeded to answer them: Who is responsible for the education of teachers? The state. Who ought to be responsible? The institutions *and* the school district. Conant proposed:

For certification purposes the state should require only (a) that a candidate hold a baccalaureate degree from a legitimate college or university, (b) that he submit evidence of having successfully performed as a student teacher under the direction of college and public school personnel in whom the State Department has confidence, and in a practice-teaching situation of which the State Department approves, and (c) that he hold a specially endorsed teaching certificate from a college or university which, in issuing the official document, attests that the institution as a whole considers the person adequately prepared to teach in a designated field and grade level.[2]

[2] James Bryant Conant, *The Education of American Teachers* (New York: McGraw-Hill, 1963), p. 210.

Another question Conant raised is, How well do state regulations protect the public against ignorant or incompetent teachers? His answer: Not very well. Why this is so is lucidly discussed and historically documented by Lucien Kinney in his treatise *Certification in Education.* Taking several states as examples, he shows how state legislatures, supported by vested interest groups, have used certification to achieve their own ends and how present practices cannot guarantee competence. Kinney's answer: Have the profession disregard and look beyond state systems and establish its own licensure system. "Only when the profession has control of the quality of its membership can it take over its proper responsibilities." [3] Kinney's proposal, like Conant's, will continue to be widely discussed (and cussed); either reaction is bound to shake up the status quo in teacher certification.

EXPERIMENTAL PROGRAMS OF TEACHER PREPARATION

Beginning in a small way in the early 1950's and continuing in an accelerated way in the 1960's and 1970's, a number of the nation's best-known colleges and universities have carried on experimental programs of teacher preparation. The Ford Foundation alone has given over $70 million to institutions to encourage them to develop and try out "breakthrough" programs of teacher education, and, more recently, the federal government has spent over $1 billion on various types of innovative teacher-education experiments. [4] Because experimental curriculums differ from standard or regular curriculums—often involving teaching internships, for example, in lieu of student teaching [5]—many of these programs initially ran head on into the inflexible requirements of state certification. As a result of the persistence of the colleges and the recognition by state authorities of the place of experimentation in teacher education, a number of states revised their requirements so that teachers prepared in other than conventional or traditional programs could be certified.

While these four developments—experimentation, political action, reciprocity, and the interest of scholars—are having the effect of liberalizing the certification requirements in a number of states, there still remains the

---

[3] Lucien B. Kinney, *Certification in Education* (Englewood Cliffs, N.J.: Prentice-Hall, 1964), p. 132.

[4] James C. Stone, *Breakthrough in Teacher Education* (San Francisco: Jossey-Bass, 1968).

[5] A teaching internship is a new type of teacher-preparation program in which (1) actual teaching (with pay and full responsibility) is substituted for practice teaching, (2) the school district and the college share supervision responsibility for the trainee, and (3) seminars drawing on the problems of teaching and designed to illuminate these problems replace formal education courses.

confusion caused by lack of interstate agreement on what it takes to become a teacher.

There exists general agreement that a teacher should be (1) well versed in the subjects he is to teach; (2) broadly educated through undergraduate study in the humanities, the arts, and the sciences; (3) professionally knowledgeable about the social and psychological foundations of education, the school curriculum, and the methods and materials of instruction; and (4) professionally "tried out" through an assignment as a student or practice teacher or teaching intern. But when it comes to the specific amount of each of these essential ingredients, states differ considerably and are generally reluctant to state their requirements. The variation among states on certification standards is not likely to be reduced in the near future.

Employment Practices

A school district's ability to compete for the less-than-adequate supply of new teachers each year depends on (1) its salary schedule, (2) its geographic location, (3) availability of its cultural advantages, (4) its physical facilities, and (5) its general reputation. It is not surprising to find that the practices of recruiting and employing teachers vary widely. Within this range of diversity, it is possible, however, to discuss employment practices that are applicable in a majority of the nation's larger, or at least "better," school districts.

Getting a Job

TEACHER PERSONALITY

"It's up to you!" This is the bold truth of the matter of getting a teaching post. Whether the individual strikes out on his own and presents himself to the superintendent unannounced (a bad practice, by the way), or whether he goes through the college placement office or the county superintendent's office (both good practices), it is the kind of person he is that counts most. *Proper grooming, good manners, cultural background, and pleasing personality are the* sine qua non *of employability.*

WHAT ADMINISTRATORS WANT

In employing new teachers, school administrators usually interest themselves in the following items:

1. Certificate held: does the applicant have a valid state certificate? What kind? Is it a regular or standard teaching license?
2. College or university attended: at what institution did the applicant prepare for teaching? (The institution's status and reputation and the administrator's experience with other teachers from the same institution weigh heavily.)
3. Student-teaching record: At what levels and in what fields did he do his student teaching? How successful was the applicant in student teaching? (Administrators have learned that the test of the pudding is in the eating!)
4. Teaching experience: Has the applicant had any? In what kinds of schools and where? With what success? (Letters of verification are necessary to prove the case.)
5. Academic interests: What subjects is the applicant best qualified to teach? What others could he teach, if necessary? (Grades earned in college in the applicant's teaching field are important, although many administrators assume that a college degree is sufficient evidence of academic or scholarly capability.)
6. Extracurricular specialties: In what extracurricular activities did the applicant participate? What other hobbies does he have? Could he supervise such activities for school-age pupils? (When other things are equal, this ability counts heavily with administrators.)

Related to the preceding six rather basic items are the findings of a survey of principals in five large metropolitan school districts.[6] The answers to the question "What characteristics do you consider most important in selecting beginning teachers?" could be grouped under these categories:

1. Professional preparation
2. Personality
3. Academic preparation
4. Interest in children
5. Related experiences—for example, scout work, camp counseling, Sunday-school teaching, and the like
6. Mental and physical health
7. Attitude toward colleagues
8. Appearance
9. Cultural and social background

[6] James C. Stone, "Factors Related to Success of Beginning Teachers," *Research Résumé,* California Teachers Association, May 1961, pp. 56ff. The study was repeated in 1969, with similar results.

10. Moral and ethical values

11. Age

The percentages of principals responding with statements that could be included in the above eleven categories are shown in figure 5. Professional preparation, personality, academic preparation, and interest in children were mentioned by half or more of the principals at each grade level (elementary, junior-high, senior-high). Professional preparation was mentioned by the largest percentage of principals at the elementary- and junior-high-school levels (87 and 95 percent, respectively). Academic preparation was mentioned by the largest percentage of senior-high-school principals (95 percent). Academic background was evidently of more concern to senior-high-school than to elementary- and junior-high-school principals. Conversely, less importance was attached to related experiences by senior-high-school than by elementary- and junior-high-school principals. At the other end of the scale, a smaller percentage of senior-high-school than of elementary- and junior-high-school principals mentioned cultural

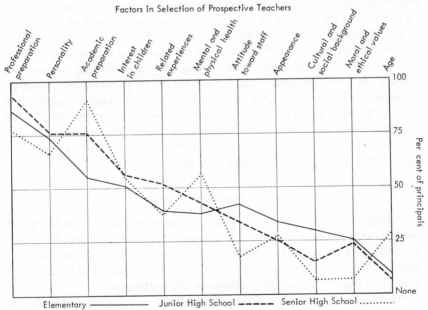

FIGURE 5. Percent of Principals, According to Grade Level, That Referred to Various Factors as Important in Selecting Beginning Teachers.

SOURCE: James C. Stone and R. Ross Hempstead, *California Education Today* (New York: Crowell, 1968), p. 48. Reprinted by permission.

and social background or moral and ethical values as important considerations in the employment of beginning teachers.

Candidates for teaching positions might well keep these divergent emphases in mind when seeking teaching positions.

APPLYING

All districts have some kind of job-application form that must be filled out. This should be done before an interview. The application usually requires official record transcripts (every applicant should have a half-dozen sets handy) and letters of recommendation attesting to the applicant's teaching experience or teaching potential. General letters "to whom it may concern" are of little value, and character references from ministers, friends, business acquaintances, or former employers are worthless unless they contain specific comments on the candidate's promise as a teacher.

THE INTERVIEW

School officials usually interview applicants if there are openings for which they are qualified. The interview serves the purpose of allowing the employer and the teacher to make a face-to-face assessment of each other. It also permits verification of the statements made on the teacher's application and gives an opportunity for securing additional information on various points. If the interview ends with any of the following phrases, the teacher can cross the school district off his list of possibilities: "We'll get in touch with you if (when) . . ."; "Have you thought of applying at . . ."; "Perhaps you'd be interested in being on our substitute list." If, on the other hand, the interview concludes with "We'll call you as soon as we receive your confidential file from your college-placement office" or "We'd like to offer you a contract," then you're in!

PLACEMENT AGENCIES

Colleges and universities preparing teachers maintain a teacher-placement service. In small colleges, the service is rendered as a part of the Department of Education. In large colleges and universities, either there is a separate teacher-placement office, or the service is rendered by a general placement bureau serving all graduates of the institution.

An additional placement service is rendered in some states by the employment agency of the United States Department of Labor. Another placement agency in most states is the state education or teachers' association, which usually charges a fee of 1½ to 5 percent of the first year's salary.

How It Works

The purpose of the college placement office is to serve as middleman between employer and applicant. Prospective employers make known their openings, known as "calls," to the placement office, which nominates for each call those persons in its files whom it deems best qualified and forwards a set of their confidential papers to the prospective employer. The employer reviews the papers and notifies the placement office of those in whom he is interested. Interviews are then arranged, generally at the placement office. Usually a school employing official will have interviews with applicants from several colleges before arriving at a decision. He then notifies both the candidate and the placement office of his decision.

The Confidential File

In every college placement office, there is a qualified professional person in charge who knows the education field and the importance of establishing a confidential file or dossier. The forms to be filled out by the teacher candidate are extensive and time consuming, and the pages of information the candidate must give (and he should do so with great care) will require several hours of work. Once done, however, the task usually is finished for one's professional life (except for keeping it up to date as the teacher secures advanced degrees and becomes qualified for advanced non-teaching positions in guidance, supervision, administration, and the like).

Letters of Recommendation

The final step in the establishment of the confidential file is securing letters of recommendation. The placement officer will furnish each candidate with envelopes and forms on which the letters of recommendation are to be written. The completed forms are mailed directly to the office by the writer of the letter.

No candidate should merely drop such forms off to selected people or have the placement office send them for him, unless he has first asked individuals if they will be willing to write a letter of recommendation for him. This is not only common courtesy; it also avoids the embarrassment of having letters filled with generalities, which might be interpreted negatively by the employing official. The candidate should remember that these letters are confidential and that, once received, they are the property of the placement office, to be used as the placement director, in his professional role, may see fit.

All these admonitions emphasize the importance of securing the right kind of letters. The beginning teacher should seek letters from (1) the public-school teachers under whose supervision he did his student teaching and (2) college or university supervisors of student teaching. Letters from other college-faculty members who can attest to the candidate's promise as a teacher are an appropriate supplement, but are never a substitute for those written from firsthand experience about the candidate's abilities in actual teaching situations.

The experienced teacher should secure letters from (1) officials of the school district in which his last teaching was done and (2) as a good supplement if the past teaching experience was in a state other than the one in which the candidate is now applying, general letters from local residents attesting to teaching promise.

The intern-program candidate should use (1) academic faculty who know him well enough to tell how acceptable he might prove as a teacher and (2) former employers or lay leaders who also know him well enough to tell how promising he might be as a teacher.

Selective Placement

Mention has been made of the professional qualifications of the placement officer and of his role in the handling of confidential letters. One additional aspect of his professional role should be made clear: his responsibility for *selective placement*. This responsibility enables him to reserve the right to exercise his professional judgment in recommending candidates to employers for available positions. If, for example, he has ten kindergarten-teacher candidates and only one call for kindergarten teachers, it is his privilege to recommend to the employing official the two or three candidates he thinks are best qualified for the job. A candidate not nominated may request that his papers be forwarded to the school employer for consideration. Papers so sent, however, are marked "Sent at candidate's request."

Out-of-state Reciprocity

Most college and university teacher-placement agencies belong to the National Institutional Teacher Placement Association. Through the national agency, affiliated institutions have agreed to assist the graduates of an out-of-state institution who wish to seek positions in their state. To secure the assistance of the in-state institution, the candidate's out-of-state college or university placement office must initiate the request to the in-state institution of choice. There usually is no charge for this reciprocal service.

FOLLOW-UP SERVICES

Placement offices usually carry on follow-up studies of their graduates. One reason for this activity is sheer interest in their alumni, but another is to secure information to feed back to the college in order to improve its program of preparation. Studies of the number of students each year who qualify for certificates but do not enter teaching are examples of placement offices' follow-up work. Another is the study of reasons why candidates are not placed.

School-District Selection Procedures

SMALL DISTRICTS

In small school districts the governing board itself selects the teaching staff, without professional assistance, since districts of this size usually do not employ a superintendent. If the district is large enough to employ a superintendent, it may delegate to him the responsibility of selecting teachers. In most cases, the board acts in matters of personnel selection only on the recommendations of the superintendent.

MEDIUM-SIZED AND LARGE DISTRICTS

In medium-sized and large districts, central-office personnel do the initial screening of teacher applicants. Such persons have various titles—assistant superintendent, personnel director, or curriculum coordinator. The most likely candidates chosen by the central-office staff usually are then interviewed by the principal in whose school the vacancy exists. Since the principal is the person who will be responsible for the teacher's success or failure, his decision is the critical one.

A growing trend in both medium-sized and large districts is the use of personnel-selection committees made up of both teachers and administrators. These committees do the "second stage" interviewing and prepare priority lists for consideration by the central office in making recommendations for board action.

In some of the nation's largest urban districts, such as New York and Los Angeles, written examinations are required as a part of the screening process. On the basis of the written examination and a selection committee's interview, each applicant is assigned a position on an eligibility list.

Recommendations to the board are then made by the central-office staff on the basis of placement on the list.

CONTRACTS

When a teacher has been selected for employment, he usually is offered a contract, a legal document specifying the terms of employment, conditions of work, and compensation. The terms of the contract are legally binding on both parties and may be enforced by court action, if necessary. In any event, the contract can be terminated only by mutual agreement of both parties. Before signing a contract, a teacher should carefully consider its provisions, because failure to live up to them may be cause for revocation or suspension of his credentials.

It is not unusual for a teacher to sign a contract one day, only to learn the next day of a position he would prefer. Nor is it unusual for a teacher to sign a contract and, upon later visiting the school and the community, wish he had not acted so hastily. Such "20/20 hindsight" may be avoided if, before signing on the dotted line, the teacher weighs carefully such items as (1) the terms of the contract, (2) the kind of community, (3) the climate of the school, (4) the type of assignment, and (5) the available housing and cultural opportunities.

Promotion, Transfer, Mobility, Professional Mortality, Tenure, Retirement

ASSUMED PROMOTIONS

Despite the single salary schedule (equal pay for equal qualifications regardless of grade level taught), unfortunately the idea still persists in the minds of some people that a person is a "better" teacher if he teaches at the higher grade levels. In all too many districts, moving from elementary to junior high is assumed to be a promotion, as is moving from junior high to senior high or from senior high to junior college.

RECOGNITION PROMOTIONS

Recognition-type promotions are the kind associated with being named department chairman (junior high school, senior high school, or junior college); a supervising teacher of student teachers; a demonstration teacher; an institute, extension, or college summer-session teacher; or a consultant teacher (for elementary-school music, art, physical education, exceptional children). Usually a modest additional stipend is paid for such services.

REAL PROMOTIONS

Actual promotions, which involve substantial salary increases, are those in which the successful and experienced classroom teacher is appointed to an administrative position, such as counselor, assistant principal, dean, curriculum coordinator, principal, superintendent, and the like.

TRANSFERS

Transfers from one school to another *within* a district are common. Request for transfer may be initiated by the teacher to the superintendent. It is wise for the teacher to discuss with his current principal his desire to transfer, since few districts will honor such a request unless the teacher's present principal approves. Acceptable reasons for transfer include moving to a school which (1) is near the teacher's home or a college or university, (2) provides a welcome change of student or faculty climate, (3) avoids his having a personality conflict with principal or colleagues.

A transfer also may be initiated by the principal and the central office. Typical reasons are personality conflicts, inability to work well with certain cultural or socioeconomic groups, parental discontent, and the need to balance school staffs between young and old teachers, strong and weak, expert and inexperienced, men and women. Some districts make it a practice to transfer a certain proportion of their experienced teachers as a means of in-service education.

A transfer *between* school districts can be made only by resignation in the teacher's current district and employment in the new district.

MOBILITY

Like Americans generally, teachers are a mobile group.

In the category of *professional mobility,* an undetermined proportion of the nation's teachers (1) move from lower grade levels to higher levels and from teaching to advanced nonteaching responsibilities, and (2) move in and out of the profession. Since a majority of America's public-school teachers are women, this possibility is one of teaching's recruitment incentives. Young married women resign to raise a family, but many return to teaching at a later date.

In the category of *geographic mobility,* an undetermined proportion of the nation's teachers (1) move from school to school or from one district to another within the state, or (2) move from one state to another.

PROFESSIONAL MORTALITY

The professional mortality rate among teachers is believed to be high, especially at the beginning stages of service. The drop-out rate of teachers who complete preparation but do not take a teaching position is approximately 27 percent. The current rate is considerably better than it was five to seven years ago, when studies showed that 50 percent of secondary- and 25 percent of elementary-certificate candidates did not take teaching positions. The improved holding power of the teaching profession today may be due to higher salaries and increased status.

TENURE

One of the significant protections of public school teachers in many states is the tenure law. This statute probably has contributed more to the stability and general health of the teaching profession than any single factor. "In 1920 only five states recognized by law the principle of permanent tenure for public school teachers. By 1955 there were 32 states with tenure laws." [7] And by 1968, thirty-seven states and the District of Columbia had tenure laws. [8]

Although, like certification, tenure regulations vary in details from state to state, a teacher usually has tenure after three years of teaching in a state. Typical reasons for dismissal of tenured teachers include (1) dishonesty, (2) incompetence or other evident unfitness for service, (3) persistent violation of or refusal to obey regulations, (4) immoral or unprofessional conduct, (5) conviction of a felony or of a crime involving moral turpitude, (6) membership in the Communist party, the refusal to answer questions regarding same, or the indoctrination of pupils with communism.

Two actions to dismiss a permanent teacher were filed recently by a board of education and consolidated for trial. The first action charged the teacher with immoral conduct, unprofessional conduct, and dishonesty. All three charges were based specifically upon the fact that the teacher, in order to sustain adequate enrollment figures in her class for adults and prevent its discontinuance for lack of pupils, intentionally falsified the attendance records by signing the names of absent students. The second action, charging evident unfitness for service and unprofessional conduct, was

[7] Edgar B. Wesley, *NEA: The First Hundred Years* (New York: Harper, 1957), p. 337.

[8] The states without tenure provisions are Arkansas, Nevada, North Dakota, Oklahoma, South Dakota, Virginia, Mississippi, North Carolina, South Carolina, Texas, Utah, Vermont, and Wyoming. Those states in which tenure is available only in certain places are Georgia, Kansas, Missouri, Nebraska, Oregon, and Wisconsin.

based upon letters written by the teacher that contained statements of a defamatory and degrading nature concerning her associates and administrative superiors. These letters also revealed such violent prejudices that she could not have been expected to deal fairly with mixed classes.

Each of the charges, supported by evidence, was held to be grounds for dismissal. In this case the falsification of records constituted immoral conduct, unprofessional conduct, and dishonesty; the defamatory statements constituted unprofessional conduct and evident unfitness for service.

Over the years, tenure decisions have been made by the courts to the extent that (1) it has become forbiddingly costly for a district to dismiss a tenured teacher, and (2) it has become almost equally costly to dismiss a probationary teacher from a regular position prior to the expiration of his annual contract, because such dismissal must be for the same causes and follow the same legal procedures as for tenured teachers.

Recognizing these facts about the dismissal of teachers, many groups acting on behalf of governing boards have advocated greater flexibility in tenure laws.

RETIREMENT

Before 1917 no state had a retirement plan for teachers, by 1957 such plans were operating in 45 states,[9] and today all states have retirement plans. A number of trends and changes are evident:

Adoption of social security coverage for all or some teachers in 37 states. An estimated 50 to 60 percent of all instructional employees in the nation's public elementary and secondary schools are now covered.

Adoption of survivor benefit programs in 14 states whose teachers have no protection under the survivors' insurance provisions of the social security system. These programs are designed to provide monthly payments to dependent survivors of members who die while in active teaching service. Seven states added this feature to their retirement laws since 1958. Only Alaska and Puerto Rico have yet to provide such survivor benefits although Puerto Rico continues monthly payments of part of the life annuity of a deceased retired teacher to the surviving widow and minor children.

At present 23 state retirement systems pay a lump-sum death benefit in addition to refunding the member's accumulated contributions to the estate or beneficiary of a member who dies before retirement. In 1950 only seven states did so.[10]

The California State Teachers' Retirement System—which we shall discuss as a typical, although somewhat generous, plan—requires a minimum

[9] Wesley, loc. cit.
[10] *NEA Research Bulletin,* December 1964

of five years' teaching service within the state. Service outside the state is noncreditable. A teacher must have reached the age of fifty-five to be eligible for retirement benefits. There is no mandatory retirement age, although a teacher loses his tenure status at the age of sixty-five.

A teacher's retirement pay is based on the average of the highest salary earned over his "best" three years. Upon retirement:

1. At age sixty, with twenty years of service, a teacher receives twenty-six-tieths (one-third) of the average of the "best" three years.

2. At age sixty, with thirty years of service, a teacher receives thirty-six-tieths (one-half) of the average of his "best" three years.

3. At age sixty-five, with twenty-two years of service, a teacher receives one-half of the average of his "best" three years.

4. At age sixty-five, with thirty years of service, a teacher receives two-thirds of the average of his "best" three years.

5. At age sixty-five, with forty-four years of service, a teacher receives 100 percent of the average of his "best" three years.

A teacher may retire for disability at any age. In general his benefit is about equal to one-fourth of his annual compensation.

If the teacher dies before retirement, his beneficiary may receive a lump-sum payment that is equal to (1) all his contributions with interest and (2) one-twelfth of his annual salary at the rate at which he was last employed but for no longer than six years. In addition, if the surviving spouse has one child under eighteen, the spouse will receive $180 per month; two or more children under eighteen, $250 per month. When the retired teacher dies, his estate receives $400 in addition to the other benefits to which he is entitled.

Should the teacher decide to drop out of teaching after five or fewer years of service (and many do), he must withdraw all his retirement contributions with interest. Should he drop out after five years of service, he may either remain in the system or withdraw all his retirement contributions with interest. Upon reentry into teaching service, a teacher may redeposit his withdrawn contributions plus interest if he so chooses, thus gaining for retirement the benefits of his previous years of service.

In-Service Growth

In-service education is the *planned* education, after service begins, which continues to promote professional growth. Professional growth, in turn, encompasses activities that extend one's liberal education, increase his competence in a subject area, enlarge his professional knowledge, and refine his professional skills.

This definition admittedly is a broad one and runs counter to the conception of in-service education in some school districts, which define it either so narrowly as to limit it to upper-division or graduate courses or so broadly as to include almost anything a teacher does outside the walls of his classroom.

INDIVIDUAL RESPONSIBILITY

As professionals using a specialized body of knowledge and technical skills, it is incumbent on teachers to maintain, improve, extend, and update their store of knowledge and technical skill. And it is the individual teacher's own responsibility to make himself a more competent professional practitioner. Expertness is acquired through consistent, organized, and purposeful professional study, which is central to the teacher's claim to membership in a profession.

SCHOOL-DISTRICT AND COLLEGE RESPONSIBILITY

Since most school districts measure teacher merit for salary increases by units of credits held and by successful teaching service, it follows that school districts share some responsibility for providing organized opportunities for teachers to meet these salary hurdles.

A practical guideline for evaluating a school district's in-service offerings follows:

1. Individual teachers should have opportunities to work on their own problems. (This includes opportunity to plan for themselves, to participate voluntarily rather than be required to do so.)

2. The regular administrative and supervisory organization of the school system should be fully utilized. (This includes curriculum development, instructional-improvement programs, workshops, institutes, conferences, and the special assistance of principals, supervisors, and department heads.)

3. The school system should insure time, facilities, and resources to stimulate and strengthen the program. (This refers to time for curriculum-study groups within the teacher's normal work day, conferences within the normal work week, use of specialized resource personnel, and the like.)

4. The program must provide for communication and interaction among all persons in the school system. (This includes all grades, all subject

fields, all teachers and principals, and representatives of laymen, such as board and PTA members.)

5. The role of the chief administrative officer in the school system should be that of facilitator and coordinator, as contrasted to "guiding and directing genius." (This refers to encouraging development of good organization and procedures for in-service education, facilitating the work of groups, and creating a climate for professional growth.) [11]

Usually school districts provide opportunities for in-service education in cooperation with higher-education institutions. In part, this is done to eliminate the squabble in the district over the credit problem—that is, what an acceptable unit of in-service credit is. Many colleges and universities have extension services specifically designed to provide off-campus courses within the proximity of school districts. In some states the county superintendent, too, plays a significant role in arranging in-service training opportunities.

TYPICAL SCHOOL-DISTRICT PROGRAMS

A recent survey of the in-service education programs of 383 school districts showed that the most frequent activities were (1) faculty meetings, (2) conferences, (3) workshops, (4) use of consultant services, (5) teacher-orientation programs, (6) institutes, and (7) preparation and evaluation of instructional materials. These seven forms of in-service education were reported to be the preference of 60 percent or more of the districts included in the survey.[12]

TEACHER PREFERENCE

A survey of all teachers in one city-school district showed that teachers themselves expressed somewhat different preferences for in-service education activities. It also showed some interesting differences between elementary and secondary teachers.[13] These preferences are shown in figure 6.

By combining similar activities (i.e., "extension course" with "college course" and "observe demonstration teaching" with "observe teaching in other districts"), the teachers' in-service education preferences appear in this order of priority: (1) observe teaching, (2) take college extension or campus courses, (3) participate in workshops, (4) visit exhibits of instruc-

[11] National Society for the Study of Education, *In-service Education* (Chicago: University of Chicago Press, 1957), pt. I, chap. 12.

[12] "District In-service Training Programs—A Survey of Policies and Practices," *Research Bulletin,* California Teachers Association, April 1959.

[13] Unpublished study, Office of the Superintendent of Schools, Martinez City Schools, Martinez, California.

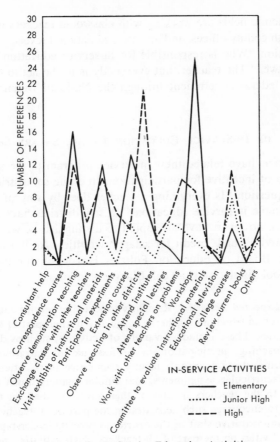

FIGURE 6. Teachers' Preferences for In-Service Education Activities.

SOURCE: James C. Stone and R. Ross Hempstead, *California Education Today* (New York: Crowell, 1968), p. 214. Reprinted by permission.

tional materials and devices, (5) work with other teachers studying special problems.

ACADEMIC ORGANIZATIONS

A number of nationally organized academic groups are active in the in-service field. These include the National Council of Mathematics Teachers; the National Council of Teachers of English; and the American Association for Health, Physical Education, and Recreation, to name a few. These organizations conduct workshops, conferences, institutes, and summer-session programs for teachers.

In addition, college and university professors who are authorities in various academic fields are working with classroom teachers in school districts, through county offices, and at state and national levels.

The question "Who is responsible for in-service education?" begets the qualified answer "The teacher, but everybody is in the act to help him, including the federal government through the National Defense Education Act."

RELATION OF IN-SERVICE EDUCATION TO THE SALARY SCHEDULE

Most districts have related their in-service program to the salary schedule as a form of incentive for participation. In doing so, districts have had to face the question "Is everything a teacher does by way of professional growth creditable in-service education?" A few districts have decided yes. More districts, however, have attempted to distinguish between "regularly expected" activities and "credit for salary" activities. An illustrative example from the Board of Education Policies Handbook for the imaginary "typical" school district we shall call Bluegrass follows:

1. *Regularly Expected Activities.* Regularly expected in-service education activities are those in which all teachers engage as a normal part of their assigned responsibilities. These include a variety of activities, such as daily preparation for teaching, participation in professional organizations, observing teaching demonstration lessons, faculty committee work, attending conferences, extracurricular assignments, and similar matters. Such activities are rewarding to the teachers in and of themselves. It shall be the policy of this board to encourage such activities on the part of all teachers and to expect the administrative staff of the district to provide leadership and support for such activities on the part of all teachers. Such activities, however, shall not normally be considered for salary credit.

2. *Credit for Salary Activities.* As professional practitioners, teachers are expected to participate in extensive and formal study and comparable forms of professional growth. These types of in-service growth activities are clearly those which are not normally done by teachers in the regular performance of their assigned responsibilities. The purpose of such activities is to increase teaching abilities and broaden teachers' educational backgrounds, thereby increasing their worth to the district. These activities shall be of a type meriting *either* or *both* classification and/or hurdle credit [credit that must be earned to obtain the normal increment] on the salary schedule. Since these in-service growth experiences will vary with the individual needs of teachers, they may encompass a wide range of activities such as college and university courses, travel, community services, organized workshops, curriculum committees, and the like. Such activities shall extend over a recognized period of time and be of a comprehensive nature. It shall be the policy of this board to delegate the approval of credit for these activities to an evaluation committee.

Districts using policies of either the limited or the comprehensive type establish evaluation committees of teachers and administrators to determine the amount of credit to be given for noncollege work and the criteria to be used in making such judgments. Bluegrass school district, which has adopted the following criteria, grants credit if:

1. The overriding purpose of the activity is clearly one of increasing the teacher's professional competence.
2. The activity extends over a definitely recognized and designated period of time, is of a comprehensive nature, and, if repetitious of a previously engaged-in activity, is clearly justifiable by new conditions.
3. The activity is planned and undertaken in an organized manner, in contrast to one in which participation is unorganized, informal, or incidental.
4. The activity is clearly related to the needs and interests of the teacher so that he may become a more competent practitioner and is designed to provide an opportunity for the fulfillment of these needs and interests in a systematic way.
5. The activity is not only of value to the individual teacher but also to other teachers in the district with whom it is shared.

Conclusion

In this chapter, we have discussed "the system," that is, the manner in which public education is organized in the United States, including local, state, and national agencies, and professional processes like placement, tenure, in-service education, certification, and accreditation.

Taken together, the dedicated people who make up the organizational structures of these various agencies and who are responsible for these processes have been referred to as "the apparatus" by Conant in his critical review, *The Education of the American Teacher*. Like any organized activity of importance on the American scene, the profession's zeal for better schools has brought with it loyalties and interrelationships that appear to the outsider to constitute an interlocking directorship. However, even a critic like Conant recognizes that it is the dedication and loyal service of these professionals that have given teaching in America its stability and its powerful voice at local, state, and national levels.

Questions for Discussion

1. How do you explain a statement of the Rockefeller Brothers Foundation to the effect that all problems in education lead us back sooner or later to the basic problem of financing?

2. What procedure does a prospective teacher take to become licensed in the state in which you plan to teach? Does your state grant life certificates? How are they obtained? What is your opinion of teaching licenses granted for life?

3. What is your reaction to the idea of merit ratings for teachers? Of relating salary increases to merit ratings?

4. What resources are available to you in your college community that would be helpful to you in your growth toward becoming a teacher? Explain how you have taken, or could take, advantage of these resources.

5. Do you favor state teacher tenure laws? Why or why not? Why do you think some states have them while others do not?

6. What kind of teacher retirement plan would not penalize teachers who wish to move from one state to another?

7. Why are in-service education programs important to experienced teachers? Which of several techniques and media used in in-service programs seem to you of most value to teachers? Why? Should in-service education be related to salary schedules? Why?

8. What are the advantages and disadvantages of having a state chief school officer appointed by the state board of education as opposed to having one elected by the people?

9. How do you account for the significant decrease in number of school districts in the United States in recent years?

10. Find out what institutions in your state are accredited by NCATE. Talk to a professor of education about this and then to one in a subject-matter field. Do they agree on the place of NCATE in approving institutions for teacher education?

Activities and Projects

1. Obtain current charts showing the amount of money spent by the various states for education within their boundaries and the amount of money raised to support education. How does your state compare with others? How does your state compare with the national average? How does your state compare with other states in the country and with the national average in the efforts made to support public education?

2. Obtain a copy of the latest edition of Woellner and Wood's *Requirements for Certification* (see References section below). What are the requirements for obtaining a license in several states in which you

have an interest in teaching? How do they compare in such aspects as the number of years to complete the license, the degree needed, the number of semester hours required in professional-education courses and in the liberal arts, and the requirements for teaching in elementary school and in secondary school?

3. Write a news article for your community's local newspaper supporting the single salary schedule that, hypothetically, your school district is desirous of adopting.

4. Secure from your college's teacher-placement office data concerning the probable supply-and-demand figures at the level at which and/or in the subject fields that you plan to teach when you finish your college work. What can be done if the supply appears to exceed the demand in your field of interest?

5. Write to the state departments of education in three states where you have considered employment to secure information about their retirement plans. How do they compare?

6. Compare the fringe benefits available in a large district that you know of with those in a small district with which you are acquainted or that you can find out about.

7. Obtain the names of the board-of-education members in your home community. What are their occupations? How well do you think they are representative of the entire community? What are the qualifications for effective board members?

8. How is the public-school system in the community in which you live organized? Draw a chart indicating the system's organizational structure, from the board of education to the pupils, and share this with others in your class.

9. Contact the superintendent of schools in a district with which you are acquainted. If possible, arrange for him to visit your class and explain the problems he has with respect to financing education in his district and with respect to organization of the schools in the district.

References

Organization of the Schools

ANDERSON, ROBERT H. *Teaching in a World of Change.* New York: Harcourt, 1966. Pp. 3–21.

BENT, RUDYARD K., and HENRY H. KRONENBERG. *Principles of Secondary Education.* 5th ed. New York: McGraw-Hill, 1966. Chap. 3.

BOSSING, NELSON L., and ROSCOE V. CRAMER. *The Junior High School*. Boston: Houghton Mifflin, 1965.

CHAMBERLAIN, LEO M., and LESLIE W. KINDRED. *The Teacher and School Organization*. Englewood Cliffs, N.J.: Prentice-Hall, 1966. Chaps. 2–4.

CONANT, JAMES BRYANT. *Shaping Educational Policies*. New York: McGraw-Hill, 1964.

CURTIN, JAMES. *Supervision in Today's Elementary Schools*. New York: Macmillan, 1964. Pp. 3–35, 141–59, 207–32.

DeYOUNG, CHRIS A., and RICHARD WYNN. *American Education*. 6th ed. New York: McGraw-Hill, 1968. Chaps. 2–5.

FABER, CHARLES F. "The Size of a School District." *Phi Delta Kappan*, September 1966, pp. 33–35.

HALPIN, ANDREW W. *Theory and Research in Administration*. New York: Macmillan, 1966. Pp. 81–127, 253–77.

HARRISON, RAYMOND H. *Supervisory Leadership in Education*. New York: American Book, 1968. Chaps. 1, 2, 5, 7, 12.

HASKEW, LAURENCE D., and JONATHON C. McLENDON. *This Is Teaching*. 3d ed. Glenview, Ill.: Scott, Foresman, 1968. Chap. 8, pp. 356–59.

HICKS, WILLIAM VERNON, and FRANK H. BLACKINGTON III. *Introduction to Education*. Columbus, Ohio: C. E. Merrill, 1965. Chap. 10.

JOHNSON, JAMES A., HAROLD W. COLLINS, VICTOR L. DUPUIS, and JOHN H. JOHANSEN. *Introduction to the Foundations of American Education*. Boston: Allyn & Bacon, 1969. Sec. 2.

LEEPER, ROBERT L., ed. *Supervision: Emerging Profession*. Washington, D.C.: Association for Supervision and Curriculum Development of the National Education Association, 1969. Pts. 2, 4, 5.

LUCIO, WILLIAM H. *The Supervisor: New Demands, New Dimensions*. Washington, D.C.: Association for Supervision and Curriculum Development of the National Education Association, 1969.

LUNDSBURY, JOHN H., and JEAN V. MARANI. *The Junior High School We Saw: One Day in the 8th Grade*. Washington, D.C.: Association for Supervision and Curriculum Development of the National Education Association, 1964.

MISNER, PAUL J., FREDERICK W. SCHNEIDER, and LOWELL G. KEITH. *Elementary School Administration*. Columbus, Ohio: C. E. Merrill, 1963. Chap. 4.

NATIONAL EDUCATION ASSOCIATION. *Elementary School Organization*. Research Memo 1965-22. Washington, D.C.: Research Division of the National Education Association, 1965.

———. *Schools for the 60's*. New York: McGraw-Hill, 1963. Chap. 3.

RICHEY, ROBERT W. *Planning for Teaching*. 4th ed. New York: McGraw-Hill, 1968. Chap. 11.

RUSSELL, JAMES E. *Change and Challenge in American Education.* Boston: Houghton Mifflin, 1965. Pp. 7–48.

SAUNDERS, ROBERT L., RAY C. PHILLIPS, and HAROLD J. JOHNSON. *A Theory of Educational Leadership.* Columbus, Ohio: C. E. Merrill, 1966. Pp. 38–41, 132–46.

"The School as a Social Institution." In *Problems and Issues in Contemporary Education,* an anthology from the *Harvard Educational Review* and the *Teachers College Record.* Glenview, Ill.: Scott, Foresman, 1968. Pp. 199–233.

Financing Schools

BENSON, CHARLES. *The Cheerful Prospect.* Boston: Houghton Mifflin, 1965. Chaps. 11, 12.

CAMPBELL, ROALD F., and GERALD R. STRONFE. "Toward a Rationale for Federal-State-Local Relations in Education." *Phi Delta Kappan,* September 1965, pp. 2–7.

DEYOUNG, CHRIS A., and RICHARD WYNN. *American Education.* 6th ed. New York: McGraw-Hill, 1968. Chap. 16.

HASKEW, LAURENCE D., and JONATHON C. MCLENDON. *This Is Teaching.* Glenview, Ill.: Scott, Foresman, 1968. Pp. 128–31, 253–55.

JOHNSON, JAMES A., HAROLD W. COLLINS, VICTOR L. DUPUIS, and JOHN H. JOHANSEN. *Introduction to the Foundations of American Education.* Boston: Allyn & Bacon, 1969. Sec. 2, pt. 3.

MUSHKIN, SELMA J., and EUGENE P. MCLOONE. *Local School Expenditures: 1970 Projections.* Chicago: Council of State Governments, 1965.

NATIONAL EDUCATION ASSOCIATION. *Educational Responsibilities of the Federal Government.* Washington, D.C.: Educational Policies Commission of the National Education Association, 1964.

———. *Education Is Good Business.* Washington, D.C.: American Association of School Administrators of the National Education Association, 1966.

———. *Federal Policy and the Public Schools.* Washington, D.C.: National Education Association, 1967.

———. *What Everyone Should Know about Financing Our Schools.* Washington, D.C.: National Education Association, 1966.

RICHEY, ROBERT W. *Planning for Teaching.* 4th ed. New York: McGraw-Hill, 1968. Chap. 12.

STONE, JAMES C., and R. ROSS HEMPSTEAD. *California Education Today.* New York: Crowell, 1968. Chap. 5.

Certification of Teachers

ARMSTRONG, W. EARL, and T. M. STINNETT. *A Manual on Certification Requirements for School Personnel in the U. S.* Washington, D.C.: National Commission on Teacher Education and Professional Standards of the National Education Association, revised triennially.

BORROWMAN, MERLE L., ed. *Teacher Education in America.* New York: Teachers College Press, Columbia University, 1965.

BURRUP, PERCY E. *The Teacher and the Public School System.* 2d ed. New York: Harper, 1965.

COLLIER, CALHOUN C., W. ROBERT HOUSTON, ROBERT R. SCHMALZ, and WILLIAM J. WALSH. *Teaching in the Modern Elementary School.* New York: Macmillan, 1967.

COMBS, ARTHUR W. *The Professional Education of Teachers.* Boston: Allyn & Bacon, 1965.

CONANT, JAMES BRYANT. *The Education of American Teachers.* New York: McGraw-Hill, 1963.

DEYOUNG, CHRIS A., and RICHARD WYNN. *American Education.* 6th ed. New York: McGraw-Hill, 1968. Pp. 301, 516.

FRASIER, JAMES E. *An Introduction to the Study of Education.* 3d ed. New York: Harper, 1967. Chap. 11.

GRAMBS, JEAN D., and L. MORRIS MCCLURE. *Foundations of Teaching.* New York: Holt, Rinehart & Winston, 1964. Chap. 9.

HASKEW, LAURENCE D., and JONATHON C. MCLENDON. *This Is Teaching.* 3d ed. Glenview, Ill.: Scott, Foresman, 1968. Chap. 10; pp. 125, 157–58, 270–71, 275.

KINNEY, LUCIEN B. *Certification in Education.* Englewood Cliffs, N.J.: Prentice-Hall, 1964.

MISNER, PAUL J., FREDERICK W. SCHNEIDER, and LOWELL G. KEITH. *Elementary School Administration.* Columbus, Ohio: C. E. Merrill, 1963. Chap. 3.

NATIONAL EDUCATION ASSOCIATION. *Milestones in Teacher Education and Professional Standards.* Washington, D.C.: National Commission on Teacher Education and Professional Standards of the National Education Association, 1966.

RICHEY, ROBERT W. *Planning for Teaching.* 4th ed. New York: McGraw-Hill, 1968. Chap. 3.

SIMANDLE, SIDNEY. "Certification across State Lines." *NEA Journal,* December 1965, pp. 56–58.

STINNETT, T. M., and ALBERT J. HUGGETT. *Professional Problems of Teachers.* New York: Macmillan, 1963. Chaps. 18, 19.

STONE, JAMES C. "Teacher Certification, Supply and Demand." *Review of Educational Research,* October 1963, pp. 343–54.

———, and R. ROSS HEMPSTEAD. *California Education Today.* New York: Crowell, 1968. Chap. 3.

WOELLNER, ROBERT C., and M. AURILLA WOOD. *Requirements for Certification of Teachers, Counselors, Librarians, Administrators for Elementary Schools, Secondary Schools, Junior Colleges.* Chicago: University of Chicago Press, revised annually.

Employment Practices

ABRAHAM, WILLARD. *A Time for Teaching.* New York: Harper, 1964. Chaps. 2, 3.

CHAMBERLAIN, LEO M., and LESLIE W. KINDRED. *The Teacher and School Organization.* Englewood Cliffs, N.J.: Prentice-Hall, 1966. Chap. 7.

CONANT, JAMES BRYANT. *Slums and Suburbs.* New York: McGraw-Hill, 1961.

DEYOUNG, CHRIS A., and RICHARD WYNN. *American Education.* 6th ed. New York: McGraw-Hill, 1968. Pp. 301–5.

GORDON, GARFORD C. "Conditions of Employment and Service in Elementary and Secondary Schools." *Review of Educational Research,* October 1963, p. 385.

JOHNSON, JAMES A., HAROLD W. COLLINS, VICTOR L. DUPUIS, and JOHN H. JOHANSEN. *Introduction to the Foundations of American Education.* Boston: Allyn & Bacon, 1969. Sec. 2, pt. 1.

MISNER, PAUL J., FREDERICK W. SCHNEIDER, and LOWELL G. KEITH. *Elementary School Administration.* Columbus, Ohio: C. E. Merrill, 1963. Chaps. 14–16.

NATIONAL EDUCATION ASSOCIATION. *How to Get a Teaching Position in the Public Schools.* Research Memo 1964-8. Washington, D.C.: Research Division of the National Education Association, 1964.

PETERSEN, DOROTHY G. *The Elementary School Teacher.* New York: Appleton, 1964. Pts. 1–4.

RICHEY, ROBERT W. *Planning for Teaching.* 4th ed. New York: McGraw-Hill, 1968. Pp. 583, 602–5.

STONE, JAMES C., and R. ROSS HEMPSTEAD. *California Education Today.* New York: Crowell, 1968. Chap. 4.

TAYLOR, GEORGE W. "The Public Interest in Collective Negotiations in Education," *Phi Delta Kappan,* September 1966, pp. 16–22.

The services of teachers are vital for the welfare of the country and of every individual. Beyond this, the nation's teachers directly influence the quantity and quality of the services provided by all the other professions.

NATIONAL MANPOWER COUNCIL

12

The Profession

"What is teaching?" We often ask this of our beginning students in education classes. The ensuing discussion inevitably gets around to the theoretical rationale of teaching as a profession, at the end of which the group usually agrees, "Yes, teaching is a profession." When the dust has settled, I usually say, "O.K., but so what? Does it make any difference? Has this discussion meant anything to you?" Generally, the answer is, "No." "Why?" I ask. "Well," they say, "we think it's a good job, attractive work, moderately rewarding, and so why get up tight over whether it's a profession, or a trade, or a ———? It's a job."

Now we ask you, the reader, to consider for a moment the theoretical rationale of teaching as a profession. Is there a meaningful difference between a profession and a trade? Is there any longer a clear distinction between professionalism and unionism? These questions are dealt with in the first part of this chapter because, as teachers of teachers, we hold the notion that there are some differences and that these differences are important—*still*. We begin our quest for answers by referring to the dictionary. Here we find some interesting, subtle differences in definition of terms, as follows:

The American Teacher

There is no office higher than that of a teacher of youth; for there is nothing on earth so precious as the mind, soul, character of the child. No office should be regarded with greater respect. The first minds in the community should be encouraged to assume it. Parents should do all but impoverish themselves, to induce such to become the guardians and guides of their children.

WILLIAM ELLERY CHANNING

profession: an occupation requiring a formal education.

professional: a person who makes a business of something that others do for pleasure.

professionalism: the standing, practice, or methods of a professional, as distinguished from those of an amateur.

trade: a kind of work; especially one requiring skilled mechanical work.

union: a group of workers, joined together to protect and promote their interest.

unionism: adherence to a union, the system, principles, or methods of labor unions.

The Making of a Profession

Using these definitions as a starting point, it appears that the making of a profession is the developing of a talent common to some degree in all people into a distinguishing hallmark by a special group of people. For example, everyone practices medicine to some degree, but when a person is extremely ill, a physician is sought. Similarly, everyone practices arguing to some degree, but when a person is in trouble, a lawyer is sought. The parallel can be continued, whether it is sandlot baseball, religion, music, or architecture. Note that a separation occurs when these "common" or "natural" talents are developed, through an extended period of advanced training, to their fullest capacity. In this "final" state the work performed has become professional. A trade, on the other hand, is not a talent that is commonly possessed by all people to some degree. Most people do not have the knowledge necessary to build or repair a television set, an automobile, or the plumbing in a home. These are skills that are mechanical in nature and that are learned in a short period of time.

But what about teaching? Certainly everyone has the ability to teach to some degree. Probably everyone has at sometime said, "Here, let me show you." Thus they have made a direct attempt to teach. But some people seem to be able to "show you" better than others. Hence, some distinguishing hallmarks begin to emerge to characterize a special group of people called teachers. Among them are: (1) an in-depth field of knowledge, (2) an understanding of how people learn at various ages and states in their lives, (3) an understanding of the organization and development of a field of knowledge, and (4) the ability to relate both subject matter and self to the student. These qualities characterize the actions of the professional teacher. Comparable qualities characterize the physician prescribing a particular medicine for a patient or a lawyer making a particular point with a jury for his client. Teaching, in a professional sense, cannot be reduced to a mechanical process, for when a particular skill is to be taught routinely, a machine might be used to free the teacher to teach. If the activity in which a teacher engages is mechanical, then that teacher has reduced teaching to a trade. If understanding, knowledge, skill, and commitment are required, then teaching is a profession.

Professionalization

To think of teaching as a profession is appropriate as an abstract model and as a hoped-for goal. In a refreshing way, Becker argues that a profession is an abstraction—"a praiseworthy moral stance" that nowhere exists in reality—a symbol—"a folk concept"—that assumes importance to the extent it is observably recognized as characteristic of a definable group of workers.[1] The dynamic process by which an occupation changes observable characteristics in the direction of the abstract model is professionalization. In professionalizing teaching, close scrutiny is given practices, principles, and methods of operation. Out of this examination emerge some salient differences between professional associations and teachers' unions. Perhaps these differences are philosophical. Choice of allegiance must be left to the individual and his view of teaching as a profession or trade. Briefly, some of the differences deal with alliances, structure, independence, and program. In general, teacher unions operate within the framework of labor policy; include only classroom teachers (thus excluding administrators, directors, business managers, registrars, department chairmen, counselors—persons who are left in limbo with regard to membership); gear pro-

---

[1] Howard Becker, "Professional Education: Present Status and Continuing Problems," in *Education for the Professions*, Sixty-first Yearbook, pt. 2, National Society for the Study of Education (Chicago: University of Chicago Press, 1962), p. 33.

grams to policy decisions of the overall labor movement; and are committed to look to a central labor council for direction and to help with labor disputes and labor campaigns originating outside of teaching. By contrast, professional associations have developed along the line of independence in setting policies, making decisions, and planning programs; enlist all allies they can without forming alliances; and include within their membership all credentialed personnel, to function in the truest sense of collegiality.

The concept that teaching is a profession is important because it connotes a *behavioral level of expectation.* This behavioral aspect was noted by the National Commission on Teacher Education and Professional Standards of the NEA when it stated that "teaching is a profession to the degree that its members are professional." [2] Certainly being professional depends on the level of behavioral values possessed by the teacher. Note that there are four values associated with professionalism: expertise, autonomy, commitment, and responsibility.

No Other Sure Foundation

We can, I think, now state the conditions which if achieved would guarantee teaching the prestige, status and public recognition enjoyed by the traditional learned professions. The nature and importance of the teacher's task is such that its practitioners must be intellectually able, must possess a defined body of subject matter and skill, must pursue their work as a career, must undergo a long and arduous period of preparation, must be dedicated to the welfare of those they teach, must be accorded a high degree of autonomy in day-to-day practice, must participate in the development of necessary group solidarity and subject themselves to the discipline inherent in such solidarity, and must be well paid and professionally secure. This definition of what we mean when we use the term "teaching profession" becomes a statement of aims and objectives of any professional teachers organization.

Arthur F. Corey, *Your AASA in 1957–58* (Washington, D.C.: American Association of School Administrators, 1958), p. 147.

The professional-standards movement since World War II has placed great emphasis on expertise, commitment, and responsibility but has given

[2] National Commission on Teacher Education and Professional Standards of the National Education Association, *A Position Paper on Teacher Education and Professional Standards* (Washington, D.C.: National Education Association, 1963), p. 2.

little attention to autonomy until recently. One reason for the lack of attention to autonomy was alluded to in a statement attributed to Franklin D. Roosevelt, "There are too many little girls in [teaching] hanging around to get married." Teaching is now attracting many young married men and career-minded women. According to Stinnett this shift and the change in median age (up for women, down for men) indicate that teaching is becoming a permanent career choice instead of a temporary resting place.[3]

THE UNION VIEW

Our view, expressing the necessity of regarding teaching as a profession (even as a theoretical model), is not held by everyone. In fact, if the goal of professionalism is, not to improve the quality of education, but, rather, to enhance personal ego, social status, pay, and employee-oriented job requirements, then Albert Shanker, president of the United Federation of Teachers, made a very valid point when, addressing a symposium at the City College of the City University of New York, he presented a "union point of view":

The question of whether we are different from other workers or if we are the same is really a matter of snobbery. I can remember only a few years ago when the teacher served cafeteria patrol and yard patrol and everything else and he couldn't eat lunch; he had to work longer hours. And the workers in the factory across the street enjoyed all sorts of rights which the so-called professional did not. Snobbery is a great psychological thing. It's the racism of the northern white in the professions. The southern white, the poor white, can look down on the black and say "I'm superior to you," and it makes him feel great; he doesn't have a damn thing, but it makes him feel terrific. This kind of professional snobbery in New York City makes us look great. We get less than a truck driver and we get mistreated but we can say, "Boy, we are professionals." This is terrific—we get less money and our working conditions are lousier and we have no decision-making but we are terrific. I would recommend to you a piece by Arthur Koestler written some years ago on snobbery in which he re-analyzes a piece about the fox and the grapes; you know, where the foxes were sitting there looking at the grapes up there and they couldn't reach them. And they all said that the grapes were sour because they couldn't get up there. But one fox was different. He took climbing lessons at night. He went to the City University or perhaps to an extension of the Board of Education and one day got up there and he started eating the grapes. And you know something, they *were* sour. But you know, he wouldn't admit it because he had taken climbing lessons. So he kept eating the grapes and he died of a gastric ulcer. I think that

[3] T. M. Stinnett, *Turmoil in Teaching* (New York: Macmillan, 1967), pp. 34–38.

some of us in our so-called professionalism are doing practically the same thing.[4]

There is concern on the part of many educators as they view this increase of nonprofessional events and attitudes. Truly, the teaching profession today is highly vulnerable. Because of its lack of maturity as a professional entity, there is neither the backlog of precedent nor adequate professional protection for those who wish to be heard on issues vital to education and the teacher. Of course, teachers should not control education, but they should be in a position to be heard, and certainly they should govern their own profession.

AUTONOMY

It is essential that a distinction be drawn between the *control* of education and the *governance* of the teaching profession. Educators must have control of their affairs through such processes as licensure, certification, and accreditation [5] if they are to be held accountable for results— successes as well as failures—as they should be. Within teaching today there is an emphasis on responsibility and requirements that is disproportionate to the rights teachers have. Legislatures prescribe courses, set standards, and interpret and enforce requirements pertaining to the affairs of teachers, with enforcement placed in the hands of state and local lay boards. It is fundamentally inimical to the concept of a profession to have the practitioners excluded from the basic decision-making process in favor of lay control.

As teachers attempt to gain autonomy so that they can be involved in the process of educational policy, their tactics cause them to become more vulnerable: they appear militant, and their lack of maturity becomes evident. The charge has been made that teachers are probably farther away from real professionalism at this time than they would ever care to admit.

[4] Albert Shanker, "The Development of Collective Bargaining in Education— A Union Point of View," transcript of an address delivered at a symposium entitled "Critical Issues in Education" held at the City College of the City University of New York in 1970, p. 29. Used by permission of Local 2, United Federation of Teachers, American Federation of Teachers, AFL-CIO.

[5] *Licensure* is the process by which individuals are admitted to practice in a professional field. It is administered and controlled by the profession itself. *Certification* is a process by which individuals are authorized to perform specific services in the public schools of the state. It is administered and controlled by the state, usually with advice from the profession. *Accreditation* is a process of approving institutions to prepare personnel for professional practice. It is administered and controlled by the profession.

Arbuckle wonders if educators want to be professionals or tradesmen. He observes:

Teachers today appear to want the best of two worlds: the status of the professional, but the level of responsibility of organized labor; the financial return of the professional, but the hours of organized labor. They have become a group of people who, while spending their working days evaluating others, stoutly insist that it is impossible to evaluate *them*. . . .

We have a situation in which the worst get practically the same reward as the best, because, in the era of collective bargaining, the teachers demand to be rewarded on the assumption that all are highly superior professionals, and thus all deserve the highest in the way of remuneration.[6]

Evidence of this vacillation is illustrated in a number of recent collective-bargaining negotiations. Throughout the negotiations union negotiating teams waver typically between two philosophical positions. On the one hand, they contend that they are professionals, members of educational faculties, and that they have legitimate concerns above and beyond traditional collective-bargaining negotiations. On the other hand, in relation to other specific demands, they contend these specific demands are "standard" in all union contracts.

Demands such as security of employment, grievance procedures, dues check-off, agency shop, release time, and workload are union standards from which teacher-union negotiators draw. Demands such as participation in faculty appointments, selection of administrative personnel, retention, tenure, promotion, curriculum, and textbooks constitute professional standards from which teacher-union negotiators also draw.

NEA AND AFT

Arbuckle's observation supports Brenton's view on the limits of professionalism as practiced by teachers today. Limited professionalism must shoulder part of the blame for the miseducation of today's youth; all of the blame cannot be laid at the door of the legislature and lay boards. Brenton, while recognizing the history of and need for tenure, feels that "professional motivation" is not as noble as many teachers want to represent it. He writes:

It's not a question of tenure alone. It's a question of too many individuals with low job motivation—sheltered by a single salary schedule, shielded by tenure —doing work that, despite its apparent challenges, can easily become routinized—coasting along. [It] is ready-made for mediocrity.[7]

[6] Dugald S. Arbuckle, "Professional or Technician?" *The Educational Digest,* November 1967, p. 12.

[7] Myron Brenton, *What's Happened to Teacher?* (New York: Coward-McCann, 1970), p. 250.

A Table of Contrasts

IN THE EDUCATION PROFESSION:	IN OTHER PROFESSIONS:
The practitioner works with 30 or more clients simultaneously.	The practitioner deals with one client at a time.
The relationship is adult to child.	The relationship is adult to adult.
Treatment is conducted in a classroom with 29 or more other clients observing and hearing all that takes place.	Treatment is conducted in a private office.
Treatment continues six hours a day, 180 days a year.	Conference is held by appointment, and the period is normally brief.
A multitude of problems must be dealt with continuously and constantly.	The client consults the expert usually regarding one specific problem.
Results of treatment are long range and not immediately evident.	Expert's advice usually brings immediately identifiable results.
Results are intangible, concerning attitudes and behaviors.	Results are tangible, even immediately visible.
Compensation derives from public funds.	The client is expected to pay the expert directly.
The client is required to submit to treatment by law.	The client voluntarily seeks expert services.
Legal responsibility for the welfare of children is complex, i.e. involving parents.	Legal responsibility is direct and from adult to adult.
The client has little or no choice in the selection of the practitioner.	The client chooses his expert, changing his choice at will.
Communication to the adult world is through the minds of children, creating misunderstandings.	Communication is adult to adult, with no intermediary.

Eva Washington, in *California Teachers Association Journal,* May 1969, p. 18. Reprinted by permission.

Thus, there is a need for major reform even as the dynamic process of change occurs that can transform teaching into a true profession. Historically the professionalization of any occupation is preceded by systematic attention to the problems of professionalization by the practitioners. But the question of leadership becomes confusing, for, in light of recent policy shifts in the NEA, one can scarcely find substantial differences between their professional negotiations and the collective bargaining of the American Federation of Teachers (AFT) in teacher-board conflict. Both organizations support aggressive militancy for teachers. Both claim that right and justice are with them and their teachers. Both hold out the strike threat as their ultimate weapon. In many ways, their organizational paths have merged. "To claim substantial differences between the ultimate tactics of the two organizations is little more than semantic gymnastics. Stripped of party-line rhetoric, this may well be a classic example of a distinction without a difference." [8]

This similarity of tactics and these alliances is evident from the teacher strikes throughout the nation. The umbrella merger of NEA's local affiliate, the Association of Classroom Teachers–Los Angeles (ACT-LA), and the Los Angeles branch of the American Federation of Teachers (AFT-LA) resulted in a month-long strike during the spring of 1970. When the strike was called off, it was not clear how the closing of the schools for a month had helped improve their "deteriorating conditions." The originally stated goals of the strike had not been realized, and the teachers voted to return to work over the protest of their leaders. It is still necessary for educators, lay board, and citizens to find honest solutions to the deteriorating conditions by way of dialogue, maintaining the deepest respect for human relations.

Several national educational organizations want to keep a united profession of teachers and administrators who can work together on social and educational problems affecting the welfare of children. They do not wish to see a merging of AFT and NEA. These organizations (NEA national affiliates) argue for a different type of decision-making operation from that used by private industry. They point out that the concept of shared authority and joint decision making has long been accepted by boards of education. They believe that the tripartite nature of teacher-school board-administrator relationships in our public schools needs to emerge more clearly and strongly.

In industry, bargaining is between labor and management. In education, negotiation is among teachers, board and administration. The superintendent is the key to the distinction. It may be predicted that in most places the superintendent will end up being not just a special agent of the board, but rather a joint

[8] William R. Hazard, "Professional Negotiations and Collective Bargaining," *School Board Journal*, October 1967, p. 19.

Learning to Use the Power

At present, teachers are concerned with gaining power through negotiations processes for the primary purpose of improving salaries, fringe benefits, and working conditions. But these three areas are not likely to remain the exclusive concerns of teachers for very long. The interest of teacher negotiators will soon turn to all areas of school management, control, and operation. This expansion of areas of concern has occurred in a few cities already. Teachers are learning that through negotiations they can gain power and that to have power is very advantageous. They are learning how to use their power effectively and how to play the game of formal face-to-face negotiations much more rapidly and effectively than are administrators and board members.

It is not uncommon for administrators, board members, and others to claim that all of the aspects of school planning, decision-making, and operation were shared with teachers long before collective negotiation procedures became prevalent. However, the difference today is that the sharing is no longer a matter of *permitting* teachers to participate in decision-making and planning. Sharing is seen by a large number of today's teachers as a matter of formal and often legislated right, rather than privilege. Administrative *noblesse oblige* and unilateral veto power, with no strings attached, are increasingly becoming things of the past.

The period during which this inevitable process of power accommodation is achieved can easily become a dismal era for education. It can be a period of sharp change in which grave damage is done to the image and foundations of public education. However, this period can also become one of tremendous advancement in education—if this is to happen, both sides in the present power struggle will have to behave more flexibly, more honestly, and more openly than they ever have before in the history of education. If both sides can produce these kinds of behavior, shared decision-making, increased power and prestige for teachers, regulation of the teaching profession by teachers, and many other worthwhile changes could well lead to a golden era of improvement in education.

John J. Horvat, "The Nature of Teacher Power and Teacher Attitudes toward Certain Aspects of This Power," in *Theory into Practice* (College of Education, Ohio State University), April 1968, pp. 51–56. Reprinted by permission of the author and the publisher.

leader, a bridge, a catalyst, a mediator, a human engineer helping to bring about the attainment of consensus and true meetings of the minds.[9]

NEW MOVES

While some teachers and their educational organizations do not desire professionalization or have changed their sights from it to unionization, it is refreshing to see a state legislature attempt to move the other way. The state of Washington took a bold step to move from state teacher-education standards that are lists of courses and credits applied identically to all cases, regardless of their relevance, to standards that are individual and contextual, based upon the idea that human differences are to be valued and that change is inevitable. This action of Washington's holds promise of *viewing professional performance professionally*. It requires that preparation agencies look at the real test of their efforts—the way children are treated in school—and that the state education agency, too, become relevant. Washington's preparation standards are now based upon the following ideas: (1) preparation should continue throughout the career of educational personnel; (2) preparation should be individualized; (3) preparation should be based upon performance; and (4) professional associations and school organizations, as well as colleges and universities, should have responsible preparation roles. The direction is good. If this philosophy can permeate all legislative bodies and go one step farther, allowing teachers the autonomy commensurate with their responsibilities, expertise, and commitment, then teaching can become a profession in the truest sense.

Individual Responsibility

The benefits of professionalization should be quality education. We believe the welfare of children, society, and teachers is intimately interrelated. As the intimate relationships among the three are more clearly understood, the power that lies in the sense of mission of more than a million American teachers will more and more come to be realized in the achievement of standards that are in every sense professional. For this to be achieved, each member of the profession must share the responsibility for each of its overall problems and tasks. A list of the specific competencies required of each individual practitioner in his role as member of the profession appears on pages 346–47. *Now the issue is no longer a theoretical one of whether education is a profession, but rather, how to bring all the individ-*

---

[9] Robbins Barstow, "The Decision-making Apparatus in Public Education," in *The Teacher Dropout*, ed. T. M. Stinnett (Itasca, Ill.: F. E. Peacock, 1970), p. 58.

uals and groups in the profession to accept their professional obligations.
Any one of several approaches could lead to this same conclusion. Our
point of view is that professional tasks require the cooperative efforts of
the entire membership for their achievement, under the leadership of qualified individuals and groups. It would be equally valid to point out that
failure to perform these tasks affects the welfare of each individual in the
profession, and that in the interests of his own welfare it is incumbent on
him to see that the tasks are performed adequately. When ineffective certification and accreditation practices result in the admission of unqualified
members, each member of the profession shares the consequences in lowered prestige and in criticism. Failure to test our professional procedures
subjects each member to public suspicion that he is following fads and
speaking jargon. The initiative in attacking the problem rests with the
membership as well as the leaders; and if the leaders drag their feet, they
ought to be stimulated or replaced.

While each individual shares responsibility in building the teaching profession, Palmatier's penetrating remarks aptly express the goal of professionalization:

Professionalization is not built on individuals' attitudes, but rather professionalization provides structure where the reverse is true; i.e. the structure and
organization guarantee that practitioners' behavior will be consistent with professional principles regardless of the teachers' attitudinal orientation.[10]

Some measure of autonomy for the profession will need to come from
state legislatures, in the form of a professional-regulation act for teachers.
This act will have to be carefully written to ensure that the various commissions and/or boards will not have conflicting legal jurisdiction. The
number of such professional bodies should be kept to a minimum and be
broadly representative of the profession as a whole. When the profession is
involved in licensure, certification, and accreditation, then the maturity
with which it functions will be of paramount importance. In an allied profession, the process of

accreditation has been likened to the stamp of sterling on silver. It [hospital
accreditation] assures the patient that within the hospital a stimulating climate
exists in which physicians subject themselves to the scrutiny of other physicians
and in which they are continually educating themselves in better methods of
providing care.[11]

[10] Larry Lee Palmatier, *Teacher Power and Professionalism in California* (Burlingame, Calif.: California Teachers Association, 1970), p. 8.

[11] Roger Olin, "The Meaning of Hospital Accreditation," *Today's Health,* January
1969, p. 87.

Individual-Responsibility Competencies

[The old bromide "The chain is only as strong as its weakest link" is certainly pertinent to the matter of individual-responsibility competencies. It is only when teachers become enterprising in professional groups that they can expect to influence effectively the decisions relating to the standards of their profession. The extent to which teachers are charged with the obligation to assume individual responsibility for strengthening the image of the profession is illustrated in the following conception of the truly professional teacher:]

A member of the profession

1. Demonstrates an appreciation of the social importance of the profession.
   (a) Renders appropriate service to society beyond that for which he has contracted.
   (b) Contributes to the honor and prestige of the profession by his personal conduct.
   (c) Actively seeks to upgrade professional standards through selective recruitment and retention programs.
   (d) Interprets to others the goals and practices of the profession.
2. Contributes to the development of professional standards.
   (a) [Helps to develop] a functional code of ethics.
   (b) Adheres to the accepted code of ethics.
   (c) Helps to enforce the code of ethics in upgrading standards of professional behavior.
   (d) Supports an adequate system of certification and accreditation.
   (e) Helps improve pre-service and in-service programs of preparation.

New Careers, Roles, and Staffing Patterns

In the movement toward true professionalization of teaching, the current and traditional role of all personnel must be carefully reexamined; new careers in education must be defined. Differentiated staffing should result. Time, expertise, responsibility, classroom roles, supervisory duties, public relations, professional participation, administrative duties, secretarial responsibilities, and commitment all are factors to be reconsidered. The erroneous idea that all teachers can be prepared alike and will perform alike throughout their careers must be discarded. The national concern for new

3. Contributes to the profession through his organizations.
   (a) Becomes a member of the organization.
   (b) Takes active part in the formulation of the organizational policies.
   (c) Supports the policy once formed until it is changed by the democratic process.
   (d) Seeks and supports legislative programs to improve the program of education as well as the economic and social status of the profession.

4. Takes a personal responsibility for his own professional growth.
   (a) Develops and tests more effective classroom procedures.
   (b) Keeps informed on current trends, tendencies, and practices in his field by use of professional literature.
   (c) Participates in conferences, workshops, etc., dealing with professional problems.
   (d) Enlarges his horizons through academic and nonacademic experiences.

5. Acts on a systematic philosophy, critically adopted and consistently applied.
   (a) Expresses a systematic philosophy of education held with deep personal conviction.
   (b) Identifies and clarifies the philosophical assumptions underlying various and conflicting policies for his work. . . .
   (c) Utilizes explicitly his philosophical view in making consistent choices of educational policies and practices.

Lucien B. Kinney, "A Member of the Profession," in *Six Areas of Teacher Competence* (Burlingame, Calif.: Commission on Teacher Education of the California Teachers Association, 1964), pp. 25–26. Reprinted by permission.

careers to relieve unemployment and to provide opportunities for victims of poverty and racial discrimination has furnished the profession an opportunity to meet a real human need while at the same time building a stronger profession.

DIFFERENTIATION

Differentiation of the teaching role means that some individuals may enter teaching at a simple level. Differentiation of the instructional staff is necessary to make the most efficient use of well-trained and effective teachers. The highly competent teacher must be given greater responsibil-

Re Status

The status of the teacher in American society does merit our concern and attention. Plato observed that "what is honored in a country will be cultivated there." If one measures honor by emoluments, then teaching, and by extension education, is not honored here.

The current tendency to suspect education as a center of subversion is a demonstration, not of honor, but of a disrepute which has dangerous implications for our country. For either education is to be cultivated here or we are lost. In Whitehead's phrase: "In the conditions of modern life the rule is absolute, the race which does not value trained intelligence is doomed."

The problem of the teacher is a complex one, and defies the laws of supply and demand. He is in short supply; he is underpaid; he lacks status. It is common to explain the first and third by the second. But to give him greater income he must first win the respect of the public, for the public pays the bill. Status then seems to control. But it is argued status is a reflection of income; so we box the compass but make no progress toward solving the problem.

Status and money will follow when in his profession the teacher can command respect. He professes knowledge. We would try to break the circle by making the teacher more wise. When his neighbors turn to him for advice as naturally as they now turn to the physician and banker the battle will be half won.

O. Meredith Wilson, "Re Status," in "Report of the Fund for the Advancement of Education," *Report of the General Session,* California Council on Teacher Education, April 1953, pp. 33–35. Reprinted by permission.

ity for planning programs of instruction and for directing the education of a unit of pupils larger than the ordinary classroom. However, care must be exercised so that his close relationships with individual pupils are not broken down by this extension of his responsibilities. To prevent this and to safeguard his other functions, the competent teacher leader must be supplied with an adequate staff of assistants who have varying levels of skill and understanding. In fact, the teacher aide, the student teacher, the intern teacher, the beginning teacher, and other teachers must be called upon to do much of the program planning in cooperation with the teacher leader.

The restructuring of the teaching profession must clearly concentrate upon improving the quality of educational services to all children and youth. Who will take the lead in moving in this desired direction? The

profession? The public? The students? Private industry? Now that education has become big business (millions of dollars' worth of books, films,
games, audiovisual equipment, and the like), perhaps the needed push will
come from the captains of industry. Certainly we have observed that as
private industry enters the education field, it focuses attention on the quality of the educational service it will furnish and how that quality will be
evaluated. This is done through a process called a "performance contract":
if the student fails to achieve ("perform") at the desired level within a
specified time period, the school does not pay for the service rendered.
More specifically, in a written contract the company lists: (1) the physical
conditions under which its personnel will teach, (2) who will teach, (3)
how they will teach, (4) how many hours of instruction each student will
receive, (5) how success will be measured (any violation of 1–4 absolving
the company from responsibility for failure), and (6) the cost to the school
in terms of the measurements of success. If profit-minded private industry
believes it can base its reputation and remuneration on measurements of
success, then perhaps professional educators need to change their attitude
toward evaluation and accountability.

The concept of the self-contained teacher in the completely self-contained classroom, created to serve administrative convenience half a century ago, has lived past its time. It embodies so many contradictions in
terms of today's demands for teaching and learning that it must soon be
abandoned. New patterns need to be adopted to permit school personnel to
move up a career ladder, with opportunities for advancement along with
increasing prestige and appropriate compensation. The career-ladder approach, which is being developed in school systems around the country, allows low-income people, including veterans, to start as aides or technicians
while they prepare to qualify as regular teachers or for other jobs in the
profession. It permits talented college graduates who majored in fields
other than education to combine work in the school with part-time graduate study leading eventually to full qualification for teaching or specialized
leadership positions in education.

The aim of such a movement is toward more effective development of
the school staff, with professionals and paraprofessionals in a variety of
different assignments. Such an arrangement puts the teacher on an instructional team, working with specialists and supportive aides. Differentiated
and flexible ways to organize and use time and talent are essential to a
more efficient learning operation. Through more effective deployment of
the staff, the net need for additional personnel can be reduced; through
creation of a variety of specialists, a fair share of the bright, energetic
young people who now see education as a dead-end career can be attracted
into the profession. "We would be able to say, 'You can start at the bot-

tom of a career ladder, or at any other rung you are prepared for, and there will be opportunities for advancement in terms of responsibility, status, and salary.' " [12]

These ideas of low entry are not new, nor are they universally accepted. The ideas have been around for over thirty years, but it typically takes fifty to a hundred years to incorporate major changes into the educational establishment. The use of paraprofessionals, the training and utilizing of unskilled people in public service, was an aim of the National Youth Administration (N.Y.A.) and the Work Projects Administration (W.P.A.) in the Great Depression of the 1930's. Particular emphasis was placed on this concept in the N.Y.A., which trained unemployed out-of-school youth or potential dropouts and placed them as nonprofessionals in schools and other social-service agencies. Now the inclusion of paraprofessionals in the educational system and the concept of differentiated staffing should result in reshaping the school to respond to the requirements of individuals and to be an institution in and of the community it serves.

IMPLICATIONS OF DIFFERENTIATION

The concept of differentiated staffing implies that education personnel should be selected, educated, and deployed in ways that make optimum use of interests, abilities, and commitments and afford them greater autonomy in determining their own professional development. A differentiated staff would include teachers and a variety of special-service personnel, subject-matter specialists, administrators, student teachers, interns, persons from other professions, craftsmen, volunteers, and several categories of paraprofessionals and teacher aides. Within the classroom-teaching ranks, some professionals might serve as leaders, responsible for induction of new teachers, coordination of teams of associates and assistants, and general management of the learning setting. Others might function mainly as diagnosticians of learning difficulties, constructors of individualized programs for pupils, developers of interpersonal attitudes and behaviors, and the like.

Status and financial reward would be based on the complexity and intensity of the task the individual chose to prepare for and assume. The goal of a new form of merit pay would be achieved, because individuals would be paid differently for assuming different responsibilities, as compared to being paid differently because they were judged to be performing similar

[12] Don Davies, "Education Professions Development," *American Education,* February 1969, p. 9.

tasks at different quality levels. Thus, differentiated staffing can provide "a plan for recruitment, preparation, induction, and continuing education of staff personnel for the schools that would bring a much broader range of manpower to education than is now available." [13]

As these roles develop, it is of paramount importance that they are conceived to provide quality personal education for our children and youth and not to become a new hierarchy for the teaching profession. Wirth, in analyzing these ideas, warns, ". . . while the plan—a brainstorm of an NEA commission—does have some merit, a cautious attitude ought to greet any quickly devised nostrum offered as a cure for the overworked condition of the classroom teacher." [14] Wirth's warning should be, and has been, well heeded. Much careful, in-depth planning and experimentation has been done. Thoughtful dialogue has been stimulated by the United States Office of Education in two ways: first, through the creation of the Task Force of the National Institute for Advanced Study in Teaching Disadvantaged Youth, the work of Smith and his committee focusing on needs in teacher education, differentiated staffing, and finance; [15] and second, by developing differentiated staffing plans in such diverse communities as Temple City, California; Beaverton, Oregon; Kansas City, Missouri; and Greece, New York.[16] Enabled by the Education Professions Development Act (EPDA), these school systems created a career ladder beginning in some cases with part-time student aides and progressing through a series of preprofessional positions (aides, assistant and associate teachers, and teaching interns) and professional positions (teachers, staff teachers, senior teachers, and teacher leaders). Each differentiated position in such a hierarchy has its own salary schedule; and, at the highest level of the teacher-leader scale, it is possible for a teacher to be paid as much or more than most administrators in the school system. In addition, decisions about curriculum matters are left to senior teachers and teacher leaders, rather than administrators. Such staffing eliminates a number of the present barriers to recruitment and retention of quality personnel.

[13] "A Position Statement on the Concept of Differentiated Staffing," in *A Position Paper on Teacher Education and Professional Standards* (Washington, D.C.: National Commission on Teacher Education and Professional Standards of the National Education Association, 1969), p. 7.

[14] Arthur G. Wirth, "A New Hierarchy for the Teaching Profession?" *Changing Education,* Winter 1967, p. 3.

[15] B. Othanel Smith, *Teachers for the Real World* (Washington, D.C.: American Association of Colleges for Teacher Education, 1969), p. 137.

[16] John Chaffee, Jr., "First Manpower Assessment," *American Education,* February 1969, p. 2.

TEACHER-PREPARATION IMPLICATION

While these new staffing patterns have opened up a vast array of pre-viously untapped resources, they have also exposed the obsolescence that exists among current teachers in their understandings, skills, attitudes, and commitment. New concepts of teaching and learning have been developed through research and experimentation. If teacher education is to be com-patible with these new concepts, it must be reconstituted. Teacher educa-tion must equip teachers with the concepts, the attitudes, the knowledge, the understandings, the skills, and the sympathy to perform new roles under new and unfamiliar conditions. But the challenge to reconstitute teacher education lies not just in transforming the curriculum for the new or prospective teacher, but in providing new and better ways to reeducate and update the experienced teacher. If in-service education is now to change teacher behavior in the direction that seems necessary, it must junk our present obsolete educational model—the college or university. As one of the coauthors of the present volume has said elsewhere, "We are shadow boxing with the real problem unless we are willing to develop new structures . . . for the education of our teachers. . . ." [17]

There are several alternatives to the present educational model. Burns suggests the responsibility should be given to the public schools: " [Let] the schools provide for the professional preservice education of teachers as they now provide for the inservice training of their personnel." This would involve a central-office person in charge of staff development. [18]

Smith suggests the responsibility should be met by way of college-school-community centers: "Since training programs . . . require easy ac-cess to children, youth, and adults who represent a wide variety of cultural orientations and racial origins [there is need now for] a new social mecha-nism . . . the Training Complex." The complex would be a teacher-education center, involving the cooperative participation of existing agen-cies, namely, the schools and colleges. [19]

Stone suggests that the Education Professions Institute is the solution: "The EPI would be a new, *separate* and *independent* agency of higher ed-ucation with a distinct, *unique,* and differentiated function. The unique purpose would be to provide professional training for teachers-to-be, teacher aides, associate teachers, intern teachers, regular teachers, master

[17] James C. Stone, *Breakthrough in Teacher Education* (San Francisco: Jossey-Bass, 1968), p. 190.

[18] Hobert Burns, "Teacher Education Programs—Their Structure and Flexibility," in National Institute for the Study of Disadvantaged Youth, National Defense Edu-cation Act, *Special Bulletin,* December 1967, p. 1.

[19] B. Othanel Smith, op. cit., pp. 95–96, 137.

teachers and teachers of teachers. . . ." It would be organized and governed by representatives from the groups it served—students, staff, community, and profession—and financed by a federal voucher system.[20]

Choosing viable alternatives to professional preparation is important to each individual in the profession. Continuing education has long been a recognized imperative for the teaching profession, but current developments and future possibilities are very rapidly expanding its scope and complexity. The individual teacher is basically responsible for continuing his education throughout his career. He commits himself to diagnosing, to evaluating, and to formulating immediate and long-range goals. He is responsible for devising and initiating his own personal program for continuing his professional growth in general and specific knowledges and technical-professional skills. If he fails to grow professionally to meet the demands of a developing, expanding society, he fails the students, the profession, and the public.

Commitment

The profession of teaching invites persons with the brightest minds, the most outstanding personalities, and the soundest moral commitments. Since teaching is not only the oldest of the professions, but is also the nurturer of all the others, it is imperative that only the best choose this field of endeavor. Educators, now recognized as professional leaders in their communities and as important agents of change, engage in complex and demanding work and thus must possess and develop a large number of varied competencies.

Elsewhere in this book, in chapters dealing with the pressures and problems of teachers, the authors point up the importance of good physical and mental health of teachers. In this section we discuss the necessity for teachers to develop other kinds of competencies and commitments.

AN AWARENESS OF THE IMPORTANCE OF EDUCATION

To be a really professional person, a teacher must have great faith in education—greater even than that of Americans generally, whose belief in free public education is so strong that they entrust their dearest possessions to it. It is imperative for the professional educator to recognize that

---

[20] James C. Stone, *Teachers for the Disadvantaged* (San Francisco: Jossey-Bass, 1969), pp. 202–7; *Education Vouchers: Financing Education by Grants to Parents —A Preliminary Report* (Cambridge, Mass.: Center for the Study of Public Policy, 1970).

teaching is essential in the development of man's intellectual, social, economic, and ethical life if he is to progress and survive. An informed individual possesses tremendous power for good in an enlightened society, and as a molder of that society's future.

When a society supports schools so that children, youth, and adults can become educated, it expresses the belief that such schools will enable members of the culture to perpetuate its traditions and values and will also change and improve the society itself. Teachers, above all in the social organization, must be aware of and have faith in the significance and potential of education, and guide their actions and evolve their values with the importance of the profession in mind.

A KEEN SENSITIVITY TO THE NEEDS, INTERESTS, AND WELFARE OF CHILDREN

A good portion of this book is devoted to the importance of meeting the needs and interests of children and providing for their general welfare and of the teacher's role in this endeavor. What happens during the twelve or more years that children are in the public-school classrooms will have a lifetime effect upon their lives. Each year a child spends in school adds to, or detracts from, his total stature.

The chief responsibility of the teacher is that of freeing young people to help themselves, of helping them define their most pressing needs, interests, and problems, and of helping them understand their environment and how to cope with it. The teacher must help children learn how to learn, how to relate the facts they discover in their learning experiences to their everyday lives.

A DESIRE TO BE IN A "SERVICE" FIELD

Inherent in almost everyone's makeup is the urge to be of service to mankind. What nobler goal could one have than that of living and working so as to help fellow human beings in their struggle to meet life's problems and vicissitudes? For the person with such a philosophy, there are probably few, if any, types of work that offer the opportunities for fulfilling life's goals the way teaching does.

> Teachers act as if the chief concern of education were illiteracy, rather than inhumanity, injustice, and irresponsibility.
>
> JAMES C. STONE

There is never a day, and seldom an hour, in the life of a teacher that does not present countless opportunities to help some boy or girl or adult to meet some problem. And as any experienced teacher will attest, these opportunities are not just in the area of the intellect but in the areas of physical, social, emotional, and spiritual development as well.

A WILLINGNESS TO CARRY ON CONTINUED STUDY IN THE FIELD

Education is dynamic! It is changing, and it is changing society! Nothing is so constant as change in the teaching field, where each new year brings added knowledge in such abundance as to challenge the brightest of minds. Teaching is one field in which continued study is not only suggested but demanded. New knowledge of how children grow and develop and learn is evolving at a very rapid rate; new techniques of teaching are being tested in increasingly larger numbers of schools each year; information in all fields of knowledge is forthcoming with such rapidity that much in this year's textbooks is already obsolete. Today we are as concerned with affective as with cognitive learning. Those persons charged with guiding the learning activities of children must be familiar with as much new knowledge as possible. The only way one may gain this awareness is through continued formal or informal study.

A BROAD LIBERAL-ARTS BACKGROUND WITH DEPTH IN SUBJECT MATTER

Of all persons in our society, a teacher must be the best educated. This demands of one a broad background in all subject or academic areas and depth of subject matter in the area or areas he teaches. Since the active minds of children are forever conjuring up ideas and questions that bear on academic areas outside the particular class or subject with which they are presently involved, the teacher must be prepared to follow their thinking to any field of knowledge. Then, too, for his own personal self-realization, a teacher must have a solid background in subject areas fundamental to his well-being in our society.

Between 75 and 90 percent of the prospective teacher's college academic work toward the baccalaureate degree is spent in the liberal arts, including course work in general education—the humanities, communication, social studies, natural science, and personal health and development—and in his major subject area.

AN ADEQUATE BACKGROUND IN PROFESSIONAL PREPARATION

It is easy enough—and obvious enough—to say that an adequate preparation is necessary in any field in which one will practice. The prob-

Teaching Is More an Art Than a Science

I believe that teaching is an art, not a science. It seems to me very dangerous to apply the aims and methods of science to human beings as individuals, although a statistical principle can often be used to explain their behavior in large groups and a scientific diagnosis of their physical structure is always valuable. But a "scientific" relationship between human beings is bound to be inadequate and perhaps distorted. Of course it is necessary for any teacher to be orderly in planning his work and precise in his dealing with facts. But that does not make his teaching "scientific." Teaching involves emotions, which cannot be systematically appraised and employed, and human values, which are quite outside the grasp of science. A "scientifically" brought-up child would be a pitiable monster. A "scientific" marriage would be only a thin and crippled version of a true marriage. A "scientific" friendship would be as cold as a chess problem. "Scientific" teaching, even of scientific subjects, will be inadequate as long as both teachers and pupils are human beings. Teaching is not like inducing a chemical reaction: it is much more like painting a picture or making a piece of music, or on a lower level like planting a garden or writing a friendly letter. You must throw your heart into it, you must realize that it cannot all be done by formulas, or you will spoil your work, and your pupils, and yourself.

Gilbert Highet, *The Art of Teaching* (New York: Knopf, 1950), pp. vii–viii.

lem comes in defining what an adequate preparation is, as shown by the considerable controversy of recent years over professional-education courses. There is a wide variety of opinion as to the actual amount of professional work necessary in a prospective teacher's college preparatory program. Most authorities claim, however, that out of a four- or five-year preparatory program, the largest part of one year should be enough for professional work. This would provide adequate preparation in foundation courses, directed teaching, and methods and materials. It is interesting to note that, whereas the requirements in liberal-arts courses over the past hundred years have been increasing in numbers of units of work, the requirements in professional education in a prospective teacher's program have remained approximately the same since the days of Horace Mann.

The Profession Tomorrow

Teaching is a profession, or at least it is in the process of becoming a profession. The abstract model does exist. It serves a purpose: it represents the goal toward which we must strive. The dynamic process of change is moving us forward toward that model. As teachers gain the authority to police their own profession, they will not tolerate the bargain-basement teacher-education programs that exist today in too many universities and colleges, public and private. Approximately 80 percent of the nation's future teachers are being prepared at institutions that are rated C or D on the American Association of University Professors faculty-salary scale; nearly half attend D-level institutions. On the other hand, less than 4 percent are being prepared at colleges or universities rated A or better on the AAUP scale. The assessment indicates that higher education has not made a substantial investment in teacher education. The cost of preparing dentists or physicians may range from five thousand to twelve thousand dollars per student per year; the cost of training teachers averages less than one thousand dollars per student per year.

In addition, or perhaps as a result, teacher-preparing institutions seem to have a penchant for producing graduates whose competence is judged solely by the successful completion of courses too frequently bearing little relationship to the realities of classroom teaching. The success of a teacher of disadvantaged children, for example, depends significantly on such inherent or acquired characteristics as openness, humanity, and a capacity to love. And yet there is no way to prevent those who lack these characteristics from entering the teaching field.

Let us hope that as teachers gain *authority* to police their own profession, they will subscribe to a uniform code of ethics of the teaching profession (like the one for California reproduced below), which will include maintaining current *expertise* and proper *commitment* to the student, the public, and the profession and will recognize the magnitude of the *responsibility* the teacher has accepted in choosing a career in education. Only with this type of structure and organization can society be guaranteed that the practitioners' behavior will be consistent with professional principles. Finally, teachers can be expected to make rapid strides toward improving the professional character of their service. At least the following steps seem to be warranted: (1) Teachers themselves must take more responsibility for controlling entry into the profession through having a voice—the main voice—in such professional processes as certifica-

The Code of Ethics of the
California State Board of Education

Article 1. Code of Ethics of the Teaching Profession

5480. *Preamble.* The educator believes in the worth and dignity of man. He recognizes the supreme importance of the pursuit of truth, devotion to excellence, and the nurture of democratic citizenship. He regards as essential to these goals the protection of freedom to learn and to teach and the guarantee of equal educational opportunity for all. The educator accepts his responsibility to practice his profession according to the highest ethical standards.

The educator recognizes the magnitude of the responsibility he has accepted in choosing a career in education, and engages himself, individually and collectively with other educators, to judge his colleagues, and to be judged by them, in accordance with the provisions of this code.

5481. *Principle I: Commitment to the Student.* The educator measures his success by the progress of each student toward realization of his potential as a worthy and effective citizen. The educator therefore works to stimulate the spirit of inquiry, the acquisition of knowledge and understanding, and the thoughtful formulation of worthy goals. In fulfilling these goals:

(a) He encourages the student to independent action in the pursuit of learning and provides access to varying points of view.

(b) He prepares his subject carefully, presents it to his students without distortion and—within the limits of time and curriculum—gives all points of view a fair hearing.

(c) He protects the health and safety of his students.

(d) He honors the integrity of his students and influences them through constructive criticism rather than by ridicule and harassment.

(e) He provides for participation in educational programs without regard to race, color, creed, or national origin—both in what he teaches and how he teaches it.

(f) His professional relationships with students shall not be used for private advantage; the educator neither solicits nor involves them or their parents in schemes for commercial gain.

(g) He shall keep in confidence information that has been obtained in the course of professional service, unless disclosure serves professional purposes or is required by law.

358

5482. *Principle II: Commitment to the Public.* The educator believes that democratic citizenship in its highest form requires dedication to the principles of our democratic heritage. He shares with all other citizens the responsibility for the development of sound public policy and assumes full political and citizenship responsibilities. The educator bears particular responsibility for the development of policy relating to the extension of educational opportunities for all and for interpreting educational programs and policies to the public. In fulfilling these goals:

(a) He has an obligation to support his profession and institution and not to misrepresent them in public discussion. When he criticizes [them] in public he has an obligation not to distort the facts. When he speaks or writes about policies he takes adequate precautions to distinguish his private views from the official position of the institution.

(b) He does not interfere with a colleague's exercise of political and citizenship rights and responsibilities.

(c) His institutional privileges shall not be used for private gain. He does not exploit his pupils, their parents, his colleagues, nor the school system itself for his private advantage. He does not accept gifts or favors that might impair or appear to impair professional judgment nor offer any favor, service, or thing of value to obtain special advantage.

5483. *Principle III: Commitment to the Profession.* The educator believes that the quality of the services of the education profession directly influences the nation and its citizens. He therefore exerts every effort to raise professional standards, to improve his service, to promote a climate in which the exercise of professional judgment is encouraged, and to achieve conditions which attract persons worthy of trust to careers in education. In fulfilling these goals:

(a) He accords just and equitable treatment to all members of the profession in the exercise of their professional rights and responsibilities.

(b) He does not use coercive means or promise special treatment in order to influence professional decisions of colleagues.

(c) He does not misrepresent his own professional qualifications.

(d) He does not misrepresent the professional qualifications of his colleagues, and will discuss these qualifications fairly and accurately when discussion serves professional purposes.

(e) He applies for, accepts, offers, and assigns positions or responsibility on the basis of professional preparation and legal qualifications.

(f) He uses honest and effective methods of administering his educational responsibility. He conducts professional business through proper channels. He does not assign unauthorized persons to educational tasks. He uses time granted for its intended purposes. He does not misrepresent conditions of employment. He lives up to the letter and spirit of his contract.

5484. *Unprofessional Conduct.* This code is a set of ideals which the teaching profession expects its members to honor and follow. Any violation is unprofessional. However, to constitute unprofessional conduct and cause for suspension, revocation or denial of a certification document, or renewal thereof, such violations shall be only those which either involve jeopardy to student welfare; evidence malice, serious incompetency or bad judgment; or show a consistent pattern of misconduct.

This code of ethics is not an exhaustive enumeration of acts or conduct which constitute unprofessional conduct.

5485. The provisions of this article do not apply to any person while serving in grades 13 or 14 or in any course taught under the jurisdiction of a community college. Such person, however, may be subject to disciplinary action for unprofessional conduct when the person or agency having responsibility therefor independently determines such person has committed an act or acts involving unprofessional conduct irrespective of whether such act or acts are or are not prohibited by this article.

tion, accreditation, licensure, and personnel selection and retention. (2) Teachers must accept the sometimes distasteful, but most essential, task of policing their own membership. (To do this effectively means agreeing on the criteria of satisfactory professional performance and then courageously and judiciously applying them.) (3) Teachers must refine and add to their stockpile of esoteric knowledge. (This step will not be an easy one, judging from the difficulty experienced in the past in deciding on the content of professional education and convincing college colleagues and the lay public that it is an academic-subject-matter area of study.) [21]

[21] A law in California (Education Code Section 13188) declares: "Academic subject matter area refers exclusively to the natural sciences, the social sciences (*other*

Finally, and in conclusion, what is at stake here? The concept that teaching is a profession, however short it may fall in practice, is important to society and its future well-being. Professions organize and, through their organization, help to regulate the service rendered to society. Professions also work to increase the quality of services they render. A profession can perform these functions for society better than society can do them for itself.

> I am not willing that this discussion should close without mention of the value of a true teacher. Give me a log hut, with only a simple bench, Mark Hopkins on one end and I on the other, and you may have all the buildings, apparatus and libraries without him.
>
> PRESIDENT JAMES A. GARFIELD

Questions for Discussion

1. Reread the statements regarding teaching as a profession and as a trade. Where do you stand on this issue? Why?

2. What is good teaching? Is it the same for all grade levels and subject-matter fields?

3. Does "essentiality of the service" of a profession give it the right to strike or deny it this right?

4. Do you agree with Wilson (page 348) that "it is common to explain the first and third by the second"? Does the change from an undersupply to an oversupply of teachers "unbox" the compass?

5. Are the importance of education and the status of teaching rising? Marshal the evidence to support your conclusion.

6. Teaching has been described as "like nursing—a woman's profession." What implications does this have for the reality of Kinney's definition of the role of a teacher as member of the profession (pages 346–47)?

7. Is education an academic discipline? What are the implications of your answer for teaching as a profession?

8. What are the major roadblocks education faces in its striving for more complete professional status?

---

than education and educational methodology), the humanities, mathematics, the fine arts."

9. Is professionalism the opposite of amateurism? What, then, is the consequence for the role of the teacher in our society?

10. Is intellectualism the cornerstone of professionalism? If not, what is?

11. Teachers no longer should be "recruited"; they should be selected. What differences are implied here?

12. Reread the quotation from Corey (page 337). Is this simply "sounding brass and a tinkling cymbal," or is it a meaningful goal?

13. What are the major advantages of differentiated staffing? The major disadvantages?

14. Compare the California State Board of Education's Code of Ethics (pages 358–60) with one in your state or with the NEA's.

Activities and Projects

1. In the company of two other students, observe several experienced teachers of the same grade level or subject field. To what extent do you agree that each is a "good teacher"?

2. Interview the superintendent of a school system of your choice. Find out how he selects new teachers and how he evaluates their success.

3. Visit a local teachers' professional association or union meeting. What were their chief concerns? How does your conclusion fit the professional image?

4. Conduct a survey among PTA members on their image of teachers. How does it square with your own image?

5. Interview a doctor or a lawyer about his "role" as a member of the profession. How does it compare with the competencies listed on pages 346–47?

6. Talk to a union member and find out what his union does for him, how he feels about it, and what part he takes in decision making in the organization.

7. Ask the principal of a school of your choice to read and react to Albert Shanker's statement on pages 338–39.

8. Write to the United States Office of Education for materials describing some of their innovative programs of teacher education. Prepare a report on the significance of these experiments.

9. Investigate what such organizations as the following do for education as a profession "in the process of becoming": Phi Delta Kappa, Kappa Delta Pi, and Student NEA.

References

Status, etc.

BARZUN, JACQUES. *The Teacher in America.* New York: Doubleday, 1959.

BRENTON, MYRON. *What's Happened to Teacher?* New York: Coward-McCann, 1970.

CAMPBELL, ROALD F., LUVERN L. CUNNINGHAM, and RODERICK F. MCPHEE. *The Organization and Control of American Schools.* Columbus, Ohio: C. E. Merrill, 1965.

CARR-SAUNDERS, A. M., and P. A. WILSON. *The Professions.* Oxford: Clarendon, 1933.

DORROS, S. *Teaching as a Profession.* Columbus, Ohio: C. E. Merrill, 1968.

JAMES, DEBORAH. *The Taming: A Teacher Speaks.* New York: McGraw-Hill, 1969.

KINNEY, LUCIEN B., and L. G. THOMAS. *Toward Professional Maturity in Education.* Burlingame, Calif.: California Teachers Association, 1955.

LIEBERMAN, MYRON. *Education as a Profession.* Englewood Cliffs, N.J.: Prentice-Hall, 1956.

POSTMAN, NEIL, and CHARLES WEINGARTNER. *Teaching as a Subversive Activity.* New York: Delacorte, 1969.

STINNETT, T. M., and ALBERT J. HUGGETT. *Professional Problems of Teachers.* New York: Macmillan, 1963.

Professional Education

BORROWMAN, MERLE L., ed. *Teacher Education in America.* New York: Teachers College Press, Columbia University, 1965.

COLLINS, J. F. "The Teacher Education Center Concept." *Educational Leadership,* February 1970, 544–47.

CONANT, JAMES BRYANT. *The Education of American Teachers.* New York: McGraw-Hill, 1963.

EDELFELT, ROY A., ed. *Innovative Programs in Student Teaching.* Baltimore: Maryland State Department of Education, 1969.

ELAM, STANLEY, ed. *Improving Teacher Education in the United States.* Bloomington, Ind.: Phi Delta Kappa, 1967.

GUTEK, GERALD. *An Historical Introduction to American Education.* New York: Crowell, 1970. Chaps. 6, 7.

KINNEY, LUCIEN B. *Certification in Education.* Englewood Cliffs, N.J.: Prentice-Hall, 1964.

KOERNER, JAMES. *The Miseducation of Teachers.* Boston: Houghton Mifflin, 1963.

McKENNA, BERNARD H. *School Staffing Patterns.* Burlingame, Calif.: California Teachers Association, 1967.

ROGERS, CARL. *Freedom to Learn.* Columbus, Ohio: C. E. Merrill, 1969.

SELDEN, WILLIAM K. *Accreditation.* New York: Harper, 1960.

SMITH, B. OTHANEL. *Teachers for the Real World.* Washington, D.C.: American Association of Colleges for Teacher Education, 1969.

STONE, JAMES C. *Breakthrough in Teacher Education.* San Francisco: Jossey-Bass, 1968.

———. "Teacher Education by Legislation." *Phi Delta Kappan,* February 1966, pp. 287–91.

———. *Teachers for the Disadvantaged.* San Francisco: Jossey-Bass, 1969.

Teacher Organizations

AMERICAN FEDERATION OF TEACHERS, COMMISSION ON EDUCATIONAL RECONSTRUCTION. *Organizing the Teaching Profession.* Glencoe, Ill.: Free Press, 1955.

CALIFORNIA TEACHERS ASSOCIATION. *We Meet to Confer.* Burlingame, Calif.: California Teachers Association, 1966.

LIEBERMAN, MYRON. *Education as a Profession.* Englewood Cliffs, N.J.: Prentice-Hall, 1956. Chaps. 9, 10.

———. *The Future of Public Education.* Chicago: University of Chicago Press, 1960. Chap. 9.

MACCHIAROLA, FRANK J., ed. *Critical Issues in Education.* New York: Bernard M. Baruch College, City University of New York, 1970.

NATIONAL EDUCATION ASSOCIATION. *NEA Handbook for Local, State and National Associations.* Washington, D.C.: National Education Association, published annually.

PALMATIER, LARRY LEE. *Teacher Power and Professionalism in California.* Burlingame, Calif.: California Teachers Association, 1970.

SHILS, EDWARD B., and C. TAYLOR WHITTIER. *Teachers, Administrators, and Collective Bargaining.* New York: Crowell, 1968.

STINNETT, T. M., and ALBERT J. HUGGETT. *Professional Problems of Teachers.* New York: Macmillan, 1963. Pt. 3; chap. 15.

THOMAS, L. G., L. B. KINNEY, A. P. COLADARCI, and H. A. FIELSTRA. *Perspective on Teaching.* Englewood Cliffs, N.J.: Prentice-Hall, 1961. Chap. 16.

WESLEY, EDGAR. *National Education Association: The First Hundred Years*. New York: Harper, 1957.

Professional Responsibilities, Privileges, and Obligations

CALIFORNIA TEACHERS ASSOCIATION. *Six Areas of Teacher Competence*. Burlingame, Calif.: Commission on Teacher Education of the California Teachers Association, 1964.

KROLL, ARTHUR M., ed. *Issues in American Education*. New York: Oxford University Press, 1970.

LEE, CALVIN, ed. *Improving College Teaching*. Washington, D.C.: American Council on Education, 1967.

LIEBERMAN, MYRON. *The Future of Public Education*. Chaps. 8, 13.

MAYOR, JOHN B. *Accreditation in Teacher Education*. Washington, D.C.: National Commission on Accreditation, 1965.

NATIONAL EDUCATION ASSOCIATION. *A Position Paper on Teacher Education and Professional Standards*. Washington, D.C.: National Commission on Teacher Education and Professional Standards of the National Education Association, 1963. Pp. 1-33.

STINNETT, T. M., ed. *The Teacher Dropout*. Itasca, Ill.: F. E. Peacock, 1970.

STRAUSS, GEORGE. "Professionalism and Occupational Associations." *Industrial Relations*, May 1963, pp. 7-31.

Index

ACT-LA, *see* Association of Classroom Teachers–Los Angeles
AFT (American Federation of Teachers), 340–42
academic organizations, teachers', 325–26
academies, 236–37
achievement tests, 162
Adams, Henry, quoted, 141
Adler, Mortimer J., quoted, 265
administrators, school, 104, 106–7
age, pupil, 171–72
Aims of Education, The (Whitehead), 33–36
alienation, societal, 12–13
Allen, James C., 29, 46
American Association for Health, Physical Education, and Recreation, 325
American Association of School Administrators, 75
American culture, *see* culture
American Federation of Teachers (AFT), 340–42
American Institute for Research in the Behavioral Sciences, 77
American Journal of Education, 236
American Legion, 103
aptitude tests, 162–63
Arbuckle, Dugald S., 340
Aristotle, 251
    quoted, 28
Arnold, Matthew, 6
Art of Teaching, The (Highet), quoted, 356

assessment-of-education program, 163
Association of Classroom Teachers–Los Angeles (ACT-LA), 342
Association for Supervision and Curriculum Development, 177
Athens, ancient, education in, 226–27
Ausubel, D. P., 73
Autobiography of Malcolm X, quoted, 212–13
average pupil, teaching of, 176–77

Backwoods Utopias (Bestor), 43
Baldwin, James, quoted, 204
Baldwin, James Mark, 158
Barnard, Henry, 236
basic subjects, 28
Becker, Howard, 336
Beecher, Catherine, 238
behavioral trends, 9
Benjamin, Harold, 15–16
Berlyne, Daniel E., 158
Bestor, Arthur, 43–45, 251
blacks
    color caste and, 204–9
    education of, 238, 246
black liberation movements, 12
Bluegrass school district (imaginary), 285, 326–27
boards of education, 104, 301
Bode, Boyd Henry, 243
books, *see* textbooks, adequacy of
Boston, early schools of, 232, 237
Boy Scouts, 82, 101, 103
Brenton, Myron, 340
British Infant Schools, 215

Brogan, Denis, 42
Bronfenbrenner, Urie, 258–59
Bronx High School of Science (New York), 180
Brooklyn Technical High School (New York), 180
Broudy, Harry S., quoted, 14, 280–81
Brown University, 238
Bruner, Jerome S., 46–47, 144, 155, 158
Buber, Martin, 289
Bugenhagen, Johann, 228
building principals, see principals
buildings, school, 123–24
Bureau of Indian Affairs, United States, 239, 240
bureaucracies, growth of, 11–12
Burns, Hobert, 352

CAI (computer-assisted instruction), 74–78
California State Board of Education, Code of Ethics of, 358–60
California State Teachers' Retirement System, 321–22
Calvin, John, 228
campus disorders, 5
Carmichael, Stokely, 206, 218
Carroll, J. B., 73
caste
  color and, 204–9
  pupils and, 196–223
certification, teacher, 303–9
Certification in Education (Kinney), 310
Chamber of Commerce, United States, 103
Channing, William Ellery, 337
Chase, John B., Jr., quoted, 288
Chavez, Cesar, quoted, 205
Chemawa Indian School, 240
Chiloco Institute, 240
Cicero, 229
civic responsibility, 38–39
Civil Rights Act (1964), 214, 250
Civil War, 234, 242

Civilian Conservation Corps Act (1933), 245, 247
class, 41, 198–99
  color and, 204–19
  pupil differences and, 185–86, 196–223
"Classical Realist View of Education" (Broudy), 280–81
classrooms
  adequacy of, 124–25
  management of, 96–97
Cleveland, Frank ("Clorox"), 208–9
Clifford, W. K., 283
"Clorox," see Cleveland, Frank
Code of Ethics, California State Board of Education, 358–60
Coleman, James, 216
Coleman Report (Equality of Educational Opportunity), 216–18
College of William and Mary, 235, 238
colleges
  early, 235, 236, 238, 245
  teacher certification and, 305–8
  see also specific institutions
colonial education, 232–40
  teachers and, 224–26
color caste, 204–9
Columbia University, 238
Comenius, John Amos, 229–30
Commager, Henry Steele, quoted, 297
Commission on Reorganization of Secondary Education (1918), 33
Committee of Ten on Secondary School Studies (1893), 245
Committee of Thirteen on College Entrance Requirements (1895), 245
Committee for the White House Conference on Education, A Report to the President, 40–42
common school, 235
communications, revolution in, 11
Community Chest, 101
community groups, teachers and, 101–4

compulsory education, 247
computer-assisted instruction (CAI), 74–78
Conant, James B., 251, 309, 327
conformity, pupils and, 186–87
Confucius, 250
Corey, Arthur F., quoted, 337
Council for Basic Education, 42–45
Crabtree, Amanda, quoted, 97
"credibility gap," 12
culture, 1–27
    changes in, 1, 7–18
    definition of, 3–5
    demoralization in, 5–7
    origination of, 2–3
    politics and, 5–7
    survival and, 18
    values of, 5
curriculum, tyranny of, 115–23
Curriculum Principles and Social Trends (Gwinn and Chase), quoted, 288
customs, 3
cynicism, students', 6–7

"dame schools," 225, 233
"Dangerous Parallel," simulation game, 79
Dartmouth University, 238, 246
Daughters of the American Revolution, 103
Davis Enterprise, 49
Davis (California) School System, 48–49
democracy, 5–7
Democracy and Education (Dewey), 243, 244
Democratic party, 103, 246, 248
DeMolay, 103
demonstration teaching, 107
Department of Health, Education, and Welfare, United States, 103, 246, 248
Depression, Great, 5, 36
Deterline, William A., quoted, 145

Dewey, John, 31, 35–37, 39n, 243–44, 251–52, 279, 284
Dillard University, 238
disadvantaged pupil, teaching of, 351
discovery technique, 72–73
    learning and, 154–56
    see also Whitehead, Alfred North
discrimination, educational, 210–19
"Dover Beach" (Arnold), 6

economic depression, 5, 36, 350
economic efficiency, 38
economic ideals, 5
Economic Opportunity Act (1964), 118, 249
education
    definition of, 1, 244
    discrimination in, 210–19
    goals of, 28–54
    history of, 224–64
    new, 34–36, 45–50
    philosophies of, 265–96
    politics and, 5–7
    questions on, 250–60
    students' attitudes toward, 6–7
Education of the American Teacher, The (Conant), 309, 327
Education: An Instrument of National Goals (Hanna), 21
Education of Man, The (Froebel), 231
Education Professions Development Act (1967), 249
Education Professions Institute (EPI), 352
Education, United States Office of, see Office of Education, United States
Educational Forum, The, 14
Educational Policies Commission, NEA, 36–39, 44
educational systems, 297–333
    employment practices and, 311–22
    in-service growth of, 322–27
    school organization and, 297–303
    teacher certification and, 305–9
Educational Wastelands (Bestor), 43

educators
American, 243
early European, 230–32
Eells, Kenneth, 200–2
Eisenhower, President Dwight D., 248
Elam, Stanley, 258
elementary schools
certification and, 305–8
classroom and, 124–25
computerized, 74–76
daily schedule for, 119–21
experience of, 89–91
teaching in, 67–69
Elementary and Secondary Education
Act (1965), 117–18, 211, 249,
250
elites, education and, 20
Emile (Rousseau), 230, 231
employment practices, educational
system and, 311–22
English High School (Boston), 237
enrichment programs, 179–80
environment
culture and, 3
learning and, 148
motivation and, 156–57
pollution and, 11
egualitarianism, 5
Equality of Educational Opportunity
(Coleman Report), 216–18
Erasmus, Desiderius, 227
ethnic minorities
color caste and, 204–9
education of, 238–42
Euclid, 45
evaluation, pupil, 161–63
existentialism, 285–90
Experience and Education (Dewey),
243
experimentalism, 279–85, 290
expository technique, 72–73

facilities, adequacy of, 123–28
family life, 41
Farber, Jerry, 6
fatigue, teacher, 128–32

Federal Broadcast Act (1967), 249
Federal Emergency Relief Act (1933),
247
federal government, education and,
28–39, 117–18, 211–14, 245–
50, 299–300
see also Office of Education, United
States
finance, school, 299–300
Follow Through, Project, 211
Foreign Policy Association, 79
Fortnightly Club, 103
Foshay, Arthur W., 156
4-H, 103
Franklin, Benjamin, 234, 236
free enterprise, 5
Freedmen's Bureau, 246
Froebel, Friedrich, 231, 243
Fulbright, J. William, 248
furniture, classroom, 125

Gallup survey, 252–53
games, simulation, 78–79
Gardner, John W., quoted, 13
Garfield, President James A., quoted,
361
Garvey, Marcus, 208
Gauss, John, quoted, 105
Gautier, Théophile, 279
generation gap, 12, 14
George-Deen Act (1937), 247
George Miller Junior Education Act
(1968), 115
Gesell, Arnold, 157
GI Bill of Rights, 245, 247–49
gifted pupil, teaching of, 179–81
Girl Scouts, 82, 101, 103
Goethe, Johann Wolfgang von, quoted,
79
government, *see* federal government
Gray, Jenny, quoted, 131
Great Depression, 5, 36, 350
Great Didactic, The (Comenius), 229
Greece, ancient, education in, 226–
27

grouping of pupils, 181–84
Gwynn, J. Minor, quoted, 288

Hall, G. Stanley, 243
Halsey, A. H., quoted, 4
Hamilton, Charles V., 206, 218
handicapped pupil, teaching of, 177–78
Hanna, Lavone A., 119, 120
Harris, Louis, 63
Harris, William T., 243
Harris poll, 63
Hartford (Connecticut) Female Seminary, 238
Harvard University, 33, 158, 238
Haskell Institute, 240
Hatch Act (1887), 247
Head Start, Project, 211, 214, 249, 259
Health, Education, and Welfare, United States Department of, 103, 246, 248
Heidegger, Martin, 285
Hemingway, Ernest, 18
Henle, Robert J., quoted, 274–75
Herbart, Johann Friedrich, 231–32, 242
Herman, George, quoted, 8–9
Hersey, John, quoted, 114
Hi-Y, 103
High School of Music and Art (New York), 180
high schools, early, 237
  see also secondary schools
Higher Education Act (1965), 118
Higher Learning in America (Hutchins), 273
Highet, Gilbert, quoted, 356
Honors program, 179–80
Horne, Herman H., 268, 271
Horvat, John J., quoted, 343
How Gertrude Teaches Her Children (Pestalozzi), 230
Howard University, 238
Howe, Harold, II, 75
Hullfish, Henry G., 281

human development, 157–61
human relations, 37–38
"Humanist Goals" (Lerner), 20–21
Hutchins, Robert Maynard, 273

idealism, 267–71, 290
Indians, American
  color caste and, 204–9
  education of, 239–41
individualism, 5
individualized instruction, 74–78
Individually Prescribed Instruction (IPI), 74–76
inquiry technique, 72
  methods of, 152–56
Institute of American Indian Arts, 240
instructional games, 78–79
integration, segregation and, 214–19
intelligence, pupil, 173–74
interest tests, 163
Introduction to Education, An (Richey), 122
Introduction to Programmed Instruction, An (Deterline), 145
IPI (Individually Prescribed Instruction), 74–76

Jackson, Arthur, quoted, 196
James, William, 243
Jaspers, Karl, 285
Jefferson, Thomas, 234–35
John Dewey Society, 243
Johnson, Lyndon B., 239
junior high schools, teaching in, 69–70

Kalamazoo case (1874), 237, 247
Kierkegaard, Sören, 285
Kilpatrick, William Heard, 243, 282
King, Martin Luther, Jr., quoted, 219
Kinney, Lucien B., 310, 346–47
Kiwanis, 103
Kneller, George F., 286
Knights of Columbus, 103
Knox, John, 228
Koerner, James D., 42–43

Kohl, Herbert, 215
Korean War, 79

labor unions
  education and, 103
  see also unionism, teaching and
Latin grammar school, 232, 236
League of Women Voters, 103
learning, process of, 141–69
  discovery, 72–73, 154–56
  evaluation and testing, 161–63
  inquiry, 152–56
  problem solving, 149–52
Learning Research and Development
  Center, 75
legislation, see federal government;
  specific legislation
Leonard and Gertrude (Pestalozzi),
  230
Lerner, Max, 20–21
lesson plans, 118–23
"Letter from Delano" (Chavez), 205
Letters Dealing with the Application
  of Psychology to the Art of
  Teaching (Herbart), 231–32
letters of recommendation, teachers',
  315–16
Lewin, Kurt, 143
liberation movements, 12
licenses, teachers', 225–26
  certification and, 303–9
Life magazine, 63
Lincoln, Abraham, 244
Lindquist, Clarence B., 258
Linton, Ralph, quoted, 2–3
Lions (club), 103
Lunt, Paul, 197, 198
Luther, Martin, 228
Lyon, Mary, 238

McCollum case (1948), 248
McKean, Robert C., 122
McLuhan, Marshall, 45–46, 254

Major Work–Honors program (Cleve-
  land), 179–80
Making of a Counter-Culture, The
  (Roszak), 15
Malcolm X, quoted, 212–13
Mann, Horace, 89, 236
Marcel, Gabriel, 285
Marc, Franz, quoted, 16
Masons, 103
Massachusetts School Law (1642), 233
materials, adequacy of, 125–27
Mead, Margaret, 12
media
  new education and, 46
  revolution in, 11
Medlin, William K., 258
Meeker, Marchia, 200–2
Melancthon, 228
"Member of the Profession" (Kinney),
  347
methodology, in teaching, 72–73
Mexican-Americans
  color caste and, 204–9
  education of, 239, 241–42
middle schools, 70–71
Military Academy, United States
  (West Point), 246
minorities, education of, 238–42
mobility
  social, 199–204
  teaching and, 319
morality, changes in, 14
Morgan, Joy Elmer, quoted, 99
Morrill Act (1862), 244, 246
mortality, professional, 320
motivation, environment and, 156–
  57
Mount Holyoke Seminary, 238

National Advisory Commission on
  Civil Disorders, 205–6
National Association of Manufacturers,
  103
National Association of Secondary
  School Principals, 39–40, 45

National Commission on Teacher Education and Professional Standards, NEA, 337

National Congress of Parents and Teachers, 102

National Council for the Accreditation of Teacher Education (NCATE), 304

National Council of Mathematics Teachers, 325

National Council of Teachers of English, 325

National Defense Education acts (NDEA), 117, 245, 248, 250, 326

National Education Association (NEA), 36–39, 64, 80, 81, 101, 245, 337, 351
   AFT and, 340–42

National Institute for Advanced Study in Teaching Disadvantaged Youth, 351

National Manpower Council, 334

National School Lunch Act (1947), 248

National Teacher Corps, 118, 249

National Youth Authority (1935), 245, 350

nationality differences, 174–75

"Nature of Teacher Power and Teacher Attitudes toward Certain Aspects of This Power, The" (Horvat), 343

Naval Academy, United States (Annapolis), 246

NCATE, see National Council for the Accreditation of Teacher Education

NDEA, see National Defense Education acts

NEA, see National Education Association

NEA Journal, 97

Negroes, see blacks

new education, 45–50

New England Primer, The, 234

Newsletter, The (Dade County, Florida), 60

normative human development, 157–58

Oakleaf Elementary School (Pennsylvania), 74

Office of Education, United States, 63, 75, 77, 246, 248, 249

"Old Deluder Satan Law," 233

Orbis Pictus (Comenius), 229

ordinalist concept of human development, 157–61

Oregon case (1925), 247

Orientals, color caste and, 204–9

Palmatier, Larry Lee, 345

parents, teachers and, 97–98, 101–4

Parker, Francis W., 242

Passion for Life (film), 265

patriotism, 5, 13, 14

Paul VI, Pope, 275–76

Peace Corps, 248

Peirce, C. S., 243

Pennsylvania, University of, 29, 238

Person to Person: The Problem of Being Human (Rogers and Stevens), 16

personality differences in children, 184–85

personality tests, 163

Pestalozzi, Johann Heinrich, 230, 242

Phi Delta Kappan, 105, 258

philanthropic foundations, 245

Phillips, Romeo Eldridge, quoted, 64

philosophies, educational, 265–96
   existentialism, 285–90
   experimentalism, 279–85, 290
   idealism, 269–71, 290
   realism, 276–79, 290
   scholasticism, 271–76, 290

Philosophies of Education (Phenix), 275, 281

physical education, 41

placement, teacher, 316–18

Piaget, Jean, 144, 157–61
Piercy, Malcolm, 158
placement agencies, teacher, 314–15
PLAN, Project, 76–77
planning
  daily, 95–98
  student-teacher, 73–74
Planning for American Youth, An Educational Program for Youth of Secondary School Age, 39–40, 45
politics, effects of, 5–7
pollution, 11
Polya, G., problem-solving formula of, 150–52
population, aspects of, 10–15
Postman, Neil, 7–8
  quoted, 18, 47
pragmatism, 283
prayer, schools and, 249
Princeton University, 238
principals
  description of, 301–2
  teachers and, 106–7
problem solving, 149–52
Process of Education, The (Bruner), 144
professionalism, teaching and, 334–65
  autonomy, 339–40, 345
  California Code of Ethics, 358–60
  commitment to, 353–56
  future, 346–53
  responsibility and, 344–46
  union view of, 338–39
progressive education, 39, 283
Progressive Education Association, 243
promotions, teacher, 318–19
Protestant Reformation, 228–30
psycologie de l'intelligence, La (Piaget), 158
Ptolemy I, 45
public relations, teachers and, 101–4
public schools, history of, 233–50
pupils, 132–33
  average, 176–77

pupils (*cont.*)
  differences among, 170–95
  gifted, 179–81
  handicapped, 177–78
  learning and, 141–69
  societal decisions among, 196–223
pupil-teacher ratio, 177
Purposes of Education in American Democracy, The (NEA), 36–40
Pursuit of Excellence, The (Rockefeller Brothers Foundation), 259

race riots, 204–5
Rafferty, Max, 29
Rainbow Girls, 103
"Re Status" (Wilson), 348
reading, computerized teaching of, 75–76
realism, 276–79, 290
Red Cross, 101
reflective thinking, 146–47
Reformation, Protestant, 228–30
reinforcement, 145
religion, education and, 227–30, 239–40, 271–76
Renaissance, 227–28
"Report of the Fund for the Advancement of Education," 348
Republican party, 103
Reserve Officers' Training Corps, 247
Restoration of Learning (Bestor), 43
retirement of teachers, 321–22
Richey, Robert W., 122
Rickover, Admiral Hyman G., 251, 257
Right to Read program, 29
riots, race, 204–5
Rockefeller Brothers Foundation, 259
Rogers, Carl, 16
"Roman Catholic View of Education" (Henle), 274–75
Roosevelt, President Theodore, 247
Roszak, Theodore, 15
Rotary, 103
Rousseau, Jean Jacques, 158, 230, 231

Rutgers University, 238

Saber-ToothCurriculum, The(Benjamin), 15–16
salaries, teachers', 81
  past and present, 225
San Francisco Chronicle, 204
Sartre, Jean-Paul, 285
schedule, daily, 118–23
Schmitt, Marshall L., 258
scholasticism, 271–76, 290
"School Goals Get Approval" (*Davis Enterprise*), 48–49
School and Society (Dewey), 243
schools
  facilities of, 123–28
  gifted pupils and, 179–81
  handicapped pupils and, 177–78
  organization of, 297–303
  pressures and problems in, 114–40
  purposes of, 29–51
  restructuring of, 45–50
  student criticism of, 6–7
  teaching in, *see* teachers
  see also educational systems; *specific types of schools*
secondary schools, teaching in, 69–72
  classrooms and, 124–25
  experience of, 91–92
  lesson planning for, 121–23
SEE (Self-Enhancing Education), 78
segregation, integration and, 215–19
Self-Enhancing Education (SEE), 78
self-realization, 37
self-reliance, 5
senior high school, *see* secondary school
Servicemen's Readjustment Act (1944), 245, 247–48
Seven Cardinal Objectives, 33, 245
sex of teachers, 225
sex differences, pupils and, 172–73
Sexton, Patricia Cayo, 217
Shakespeare, William, 36
Shanker, Albert, quoted, 338

simulation games, 78–79
Simulation Games for the Social Studies Classroom (Foreign Policy Association), 79
slow learner, teaching of, 177–78
Smith, B. Othanel, 351, 352
Smith-Hughes Act (1917), 245
Smith-Lever Act (1914), 245, 247
Smith-Mundt Act (1948), 248
social class, 185–86, 196–223
social heritage, 3–4
social mobility, 199–204
social order, 11–15
Society for the Propagation of the Gospel in Foreign Parts, 239–40
"Sociology of Education, The" (Halsey), 4
Sociology: An Introduction (Smelser), 4
Socrates, 250
Soviet Union, education in, 258–59
Sparta, ancient, education in, 226–27
specialized high schools, 180
specialty teachers, 127–28
Spencer, Herbert, 30–32
Sputnik, effects of, 28–29
states
  education and, 302–3
  teacher certification in, 303–9
Stevens, Barry, 16
Stinnett, T. M., 338
Stone, James C., quoted, 354
strategy teaching, 72–73
student-teacher planning, 73–74
students, *see* pupils
Study of Man, The (Linton), 2–3
Sturm, Johannes, 228
Stuyvesant High School (New York), 180
summer, teachers and, 94–95
superintendent of schools, 301
superior student, teaching of, 79–81
supervisors, 104, 106–7
supplies, adequacy of, 125–27

Talks to Teachers (James), 243

Task Force on Parent Participation (Department of Health, Education, and Welfare), 103–4

"Teacher Supply and Demand in Public Schools" (NEA), 80

teachers
  certification of, 303–9
  commitment of, 19–21
  employment of, 311–22
  fatigue of, 128–32
  influence of, 65–66
  in-service growth of, 322–27
  job of, 67–79
  organizations of, 36–39, 64, 80, 81, 101, 103, 107
  parents and, 97–98, 101–4
  past and present, 224–26
  role of, 50, 65–79, 98–104
  salary of, 81, 225
  specialty, 127–28
  traveling, 127–28
  work week of, 93–94

Teacher Corps, 211

Teacher's Survival Guide, The (Gray), 131

Teaching as a Subversive Activity (Postman and Weingartner), 18, 47

technological revolution, 11, 14

Temple, Archbishop, 34

Ten Imperative Needs of Youth, 39–40, 44

tenure, teaching and, 320–31

tests, pupil, 161–63

textbooks, adequacy of, 125–27

Third World, color caste and, 204–9, 218

Third World liberation movement, 12

36 Children (Kohl), 215

Thoreau, Henry David, quoted, 265

Toynbee, Arnold, 28

"tracking," color and, 214

transfers of teachers, 319

traveling teachers, 127–28

Troy (New York) Female Seminary, 238

Tufts University, 238

Two Worlds of Childhood (Bronfenbrenner), 258–59

Tyler, Ralph W., 170

unionism, teaching and, 334–65

United States Military Academy (West Point), 246

United States Naval Academy (Annapolis), 246

UNESCO (United Nations Educational, Scientific and Cultural Organization), 248

United Federation of Teachers, 338

United States Office of Education, *see* Office of Education, United States

Upward Bound, Project, 211

Van Doren, Mark, quoted, 55

veterans, 245, 247–48

Veterans of Foreign Wars, 103

Vietnam war, 7

VISTA, 211

Vocational Rehabilitation Act (1920), 247

vocational studies, 43

Volunteers in Service to America, 211

W. K. Kellogg Foundation, 245

Warner, W. Lloyd, 197, 198, 200–2

Washington, Booker T., 238

Washington, Eva, quoted, 341

Washington, George, quoted, 224

Watson, Goodwin, 146

Watts riots (1965), 204

Weingartner, Charles, 7–8
  quoted, 18, 47

welfare, 5

Western Female Institute, 238

Westinghouse Learning Corporation, 77

"What Am I?" ("Clorox"), 208–9

White House Conference on Children and Youth (1970), 250

White House Conference on Education (1955), 40–42, 250

Whitehead, Alfred North, 33–36

"Whose Children Shall We Teach?" (Phillips), 64

Wiener, Norbert, quoted, 1

Willard, Emma, 238

William and Mary, College of, 235, 238

Wilson, O. Meredith, 348

Wirth, Arthur G., 351

women, education of, 238

women's liberation, 12

work, as objective of education, 38

Work Projects Administration (WPA), 350

workload, teachers', 226

work week, teachers', 93–94

World War I, 33

World War II, 79, 208

WPA, see Work Projects Administration

Yale University, 238

Yankee City, study of, 197–98

youth
    legislation and, 245, 250
    needs of, 39–40
    teaching of disadvantaged. 351

Zorach case (1952), 248